CRYSTAL EASTMAN

CRYSTAL EASTMAN

A Revolutionary Life

Amy Aronson

OXFORD
UNIVERSITY PRESS

Oxford University Press is a department of the University of Oxford. It furthers
the University's objective of excellence in research, scholarship, and education
by publishing worldwide. Oxford is a registered trade mark of Oxford University
Press in the UK and certain other countries.

Published in the United States of America by Oxford University Press
198 Madison Avenue, New York, NY 10016, United States of America.

Library of Congress Cataloging-in-Publication Data
Names: Aronson, Amy, author.
Title: Crystal Eastman : a revolutionary life / Amy Aronson.
Description: New York, NY : Oxford University Press, [2020] |
Includes bibliographical references and index.
Identifiers: LCCN 2019017396 | ISBN 9780199948734 (hardback) |
ISBN 9780199948741 (updf) | ISBN 9780190912857 (epub) | ISBN 9780190912864 (online)
Subjects: LCSH: Eastman, Crystal, 1881–1928. | Feminists—United States—Biography. |
Labor leaders—United States—Biography. | Suffragists—United States—Biography. |
Pacifists—United States—Biography. | Civil rights—United States—History—20th century. |
United States—Social conditions—1865–1918. | United States—Social conditions—1918–1932.
Classification: LCC HQ1413.E A77 2019 | DDC 305.42092 [B]—dc23
LC record available at https://lccn.loc.gov/2019017396

9 8 7 6 5 4 3 2 1

Printed by Sheridan Books, Inc., United States of America

In loving memory of my mother, Winnie Aronson, who always spoke up.

CONTENTS

ACKNOWLEDGMENTS

I first encountered Crystal Eastman more than twenty years ago, when I came across some of her feminist journalism. I was twenty-six years old, and, like her at the very same age, I was finishing my last graduate degree and preparing to embark on an adult life in the world. Discovering Crystal only through excerpts and flashes, still I was struck by what seemed to be a voice calling ahead of itself, a woman trying to live a life she was also trying to usher into possibility. What she envisioned, what she demanded and took steps to design, I felt, was a world for women much closer to mine than to her own.

Over the years since, that voice has stayed with me. Her restlessness with single-issue politics spoke to me, and still does; her effort to bring people and movements together, to organize for common cause, inspires me now more than ever. With so much left unfinished, her thirst and urgency, her marbled idealism and deep humanity, would not let me go.

It has been a very long journey with her, but never a lonely one. So many people have helped and supported me over the years of work on this project that it has been a challenge to my aging brain to recapture all their names! I will begin at the beginning, with Professor Robert Ferguson of Columbia University, my dissertation adviser and first champion, who wrote more recommendations for me than I can count and convinced me with his steady confidence and endless support to believe that I could someday write this book.

When I finally got serious about trying to tackle it, I was fortunate to be able to meet with Blanche Cook, who not only introduced us all to Eastman but also continued to love her enough to give my project her blessing and to support me with letters and two sit-down interviews along the way.

Several other scholars have been incredibly supportive, each one offering me creative and substantive suggestions, a generous sounding board, and crucial feedback that shaped and improved this book. First, I must thank Peter Winnington, Walter Fuller's biographer, for the exceptionally generous input he gave me; I literally could not have finished this book without his willingness to share resources, as well as his insightful impressions and his knowledge of the wider Fuller family and the British context of the period. I am also grateful to Lucy Knight for many conversations, and to Martha Wheelock for a week of thought-provoking discussions about Crystal while filming some key sites from her life in New York City. I would also like to thank Michael Kazin for the input and encouragement he so helpfully offered me.

A silent partner in this project has been the late Carl Wedekind, an honored civil libertarian who served on the board of directors of the American Civil Liberties Union (ACLU) in Kentucky and authored two books on the death penalty. He wrote an unpublished manuscript about Eastman prior to his death in 2011, and I am so grateful to his daughter, Annie Wedekind, for giving me his work in hopes of it helping my own. I am fortunate to have had the chance to consult and incorporate his insights where I could, a charge made easy by the fact that we often saw Eastman so similarly. I wish I had had the chance to meet and talk with him more about her.

The Eastman-Fuller descendants have opened their lives and family memories to me with limitless generosity. I treasure the friendships that we've developed over these years. Thank you for everything, Rebecca Young, Charles Young, Anne Fuller, Cordelia Fuller, and Reuben Fuller. And thank you, Phil Wingard, for finding me on the internet to offer your friendship and family photos, not to mention your intrepid family research.

This project was supported by a number of institutions as well. I am so grateful for the Faculty Fellowship I received from Fordham University, and for two of the university's faculty research grants. I am also thankful to my department for repeated annual support through the Faculty Research Expense Program. This book was further supported financially by two external research awards. I would like to thank the Carrie Chapman Catt Center for Women and Politics at Iowa State University for the Catt Prize for Research on Women and Politics in 2010, and the Schlesinger Library at the Radcliffe Institute, Harvard University, for the research grant the same year.

I am also grateful for the generous assistance I received from archivists and research librarians at many institutions across the country and abroad, beginning with the wonderful staff at the Schlesinger. A special thank you as well to Charlotte Labbe at Fordham University and Laura Street at the Vassar College Libraries. I have also benefited from the experience and help of archivists at the Swarthmore College Peace Collection at Swarthmore College; the Lilly Library at Indiana University Bloomington; the Manuscript and Archives divisions of the New York Public Library; the Kheel Center for Labor-Management Documentation and Archives at Cornell University; the Seeley G. Mudd Manuscript Library at Princeton University; the Tamiment Labor Archives at

New York University; the Rare Book and Manuscript Library and the Center for Oral History at Columbia University; and the Women of Protest Collection at the US Library of Congress.

So many friends have given me their support and kept the faith, no matter how long this book took for me to finish. I am grateful to Bill and Zelda Gamson for their kind hospitality while I did research on Martha's Vineyard. I would like to thank some wonderful colleagues, and all the loving friends whom I simply could not live without: Tamar Datan, Josh Gamson, Shanny Peer, Chloe Angyl, Marty Duberman, Michael Kaufman, Michael Sheran, Eric Stewart, Louis Bayard, Don Montuori, Mitchell Tunick, Pam Hatchfield, Perry Tunick-Hatchfield, Kathryn Glass, Jon Hochman, Elizabeth Dabney, Lou Lopez, Mary Morris, Larry O'Connor, Kate Morris, Linda Stein, Helen Hardacre, Michal Hershkovitz, Jackie Reich, Jennifer Clark, Margaret Schwartz, Claudia Rivera, Gwenyth Jackaway, Brian Rose, Father Michael Tueth, Micki McGee, James Van Oosting, Dawn Williams, Abby Goldstein, Patricia Belen, Fred Wertz, Greg Kenny, Maria Sanabria Kenny, and Lisa Eldridge. A heartfelt thank you to my mother-in-law, Barbara Diamond, and my sister- and brother-in-law, Sandi Kimmel and Patrick Murphy, for their constant encouragement, and to Madeline Aronson.

This book benefited so much from the input of my editor, Nancy Toff. I am also grateful for the work of her helpful assistants, Lena Rubin and Elizabeth Vaziri. My thanks as well to my patient and supportive production manager, Julia Turner.

My deepest thanks to Joy Harris, who has always understood me like almost nobody else.

I am forever thankful for the time I had with my sister, Nancy Aronson (1960–2012), and my mother, Winnie Aronson (1934–2018), who passed away while I was finishing this book. Their memory will always inspire me and give me strength.

And to my boys, Michael and Zachary, who fill me every day with gratitude that approaches awe. I love you with all my heart.

All of these people and more have helped carry me to today. Having tracked down Eastman's extant works and utterances in disparate archives over many years—having found all I can of her remains—this book, at the end, can lay her to rest. I hope this project will encourage new scholarship well beyond my own. I hope it can spark thinking and inquiry that can carry us closer to the understanding and the answers we are still seeking that Eastman was unable to find. I offer this book as a start, an invitation to scholars and students, to readers in many disciplines and areas of concern—to all those who might have otherwise encountered glimpses and whispers of her in so many texts and contexts, and wished for more.

INTRODUCTION

SEARCHING FOR CRYSTAL EASTMAN

Given the distance traveled, it is surprising there was no nameplate, no marker, no badge. And the surviving records from the A. P. Burton & Sons Funeral Home only amplify the mystery. They show that Crystal Eastman's remains were sent from Erie, Pennsylvania, to Buffalo, New York, on July 28, 1928, the same day she passed away. The train departed at 5:30 p.m., rush hour, en route to the busiest transport hub in the Northeast. But it was a Saturday, so a rare quiet marked her passage.

Only two scant documents accompanied her. A registrar's permit granted transport across state lines. Then there was a funeral slip, with spaces for information that might have begun to convey her life to memory. Of the seventy-eight lines on the slip, though, most are blank. And of the twenty-six spaces on which something is written, half record only perfunctory details—name, age, occupation, marital status. "Catherine Crystal Eastman Fuller." Her name is the longest entry. But she always knew herself by just the two identifiers at the heart of it, the name her mother designated for her: Crystal Eastman. "Marital Status: Widowed (Walter Fuller)"—factually true, but it overlooks the feminist revolution she fomented in marriage and the family, a significant part of her unending effort to live a woman's life on her own terms. "Occupation: Editor." Perhaps that was the simplest job to name, but it misconstrues her life's work: she was an activist and initiator, a leader and champion who left her mark on many of the great social justice movements that defined the twentieth century—labor, feminism, internationalism, free speech, peace.

After that, almost all the requested information is missing entirely. "Kind of Grave"—blank. "Cemetery"—blank. There are scattered spaces that have been filled in, with capital letters, but the words read like emphatic refusals that only seem to barricade the way to Crystal Eastman's story. "Date of Funeral: NONE." "Notices: NONE."

Crystal Eastman. Amy Aronson, Oxford University Press (2020).
© Oxford University Press.
DOI: 10.1093/oso/9780199948734.001.0001

And then, at Buffalo, she disappears. The records show that another funeral home, E. L. Brady & Sons, was to take possession of her casket at the railroad depot and carry it, by the Spartan Silver handles that were its only distinctive trait, to some destination that is now unknown. In 1928, the train terminus in Buffalo connected thirteen different railway lines and the vast shipping networks of the Great Lakes. From a nerve center like that, hundreds of destinations were within reach.

Where might she have gone from that junction? Where would her brothers, Anstice and Max, both present when she died, have chosen to lay her to rest? Where was her truest home?

Traced from Buffalo, the locations that composed Crystal Eastman's life map like a comet across the expanse of New York State. Following its path, one comes first to Glenora, New York, where in the spring of 1898 the Eastman family purchased one hundred acres of farmland on Lake Seneca and a summer cottage they named Cherith, after the brook where God sent Elijah to learn the value of the hidden life. Crystal adored Glenora, the only place the family could be together for a time each year; she visited there with friends and colleagues, boyfriends and future husbands, partly appraising their place in her life by the degree to which they loved it too.

Or she may rest thirty-three miles south, in her hometown of Elmira, where she grew up the only daughter of an extraordinary American family. Eastman's rural childhood was steeped in nineteenth-century reformism led primarily by her unconventional mother, Annis Ford Eastman. The family matriarch was an ordained Congregational minister who succeeded the abolitionist Thomas Beecher to become pastor of the prominent Park Church and lead a flock that included Mark Twain's family. Indeed, Annis Eastman wrote Twain's eulogy.

Then again, her final resting place could be Greenwich Village in lower Manhattan, where Crystal came of age. In the stirring first years of the twentieth century, as nineteenth-century notions of liberalism and genteel social reform lost momentum, this downtown "bohemia" became the wellspring of a new era. In Eastman's time there, old-world ways in arenas from international relations to interpersonal morality were giving way to new conceptions of society, new freedoms, new artistic directions, new ways of life. American urban life in general, and New York's in particular, seemed rife with transformative energies and opportunities.[1] The defining sensibility in Crystal's world—"noble, crazy, glorious," as Max Eastman would remember it—was that *everything* could be different.[2] It was a feeling she never fully outgrew or let go.

Or she could rest on Mt. Airy Road in Croton-on-Hudson, then a country swath in Westchester County, where she owned a simple, yellow clapboard house at the slope of a grassy hill. Eastman lived there with her young family among a small group of radical friends and fellow travelers. Her brother Max, always her most intimate companion, had been first to buy a house in Croton in 1915; she arranged to live very near him, as she would throughout her adult life whenever she possibly could.

Croton seems to have been the home where Eastman's children wanted to remember and keep their mother. The only other relevant document, a letter held by the family, reveals that four years after her death, her then-teenage son, Jeffrey Fuller, planned a memorial plate to be mounted at Croton. The plaque was to be installed over Thanksgiving, 1931, but by November 10 it was clear the project could not be finished in time. In fact, it may not yet have been started. A severely limited budget, always an insistent problem for the family going back to Crystal's own childhood, had stalled the purchase of the necessary tools. Margaret Lane, Eastman's longtime friend and ally in several organizations, urged Jeff to postpone his trip from Manhattan up to Croton until Christmas, or maybe after the first of the year. In the meantime, Lane wrote him, he "could be designing . . . "—but there the letter breaks off. It's a fragment, and no further mention of the plan or the plaque has survived.[3]

Today, none of Crystal's four surviving grandchildren knows where she is buried, and nothing, as far as they know, marks the ground where she rests. In both personal and public contexts, her place remains obscure, her imprint too easy to overlook, misunderstand, or miss almost entirely.

* * *

In the early twentieth century, Crystal Eastman was one of the most conspicuous Progressive reformers in America. Her militant suffragism, insistent antimilitarism, gregarious internationalism, support of the Russian Revolution, and uncompromising feminism led some in the press to brand her notorious. Yet more than a century later, none of these paths to recognition has carried her to significant historical remembrance. Today, she is less known than might be expected, especially given the rarity of a woman with such wide political influence and her continuing institutional legacy in so many high-profile struggles.

Eastman drafted the nation's first serious workers' compensation law, and it became a model for many other states. She helped found the Congressional Union, later to become the National Woman's Party, the world's first women's political party and the group whose unyielding pressure politics finally leveraged universal suffrage in America. And after the vote was won, Eastman has been widely credited as a coauthor of the Equal Rights Amendment (ERA), the party's signature next-wave goal. As the world hurtled toward its first global war, Eastman's integral roles in two major peace organizations made her the most important organizer of the radical internationalist movement in the United States.[4] She facilitated the founding of the Woman's Peace Party, today the Women's International League for Peace and Freedom (WILPF), initiating the recruitment of a reluctant Jane Addams to head the national organization while she formed and led the more audacious New York branch. At the same time, she served as executive secretary of the American Union against Militarism, where she shaped and often catalyzed the only American peace group ever to demonstrate that citizen diplomacy could avert war. The democratic action that accomplished that feat? It was Eastman's brainchild. Then, beginning in 1918, she copublished the *Liberator*, the magazine that became the intellectual rallying point and postwar paper of record for revolutionary movements worldwide. And all this occurred after she had engineered the founding of the American Civil Liberties Union (ACLU).

Yet even all these achievements are only parts of the story. Eastman advocated a politics of private life as far-reaching as her public agenda. Divorced in 1916 after learning of her husband's infidelity, she refused alimony, telling newspapers at the time that "no self-respecting feminist would accept alimony—it would be her admission that she can't take care of herself."[5] When she remarried, to the English pacifist and publicist Walter Fuller, who would become the father of her two children, she expanded her search for feasible solutions to feminist dilemmas in marriage and family life. Her practical experiments in egalitarian marriage and work-family balance accompanied her writing in this area, advancing cultural and feminist conversations on subjects still pressing today: reproductive rights, paid parental leave, economic partnership within marriage, wages for housework, single motherhood by choice, and even the silenced longing of married mothers for substantive work outside the home, a yearning that almost exactly iterates Betty Friedan's "problem that has no name"—nearly half a century before the breakthrough of *The Feminine Mystique* (1963).

In her comparatively short life, Eastman attained wide influence and unusual access. Her aspiration for social justice took her into the heart of progressivism, the final triumph of universal suffrage, the opening battle for birth control, the cataclysm of World War I, the passion and muscle of revolutionary feeling in Europe as it grew. She saw the rise of big media and celebrity culture, the popularization of Freud, the ascendance of the corporation in American life.

Eastman worked side by side with many of the most acclaimed reformers of her time: national and international suffrage leaders including Anna Howard Shaw, Carrie Chapman Catt, Alice Paul, and Lucy Burns, as well as Progressive champions such as Lillian Wald, founder of the Henry Street Settlement and the Visiting Nurse Service of New York; Florence Kelley, social worker, attorney, and general secretary of the National Consumers League; and Jane Addams, the eminent public philosopher, pioneer in the American settlement house movement, and internationally esteemed champion of women's suffrage and world peace. She also worked closely with important men, including Paul Kellogg, the Progressive journalist and urban reformer; John Reed, the revolutionary writer and activist; and Oswald Garrison Villard, grandson of the abolitionist William Lloyd Garrison, publisher of the *New York Evening Post* and later *The Nation*, the man who sketched the blueprint for the National Association for the Advancement of Colored People (NAACP) and then financed it.[6]

Eastman's letters and surviving phone book document the range of her involvement with giants and icons: Charlotte Perkins Gilman—for many, the preeminent theorist of twentieth-century feminism; Inez Milholland, remembered as the symbol and ultimately the martyr of the battle for the vote. Eastman knew the muckrakers William Hard, Lincoln Steffens, Jacob Riis, and Ray Stannard Baker, and millionaire reformers such as Mrs. Malcolm J. Forbes and Henry Ford. She worked with prominent politicians including the anticorporate Progressive Wisconsin governor and US senator Robert "Fighting Bob" LaFollette; his formidable wife, Belle Case LaFollette; and Victor Berger, the first Socialist elected to the US House of Representatives. Her close colleagues included institution builders such as Stanford's first president David Starr Jordan; Morris Hillquit, a founder of the Socialist Party of America; and the Zionist leader and reform rabbi Stephen S. Wise. And across her life and career, she traveled in the company of a transatlantic crew of boundary breakers and innovators, including Charlie Chaplin, Helen Keller, Ida B. Wells-Barnett, Clarence Darrow, John Dewey, Frances Perkins, Louis Brandeis, Jeannette Rankin, F. Scott Fitzgerald, Rudolph Valentino, Rebecca West, H. G. Wells, Bertrand Russell, Sir Norman Angell, George Bernard Shaw, and Leonard and Virginia Woolf.

In all these circles, Eastman seems to have made an impression on everyone she met. She loved to laugh and was nearly six feet tall; athletic on land, court, water, and horseback; and ebullient in verbal style. She "always reminds you of hill-tops and open spaces," her sister-in-law Dorothy Fuller commented in 1916. "She has a fine vivid character. . . . Bright colors suit her well."[7] While newspaper photos do not typically show devastatingly good looks, reporters who interviewed Eastman were frequently taken by her beauty. She was "one of the leading spellbinders," according to the *Washington Herald*, "the suffragette who proves there is beauty as well as brains among the American women who seek the ballot," said the *Mail Tribune*.[8] She possessed "a trinity of virtues," according to *Pearson's* magazine, "beauty, brains and a monstrous faith in humanity."[9] Colleagues and comrades also often found her dazzling. The Harlem Renaissance novelist and poet Claude McKay, whom Eastman discovered and brought to the *Liberator* when he was working on the railroad as a Pullman porter, called her "the most beautiful white woman I ever knew."[10] Her civil liberties colleague Roger Baldwin remembered her warmth coupled with an electric energy. "Crystal was a very beautiful woman in a very arresting sort of a way. A photograph wouldn't show it . . . because it was largely manner, and expression, and the quickness of her response. Her eyes flashed. She had a very pretty smile. Dimples at the corners. A very endearing way of looking at you. She was very responsive. A very mobile face."[11]

Those closest to her often sensed something powerful in her "magnificent presence," as McKay put it. She seemed to carry meaning with her, to signify some cherished promise or hope. McKay, who for years carried a note from Eastman in his breast pocket, saw her "embodying in her personality that daring freedom of thought and action—all that was fundamentally fine, noble and genuine in American democracy."[12] She "sails into a room with her head high," the sculptor Clare Sheridan commented in her diary, "and the face of a triumphant Victory."[13] To her husband Walter, this "strange, wonderful dazzling creature is a much finer woman than I am a man."[14] Her friend Jeannette Lowe marveled simply, "You wouldn't believe how free she was."[15]

In virtually every arena she entered, Crystal Eastman stood for something. "Outspoken (often tactless), determined . . . and courageous," as Baldwin remembered, she was often controversial, but she always declared herself.[16] Whether addressing government officials, capacity crowds, or the most influential papers of the American press; whether confronting colleagues in internal debates or organizing in opposition to adversative policies, institutions, or groups, she did not demur from speaking out—some would say to a fault. But whether celebrated or criticized, her presence was palpable and difficult to ignore. "When she spoke to people—whether it was to a small committee or a swarming crowd—hearts beat faster and nerves tightened as she talked," the famed *Nation* editor Freda Kirchwey recalled in her obituary.[17]

Eastman radiated an unmistakable vitality and dynamism, striking yet hard to pin down. A decade before her death, she called herself a "militant idealist," a handle that suggests the organizing idea of her life.[18] Her wholehearted ideal was to bring together all the great social movements of her era into a grand campaign for global equality and justice. Direct action militancy, both spectacular and bold, was her method and her mantra; she applied it at the highest levels, without equivocation or reserve. Fierce yet deeply kind, as affectionate as she was uncompromising, Eastman was one of the most resounding women known to her allies and adversaries alike. In 2000, she was inducted into the National Women's Hall of Fame, yet today she is still commemorated, paradoxically, as one of the most neglected feminist leaders in US history.[19]

What accounts for this paradox? Why would a feminist star so visible to so many in her time have become so difficult to recognize in our own? As it turns out, the question of Eastman's peculiar obscurity yields distinct insights about why she merits remembering today.

Part of the explanation is methodological. Eastman left a patchy record of personal papers behind. The only collection of her letters is mainly concentrated in her adolescent and college years, tapering off during graduate work to almost nothing by the time she began her first job. This dwindling of personal correspondence is largely the result of her relative proximity to the main correspondents of her life, her mother and brother. In 1907, Max Eastman followed his big sister to New York City, where they lived and worked together much of the time. Then, in 1911, their mother passed away. Crystal largely discontinued letter writing at that point, depriving the historical record of her personal accounts of the activities and ideas that occupied much of her adult professional life. Information about her most pivotal years must therefore be gleaned second-hand, from the memoirs and recollections of those she knew, or from the archives of others—the organizations with which she was involved or affiliated and the papers of her colleagues, allies, and political foes. While this dispersion of material attests to the range and variety of her work, it also diffuses her political voice, eroding our ability to recognize the salience of her contributions.

But this scattered archival record evokes a subtle yet more indicative phenomenon. Since the 1970s, when the historian Blanche Wiesen Cook anthologized important selections of her writing, Eastman has actually surfaced in scholarship many times.[20] In fact, her arguments often flash into narratives as some of the most bracing and memorable moments in relevant biographies and histories. Yet she typically appears for just moments, as a cameo in stories in which she actually played a more meaningful part. Such intermittent visibility has rendered Eastman both familiar and elusive. Glimpsed as a walk-on, she can seem almost out of context in the very organizations and movements she helped to found and to lead. At times, she even seems to arise as a problematic or desultory figure, errant within the very arenas where her input was significant. She becomes a walking ambiguity—conspicuous yet obscure, principal yet somehow peripheral to the main plot and players.

Cook has explained Eastman's position as a nearly direct result of her radical politics and militancy. She rightly described Eastman as an exceptionally bold and assertive woman, and suggested her leftist revolt against the political and economic power structure all but ensured her exile from history. As Cook succinctly put it, "History tends to bury what it seeks to reject."[21]

Cook situated Eastman as an early precursor to what second-wave feminists dubbed "Socialist feminism"—a type of feminism that married women's rights to a critique of capitalism and the social problems associated with it. This was contrasted to "liberal feminism," which cast women's equality almost entirely in the discourse of expanding opportunities and choices, and to "radical feminism," which saw the oppression of women as the central and fundamental oppression from which all others derived. At the turn of the twentieth century, as now, liberal feminism would have enlarged women's individual choices—to vote, to work, to obtain an education. Radical feminism in the 1970s cast women's subordination as the foundation of all other forms of oppression, focusing on those acts of subjection that men "do" to women (sex, violence, rape); in Eastman's day, it insisted on organizing *as women* into political parties entirely devoted to women's issues.

Both Socialist feminists and liberal feminists have spent less time on interpersonal politics—love, marriage, sexuality, balancing work and family—though Cook does tacitly suggest that Eastman's marginalization also stemmed from her sexual radicalism, particularly implying the possibility that she may have been lesbian. While it is true that Eastman was embedded in the permissive world of Greenwich Village and, later, tied to Bloomsbury sexual radicals, she seems to have been a practicing heterosexual. In fact, some evidence suggests she practiced her heterosexuality more freely than most. The perception that Eastman was overly or improperly engaged with men followed her from graduate school through her public career, and pooled particularly within some circles of her women colleagues.[22] Crystal confided to her brother Max that her heterosexual desire felt ineluctable and propulsive at times. On the eve of her first marriage just shy of her thirtieth birthday, she sought out Dr. A. A. Brill, the first psychoanalyst to open an office in the United States. She wanted "help in bringing her 'libido' down," Max recalled; she felt its power drawing her irresistibly to her first husband, a sporty and faintly rakish man she knew did not offer the "companionship in idealism" she would seek when she wed for the second time.[23] And throughout Eastman's career, many ideas that distinguished her—particularly her arguments for contraception in the context of female desire, but also her efforts to create egalitarian marriages and balance work and family—further suggest a heterosexual consciousness at work.

Eastman's leftist militancy is certainly the framework of the answer, but documents once buried in disparate archives and collections now suggest additional dimensions of her radicalism. New evidence suggests her most revolutionary attitude, in fact, may have been her resistance to orthodox political categories at all. In her feminism, for example, she felt the pulls of multiple strands of feminist thinking—today's Socialist, liberal, and radical—and said so, despite the dominant philosophy of her wing of the movement. Indeed, across her political life, Eastman's impulse was to question or challenge doctrinal requirements almost as an organizing principle in itself. She tended to see such requirements as antidemocratic and stifling, detrimental to the successful pursuit of social justice through grassroots social change. Eastman never considered joining the Socialist

Party or, later, the Communist Party, even though she first identified herself as a Socialist while still a college student, publicly blessed the Russian Revolution in 1917, and befriended prime movers of the Communist Party in Britain when she lived there in the 1920s.[24] After Max briefly joined the Socialist Party in the winter of 1912, she applauded his iconoclastic letter published in the Socialist daily, the *New York Call*, precisely for its challenges to collective complacency and any emergent dogma. She encouraged him in a principled nonconformity she would exemplify herself, telling him, "I'm glad of it. They need somebody like you."[25] Six months later, when the January 1913 issue of *The Masses* published a critique of party reasoning, she similarly commended the political and organizational value of candor and independent thinking in the face of whatever the party line. "That straight talk to the Socialists," she said, "does us all good."[26]

Eastman consistently resisted lining up categorically with single organizations or schools of thought. She claims a legitimate place in the leadership of many leftist movements but never allocated her energy to one at a time. She had decided early on that you cannot fix one social problem without fixing the others. From the age of twenty-six, armed with a BA from Vassar, an MA from Columbia, and a law degree from NYU, she went on to pursue a dream to do it all. At the time, she envisioned herself as "one of these circus-chariot-ladies," with "one hand driving a tandem of the arts and the law [and] the other hand holding aloft two streaming banners,—love and liberty."[27] Traversing the "disciplinary" boundaries of arts and the law, as well as the public and private arenas—love and liberty—she positioned herself as a multimovement activist with a foot in many quarters. Eastman understood sexism, exploitation in the class system, racism, and the antidemocratic practices of militarism, imperialism, and war as linked social maladies. Each was a ruthless expression of self-interested power by the privileged few over the many—arbitrary, inhumane, oppressive, wrong. And since she believed each helped reinforce and perpetuate the others, she refused to divide or prioritize them. Steering under the banners of numerous movements at once, she committed herself to the pursuit of their equal and simultaneous redress.

From the dawn of her public life, Eastman worked to confederate social struggles and to coalesce her own heartfelt investments in their intersecting ideals, allies, interests, and constituencies. She talked about gender with the Socialists and the antimilitarists, about class and imperialism, internationalism and also maternalism with the feminists. At juncture after juncture in her political career, she pushed to enlarge connections among social justice movements by forging ties among shared experiences of inequality. She repeatedly confronted the complex relations of oppression and privilege among and within activist groups, all in an effort to link organizational agendas and collective actions under one vast emancipatory rubric.

In this persistent drive, she was politically notable, and also ahead of her time. More than seventy-five years before black feminism defined the concept of "intersectionality," Eastman was reaching toward what might now be characterized as intersectional activism. She intuitively understood that there are interconnections among systems of oppression that must be attended to simultaneously.[28] Gender inequality, for example, could not be redressed without considering other aspects of identity: class was particularly salient to her, but nationality and race were also in the mix of her thinking. It is important to note that while Eastman deplored racial injustice, she did not always emphasize racism per se when itemizing the sources of oppression in her social critique. At times, she incorporated racial inequality into other contexts, either her Socialist concerns with class struggle and anti-imperialism or her feminist and pacifist concerns with antiviolence and antimilitarism—and sometimes a combination of these.[29] Nevertheless, current work on intersectionality invites comparison with her political sensibility. Eastman perceived the interlocking structures that arrange and maintain inequality and strived to create a coalition identity and public actions to combat them in concert.[30]

Contemporary historians now reflect that Socialist feminists of the second wave were reaching in the 1970s for intersectional connections among the social movements around them—connections like those Eastman pursued beginning in the 1910s.[31] These recent observations alert us to the complexities of Eastman's position and her efforts in her time. In a much earlier era, she too tried to engage cross-movement policy ideas and mobilize actions designed to harmonize the aims of multiple groups. Yet then as now, history, exigency, and interpersonal alliances kept asking her to choose: one single-issue campaign; one struggle to create a better world; one identity—laborite, suffragist, Socialist, pacifist, or internationalist, militant or mother. But Eastman did not see herself that way, and she had always been taught that the sacrifice of her own vision was tantamount to a deadly sin.

Expansive, straddling, disquieting to dominant perspectives and institutional rank, Eastman was transgressive in ways that have been less apparent in the past. Her militant idealism, sustained by intersectional arguments, made her an iconoclast or gadfly within every organization she knew. Its competing demands within a world of practical politics and organizational dynamics positioned her more precariously than many of her colleagues. Indeed, her arguments at times left her stranded, as if she had tried to build a bridge from the middle of the water, rather than solidly anchored on one side or another.

Yet this approach, and the far-reaching freedom and justice she always believed it would bring, remained the defining paradigm of her life. Eastman consistently carried forward and attempted to mesh the perspectives and objectives that emerged in each chapter of her career: labor into feminism; feminism into peace; world peace into revolutionary change; feminist politics into family life. In light of the scope of her political involvement, her cumulative vision ultimately became aggregative, or, to adopt an image with which some scholars have conceived history itself, *kaleidoscopic*: she moved among a constellation of ideas and interests, reconfiguring the mix as historical, political, and personal conditions shifted before her eyes.[32] The overall set of relevant issues remained constant, but the mergers and interconnections, the focal points and emphases, changed as the force and flow of dramatic events called different combinations to the forefront of her view.

However compatible this politics may have been with her idealist vision, in practice Eastman's resistance to the reputational anchors offered by single causes or dominant affiliations raised "definitional dilemmas," a problem often connected with intersectional thinking and activism today.[33] A clearer relationship to recognized individual movements or organizational leaders might have better located her, securing her political identity and historical memory.[34] Even her transgressive qualities might have produced reputational benefits had they been more deferential to one cause over others. Properly situated and supported, cultural rebels are often carried to historical recognition and renown.[35] But Eastman lacked the contextual clarity that might have allowed a reputation as rebel to take hold and endure. Her positions too often opened quandaries—over principles, priorities, strategies, tactics, organizational identity itself—even among her allies. Her intersectional arguments seemed to challenge the process of self-definition, already more precarious and hard-won for these groups, from within.

The very ambition and intensity of Eastman's idealism vexed her status within the array of social change organizations she always identified as her collective political home. As Eastman bridged movement contexts and agendas, surging by turns as a dynamic champion and challenging voice, all the while balancing work and family, she complicated the political affiliations and interpersonal alliances from which historical recognition and renown are built. The tandem she was driving at the dawn of her career ultimately came apart beneath her feet. She fell through the main planks of historical memory.

Yet Eastman's perspective and experiences give her story uncommon relevance and value today. A fuller picture of her life gives us access to not just one uncommon story but several of them. And in almost every connection, Eastman's politics made her stands especially provocative and revealing. To see her now is to discover more than a few canny observations, promising cultural and political roads not taken, and a number of still-relevant ideas, all born with the onset of our time.

In so many respects, Eastman's story both backlights and illuminates current issues. From reproductive rights to the ERA, her advocacy for gender equality particularly put her at the leading edge of the policy curve. Indeed, these stands arguably put her on the front lines of feminist activism today. The same may be said of her positions on feminism and family life. In the twenty-first century, the personal has become profoundly political; questions of identity, equality, and empowerment in sex, love, marriage, family, child-rearing, and more are pronounced concerns for contemporary women. Further, men and masculinity, subjects she discussed discerningly time and again, have entered the agenda of equality movements worldwide. Eastman was one of the few women of her era to consistently press the concerns of private life into public affairs. And she was a leading voice in warning that if the private sphere was not transformed along with the public, the gender revolution that promised to let women live freely and fulfilled as complete human beings would stall out, half-finished. She anticipated by a century, and counting, the "unfinished revolution" documented by feminist sociologists,[36] the "forgotten fight" spotlighted by feminist historians[37] to this day. "Life is a big battle for the complete feminist," she declared in 1918, and she advanced that struggle into today's world through her often-startling perceptions and initiatives on the home front.[38]

The media activism that Eastman prized has risen to nearly equal footing with more traditional forms of democratic participation and public action today. Eastman had an instinct for the latest popular platforms of her time, the moment when the modern revolution in electronic media began. Following that impulse, she organized an assortment of spirited public interest campaigns. When she teamed up with her husband Walter, she involved herself in more immersive and even more far-reaching efforts. In the wartime era that saw unprecedented government propaganda organized to manufacture consent, Crystal facilitated, and Walter designed, new media campaigns to manufacture *dissent*, ingeniously cultivating the deep human desires for peace and fellowship they believed could spur resistance and sustain fundamental social change. Such aspiring efforts offer us new insights and opportunities, as they anticipated both modern participatory media approaches and some key precepts of persuasion and public opinion formation still operating to this day.

Finally, intersectional thinking has now become a principal mode of understanding, and an applied concept in social movement organizing across the globe. Today, both in academia and the activist world, marshalling the energies of diverse political groups is a matter of considerable and consequential concern. We are among many democratic cultures confronting challenges to political processes that recall Eastman's experiences, from the question of defining similarities in ways that can draw differently situated individuals and groups into common cause,[39] to the need to attend to variations in principles, priorities, tactics, and modes of organizational governance to bring—and keep—diverse coalitions together.[40] Eastman's efforts, and their outcomes, can contribute to current research and debates about political equality connected to social identity and change organizing alike. Indeed, her story has something to offer to our most profound questions about living together equitably and authentically in diverse democratic societies writ large.

For all her multimovement vision and activity, Eastman's singular aspiration was the achievement of global social justice. The great drama of her life was the effort to bring people together to battle the great forces that keep them down. Her urgent social conscience propelled her to great heights and subjected her to some piercing losses, but it would not let her rest or remain silent. The tragic irony was the way her voice sometimes seemed to divide people, to divide loyalties. But whatever the complications of her stands then, and her historical recognition since, there is no mistaking the fact that Crystal Eastman was her own woman. She knew, as she emphasized in her very first public speech on feminism in 1914, that for women to claim full selfhood, "the biggest battle will be with ourselves."[41] Through every challenge and chapter, she stayed true to herself, even when the political ground shifted, sometimes violently, what her causes would connote. Even as the balancing of her cross-movement identity—"equalitarian labor lawyer," "pacifist revolutionary," "working mother," "feminist, activist, wife"—pushed her from the very fields of struggle it also beckoned her to charge.

That indomitable spirit makes Eastman a woman leader worth knowing at any time, but perhaps especially now. As thrilling as she could be challenging, she was a force to be reckoned with. And for all the ways that definitive quality can inspire us, it can also frustrate our strategic impulses to celebrate more straightforward models of women's leadership. Eastman was a persistently significant voice, unsettling premises and challenging those around her to confront the unexamined biases in their thinking and policies. Hence, her story sometimes complicates the terms of remembrance—even newer, revised terms wrestled into respect since the second wave—on which we have come to rely. But just as she did with her contemporaries, she may now challenge us, as readers, thinkers, and citizens, to examine our expectations and reflexes. She may offer us another call to confront our differences, to come to terms with the organizational gadflies among us, to critically engage the logic and reception of all those whose perspectives, for whatever reasons, raise questions from within. In Eastman's case, heartfelt questioning has so far come at the cost of a recognized resting place in public memory, of a settled historical home. But such pressures can be mechanisms for both evolution and accountability, a means for keeping participatory democracies and organizational policies relevant and responsive over time, just as she hoped they would be.

Collective memory shows a tendency to compose either the great or the evil, socially constructing remembrance around those seen to do one big thing wrong (who then can do little that is right), or those who do one big thing right and so can do no wrong.[42] This predilection leaves too little room for complicated stories of various kinds, and thus for a richer and more thought-provoking reading of ourselves. Perhaps Eastman's life, in its achievements and its altercations, can help us claim an era when women might accomplish recognition and remembrance even if their significance comes swathed in restless narratives or troublesome stands. To move forward in challenging times, we need challenging women among us. We need to know leaders who are human and real—who blaze a trail by leaving us goals and road maps and also make plain some critical hurdles and hazards along the way. If we come to recognize more complicated women as our allies and champions, we gain the mettle to forge a stronger way forward. And perhaps more of us may even dare to dream big the way Eastman did, to unite in struggles that embody and strengthen humanity, to attempt great things ourselves.

This book strives to recover that kind of complex, searching, quenchless American woman. I have tried to emphasize the category-defying ambit and eclecticism of her life's work. Eastman wore so many hats. She was a policy innovator, media activist, speaker, organizer, executive, publisher, writer, working mother, and provocative voice in many debates that shaped her world—and ours. I seek to bring out her distinctive point of view, quoting often, and as much as possible from speeches, meeting minutes, press rejoinders, surveillance reports, and her unpublished manuscripts, sources that particularly convey her personal accent.

Eastman's politics gave her life an episodic quality that has left her vulnerable to fragmentation and misunderstanding over time. It is my hope that this biography can render the patterns in her thinking and continuities in her work recognizable and available to a new generation. I have also tried to capture the cultural parameters of her militancy, the righteous ingenuity of her fierce, "in your face" attitude that has once again emerged as the cornerstone of social change advocacy.[43] Most of all, I have strived to impart her voice in the way she herself exercised it in life: in debate and conversation, in candor, contention, and unceasing hope.

Eastman dared to speak truth to power—and even to herself—while knotty allegiances in work and family, love and politics, challenged her alliances, her finances, her hopes, her health. She died young, still trying to live in a world she longed for and had labored to call into being. Yet the social justice issues she cared about—gender equality and human rights, nationalism and globalization, political censorship and media control, worker benefits and family balance, and the monumental questions of war, sovereignty, force, and freedom—remain some of the most consequential questions of our own time. And her struggle at the intersections of multiple identities and allegiances, and to abide with integrity and wholeness across private and public affairs, summons her story to life not just in her time but also in our own.

1 ORIGINS

In her last piece of public writing, published anonymously in *The Nation* in 1927, Crystal Eastman took stock of her own life for the first time. She contributed an autobiographical essay to a series called "These Modern Women," in which seventeen feminists recounted their life stories to the world.[1] The whole project was the brainchild of *Nation* editor Freda Kirchwey, her longtime friend and colleague from the suffrage and women's peace movements who would soon write her obituary.[2]

"The story of my life," Eastman began, "is the story of my mother."[3] Writing just fifteen months before her own death, Eastman felt her maternal inheritance so emphatically that her only writing ever to recount it breached its own genre: Crystal's autobiography quickly passed into her mother's biography. In memory as in life, her investments in her mother's story blurred the boundaries of her own.

Crystal Eastman was a child of restive forces. She was born simultaneously into a rising political reaction against the inequality and human suffering wrought by American industrialization and a dynamic American family. Those closest to her wielded a blend of social reform, communitarian Socialism, and women's rights, all stirred with a searching millennial zeal. Eastman's mother was the principal source of this solution to her. Annis Ford Eastman was a Congregational minister, the first woman ever ordained in New York State. Her spiritual politics and personal charisma not only led to regional renown as a preacher and reformer but also settled her in a powerful place as both the economic and the emotional engine of a family that might otherwise have been driven and defined by men.[4]

Eastman's father was Samuel Elijah Eastman, a tall man of dusky complexion whose second name recalls the prophet who was taken up to heaven in a whirlwind. Sam was in the prime of his young manhood when he met the woman who became his wife, but he was fragile. He had lost a lung at nineteen, a sacrifice in service to the Union army in 1865. During a battle near Richmond, he had collapsed on the field

Crystal Eastman. Amy Aronson, Oxford University Press (2020).
© Oxford University Press.
DOI: 10.1093/oso/9780199948734.001.0001

from what was termed typhoid pneumonia, and the high fever he suffered damaged his lung and sapped his health and stamina for the rest of his life.

The Eastmans had three sons. Their firstborn was Morgan, a gentle and adored child whose "exuberant sweetness [and] rare gift of sympathy made [him] seem divine," Max recounted.[5] His death from scarlet fever at the age of seven forever sealed his seraphic image in family memory. Next was Anstice, known for his intelligence and his physical endurance.[6] "Rash, reckless, agile and muscular," as Max described him, Anstice excelled at masculine sport with a militant quality— "spearing bullfrogs, shooting birds and squirrels with an airgun, playing 'I'm the king of the castle'" activities, Max noted, that were enhanced by his insistent "quaff of anger." His outward penchant for making trouble, however, masked a kind and even sentimental heart, which Anstice hid underneath.[7] A second son, Anstice persistently confounded his mother's love—the two "would go into surly glooms against each other like two lovers quarreling," Max remembered.[8] But he felt no such tensions with his sister, the other woman in the household. Anstice, like Max, felt Crystal's "gift for loving-kindness . . . so spontaneous and tranquil that . . . it seemed like musical or mathematical genius." Anstice used to call her "an angel sister, almost."[9] Last came Max, the baby, who proclaimed himself a "mama's boy" and at different times called his mother and his sister his hero.[10] Max was emotionally entwined with the two women in the family for as long as they lived. "Of all Freud's plain and fancy inventions," he wrote toward the end of his life, "the concept of the 'incest barrier' is one of the most easily verifiable in my experience."[11] The three of them formed a tight and tangled inner core of the Eastman clan. Annis once told Crystal, "You will have to take my place with [Max] some day [sic]. . . . Be always tender to him and save him from himself."[12]

Eastman titled her article "Mother-Worship," an apt headline that captured the attitude of the entire family. They all adored what Max described as her "originality and impulsive candor," her "vivifying mind and voice," temperamental qualities that dictated the timbre and rhythm of Eastman family life.[13] Each day, it seemed, she "lifted and launched anew some vividly conceived scheme . . . for making life a great thing."[14] But they also experienced the darkness that frequently intruded without warning, "the sharp, grievous sense of unworthiness," as Max characterized it, which visited the family matriarch unbidden in the midst of her hopes.[15] Her restless energies and shifting emotional currents, in all their thrilling prospects and threatening doubts, affected Crystal, the only daughter, even more than anyone else in the family.

Yet what that immense maternal relationship ultimately meant to her has been in dispute since the day "Mother-Worship" appeared. Kirchwey revised the article's original ending, altering the most revealing conclusions Eastman ever expressed about her origins and herself. In the months that followed its publication, she told family members that the essay "was much better the way I wrote it." It was "more honest," she said, and "therefore, more interesting."[16] The actual content of Crystal's original conclusion has been missing until now, left behind with the last bits of her literary estate still in the hands of her descendants. What was cut or changed in that last published essay, her only sustained autobiographical utterance in print, may be nearly as revealing as what appeared on the page. From the elisions and revisions, the foundation of her story emerges.

* * *

Bertha Annis Ford first encountered Samuel Eastman at a boarding house at Oberlin College, in a dining commons where students ate their meals. It was 1873, and Oberlin was the first college in the country to give women the opportunity to earn a degree alongside men. When they met, Samuel was slim and rangy, his straight, forthright mouth almost perfectly horizontal except for the slight lift created by upright crescent dimples at each end. Led by an unbending nose, his face was balanced and open from the front, yet appeared angular when viewed sidelong. As a student, he wore his sideburns full and wiry, almost reaching his jaw, but he cut them short once he married and became a family man. At twenty-six, he had entered divinity school to please his father, an evangelist whose voice was insistent in his ears.

Bertha, as she called herself then, was eighteen and in her first year of college, the one year for which she had the money. When that year was over in June 1874, she had to leave Oberlin, and she found a job teaching school. Samuel wrote to her. She replied. Soon they were engaged. They married in Peoria, her hometown, in 1875, on August 25—a Wednesday. It must have seemed unusual to some—a midweek wedding—especially for a young minister and his bride.[17]

But the Eastmans were an unconventional couple in several respects. For one thing, Sam was not by nature a patriarch (nor particularly a breadwinner), and Bertha held onto her "early yearning to *be something*," as Max put it, beyond the home.[18] In their first years together, the couple lived an itinerant life, striking out in various directions not only for a parish for Sam but also for a way of living they could share together. In the course of eight years, they relocated four times, roaming more than two thousand miles from North to South and back again. From Swampscott, Massachusetts, a beach town north of Boston where Sam had his first job at the Congregational church, they moved more than eight hundred miles to Newport, Kentucky, in 1877 or 1878; soon they headed back up north to Marlboro, Massachusetts, in early 1879. Eighteen months later they relocated to Canandaigua, New York, where Sam became pastor of the First Congregational Church in the autumn of 1881.

At each place, the family grew. Morgan was born in Kentucky, with Anstice not far behind. Then Bertha's sister Elmina committed suicide, and the couple took in her twin infant sons, Chambers and John Stettinius. The group was shortly joined by Bertha's aunt, Catherine Stehley, who had separated from her domineering husband, George Ford. Then came Bertha's dearest friend from Oberlin, Mary Landen. Mary joined the family to help with the children perhaps, but also to give Bertha "what she so desperately missed in her all-too-perfect husband—a friend of her intuitions and her wit," Max recalled. Mary was single, perhaps lesbian—in the 1960s, Max described her as "a spinster foreordained by God"—and an excellent tutor; she was freer than most women to live where she wanted. And Bertha had begged her to come. As a young wife, Crystal's mother had struggled from the start of her marriage with "her disappointment in the intimacies of love which was so commonly the lot of women in that day when ignorance was holy," Max said. "Aunt Mary" joined the household to provide companionship that Bertha did not seem to experience with her husband, to make her feel, as she described it, "at home." Aunt Mary stayed in the Eastman household for the next fifteen years—until Crystal herself, as Max saw it, "grew up and replaced Mary Landen as my mother's closest friend."[19]

For Bertha, now settled in a female-centric family unit, a feeling of transcendent joy arrived with the dawn of motherhood. She would always look to her children to meet many of her emotional needs. With her first-born, Morgan, she described nearly ecstatic experiences in the everyday. Rocking him to sleep, for example, "with no other light in the room," she would look down "at his face with its wonderful eyes," seeing in them "stars and suns and every shining thing."[20]

But for Sam, the early, unmistakable signs of intimate alienation by his wife, coupled with his breadwinner responsibilities in a family unit suddenly grown into a company consisting of a triangle of adults, an elder in-law, and three very young children, became overwhelming. Already fragile physically, he grew ill and nearly died in Kentucky. It was the first of numerous breakdowns, as the family termed them, which he experienced throughout his prime years of career building, fatherhood, and family life. As Max remembered, only when "his lustihood" declined with age did his health grow more stable.[21]

Sam searched for his place as a father just as he did as a husband; he "could not find the poise she found in the love of their baby," and as he "tried to deny and drive down his grief," Max recalled, "it took revenge on his body."[22] In the infancy of his second son, he announced that the southern climate was causing his declining health, and returned the family to New England. Then came Marlboro, where Crystal, the daughter Annis always wanted, came along in June 1881. Two months later, they moved on to Canandaigua, and Max was born, in 1883. At

Max's birth, Bertha ended her sexual relationship with her husband—never, so far as we know, to share a bed with him again.

Crystal had just turned three when they lost Morgan to scarlet fever, a life-changing event for the whole family that her mother called "the shadow in my soul."[23] Annis relived every detail in her diary. It happened just after Independence Day. Sam, an outdoorsman—he would later sleep in a tent he pitched in the woods near the Eastman home unless weather prevented it—liked to take his children on excursions into the countryside. Bertha had put Crystal to bed one evening as she awaited his return. Suddenly, the door flung open and she looked up to see Sam with seven-year-old Morgan in his arms. The child's body seemed lifeless and his eyes were glassy and blank.

Over the next two days, Morgan seemed to improve, but then he took a turn downhill; he developed chills, and then began vomiting. The doctor came to the house more than once and diagnosed a simple summer cold. They all thought it would run its course. When the symptoms did not ease, Bertha called another doctor, who noticed the telltale rash on Morgan's chest.

The next afternoon, Crystal became ill. Bertha could barely cope with her worry and dread; for the rest of her life, she was on guard if Crystal showed the slightest signs of illness of any kind. Morgan cried out for his mother "in a sharp voice that thrilled me through," she recorded in her diary. She left Crystal with the nurse and rushed with her husband to Morgan's bedside.

"Oh how we tried to get him still," Annis recounted—"putting heat to his feet, bathing his head, holding his hands. But all was to no avail. He must toss on now until the stillness of Death overtook him."

"Bring him to me," she said at last, "and let me hold him in my arms. Let him be Mamma's baby again."

Morgan murmured, " 'yes,' and held out his arms."

"His father brought him and laid him in my arms," she wrote, and "at that very instant he straightened out and was still, his breath coming only a few seconds longer in painful gasps."[24] Morgan died gazing up at her.

The next day at 5:00 p.m. his small body was carried out for burial. But Crystal "was then in the first and nervous stages of the fever when she could not be left for a moment," her mother remembered. "I could only go a few minutes while Dr. John watched her, to say goodbye to the form I loved so passionately, and to kneel with his father beside the little white casket so soon to be hidden away from mortal sight."[25]

Crystal battled the infection for days and ultimately overcame it. But the damage it had done to her young kidneys, unknown to doctors or her parents at the time, would linger throughout her life. While Crystal appeared to have recovered, her mother did not. The loss of Morgan brought on a period of grief that consumed her for more than a year and would recur on the anniversaries of his death. Then, by the time she managed to emerge from her initial mourning, it was Sam who collapsed. Bertha began writing his sermons for him, his prayers and letters, too; as Max recounted, she "eased and supported him in every way but the one that a woman can."[26]

By the end of the summer of 1886, Sam was unable to continue as a pastor. He "began, as mysteriously as though sucked by a vampire, to lose his small vigor and fade out into the frail, hollow, weakly gesturing, half whispering ghost of a minister," Max remembered.[27] In August, Sam resigned from his position at the Congregational church. Annis wrote his letter of resignation for him.[28]

The family had to leave the parish house. With Sam no longer working, the Eastmans had no income. The books were sold; the home that had held together an extended household was broken up. When two of Sam's former parishioners, Antoinette and Josephine Granger, offered Bertha a teaching position, she took it immediately. At that moment, when she became the breadwinner for the family, she elected to become Annis Ford Eastman. Bertha Eastman was gone forever.

Within two weeks, Annis began teaching English and history at the Granger Place School, a finishing school for young ladies outside Canandaigua that promoted itself in magazine advertisements for its college preparation and attention to the health of each pupil.[29] Crystal would later attend, graduating in 1899. For now, Annis took seven-year-old Anstice with her to study. Sam took Crystal, five, and Max, three and a half, and their twin nephews to live effectively as boarders—though they paid no rent—with the Pratt family on their farm on one edge of town.

The turn of events affected Crystal cruelly. She "felt bitterly the breaking up of her much brooded-over family," Max recalled.[30] She wanted her mother, and a home where they could all be together, perhaps more than anyone else in the family—and perhaps more than life itself: at the time, she used to play a game where she pretended she was a peddler selling a special kind of candy that would make the whole family die together.[31] "And how Crystal suffered with her dear loving heart," Annis wrote in her diary. "Once she said to me: 'Before you go, won't you and Anstice and Papa and Max come up into our room a little while?' I asked her for what, and she said, with quivering lips: 'Oh, so we can have our *family* all together!'"[32]

* * *

One of the most subtle changes Kirchwey made to "Mother-Worship" pertains to Crystal's commentary about her father. In her original, Crystal gave a separate paragraph emphasizing his exceptional empathy. Sam Eastman, she explained, "honestly want[ed] other people to have as good a time as he would like to have himself." And for him, "people" included women, without question. When it counted, Sam's innate "generosity," as Crystal named it, overflowed his generally formal demeanor and his tendency to rest on "ritual aspects of righteousness," temperamental traits that openly exasperated his wife.[33] Nevertheless, Sam stood by his wife and his daughter in every feminist act, "from the time when I wanted to cut my hair off and go barefoot to the time I began to study law," Crystal recounted. "When I insisted the boys had to make their beds if I had to make mine, he stood by me. . . . And when I declared that in our family there was no such thing as boys' work and girls' work, and that I must be allowed to do my share of the wood-chopping and outdoor chores, he took me seriously and let me try."[34]

Through the early years of marriage, as Annis grew to find her voice, Sam struggled to maintain his. He groped for a sense of himself as a man who was compatible with his wife. To a certain extent, he eventually found it as a father. By the fall and winter of 1886, Annis was a working mother with Anstice in tow at Granger Place, and Sam a single parent to the younger children. To keep the second household going, Sam bought live ducks and chickens, dressed them, then sold them door to door. He survived the local embarrassment by keeping an eye forward. Within a year, he had managed to buy a farm about half a mile from the Granger Place School. It was a big risk—borrowing $6,500 for forty acres of soil, plus pasture lands and a meadow and what Max described as "a muck of a lot"—but the goal of reunifying the family superseded everything. Actually, Sam often took chances on land to create a home for the family—first here in Canandaigua, later in Elmira, and in two summer settings on Lake Seneca, including the land in Glenora where the Eastmans built their cherished summer retreat. It was not Sam but Annis who fretted over borrowing money, whether for a mortgage or anything else; she persistently suffered family debt as a "dismal fact," both humiliating and wrong.[35] "We have no right to trade on our future prospects," she would say.[36]

Leaving the Pratt family farm for one of their own probably felt like a dream to Crystal. On the day they moved in at Canandaigua, she rode at the crown of a mound of furniture piled on top of a horse-drawn wagon all the way down a long hill, past Canandaigua Lake, and up through the main street of town. Her mattress was placed at the apex of it all where, dressed in her nightgown, she was tucked away in bed.[37]

By the time Crystal was seven, the Eastman farm in Canandaigua was home to twenty head of cattle and a stationary engine. Sam employed a hired man named Ownie Clark and built the first silo in Ontario County, a feat that spread his name throughout the region. Crystal and Max each had a pet calf to take care of; Crystal named hers Daisy. Later Crystal inherited a little bay mustang her father originally brought home for Max, who was too scared to ride it. Max would recall his sister's intrepid heart and natural athleticism as she "careen[ed] around town and country on a man's saddle in fluttering vast brown bloomers."[38] In these years, Sam regained his health and was able to preach sometimes. In 1888, he wrote to his father that preaching one Sunday had brought him a "tidal wave of sweet and tranquil joy" all the preceding week.[39] But by 1890, he wrote again to his father, "I am trying to face the fact that I may never be able to speak continuously in public again!"[40]

It was in 1890 that Annis was ordained. It is unclear how or why the idea came to her that she could preach, but her "thirst for wider experience and fresher wisdom" that Max likened to "a perpetual change of seasons" probably contributed.[41] Besides, she knew something about preaching after helping her husband with his sermons all those years. As Annis remembered it, one day she proposed the notion out of the blue, and "it had the effect of a galvanic shock." But Sam, struck all at once by his empathy for the equal person he had married, "raised himself up quickly, with the dazed air of one making a surprising discovery, [and] replied, 'It was what you were made for!' "[42]

Weeks of consultation with local and clerical authorities resulted only in discouragement, but Sam's persistent investment of his "coaching and local prestige," as Crystal recalled, boosted her mother's prospects.[43] Finally, a letter arrived telling Annis of "a church which had fallen among thieves and robbers and was left more than half dead."[44] No ordained minister, no man with other choices, it seems, could be found for a church so destitute and failing. They had little but a leaky roof, a sizeable debt, "several antiquated church quarrels and about twenty-five members," Max recounted. Still, Annis was told, "they will have you for one Sunday but promise nothing after that."[45] That first Sunday stretched to nearly three years, a new roof on the church, repaired stairs at the entryway, and a much larger congregation.

The derelict church was in Brookton, near Ithaca. Annis commuted to her work, leaving her family on Saturday and returning again on Monday to be, as Max put it, "our mother again."[46] Crystal ministered to her little brother through the tearful separations. Although she did not acknowledge it, she assumed a mother's role as much for her own mother's sake as for her little brother's. "I have a vivid memory of my mother when I was six years old," she recalled:

> We are standing, my brother and I, in front of a run-down farmhouse on the edge of town which had become our home. We have just said goodby [sic] to our mother and now are watching her trip off down the hill. . . .

She turns to smile at us, such a beaming smile, such a bright face, such a pretty young mother. When the charming, much-loved figure begins to grow small in the distance, my brother, who is younger and more temperamental than I, begins to cry. He screams as loud as he can, until he is red in the face. But he cannot make her come back. And I, knowing she will be worried if she hears him, try to drag him away.[47]

It was the Brookton congregation that encouraged Annis to seek ordination. That event occurred in Brooklyn, New York, with a sermon preached by the famed abolitionist minister Thomas Beecher. At first, Beecher had refused to ordain a woman. Despite "knowing and esteeming the Rev. and Mrs. Eastman," he commented, he nevertheless left for the ceremony saying, "I shall have nothing to do with ordaining Mrs. Eastman because I do not believe in a woman's preachings." But afterward, when word got out that he had assisted in the service, Beecher made a qualification. "I stand just where I did when I left home. I do not believe in ordaining women to preach, but I do believe in ordaining Mrs. Eastman."[48] Four years later, Beecher would bring Annis to his Park Church as copastor. He would say many times that Annis Eastman preached the greatest sermons he ever heard.[49]

Prior to that, however, Annis was formally called to her first real parish in West Bloomfield, a small town west of Canandaigua then consisting of two hundred houses scattered along a dirt road. She liked to joke that the town boasted "a fish pond, a skunk farm and a woman minister."[50] Her job came with a parsonage for the family that sat on a crossroads. As the second Reverend Eastman gained a following, Sam sold the farm and opened a grocery store in town, to which he commuted thirteen miles each way on a local train affectionately called "the peanut line." He shouldered the marriage his wife and family needed. Annis's salary was $800 a year, almost exactly the same amount as the $12 to $15 a week her husband brought home from his grocery business.

* * *

Other than the changed conclusion, Kirchwey's largest editorial intervention in "Mother-Worship" was the removal of a paragraph in which Crystal witnessed her mother's rise to renown as a minister. By all accounts, Annis was riveting when she preached—"gay, sparkling, humorous, intimate, adorable," as Crystal described her. She could be exceptionally charismatic interpersonally, as well as in front as a crowd, a natural spellbinder, just as her daughter would be. But to Crystal, her mother's preaching rose to the sublime. To listen to her, she suggested, was to have opposing emotions held together in equipoise, to be roused by inspiration yet firmly assured at the same time. "There was never a moment of anxiety or concern," Crystal wrote; "she had the secret of perfect platform ease which takes all strain out of the audience." Her mother's "voice was music," she felt, "and what she said seemed to come straight from her heart to yours."[51]

Yet a crucial autobiographical dimension of this memory—cut by Kirchwey—recounts Crystal's emotional response as she watched her mother preach. Listening raptly from the third row, she started to weep. As Annis spoke, a brass band had struck up behind the pulpit. Crystal was not shedding tears of joy over her mother's message, or the image of a high-spirited ensemble seeming to trumpet her mother's glory. Rather, she cried out of fear that the sounds of celebration would cause one of the terrible headaches Annis suffered beginning at the time she was ordained.[52] Often, they came on Mondays. Crystal, then just a teen, always attended to her mother's suffering above all else.

The headaches were only one eddy that formed amid the churning emotional tides that accompanied Annis's rise to fame. The first of several debilitating breakdowns occurred in July 1892, after six months at West Bloomfield. She checked into the Gleason Sanitarium, the same place Sam went for help.[53] By December, Annis was on the upswing again, rising to speak at the Congregationalist meeting held in nearby Geddes, New York. The following year, she would address the World Congress of Religion in Chicago, one of the largest events at the World's Columbian Exhibition in 1893 and the first formal gathering of Eastern and Western spiritual traditions in interreligious dialogue.[54]

It was exactly one year later that Annis's early champion Thomas Beecher invited her to join him at the Park Church. The parish had formed when a group of worshipers broke away from the Presbyterian church over the issue of slavery, forming the Congregational church of Elmira in 1846.[55] Beecher, half-brother of the famed abolitionist minister Henry Ward Beecher and of Harriet Beecher Stowe, author of the antislavery novel *Uncle Tom's Cabin* (1852), was renowned by then—or notorious, depending on the source—across the Chemung and Susquehanna Valleys for his lifetime of free-thinking ways. Now nearing seventy, he proposed Annis be called to serve as his associate. Sam was invited to share the call but declined. "I think I could be helpful in the executive work," he responded, but serving as copastor with his wife "is too exhaustive for me to think of undertaking."[56]

The salary was $2,000 a year, and the family was to live inside the Park Church above the church parlors. The appointment settled the Eastmans in a "rare position for the growth and cultivation of the mind," Max recalled, "at the exact center of one of the most interesting clusters of people and ideas that American churchdom ever produced or found room to contain."[57] Beecher himself was "masterful, humorous, poised upon himself although impetuous, and endowed with a supreme contempt for fame, money and 'success,'" Max said, and he created a church "in his own free-moving and magnanimous" image.[58]

Beecher aroused deep animosities among the surrounding churchmen for a variety of acts they considered "blasphemies," but chief among them were two crucial traits he shared with Annis. First, "he was a man of science," Max declared. He cofounded the Elmira Academy of Sciences, a league of about fifty men whose mission was to promote a taste for scientific pursuits. Through its regular reports by standing committees and periodic scientific meetings, the organization connected local citizens with current research from eminent institutions such as the Royal Academy in London—and so with revolutionary thinkers of the day like Charles Darwin; the comparative biologist Thomas Henry Huxley, often called "Darwin's Bulldog" for his scientific support of Darwin's discoveries; and the physicist John Tyndall, whose measurements of infrared radiation provided the first experimentally grounded account of what is now called "the greenhouse effect."[59]

Second was Beecher's "absolute rejection, not of 'angular sectarianism,' but of all sectarianism whatsoever," as Max described it. Beecher's spiritual devotion lived in the world all around him. He was a trained mechanic, and he served his parishioners as carpenter, painter, paper hanger, and sewing machine repairman. He wrote a weekly column in the local newspaper. He organized a baseball team called the Lively Turtles. He played pool, loved the theater, and sang college songs, accompanying himself on the church organ. And for forty years, Beecher "wound and set the Elmira clock, keeping in pace with the sun by means of observations made with his own instruments," Max recalled. He likened Beecher's innovational delight in the rhythms and truths of human community to the "world-embracing mystic vision" of Walt Whitman, the father of free verse, who was Beecher's contemporary.[60]

The Park Church is an early example of what would later be named Christian Socialism; in its simplest essence, the church sought to bring all people together into one Christian family by dedicating itself to both community and spiritual needs. The Eastman family's "church home," as Annis called it, was a corridor of rooms situated among three interconnected buildings that included a large circular auditorium with seating for approximately a thousand people. The facilities were designed to offer a range of services. There was a kitchen equipped to serve up to three hundred, meeting parlors available to anyone who wanted to use them, a free public library, a billiard room, a dancing hall, and a children's "romp room" complete with a stage for plays and performances.[61] Every fourth Sunday was Children's Sunday, when Annis delivered some of Crystal's favorite sermons.

In "all these wildly sensible acts and this great-hearted thinking," the Park Church represented, as Max saw it, "the outlines of a cultural revolution."[62]

Both Crystal and her mother found best friends directly connected to the Park Church. Annis's kindred spirit was Beecher's wife, Julia, a sculptor, cartoonist, granddaughter of Noah Webster, and the inventor of the Beecher Rag Doll, whose sales raised considerable sums for charity each year. Mrs. Beecher was known to be "quite as headstrong as her husband in smashing through forms and conventions, and her rebellion was not only moral but aesthetic," Max said. "She bobbed her hair in 1857. She taught Sunday school wearing flat shoes." She used to "invade the parlors" of Elmira locals "like a whirlwind, clearing out the mid-Victorian junk. 'Why do you have all those little things on the wall?' she would exclaim. 'Don't you see how much better one big picture would look?' "[63] Annis and Julia's friendship often consisted of traveling together, whether to the Eastman cottage on Lake Seneca in the off season or, as Max revealed, "in the company of Emerson and William Morris and Walt Whitman, beyond the confines of churchly ethics and religion."[64]

Crystal's best friend (besides her brother Max) was Ida Langdon, the niece of Jervis and Olivia Langdon, who lived across the street from the church.[65] Ida became a relative of Mark Twain when her cousin Olivia met and married Samuel Clemens, a friend of her brother Charles. Crystal got to know Twain when he and his wife spent summers at Quarry Farm, the Langdon's property just outside Elmira. The family built him an octagonal study, with windows at each inclination, in which he wrote portions of both *Tom Sawyer* (1876) and *Huckleberry Finn* (1884).[66] Although the Eastmans were of modest means and still without a home of their own, Crystal associated with Elmira royalty—or, as Max characterized the Langdon family, "nobility": "their elevation seemed deep and old and spiritual and infinitely removed from snobbishness. They were at once princely," he recalled, "and democratic."[67]

Crystal was thirteen when she met Ida. She emerged into young adulthood at the center of a place percolating with qualities she would later attempt to reconstruct around herself. Most of all, the world she knew in Elmira cultivated a spirit of rebellion "against empty forms and conventions," Max said. Through "common sense, and democracy, and science, and reckless and humorous truth-telling," he later marveled, they formed a community of people who were "dedicated with moral courage to an ideal."[68] Crystal thrived in it. She became a "ringleader," as Max recalled, in everyday acts of gender defiance and youthful revolt. When she was a teenager, the town hero, legendary as a daring adventurer, anointed Crystal and Max "the only live people in town."[69]

Annis, who, Crystal remembered in "Mother-Worship," was "not without consciousness of neighbors' opinions,"[70] nevertheless urged this boldness and originality in her daughter. Individuality was an absolute moral value to her. Crystal developed many of her most vital ideas in living conversation with her mother. These included her suffragism and feminism; her instincts toward Socialism and antimilitarism; her devotion to both work outside the home and children; and the importance, as Emerson had taught Annis, of love grounded in a bond between people who "see the same truth."[71] But the most animating principle Annis transmitted to her daughter was to always think for herself. Never succumb to "conformity with the crowd," Annis warned her children over and over. "Conformity is beautiful until it requires a sacrifice of principle—then it is disfiguring," she said.[72] One must "learn to do without the praise of men," she preached in a favorite children's sermon, "for you will have to do without it a great many times if you do exactly what you believe to be right."[73]

The way would never be easy, but in that struggle lay inestimable value, Annis preached. In one children's sermon, she spoke about watching in horror as a man came to a humble garden "with a little, keen, shining weapon in his hand." The man "began to dig and cut among those tender green shoots in such a savage way that I thought not one of them would be spared." But, she continued, "to my surprise they all lived through it and seemed to grow faster after it, as if opposition only made them more bound to succeed." Then, Annis revealed, "I knew the meaning of it all, all growing for dear life."[74] The virtue in conquering adversity or opposition was a consistent trope in the lessons Annis delivered to children, perhaps especially to her own. "Every garden is a victory over hundreds of seen and unseen forces," she preached in another favorite children's sermon; "it is necessary, and good, to have something to overcome." In another, she professed, "I like this spirit in a garden (or a girl). . . . Every bit of beauty and goodness and love and joy in the world to-day, children, is the fruit of somebody's overcoming." In yet another sermon for young people, she concluded simply, "Men and women are born to overcome."[75]

Individual vision was the engine and the instrument of good, and it must never be compromised, sacrificed, or sold out, no matter what the obstacles to its realization. "We can scarcely find in all the story of the world a seer who would sell his vision for any price," Annis taught in another children's sermon, published when Crystal was fifteen. In it, she grouped Galileo, Bruno, Columbus, Socrates, Darwin, and Jesus together as heroes, and all for the same reason: each changed the world by staying true to himself. "What I wish you to remember is this," Annis exhorted. "That the people who see with the inner eye have a hard time. If you wish to be popular and slip through life easily, shut up that inner eye and see only what everybody else sees. But if you wish to be a hero—pray, 'Open thou mine eyes that I may behold wondrous things!'"[76]

"Trust in your inspirations & obey them," Annis urged her daughter at eighteen.[77] "Live out of yourself persistently. Become interested in all that is going on in the world and train yourself to think about it. It's better to have your own thought, even if it's a mistaken one, than to be always repeating other people's better thoughts."[78] To be righteous in the world, Annis taught her daughter, was to see for herself and stand fervently for it, come what may. If only she did that, Crystal learned from her mother, she could do no wrong.

* * *

Crystal herself made an editorial change to "Mother-Worship" that Kirchwey kept in the published version. She added a paragraph emphasizing how "thoroughly domestic" her mother was, excelling in both work and family. She "was all kinds of devoted mother," Crystal remembered, "the kind that tucks you in at night and reads you a story, and the kind that drags you to the dentist to have your teeth straightened." She seemed to do it all. "We children loved her cooking as much as we loved her preaching."[79]

By the later 1890s, conditions were right for Annis's public life to grow. Anstice was away teaching school in Idaho until he was old enough to enter the Princeton class of 1901; Crystal was away at Granger Place. In 1896 or 1897, Annis's niece, Adra Ash, joined the family, helping considerably with household management. Adra was about eleven years old at the time and would later join Crystal at Granger Place during the 1898–99 school year, the point at which the family could afford to send her.[80] Max began high school at Mercersburg Academy in the fall of 1898, a financial stretch for the family despite his scholarship. With lessening child-rearing responsibilities but increasing financial needs, Annis accepted outside speaking engagements in part for their fees— although she usually gave speeches about suffrage for free. In 1897 alone, she delivered two such speeches—one in Syracuse on "Why Do Women Wish to Vote?"[81] and another at the New York State suffrage meeting in nearby Geneva. She spoke alongside "all the great lights,"[82] as she called them, including Anna Howard Shaw, with whom Annis had been friends ever since they met as ministers delivering religious services at the National Council of Women in 1895, and Susan B. Anthony, whom Annis called "the most important person in history besides Jesus."[83]

That year, the Eastmans wanted and could afford to purchase land high on a hillside bluff overlooking Seneca Lake in the hamlet of Glenora, about thirty miles north of Elmira. A farmhouse sat four hundred feet above the shoreline, overlooking water so clear that "the cliff [went] right on down into the water and [met] another sky in its depths," Max remembered.[84] In July and August, the

Park Church held no Sunday services, so the farmhouse became their summer retreat—and their hearts' home.

Annis adopted vanguard ideas of how she wanted to live by the lake. The Eastmans invited three families with whom they were friends—the Beardsleys, McDowells, and Pickerings—to form a partnership and collective: the land was divided into four parcels, each family had its own place, and together they built a dining hall convenient to all where they would join for meals and conversation and share the chores. The Eastman home in Elmira already ran on feminist principles, where housework was shared on a rotating schedule without regard to gender. The summer retreat expanded that mindset across a communal setting. The arrangements were designed to free everyone from duty and convention, but especially the women, who normally were responsible for the endless, exhausting tasks of cooking and homemaking. "A cook was hired jointly, but the burden of keeping house, planning meals, buying meat and groceries from carts that came along three times a week, getting vegetables and fruit from the garden, collecting the money, keeping track of guests, and paying the bills, shifted every week," Crystal recalled, so "we all had the fun of eating in a big jolly group and only one or two weeks of housekeeping responsibility during the whole summer."[85]

The plan partook of architectural ideas closely tied to communitarian Socialist pioneers like Robert Owen and Charles Fourier, both of whom envisioned communal kitchens to foster community. The feminist dimensions came from Charlotte Perkins Gilman, whose brand-new book, *The Home: Its Work and Influence* (1903), discussed cooperative cooking and child care to liberate women. Annis admired the work and told Gilman so. The author was not surprised. "Women who *do things* usually see clearer on these subjects than the solely female kind," Gilman replied. She even asked if she could quote Annis's letter in the advertising circular for the book. Annis agreed, then did a little promotional work for Crystal. "Thanks for your daughter's address," Gilman responded. "I am asking her to come to lunch with me. Then we can talk. It is a keen pleasure to meet girls of that sort—who *care*."[86]

Before long, the Glenora group began an informal weekly symposium, sometimes dubbed their "supposium." Topics followed the interests of each voluntary discussion leader. Anstice, studying to become a doctor by this time, led a discussion of inflammation; Max led discussions of "Classification and Abstraction" and "A Theory of Practice."[87] Mrs. Beardsley led one on the relatively new concept of kindergarten.[88] When Crystal, age fifteen, gave her talk entitled "Woman," it was only the first of several she would lead on the subject of women and work.[89] "The trouble with women," she began, "was that they have no impersonal interests." Instead, as she wrote in "Mother-Worship," a full and complete life must bridge the public and private spheres, both work and family:

They must have work of their own, first because no one who has to depend on another person for his living is really grown up; and second, because the only way to be happy is to have an absorbing interest in life which is not bound up with any particular person. Children can die or grow up, husbands can leave you. No woman who allows husband and children to absorb her whole time and interest is safe from disaster.[90]

Everyone was invited to attend each week, and their friends and guests were too, but the extant records suggest it was mainly women who attended regularly.[91]

The Eastman family thrived at Glenora. Everyone loved it there. Anstice, a track star at Princeton, used to compete with his siblings over the question of who loved it more, writing to Crystal in the spring of his first year of college, "You aren't half as wild to get there, with all the dear people again, as I am."[92]

At Glenora, the Eastman women were prominent figures, especially Annis, whose social spontaneity and inventiveness were legendary. Once, Crystal and Ida Langdon were desperate to figure out last-minute costumes for a masquerade ball being held at the lakefront. It was already "after dinner," Langdon recalled, and "dizzy with sleep after a camping party, we went into [Crystal's] little bed-room two fairly normal, quite conventionally dressed Chemung County girls, and with the help of Mrs. Eastman, a dozen long pins, some black rags, and a couple of red fillits [sic], we emerged 'Bedegypts,' and silently, hand in hand, smothered under long black masks, glided to the Point." Once there, they "met a motley company, with whom we talked and danced and romped for an hour, behaving ourselves with the abandoned glee of the unidentified."[93]

Annis merged her personal life with that of the community, becoming central to the culture at Glenora, just as she was in her own family circle. She celebrated one wedding anniversary, for example, by organizing a morning swim followed by a picnic down at the dock. (It is not clear whether her husband was invited.) Then the group walked up to a circus, after which she invited them all to Cherith for tea. "When she gets there she finds nothing to eat, not even bread," a friend recalled, "but manages as usual to come all right for she thinks of pancakes and it was a meal to be remembered. And we kept the cook busy."[94]

Crystal exercised a similar social energy. Her warmth and wit animated the genius for friendship that would shape her political outlook, as well as her personal relationships. One summer day, after gathering both wood and flowers, then taking a swim, Crystal told friends she was still "feeling full of zeal," so she poured her surplus energy into a spontaneous escapade. She decided to go sailing with Ida, only to discover she was unable to stop the boat:

Two more unsea-worthy people never set foot in a sail boat. We uncovered the sail, untied the boat and wiggled out of the harbor. We then lowered the centerboard, too far, but we left it for more important things. Crystal raised the sail and turned the boat into a cob-web party by tying the sail ropes in the stern of the boat in place of at the base of the mast. But after we got arranged we sailed off quite smoothly. It was all right while we were sailing back and forth on the lake, but how to ever stop was more than we could tell. I suggested that we sail a little north then come down before the wind, steer close to the dock and jump off. Crystal agreed that that was just the way. But as we approached the dock it seemed that Max did not think it was, for in a very scornful tone he said "What are you trying to do?"... We admitted that we were landing. Max did not seem to think we were ... and [we] were hawled [sic] into the harbor by the children.[95]

Afterward, they had been invited for supper, which was called for 6:00 p.m. Their inability to dock made them thirty-five minutes late. Upon arrival, Crystal instantly quipped, "Why this is dinner, if I had known it was going to be dinner I would have tried to be on time."[96] The room broke into laughter, launching another evening to be remembered at the lake.

* * *

Of all the editorial changes to "Mother-Worship," only one provoked a negative reaction from Crystal—but it was volcanic. When Kirchwey revised the ending, she found Crystal "boiling with deep rage" at the changes—and not merely because they were made without her knowledge.[97] As published, Kirchwey made Crystal's piece conclude with a relatively uncomplicated continuity between Annis, the trailblazing feminist foremother, and Crystal, her successful feminist daughter. The published version began as Crystal had: "I have lived my life according to the plan." But then Kirchwey continued, "I have had the 'career' and the children and, except for an occasional hiatus due to illness or some other circumstance over which I had no control, I have earned my own living." Finally, Kirchwey added, "I have even made a certain name for myself. My mother has always been a beacon to me, and if today I sometimes feel a sense of failure it may be partly because I have always lived in the glow of her example."[98] That last claim strayed far from Crystal's own conclusion.

Kirchwey's editorial changes partly reflected her desire to clarify Crystal's story, making it more memorable to readers as an affirmation of feminism. She drew upon cultural narratives about mothers and daughters that had been circulating in the discourses of social movements, as well as in magazines and other popular media, for decades.[99] Since the nineteenth century, female reform movements had drawn upon maternal authority and leadership. To rebel against the patriarchal order of the father, many women's organizations wielded the idea of maternity, of mother-love, to warrant their policy positions and fuel their actions. This idea helped bond women across generations in revolt against the male-dominated status quo. Moreover, it also worked to revise traditional notions of the cultural responsibility of mothers toward their daughters. Now, rather than socializing dutiful daughters into traditional domestic lives, feisty foremothers pushed open doors for women's participation in political and public life for their progeny to step through.

By the dawn of Crystal's era, this powerful narrative of intergenerational ambition had set in, fostering an understanding, internal to the movement, that senior suffragists aimed to serve America's daughters, to raise the prospects of women in and for the future. Mother-daughter teams, such as Elizabeth Cady Stanton and her daughter, Crystal's friend and New York suffrage leader Harriot Stanton Blatch, could be seen as an emblem of the intergenerational story on which Kirchwey's revisions relied: what Elizabeth Cady had begun at Seneca Falls in 1848, her daughter Harriot would advance in twentieth-century New York and across the nation.

However fervently Blatch carried on the cause to which Stanton dedicated her life, she would live for nearly twenty years in England, putting an ocean between herself, her own daughter, and her venerable mother.[100] She returned to the United States in 1902, the same year her mother passed away. Blatch founded her own organization that year, the Equality League of Self-Supporting Women. The league then became the Women's Political Union in 1910, a militant group of younger women, redolent of the English suffragettes; the organization would unite with the Congressional Union for Woman Suffrage in 1916, just as the latter broke fully with its mother organization to become the National Woman's Party—the world's first independent women's political party.

Like Blatch's, Crystal's maternal inheritance was more complex than most. After all, whatever Stanton's messages in parenting may have been, her feminist politics were anything but cautious, compliant, or "motherly" in the traditional sense. And Annis too was brave and innovative in her feminism, if in more of a regional theater. But for many women in Crystal's cohort, twentieth-century women's rights activism began to entail rebellion against the animating ideas and approaches of their elders. Broadly, many daughters of Crystal's generation were drawn to the women's movement in defiance of traditionalist mothers and the patriarchal society they were seen to enforce or accept. And even as younger women entered suffrage organizing to find a generally different breed of leaders, the new generation wanted to be self-supporting women, to break away from the mentality of their mothers' movement and create instead a "sisterhood" of their peers. Disidentification with mothers became a distinct political act for feminist daughters after about 1910.[101]

In the contest for the conclusion of "Mother-Worship," both Eastman and Kirchwey acknowledged the generational rupture characteristic of the era in which Crystal came of age. Both recognized the "struggle for survival" by a younger generation that must overcome parental agendas and expectations in one form or another. But only Kirchwey's version fully affirmed the narrative of feminist progress across the generations. Only Kirchwey offered Annis as a beacon lighting the way for the even greater success of her daughter. And to support this expected story, she rendered any threat to it as conditional, tentative, merely a result of Crystal's shadowy perception and memory: *if* she sometimes felt *a sense* of failure, it *may have been partly* because of living in her mother's glow (italics mine).

But Crystal saw her own story very differently. She adored her mother. Indeed, she idolized her. Unlike so many young feminists of her generation, she never felt she needed to rebel against Annis to become herself. She never wanted to. Yet, just as she bridged multiple movements in her politics, she also occupied multiple positions in prevailing mother-daughter narratives. She lived her life as a mixture of suffrage successor, rebellious modern, and dutiful daughter—an original compound. *That* was the woman her mother led her to be. Her rage partly resulted from the simplification of her story into conformity with a standard narrative, wedging it into a single political precinct when in fact it straddled them. Crystal would angrily cross out Kirchwey's ending on every copy she gave to friends, family, and colleagues.[102] Alongside the altered final paragraph in the copy she saved in her scrapbook, she disowned it, noting for posterity, "None of this is mine."[103]

Still, Kirchwey had furnished a story that strengthened Eastman's image for the eyes of the world. Crystal's original ending had defied the expected narrative not by maternal disinheritance but by refusing to claim her own success as a feminist daughter in the end:

> I certainly have not fulfilled the promise of my youth. Neither as a homemaker nor as a professional woman have I achieved much success or distinction. I have never wavered in my feminist faith, but I must confess that I go around nowadays with a pretty constant sense of failure. 'With such a father and mother surely had had every chance!' I say to myself. But it does not always seem to work out that way.[104]

At greater length than Kirchwey retained, Crystal contemplated the effects of generational adversity, suggesting her own life with her mother had lacked hardships and obstacles, the overcoming of which equips a child to succeed. "Perhaps the children who have to fight their way out of an unfriendly environment stand a better chance than those for whom the beginning is made easy," she wrote. Perhaps then "a child's character gets the iron it needs for the struggle of life."[105]

Crystal's disillusionment and deflated self-image may have had many sources by 1927, but when she refused to acknowledge her own triumphs—and her own adversity—she herself presumed a mother-daughter story far more composed and uncomplicated than it was.

When Crystal graduated from the Granger Place School on June 15, 1899, her mother delivered the commencement address. It was thirteen days before Crystal's eighteenth birthday, and it marked a triple turning point: in Crystal's education, her adulthood, and a new century.

Annis's address was probably an undated "message to young ladies" she later published under the title "Have Salt in Yourselves!" The speech opened by acknowledging the great moment of transition they were all witnessing together. "You are a nineteenth—nearly a twentieth-century—girl," she began, "and new times bring new duties." Women must rise, and speak for themselves, she said. "It is no longer enough for women to suffer in silence, to cry to Him who seeth in secret, for the sins and sorrows of their native land and the world,—the call for action has been heard and women have arisen to obey it." Yet this new world for women, she warned, should not replace what is ageless. "Women are working at many knotty problems to-day, but none is harder than that old one which nearly every one of the Old Testament worthies failed—bringing up a child successfully according to his bent. It is an arduous calling, this of being a woman, one which should not be embraced lightly."[106]

Women must do it all, Annis urged, but how? "In view of all this, what can we say to you to make you large enough, strong enough, good enough for your opportunities?" she called out. "Have Salt in Yourselves," she answered. To make the case, she drew on the "old law concerning sacrifices," with its paradox of Christian fulfillment: embrace the salt of difficulty, for that is what gives savor to one's sacrifice and so yields perfection. Salt each sacrifice, she advised, so as to "offer it with joy."[107]

It was a message in a language Annis was increasingly struggling to apply. For her, joy was fleeting and capricious—so was the whole paradigm flawed? In these years, Crystal saw her mother experience increasing emotional volatility, at one moment glistening with optimism, eloquence, and sparkling insight, and at the next flooded by darkness, self-criticism, and self-doubt. "She had a stormy, troubled soul, capable of black cruelty and then again of the deepest generosities," Crystal revealed in "Mother-Worship." "She was humble, honest, striving, always beginning again to try to be good."[108] Years later, Max would characterize their mother's struggle with her black periods as a function of her faith, an embrace of "the most sorrowful of Christian virtues . . . perpetual repentance."[109] But by 1906, Annis would reject her religious denomination, disavowing Congregationalism in favor of Unitarian belief in the possibility of continuous spiritual, moral, and intellectual growth. Toward the end of her life, she would plan to leave the church entirely. The famed woman minister could no longer keep Christian doctrine in her heart.

Both her spiritual yearnings and later uncertainties had emerged from a fundamental emotional volatility that marked her temperament from a young age. "Annis was like an irrepressible fountain," one of her girlhood friends recalled in 1904, "always rushing forth in some unexpected way—sometimes it was cold—and sometimes it was awfully hot."[110] The two forces, psychological and spiritual, were always entwined for her, and Crystal, especially, became an essential instrument in the medley. From childhood, the daughter learned she was pivotal to her mother's well-being, indispensable in perpetually delivering her to a state of stability Annis described as salvation. Only Crystal could shepherd her mother from her dark depths and through the waves of repentance as she struggled to restore herself to absolution. When Annis would lament of "the unreality and worthlessness of it all," she would always look to her daughter as the one redeemer who could "say to dark thoughts, 'Get thee behind me, Satan.'"[111]

From Crystal's first days away from home at Granger Place, Annis received her daughter's letters "like the sacramental bread and wine—they feed my soul," she said.[112] By her senior year, Annis told her, "Do you know that for the first time in my life I felt the possibility of the virgin birth of Jesus—on reading your letter."[113] In the interim, Annis's dispatches often diagram the pattern of her thinking. Letters that grounded the mother-daughter bond in more typical psychological and emotional contexts—time, family, memory—take a turn when a flash of unworthiness would tip Annis toward the infinite. "I read your letter with tears welling up from the depths of a joy unspeakable," she told Crystal her junior year. "I will always keep this in one of the little boxes on my top bureau drawer—you will know where to find it if I should slip away—Keep it always until you can give it to your daughter when you tell her that your mother was the happiest woman in the world because of you. She may keep it to give to her daughter and so it will go on and on and never die." Then, immediately: "Not that I have earned it or for one moment deserved it—it is like the grace of God, abounding where sin most abounds—and therefore need."[114]

It must have been incredibly affirming for Crystal to hear she was the source of eternal salvation to the mother she worshipped. "You always have a tonic effect with me," Annis variously expressed to her. "I want to begin all over again to do one right thing after another. I do not think my love for you can be idolatry if it helps me to be good—do you?"[115] And if Crystal could save her mother, she did so as a deity does, simply by being herself: "the wonderful face of your love fills me with new amazement—and what you *are* makes me glad that I am what I am—as the black mold might rejoice to be ugly and unclean for the sake of the rose it has nourished for you could not be *just you* if I were not I." To Annis, such realizations were exalted: "Why should I not believe that the heavenly powers have conspired to make me glad—Why should we not believe the very *best thing* of which we can dream? Truly I know no reason—it may be the highest wisdom."[116] But these revelations, as abiding as her faith, would perpetually wither and turn to dust.

For Crystal, the attachment was nearly as immense and compelling. From college, she wrote to her mother, "Love for you is singing in my heart. And it will never cease singing, tho when I leave you it is sad. . . . Let us always rejoice in the love,—that it is and always will be, even tho' it means real pain and heartache sometimes." Later in the same letter she remarked on the mystical depths of their bond: "Our love is so precious—no one really knows how passionately I love you," she confessed. "No one could understand and I don't want them to."[117] The next month she too observed the divine in their connection. "Do you know that whenever I pray, my thoughts go to you before they go to God. Do you think that's wrong? Then my thoughts seem to go in a circle from myself, through a vast conception of infinite good, to you." The connection—circular, infinite, repeating—was simultaneously experienced as keen, brilliant, piercing: "Sort of an electric current," Crystal described, "conveying good from me to you and from you to me."[118]

This exceptional bond, vibrant and thrilling to both women, was uniquely necessary to Annis. "You *are* my life," Annis wrote Crystal at college.[119] Her identity blurred with her daughter's. "Is it not joyous that we can be so perfectly at one," she asked without using a question mark. "I often seem to live two lives—one in you—When I'm tired of my old sinful disillusioned self I escape into you and look out upon the world thro' your dear eyes."[120]

As a result, Annis become increasingly anxious at the thought of its loss or decline. "Nobody has ever loved me as you do. . . . I am sure it will never fail—but there were a few black days when I thought it must become a pitying love and you must grow weary of me," she wrote to her daughter. "It seemed to me that you could not bear it—that you must in very self defense turn from me and just endure—and find your life in other things."[121] Metaphors of life-giving redemption, of hunger and thirst, and of starvation and reprieve increasingly permeate her letters to her daughter. Continuing contact was expressed as essential to Annis's very survival, most acutely at moments of transition in Crystal's life. "I'm turning with what courage I can muster to the old, old hopeless struggle to be good—it's all that's left till your first letter comes," she wrote on her daughter's first day of graduate school.[122] "I am as dependent upon you as is a baby on its mother," she told Crystal as she completed her master's degree. "If you had been really withdrawn when I began to struggle up I could *never* have succeeded—When your card or letter comes I am 'nursed'—and satisfied and know that I will hold out until the next one comes."[123] "Will you think it silly," she asked Crystal on the eve of her graduation from college, "if I tell you that I want your letter put into my hands—when I'm dead?"[124]

Crystal would answer with testaments to her devotion. Even as a young professional beginning to come into her own, her expressions of love reproduced her mother's transcendent language, at times fusing the eternal and the romantic, the worldly and the divine. "The marvelous thing is that life grows deeper and love grows sweeter all the time—the same life and the same love," Crystal wrote Annis from her first full-time job. "Now it is goodnight to my best beloved,—with my arms held out to you in spirit, and a dozen dear, love-words rushing to my lips."[125]

This is the maternal relationship that informed Crystal's conclusion to her essay; this is the backdrop to her recurrent sense of personal deficiency in the face of the mother she glorified above all others.

Crystal's own conclusion never seems to have questioned her mother's legacy, only herself as the heir to it. Her final words imagined a dysfunctional daughter, a beneficiary who had failed to progress as she should. Her conclusion thwarted the narrative Kirchwey wanted, while deferring any understanding of it. Crystal concluded the essay in suspension, not succession. Her final sentence: "I await the verdict of a psychoanalyst."[126]

Set up as a successor, she felt she had failed to succeed. Yet she never accounted for any reciprocity in their relationship, for the many ways she herself had made her mother's story possible. Neither had she come to terms with the full depths of her maternal legacy. Both Crystal and Kirchwey avoided recognizing that while Annis surely was a beacon, she was also a flare. All Crystal's life her mother issued a flashing signal, bright to dark to bright, that was not easy to follow, or to answer.

Crystal never accounted for what that meant to her, or for the turmoil Annis brought to all those who loved her. She never acknowledged the struggle to mother her mother, or to maintain a balance of love in the family she cherished. For in the midst of her mother's radiance, a gravitational force, Annis also created an atmosphere of anguish in a family that orbited unevenly around her, with Crystal and Max bonded to her—and ceaselessly to each other for her sake—at the core, while Sam and Anstice lived lonely as satellites, sporadically welcomed to circle nearer before a change in the winds would return them to the outer reaches, to the dark and the cold. And in Crystal's feelings about her own inadequacy, she never seems to have considered the adversity of a daughter whose boundless love was imperative to rescue the mother she revered, a child who tried over and over to tend to a beloved parent's pain, yet was destined to feel herself a failure, because the blazes of torment and self-doubt, fugitive like wildfires, ultimately lay beyond her power to extinguish.

As Crystal moved forward, this titanic maternal connection could not help but influence her sensibility and mindset, her expectations of her own family, her two marriages, and her relationships, particularly with other women. Eventually, she would experience tensions or conflict with some of the most important women in her professional life, often involving interpersonal dynamics reminiscent of this complex bond—devotion and loyalty, conviction and compromise, emotional boundlessness and self-restraint. In her work with others, Crystal would never fail to apply what she had learned from her mother about being true to herself, about the immense redemptive value of her own being and vision in the world. And when her own self-expression did not organically heal strife and restore stability the way it had, at least temporarily, with her mother, she had learned from experience to escalate efforts, to devote herself with greater abandon and intensity—to redouble the kind of passionate investments that had once renewed her mother, now to her colleagues and the cause.

It was a formidable inheritance. While Annis surely was a beacon to her daughter, she emitted a strobe both enlightening and blinding, radiating inspiration that also concealed the dark side of its own light. As a guiding signal, Annis was liable to go black without warning, each time calling more urgently on the mystical energies she deified in her daughter to illuminate the way back. In the process was forged the spirit of a woman taught to recognize no limits to what she might do, as long as she invested herself infinitely, without reserve, and refused to ever forsake her ideal.

2 DISCOVERING CRYSTAL

In the fall of 1899, Crystal Eastman entered college for the first of her three postsecondary degrees on the cusp of a new millennium. For the country, and especially the generation coming of age across two centuries, it was a moment of restlessness, anxiety, anticipation, and incipient revolt.

In American politics, populism was on the rise. The three-term Nebraska congressman William Jennings Bryan had ascended as a dark horse to claim the presidential nomination of the Democratic Party in 1896. Bryan, often called the "Great Commoner," ran hard against laissez-faire capitalism and the gold standard that served the interests of employers and financiers; he had electrified delegates at the party convention by railing against what he called the crucifixion of the common man on a "cross of gold."[1] Bryan was thirty-six years old at the time, the youngest major party nominee in American history. He would go on to win the Democratic nomination twice more as Crystal advanced through her education—in 1900, while she was in college, and again in 1908, the year after she finished law school. Coupled with his youth and left-wing domestic policies, Bryan's outspoken anti-imperialism in response to the outbreak of the Spanish-American War of 1898, the country's first major colonialist move onto the global stage, sealed his appeal to her. She would march energetically in support of Bryan's second presidential bid, shouting for him against the Republican McKinley, while she was a Vassar sophomore—even though she could not vote.[2]

At the same time, Socialism was evolving in the United States and Europe as an internationalizing force. Since the mid-nineteenth century, the Socialist idea had spread through an array of interpretations and social experiments, mainly in collective and communitarian living arrangements. As a political ideology, the terrain of Socialism both divided and widened as the early twentieth century unfolded. The growing separation of orthodox "scientific" Socialists from emergent

Crystal Eastman. Amy Aronson, Oxford University Press (2020).
© Oxford University Press.
DOI: 10.1093/oso/9780199948734.001.0001

"utopian" Socialists would encourage new factions, approaches, and parties to emerge. In the same year that Crystal graduated from high school, the German theorist and politician Eduard Bernstein challenged significant building blocks of traditional Marxian thinking in his *Evolutionary Socialism* (1899), endorsing a "revisionist" or "reform" model that entailed the achievement of Socialist goals through democratic, rather than revolutionary, processes. Now known as social democracy, the reform model would shape Crystal's thinking and influence the Progressive projects that would launch her career.

Mark Twain had satirized the era that came before. In 1873, he coined the term "Gilded Age" to name a time when fierce inequality, brought on by rapid industrialization, was reflected and reproduced in a jungle of social problems—poverty, violence, greed, racism, class warfare—all masked, Twain wrote, by a veil of gold plate.[3] Twenty years later, Annis forecast a new breed of citizen who would rise in response to these ills. In an 1893 sermon at West Bloomfield, she invoked a changed human consciousness, free of the bounds and divisions of the past. "The coming man," she told her congregation, "will possess many powers of which we do not dream and many virtues in perfection which are seen only in bud among us." She predicted a new kind of citizen, internationalist and radically democratic, someone "broad in his sympathies, not naming his interests and ideals by family boundaries or race lines or sect." She presaged a political emancipator and deliverer: "He will be a citizen of the world," she said, "and the world will be the Republic of God."[4]

Annis's visionary brio, typical for her in moments of hope, seized the expectant sensibility of her daughter's generation. Maturing into adulthood while crossing into a new century, Crystal and many of her contemporaries shared a sense of anticipated destiny—as if they were arriving on the verge of something, something they had been chosen, indeed called upon, to conceive. For them, a youthful rejection of authority and received wisdom were married to ideals and experiments seeking an entirely new structure and set of values—one that would allow human potential to flourish. A "new temper of mind," Walter Lippmann would write to Max, was beginning to emerge.[5] Lippmann became a highly influential editor of the *New Republic* and the author of the groundbreaking *Public Opinion* (1923); a key Wilsonian policy shaper, he would nevertheless meet modernity with some anxiety, eventually, in the aftermath of World War I, raising questions about the viability of democracy itself.[6] Even as a young man, Lippmann was satirized by some contemporaries as too sober, as somewhat priggish and no fun.[7] But when he talked about the time in which he and Crystal would both begin their adult lives, he waxed poetic. "Instead of a world once and for all fixed, with morality finished and sealed," he felt, "we have a world bursting with new ideas, new places and new hopes."[8]

If Annis predicted a new man on the horizon, she meant it in both a general and a gendered sense. Her prognosis for a coming humanity—a new *mankind*—was predicated on the idea of a new *man*. In the 1890s, the decline of manliness had emerged as a topic of American cultural concern, raising questions, as the author Henry James would describe in 1885, about the ability of "the masculine character . . . to dare and endure."[9] The closing of the American frontier, coupled with the "overcivilization" thought to arise from new technologies like steam power and the telegraph, led political leaders and cultural pundits to call for the revitalization of a virile, indomitable manhood deemed to be wasting away. The turn of the century gave rise to health crazes in gyms and to body building; new arenas for athletics from basketball to tennis to bowling to boxing; cultural adventures involving the rugged outdoors from dude ranches to cowboy fiction; and the rapid growth of fraternal orders, in which nearly 30 percent of American men participated.[10] All of these solutions were trained on restoring the "strength, self-reliance, and determination" that Theodore Roosevelt would argue epitomized American manhood. Roosevelt gave his defining speech, "The Strenuous Life," in which he linked manly resurgence to patriotism and national character on the world stage, in April 1899, just weeks before Crystal's graduation from Granger Place.[11]

But Annis envisioned a new man who would grow in the opposite direction, embracing egalitarian values that would make him compatible with the "New Woman" already arriving on the scene. Recently available to the cultural imagination from the popular fiction of the 1890s, the "New Woman" was independent, urban, and hungry for a life of her own. In both fictional depiction and sociological fact, she defied conventional domestic roles, operating in an expanding space of cultural acceptability somewhere beyond the established categories of Victorian lady, single spinster, or woman of ill repute.[12] As Crystal progressed through her education, local variants would develop in twentieth-century New York: the "bachelor girl" or "rebel girl" began to materialize around her. Now in conscious revolt against gender convention and inherited wisdom, the rebel girl was ambitious for meaning in the world, experimental, outspoken, and determined to exercise the freedom she would heartily clamor to win. Crystal was primed to be that kind of woman. From the time she was a youngster, Max would recall, the Eastmans always referred to her as "mighty girl."[13]

For Crystal and other young women like her, higher education both fueled and responded to the anxieties and aspirations of the age. Vassar, which had struggled in recent years with competition from the opening of Smith College in 1871 and Wellesley in 1875, began to embrace new directions during Crystal's time on campus. President James Monroe Taylor oversaw an expansion in both facilities and curriculum after 1895 that gave students increased opportunity to vary from what had been a prescribed nineteenth-century course of study. Just two years after Annis foretold a new age of sympathetic solidarity and undivided human community, Vassar added new classes to help students mindfully encounter a broader world, including Russian, Spanish, economics, sociology, psychology, and political science.[14]

The advancing vision at Vassar took exception to women's suffrage, however—the very engine of human progress as far as both Annis and Crystal were concerned. President Taylor forbade any discussion of votes for women on campus. He considered it "propaganda," and while the term denoted general publicity and perhaps sensationalism at the time, acquiring its more malevolent connotations only after its use by the Nazis in World War II, Taylor considered it his moral obligation to safeguard female students from it all the same. In defiance of his attitude and policy, however, Vassar women, led by Inez Milholland, five years Crystal's junior, organized suffrage meetings in a small cemetery just beyond the college grounds. At the first meeting of what became the Vassar Votes for Women Club, Harriot Stanton Blatch, also an alumna, unfurled a bright yellow banner bearing a powerful rejoinder to Taylor and the college. Quoting the book of Isaiah, it blended the prophet's marked moral authority with the voice of an educated woman, urging: "Come, Let Us Reason Together."[15]

For the Eastmans, college admission and tuition were a family-wide effort. Financial aid would not become an organized practice for another thirty-five years, so poorer students like Crystal and her brothers continued to rely on sponsorship, charity, and patronage, the same way a rare few men, mainly those pursuing the ministry, had attained higher education in America's oldest colleges since the colonial era.[16] Crystal's tuition was cobbled together by her parents, who rallied a community of supporters, including Sam's father, the Granger family, and two wealthy women patrons, probably parishioners brought into the enterprise by Annis.[17] For years, Annis energetically amassed support to pay tuition for her daughter. "I have a $50 scholarship for you thro' Dr. Bradford's kindness," she reported in Crystal's last year at Granger Place, "and I may get one for $100."[18]

Given their hopes and the stakes, Crystal and her mother debated her college plans at length. Crystal wanted to attend a coeducational institution—perhaps Oberlin like her parents, or Cornell or Michigan, which had accepted women alongside men since the 1870s—but her mother objected. "Coeducation is the ideal, but it is not in an ideal state by any means in these days," she warned. Annis feared coeducation would be bad for women, largely because the "coming man" she predicted in the 1870s had yet to appear. She felt intuitively that women would outdo men on campus and believed their relative dominance and success would render future male coworkers and husbands threatened and angry. And from what she could tell, the inevitable male reaction to such feelings would be the abandonment of responsibility and adulthood itself. "I should say that men would be discouraged by the superior ability of women—giving instances of women carrying off the prizes in English schools (you know they have taken the very highest honors) they will give up & let the women run the field," she told Crystal. "You know it is claimed that if women work for their living men will stop working. Again men need to have somebody to look up to them—& girls are educated side & side with them. They will not be so apt to look up—so men will degenerate."[19]

Annis wanted her daughter to attend Bryn Mawr. She had lectured there in March, met M. Carey Thomas, president of the college, and quickly came to like and admire her. A leader in the suffrage movement, Thomas became the preeminent advocate for women's education at the turn of the twentieth century. In the four years since she had been appointed, she had already successfully revamped the curriculum, promoting more intensive and integrated coursework, original research, and advanced study for women. Annis was thrilled by everything she saw. "I was entertained in the president's luxurious home and was delighted with it and her," she told Crystal.[20] One of Thomas's first initiatives as president was to raise admissions standards. She made Bryn Mawr's entrance exams as demanding as Harvard's, and students were no longer admitted by certificate of graduation, even from preparatory schools like Granger Place.

Annis made some inquiries about what would be involved if Crystal agreed to apply. An acquaintance suggested "a special arrangement could be made for you to take some exams in June & some in the Fall"—adding, "they are not as dreadful as they are made out to be." Annis then rolled out a punch list of reasons the school would be a good fit for her daughter. "It is the best and the gymnasium and swimming tank are fine. You need fear no snobbishness and we'd expect to have you go to Phila. sometime with the others. It is not a bit more expensive than S[mith]. & less so in regard to travel." But she promised to leave the decision up to Crystal. "Think it all over once more carefully and decide," she told her; then, whatever school she chose, Annis would snap into action. "But when you decide let me know at once for application should be made for you at once. If you decide on B M I'll write to Dean Thomas to see if you can take some exams in Feb. If you decide on Smith you ought to apply there—Find out from Mr. Fairley whom I shall write to."[21]

No decision was immediately forthcoming, but a coed school seems to have stayed on Crystal's mind. Annis next told her daughter, "If you care for the social prestige of college, Bryn Mawr will give it to you much more effectually than any Western or coed institution. The best families (i.e. the most aristocratic) will not send their daughters to a coed school," she continued. "Bryn Mawr has the cream—and has the highest standing. Her diploma would mean more to you than any other in this country." Plus, she added, enhancing her pitch to the daughter she knew so well, "there is moreover a very democratic spirit there. The best rooms (highest priced) are right beside the lowest and there is very little difference save in size. There is almost no dress—for all wear gowns. The president said that many girls went thro [*sic*] the year with two gowns. There are almost no extras and a spirit of economy is very fashionable."[22]

But in a "very emphatic letter," Annis reported, Crystal "refuse[d] point blank to go."[23] She announced a decided preference for Smith. Her mother tried one more time to persuade her. "Are you determinedly set against Bryn Mawr? It would be very fine to have Pres. Thomas interested in you beforehand. She couldn't fail to be afterward." Nevertheless, Annis would tolerate her daughter's preferences in this. "It is a little—quite a big—disappointment to me—your decision—but I will not speak further of it," she told Crystal. "I said you might decide and I must abide by the consequences," she conceded. Still, she couldn't resist a mother's admonishing before closing the subject. "Your reasons however will not look so good to you in ten years as they do now," she remarked.[24]

It is unclear when or why Crystal ultimately decided to attend Vassar. Perhaps it had something to do with the timing or quality of entrance requirements at Bryn Mawr. Perhaps she was not accepted by Smith. "Do you know that there is some doubt about your being admitted at Smith next year?" Annis asked in October of her senior year. "I learn that they are crowded now. I wish I knew somebody of influence there. I hate to have you lost in a crowd."[25] Perhaps in the end it was Vassar's advanced gender politics—those virtues in perfection seen only in bud when Matthew Vassar removed the word "female" from the name of the college in 1867—whose time to flower had come. "When Vassar was founded," Annis would tell Crystal during her first year, "it was frowned upon by the 'best people'—a very intelligent woman—a missionary said—'Its name "a college for women" condemns it. No refined Christian woman will ever send her daughter there!'" Yet now, as a new century beckoned, things were changing. "Oh," Annis observed, "the world do move!"[26]

For all the uncertainties at this juncture in her life, Crystal knew she wanted a college connected to all that—to a world on the move. At first, she would strive as her mother's daughter. After her first month at Vassar she would tell Annis, "I want to do great things and clever things because you love me so much and because you think I have brains. . . . I want to do something to make me worthy of your love and admiration."[27] But by the time she completed her education, she would claim a sense of mission and aspiration in the world all her own. "[F]reedom is something," she would avow. The "freedom to taste the common joys,—to work, and fight and struggle, and die, with the others. . . . To live greatly," she would determine, "*that* is the thing."[28]

* * *

Crystal was feeling ready for anything the summer before she started college. She had taken full charge of the family at Glenora during July and August 1899 while her mother embarked on an educational endeavor of her own. As early as 1894, Annis had called herself an "un-denominational Christian," and on the eve of Crystal's departure for Vassar she attended the Harvard Summer School, where the more liberal wing of Congregationalist ministers tended to study. Annis delved into courses in contemporary philosophy taught by the idealist philosopher Josiah Royce, the field-builder George Herbert Palmer, and the metaphysical naturalist and writer George Santayana.[29] Crystal managed the household in her mother's place, and she seems to have managed it well. Her brother Anstice reported favorably on "the regime of Crystal."[30] She reassured her mother she was fully up to it all: "I'm feeling so perfectly well this summer that I can hardly recognize myself," she said. "I have not had to take one of Dr. Stuart's pills since I came out here. I can do lots of work and I sleep like a top."[31]

However, by the opening ceremony at Vassar in September, Crystal was struggling both physically and emotionally and felt too ill to attend. "Of course lots of people have suffered more, but that doesn't help me. If only the ache and pain would stop for long enough for me to catch my breath!" she wrote her mother. "One thing I am proud of. Although this thing has made me homesick, *wildly* homesick inside, I have not once given up to it."[32] Crystal would will herself through it, partly by thinking out loud in dialogue with Annis. "I can make mind superior over matter, but I *will* not let matter get full swing over mind," she insisted. But "oh, for a little let up on these awful aches! I must not give up." But then, "If anyone should be kind to me now or even look sympathetic, the tears would just come flooding out."[33]

Two weeks later, two older classmates gave her what she needed. In October, Crystal went on an annual trip to Mohonk Mountain, not far from Poughkeepsie, with "Miss Clapp and Miss Burns, the two Brooklyn girls who have been so good to me in my troubles."[34] The excursion was an exquisite event for Crystal. It merged a rapture in nature that rivaled her mother's with the meeting of her first real women peers. "The peace of the soul that comes over me when I suddenly come upon a beautiful view is indescribable," she once observed; "I seem to have seen a little bit of heaven and I come away rested in every way and ready to love the world."[35] At Mohonk, she experienced an even greater bliss:

> Such a glorious day as I have had! I feel as if the unalloyed delight and enjoyment of it ought to make up for all the ills I ever suffered. To explain, yesterday we went on the annual trip to Mohonk Lake. . . . First there was

a long breezy trolley ride across the river and on for miles thro [*sic*] this beautiful country. Then we changed from the car to a big four-seated carriage for the climb up the mountain. I soon noticed a way off and up on a mountain, a cliff that broke off. . . . Well, they told me that right under this cliff was Lake Mohonk. So we went, up and up winding back and forth. At every new turn a fresh view either ahead or back would strike you. . . . The sky was clear blue and the lake clear green and the sun shone warm, so we three girls lay in the bottom of a boat and drifted and dreamed and talked and sang softly, all afternoon. . . . Oh! The pure joy of it![36]

Crystal spent Thanksgiving with Elsie Clapp that year and began a friendship with Lucy Burns that would help carry her into the drive for a constitutional suffrage amendment beginning in 1913, a decade after graduation. Lucy was a year ahead of Crystal and a roommate at their off-campus boardinghouse run by an older couple named Whitlock. To Crystal, she was a leader and role model. Lucy would direct the first hall play in which Crystal had a lead role, and she majored in math, a required subject Crystal would struggle to pass despite the help of both an algebra tutor her first semester and her brother Anstice, then a Princeton premed student, the previous summer.[37]

She was intensely drawn to Lucy. "Oh my! I like that girl," she told Max halfway through her first year. "If only she liked me as much as I like her, my cup of bliss would be brimming for awhile." Her first descriptions exude sensual undertones. "She walked over from the college this noon in the pouring rain without any thing on. She came in late to lunch, her beautiful red hair was all wet and curly. Little sparkles of rain were all over it and her blue eyes were glowing and scintillating."[38] Days later Crystal told her mother, "Lucy is just the same as ever, only more attractive to look at every day I believe. She doesn't dream that I am as fond of her as I am. It gets to be almost a passion with me sometimes and then it dies down for awhile and continues to smoulder [*sic*] quietly, until some look or smile or word of hers stirs it up again in full force. I wouldn't have her know, because it would only embarrass her, and she couldn't possibly return it."[39]

There is no evidence any sexual encounter ever occurred between the two women, nor any that it did not. However, female friendships at this time were generally intimate and often quite romantic; today, these emotionally involved and sometimes sexual relationships between women tend not to be viewed strictly from a psychosexual point of view.[40] On the campuses of women's colleges at the turn of the century, "college girl crushes," or "mashes," particularly between first-year students and their older classmates, were common enough to be discussed in yearbooks, bulletins, and even campus songs.[41]

Through the spring term, Crystal often gushed over Lucy's talents. As the director of a farce called "The Bicyclees," Lucy "is a dandy," she told Max. "I never saw anything like that girl for versatility."[42] When the rooming house put out a magazine of their writing, they called it "Whitlock Whittlings," and she remarked, "the name is a creation of Lucy's of course."[43] But beginning in her first letter about Lucy, Crystal seemed to understand her feelings as a flood of admiring affection connected largely to her own temperament. "When I like people, I like them so *awfully*," she confessed to Max. "It's a rather hard lot."[44] She expressed similar responses to other older classmates, particularly those, like Lucy, who emerged as leaders. "Miss Sperry, the Sophomore President, is Miss Cutling's room mate [*sic*]," she told Annis. "She is the most interesting girl to me in the college so far. I sort of idealize her. I have to have someone, you know," she noted with an implicit wink to her mother. "One of the great needs of my nature," she added in the postscript, "is to have some one [*sic*] near me whom I can love and who loves me."[45]

Crystal and Lucy were becoming like siblings, a loving attachment not without romantic valence in the Eastman family. Annis would come to adore Lucy in her own right. "She is one of the people you want to watch every minute for fear you will miss something," she remarked during Crystal's sophomore year.[46] By junior spring, Annis told Crystal she had received a "charming—original—note from 'Lucy Burns' that makes me very happy." "I covet her," she continued. "Do you suppose she *could* be persuaded to marry Anstice? Think what wonderful grandchildren I might have!"[47] Likewise, Lucy's parents were a surrogate family to Crystal:

> Saturday I went over to Lucy's and spent the night and Sunday with them. I am wild about the family. It's a very large one—eight children between 30 and 15 years old, and father and mother. Think of it! And the jolliest, cleverest, teasing crowd you ever saw. I felt like one of them very soon, and I feel sure they liked me. It makes me happy to think of it. . . .
> . . . They told me to come any time—that the door would always be open. Imagine a dining-room table with four on a side and one at each end, for a family![48]

By the spring of her junior year, Crystal was groping for what might come after college. Her transcript was very mixed and would ultimately, in senior year, include an F in history and a D in economics, subjects she had aced as a sophomore. Her heart seemed to lie in multiple areas outside the classroom. She enjoyed theater and was involved in both the First Hall Play and the Fourth Hall Play, the latter also with Lucy Burns, in 1902.[49] She loved to sing, "sometimes almost more than I can stand," she expressed, and sang soprano in the choir as a junior and second soprano in the choral club in her senior year.[50] She would study voice with the hope of a professional singing career until well into young adulthood.[51] And she always enjoyed athletics. She was an excellent swimmer and tennis player, and in college she played catcher for an impromptu baseball team—without gloves; "it kills our hands," she told Max. In fact, she led her baseball team in introducing the sport to the campus "and now other girls from the college are taking it up."[52] An unusually tall woman, she also played a little basketball in games against other classes.[53]

Crystal increasingly reveled in group activity and social life. She was a member of several social and academic clubs, including an eating club affectionately called the Pistachio Family, and the political group Civitas, which elected her its chair in 1903, succeeding Lucy Burns.[54] By graduation time, she had been elected class historian.[55] Crystal was a little surprised by her rising popularity over the course of her Vassar career. Next to her mother, she did not "seem to be funny in my family," she told Max, yet "at school and college I am always making people laugh."[56]

By the end of her junior year, she was starting to think the subject that interested her most was human society, in all its variety and striving, tenderness and struggle. She began a diary in May 1902, the end of her junior year, and wrote in her first entry:

> Nothing except a "character book" measures up to watching a coming and going of all kinds of people and studying their faces. If occasionally it is depressing, but not usually. Most faces, even when they are tired and sad, have a gleam of kindness and goodness in them, I think. When a person spends almost all of her time in a place where she sees only one kind of people—girls—young, healthy and happy—it has been a pleasure to stand on the corner somewhere and watch humanity in all its phases. It was hot today and almost everyone looked worn, but they were all human beings and endlessly interesting. I never could understand a desire to spend one's time studying the life and character of plants, animals, etc, when we always have the great throbbing mass of humans to study.[57]

These feelings probably gave birth to her plan to pursue a graduate degree in sociology, as well as to her political identity: nine months later, she declared herself a Socialist.[58] Three months after that, President Taylor would address the 154 graduates of Crystal's class of 1903, telling them America needed an unmistakable wake-up call, the "moral equivalent of war"; the educated, he augured, are so focused on attaining wealth that they're losing sight of higher ideals.

As Crystal turned toward graduate study, she was not exactly inspired by the life of the mind as she found it. She had noted "how few people are original thinkers" the way Annis had urged her to be. "I have decided that very few people do any *independent* thinking," she told Max.[59]

In pursuing her master's degree at Columbia, she would study with two professors seen as avatars of new schools of thought. The political economist John Bates Clark had been transformed by his own graduate study, in Germany. He built his career on the renegade thinking of the German Historical School, a new stripe of economic thought at the time that explicitly rejected the laissez-faire economics and philosophy then spreading across Europe. Though Clark became less Progressive in his thinking across his career, he produced his two most assertive works, *The Philosophy of Wealth* (1886) and *The Distribution of Wealth* (1899), in the decades immediately preceding Crystal's arrival on campus. Rather than accepting inequality as a natural occurrence resulting from the economic laws of competition, both books conceptualized social and political factors involved. In 1885, the year before Clark's first big book came out, he cofounded the American Economic Association (AEA), and he served as its third president, from 1893 to 1895. The organization established its fundamental purpose as promoting a shift away from laissez-faire thinking and policies in the United States. Four years after Crystal's graduation, the AEA would play host to one of her most pointedly political speeches about the price workers and their families pay for prevailing law and policy that justified an unregulated industrial workplace, wrongly exempting owners from responsibility for the human cost of doing business.

Crystal took two courses with Clark and two with Franklin Henry Giddings, a founder of American sociology whose professional rise speaks to his innovative intelligence, as well as the play of opportunity and mentorship in his own career—resources he would pay forward as a popular teacher to his Columbia students, as long as they happened to be men. Giddings had been an undergraduate student of civil engineering who, without a degree, successfully published work on social science in both popular and academic venues. These publications caught the attention of some important men, including Woodrow Wilson, then a professor of history at Bryn Mawr. Wilson hired Giddings as a lecturer in politics in 1888, the same year Giddings belatedly received his bachelor of arts degree from Union College. Offering courses in political economy and methods of administration, Giddings rose, in just four years, to the rank of full professor in 1892. Two years later, he was given a newly established chair at Columbia, becoming the first full professor of sociology in the United States. The new position helped elevate the field from a small outpost of philosophy to a discipline of its own, and established Giddings as one of its main architects.

Giddings's definitive textbooks, *Inductive Sociology* (1901) and *The Scientific Study of Human Society* (1924), combined with his leadership as third president of what became the American Sociological Association (ASA), in 1910 and 1911, associated the emerging field with the Progressivism and rising international consciousness of the new century. In *Democracy and Empire* (1900), he called on sociology to be the source of a "rational and constructive criticism of our social values" and consequently an engine of "a realizable social ideal."[60] A student of Charles Darwin and his sociological disciple, Herbert Spencer, the father of Social Darwinism, Giddings posited an interrelationship between the social and physical sciences; what he called the "law of social choices" held that the institutions, laws, and values that constitute societies emerge from the perpetual adjustment by people to an always-changing environment.[61]

Giddings rejected what he saw as the guesswork of philosophers, favoring verifiable data to support arguments about which choices would constitute proper routes to social progress. Arguing for the application of early quantitative methods to social phenomena, he established himself as the nation's premier advocate of computational sociology and led what was later recognized as the "statistical turn" in American social science.[62] Yet while Giddings wrote strenuously about the value of data analysis for sociological argument, his own work barely practiced what he preached. His late book on methodology, published just seven years before his death, was a rare case in which he included some numeric tables; however, these tabulations consisted of basic calculations, a far cry from the logarithmic functions used in scientific fields such as astronomy at the time or the statistical concepts he advocated for his own discipline.[63] But Giddings made such consistent and persuasive statements, in his pedagogy and his public life, that he successfully legitimized statistical analysis as a primary tool of sociology, essential in formulating effective and far-reaching public policy.[64] Crystal would assiduously apply this rationale—a mandate to measure, so to speak—in her work with the Pittsburgh Survey to come. While a Giddings student, however, she probably drew little direct inspiration from a professor who ignored verifiable data about women's intellectual ability and achievements in higher education and famously disapproved of their entry in public life.[65]

She may have experienced a greater intellectual affinity with Clark, whose interests more immediately align with her master's thesis. She chose to write about Daniel Raymond, an early nineteenth-century American lawyer whose treatises, *Thoughts on Political Economy* (1820) and *The Elements of Political Economy* (1823), were the first by any American economist to examine social conditions at the rise of American industrialization. She considered that era "a critical time in our national development" and compared it to her own.[66] Eastman clearly gravitated toward Raymond's most left-leaning ideas: his interest in the problem of extreme inequality, the role of government in redressing it, and his assertion of the pivotal value of labor in creating national wealth.

Just as Clark would have, she highlighted Raymond's position as "a determined and out-spoken opponent of laissez-faire." In contrast to dominant thinkers in political economics, pointedly Adam Smith, Raymond "did not admit that individual interests are ever as a rule in harmony with the common interests of all."[67] Rather, more communally, more socialistically, Raymond posited "the nation is *one*" and expressed what she called a "broad view of national wealth." This premise informed "not only the capacity of the nation as a whole to produce," she found, but also, more important to her, "the chance of each citizen to acquire the necessities and comforts of life."[68] In her only first-person intervention in the body of her thesis, Crystal emphasized the crucial humanitarian idea expressed by this encompassing conception of American prosperity. Raymond's notion of wealth recognized the national interest in promoting the "opportunity each individual has of maintaining a comfortable existence—this, I think, is a radical departure from accepted political economy of that day," she wrote.[69]

Eastman explored Raymond's "condemnation of extreme inequality," as she put it, as one of several "important truths" of his work, detailing his insight that large disparities in wealth harm not just workers but owners as well.[70] Inequality demeans the value of labor, while it discourages industry and enterprise alike, she noted.[71] "More seriously," she continued, inequality, unchecked, will cripple the very system of free enterprise that produces it: for owners, she argued, it "leads to the production of an unreasonable proportion of comforts and luxuries . . . furnishing too great and unnatural a check [on their] productive impulses to invest, hire, compete and expand."[72] After a point, she indicated through Raymond's work, extreme wealth dams its own flow; it pools at the top and does not trickle down through the economy as it should if it is to stimulate national prosperity. As a result, she argued, building on Clark, Raymond thought it was the proper work of government to intervene in market systems to redress wealth inequality.[73] Such government action, she emphasized, would be good for the country and American society, and for all individuals concerned.

Yet Raymond had "no sympathy for systems of perfect equality," she hastened to add. Indeed, Raymond believed too much government control would check free enterprise and competition, bringing what he had called " 'a universal paralysis [to] the body politic.' "[74] Much like Giddens, Raymond accepted inequality as essentially natural, as inevitable in society and so the economy. "If one has more talents, more strength, more ingenuity, industry or a better character than another, let him enjoy the full benefits of these advantages," Crystal summarized. However, public interventions were needed to "undo" inherited advantages, as she dubbed it, hindering opportunities for upward mobility, and paralyzing or at least hobbling those who strove to rise.[75]

Here she identified Raymond's critique of the public truss of an unequal playing field—laws concerning inheritance and primogeniture, and corporations, banks, and the national debt, "contrivances or institutions which give the rich an artificial power to increase their wealth," she wrote. Overall, since the "evils come from an unnecessary and artificial degree of inequality, not from inequality itself," Crystal emphasized Raymond's assertion that government should protect and support the poor. The rich, she inferred, can take care of themselves. On this point, her own voice surfaced. Republican government, she wrote in summary, should be a "good shepherd who supports and nourishes the weak and feeble in his flock until they gain sufficient strength to take their chance with the strong, and [Raymond] does not suffer them to be trampled out and crushed to the earth by the powerful."[76]

Crystal particularly admired Daniel Raymond's commitment to his own vision. She was initially drawn to a man who "without calling himself a Political Economist, disagreed with those who were, with a sublime disregard for age, reputation, and long-standing authority, that was in its very boldness attractive."[77] However, she criticized Raymond more than once for what she saw as his "careless thinking."[78] He was "occasionally almost brilliant in his criticism and at other times exhibiting a deplorable lack of depth and understanding," she wrote.[79] In the end, she censured him with what became a somewhat characteristic complaint: that he was not thinking big enough or going far enough to really change things. "The thinker failed of patience, and had not the lively sympathetic understanding which are useful for criticism and also prevented him from coming up with a complete system of political economy of his own." The latter deficiency, she concluded with a youthful gusto whose spirit she would never really surrender, "might have been of more use to the world."[80]

As one of the very few women students at Columbia, Crystal had a perspective that was uncommon almost by definition. Although the proportion of master's degrees awarded to women rose significantly after the turn of the twentieth century, reaching 26 percent of all master's degrees in 1909–10, the raw number of degrees conferred upon women in those years was relatively small. In 1904, when Crystal's degree was conferred, only 338 other women earned degrees at that level nationwide.[81]

Like many minorities entering arenas previously closed to them, she experienced her position as paradoxical. On the one hand, her gender marked her, making her hypervisible in classes and on campus. On the other, her difference marginalized her, making her invisible as both a thinker and a peer. She recognized that she lacked an unacknowledged privilege that men enjoyed: the assumption of oneself as the standard person, free of gender and its habitual assumptions and qualifiers. "I can't make myself into a mere intelligence, going among them, and look neither to the right nor to the left but straight into the face of knowledge," she wrote to Max. "I am, after all, a girl." She experienced the worst of both worlds, so to speak, at a university overwhelmingly dominated by men. Too visible as a woman to be an intellect, Crystal was also too apparent as a classmate to be seen as a woman in their midst. Yet to her, all fellow students were both classmates and men. "Oh—so many, many, men!" she exclaimed to Max. "I look them all over and look again at the good-looking ones." Her baffling status left her isolated, alienating her from engaging either academically or socially with her classmates. "They are not glad to have me there and are not interested in me, so that I shall soon lose interest in them, no doubt."[82]

Marked yet marginal, Crystal felt intimidated and lonely at Columbia. "On Tuesday evening I have a seminar—in which I am the only woman," she told Max, out of a group of twenty "learned guys," many of whom were working toward their doctorates. "One or two are comparatively young," she continued, "[b]ut I seem to be the only ignorant one. . . . Ah me!"[83] One response was to get involved with the expanding suffrage movement in New York. In 1904, Crystal joined dozens of other young women in the just-formed College Equal Suffrage League of New York State. Founded by Caroline Lexow, later to become an organizational leader in the National Woman's Party and a campaigner for world government, the group immediately drew other up-and-coming suffragists, including Inez Milholland and her sister, Vida. It also included such established movement figures as Carrie Chapman Catt and M. Carey Thomas, who would soon agree to serve as president of the national organization. The league, then affiliated with the National American Woman Suffrage Association (NAWSA), recruited young women across the state into the suffrage cause.[84]

For much of her year at Columbia, Crystal contemplated her social life as much as sociological study. She had previously felt her "first real longing for a man" in October of her first year at Vassar[85] and began actively orchestrating dates, particularly through Max once he entered Williams College in 1901.[86] When she wrote in her diary, her private thoughts most often concerned her ideal man and mate. She envisioned a companionate relationship, a partnership of peers—what her generation would sometimes call "sibling marriage." She wanted a meeting of both hearts and minds, someone with an emotional range, depth, and candor equal to her own. She prioritized a romantic partner over a successful provider, envisioning a poetic figure who "shows a soul in his face, and whose eyes are unmistakably true." As Annis had forecast, she was formulating someone very much like her actual sibling, her brother Max. "I verily believe I would rather have an improvident philosopher kind of man, like Max, and see to earning the living myself," Crystal told her mother, "than a practical man without the finer [qualities]. No amount of worldly disappointment and poverty could be as soul destroying as to discover a poverty of fine feelings and appreciativeness in the man you must live with all your life and whose children would be yours also."[87]

Crystal seemed to thrill in the emotional profusion of attraction and connection almost as much as in her relationships themselves. "I am willing to take the risk, because I was the one to first feel a thrill of sympathy between us," she told Max about one man she was seeing in these years. "I told him that, I think. I don't remember him at all, but merely the feeling I had when I thought of him for a few days after."[88] She savored emotional experience, almost as a value in itself. "I do love to . . . search for words that just express a feeling or suggest it," she would say. "Writing notes to a person who has just left me when my feeling for him is vivid and present, for instance, is a perfect mania with me."[89] Indeed, she loved the very experience of feeling. "Rutger Green asked me to marry him," she told her mother in 1906, "and I said I couldn't. . . . On top of this, came Konrad in the evening, bringing me a great glowing armful of autumn branches he had gotten for me in the woods. His eyes were shining with happiness because I was so delighted." Then, she continued, another man dropped in, "saying nothing much but leaving me a note that made me want to cry. Altogether Sunday was a blissful day of emotions," she concluded. "I wanted to laugh and cry at the same moment when it was over."[90]

As a twenty-something graduate student, these swirling romantic feelings would sometimes pool around a strong maternal urge, which she experienced as profound and elemental, as both "psychical" and "physiological," she would say. If she felt "joyless," she would at times attribute her mood "to the fact that the mother-instinct is strong in me just now and has no fulfillment."[91]

On the eve of her Columbia final exams, Crystal found her thoughts confronting the challenges ahead for an educated woman who longed equally for love, children, and meaningful work. She recorded in her diary "my great desire to be married, my hope and even eagerness in planning for it," while acknowledging it might "stand in the way of a successful career of any kind." She lamented the impossible choice women faced, at first blaming herself for the problem: she noted "the single-minded persistence one needs" to succeed as a woman in a career yet "cannot have while I have these ever present unsatisfied longings in quite another direction."[92] In her diary, she wrestled with herself over it, trying to figure a way forward:

> The question is, how can I . . . keep way down in my consciousness, almost out, all thought of a love, of children, and a home,—for days and weeks and months and even years together! How can I keep this all out of

my head when it seems to come in so naturally? All this, my great happiness may come eventually, all unplanned and unforeseen. If it does it will take its place in my life. But for the present future there is nothing of it in sight. The reasonable thing to do is to go ahead and forget it in giving myself to work, to face a future without it, rejoicing if it comes, but being strong, courageous and happy, and full of a large definite purpose always, if it doesn't.[93]

A true resolution to such dilemmas would be hard to come by, even today, and Crystal's drives for both motherhood and career became a dominant theme of her life, her writing, and her politics. But her hunger for both work and family, experienced as vital and inborn, also typified the kind of intense emotional engagement characteristic of her in everything she did. Crystal would embrace the same excitation of feeling in her political activities as she did in her private life. "I love nothing better," she would tell Max after he spoke at a mass meeting during the election of 1900, "than to get into a certain situation, funny, solemn, romantic, sentimental, or just unusual, and *feel* myself in it with a kind of exulting joy.[94] Later she admitted, "My greatest weakness and temptation is a passion for *living* hard, especially on the emotional side."[95] To Max she acknowledged her "passion for passion," a quality she felt she shared with her brother, and which, she noted, "I don't see in people very often."[96] In the months after completing her master's degree, as she contemplated next steps, she tried to come to terms with it. "Perhaps it is my strength too," she ventured in the spring of 1905. "It must be the same thing which gives me so warm and tender a love for so many people—and that is good. Isn't it?"[97]

Crystal hoped an answer would become clearer in law school. Uptown, Ivy League Columbia had not been a great fit for her. As she reported to the *Vassar Bulletin* in 1904, "Studying Political Economy and History at Columbia, with hopes of an M.A. in June—despite the conservative influences of this institution, the days find me a confirmed Radical, still wavering on the brink of Socialism."[98] Maybe the renegade study of law, especially when pursued in Manhattan's bohemia of Greenwich Village, would let her follow what she knew of her heart.

At the time, women's place in legal education was highly uncertain, and in legal practice even more so. Columbia's Harlan F. Stone, soon to become dean of the law school and eventually a US attorney general and chief justice of the United States, was known to say female students would be admitted "over my dead body."[99] Downtown, New York University (NYU) Law School, however, had been accepting women for more than fifteen years and was becoming an incubator and haven for women in the law. When Crystal enrolled in the fall of 1905, NYU was on track to graduate more women lawyers than any other school in the country.[100] Still, she knew she was braving a monumental gamble. "Next year I'll try the 'law,'" she reported to her Vassar classmates, and wondered, "what if *all* my fond hopes turn out to be illusions?"[101]

A significant influence on her decision to pursue law seems to have been Tommy Fennell, the son of a saloonkeeper who became a lawyer in Elmira. She dated him in 1904–5, while teaching American history and English literature at the Elmira Free Academy; Crystal worked for a year to allow the family to focus on tuition payments for Max's final year at Williams, just as he had done while she attended Columbia the year before. Tommy introduced her to the real-life practice of the law. He took her "twice to court, and I am even more wild than before to be a lawyer," she told Max. "I have decided there is nothing to be afraid of, and that I can be as good at it as the next man." In fact, Tommy "says I make him work like everything in an argument and that I 'go him one better every time.'"[102]

Two months later, in February 1905, she was traveling to lower Manhattan to interview for jobs to support herself while studying law. She saw two employment agents and the Legal Aid Society about work, then took an athletics test—exercises, gymnastic apparatus, games—for a position running the evening recreation center at the Greenwich House Settlement.

Her visit was "one of the most royal good times I have ever had in my life," she reported. She took in "three good plays, had a great visit with Lucy and the Burns's [*sic*], . . . and I had a man at hand all the time . . . —it was all I could do not to have them over lap [*sic*] each other," she told Max. And the exam "was easy and hard enough for me to enjoy." She could readily see herself there. "Greenwich House . . . is the place of all places where I want to go next year," she quickly knew. "I think I'd like to have my little room over on Washington Square near the Law School and then go over to this Greenwich House, only a few blocks away, for my meals." [103]

The Greenwich House Settlement was located at 26 Jones Street in lower Manhattan, one of New York's most congested immigrant neighborhoods at the time. On that block alone lived some 1,400 people of twenty-six nationalities, all in dilapidated tenements and nine boardinghouses, interspersed with five salty saloons.[104] It had been incorporated just three years before, taking over a three-story building that had been a boardinghouse for longshoremen working on the docks of the ninth ward. The social worker Mary Kingsbury Simkhovitch, along with the writer Jacob Riis, former US senator and Secretary of the Interior Carl Schurz, and Felix Adler, founder of the ethical culture movement, had jointly launched it.

Greenwich House was part of a movement that had begun in the late 1880s, when pioneering institutions such as New York City's University Settlement (1886) and Chicago's Hull House (1889), founded by Jane Addams and her life partner, the reformer Helen Gates Starr, were established in the most destitute areas in America. Two other New York City pioneers—the Henry Street Settlement (1893) and then Greenwich House (1902)—helped lead the way as dozens of settlements spread across the country over the next two decades.[105] By the time Crystal settled into her first job, some four hundred settlement houses were operating in the United States.[106]

Settlement houses were designed to let reformers live among the poor as their neighbors, fostering cross-class bonds of understanding and shared participation in community building, social improvement, and problem solving. Although most settlements had roots in religious denominations, primarily Protestant Christianity, their very concept generally reached beyond older models of Christian charity, which focused on sympathy by the affluent to promote uplift for the downtrodden.[107] Nestled in immigrant neighborhoods of major American cities, settlement houses brought middle-class reformers to live among the poor. They functioned as meeting grounds and community centers, sponsoring a variety of educational programs to help people lift themselves up through opportunities and relationships in their own communities— albeit in defined middle-class terms. Greenwich House, for example, had a playground and library; it ran a kindergarten and children's clinic; it offered classes in painting, music, sculpture, pottery, language, and much more. Like its kin around the country, its mission was to combat fear of swelling immigrant groups by fostering their assimilation and inclusion within local communities, to agitate for social reforms in the face of corporate greed and labor exploitation, and to aid immigrants and the poor by directly providing essential services.

Overall, the movement would characterize its applied communitarianism in simple terms, now remembered as "the three Rs": "residence, research and reform."[108] But the array of settlement houses across the country came to function as living incubators of the rising collectivist and internationalist spirit in social work.[109] They helped advance the coalition building so central to the Progressive projects of the early twentieth century, while adding new dimensions to the composition and the strategies of those coalitions. Large numbers of settlement houses were established and staffed by affluent, educated women, who responded to the urgency of emergent social problems with research, philanthropy, and active new initiatives in advocacy. As a result, the settlements became vital training grounds and safe havens for educated New Women who were determined to create a political and communal place for themselves in the world. At Greenwich House, Mary Simkhovitch became a leading figure within a network of professional women who were forging new pathways for social impact and professional advancement at the time. So many women like her would build vital careers in social work that they are often credited, as a group, with professionalizing the country's social welfare system in the years to come.[110]

Mary Simkhovitch was fourteen years older than Crystal and had studied at Boston University, Radcliffe, and Columbia, and abroad in Germany. Her great-great-great-grandfather had fought with Washington at Valley Forge, and his successors had included some notable literary and social lights in Massachusetts. While in Europe, Mary had met Vladimir Gregorievitch Simkhovitch, a Russian seven years her junior, who was then getting his doctor of philosophy degree at the University of Halle. Before she left for home they became engaged, and as soon as he could, he followed after her. By the fall of 1902, the Simkhovitch family was among the first fifteen residents of Greenwich House. On Thanksgiving Day, they sat down for their first meal together in a settlement dining room that had once served as the official headquarters of the Anarchist's Society—Vladimir; their eleven-month old son, Stephen; and Mary, who was seven months pregnant.[111] Their daughter Helena was born in January 1903.

Greenwich House began developing classes and clubs in 1905, the same year Crystal was hired for sixty-five dollars a month to run the recreation center four nights a week. "With *my* economy," she would tell Max after she got the job in April, that "is a comfortable living wage."[112] The settlement would introduce Crystal to many of the most important Progressive reformers of the era, people who became her colleagues and mentors in the labor, suffrage, and peace movements. It was a magnet for them. "Sooner or later every really interesting up and doing radical who comes to this country gets down there for a meal," she told Max.[113]

It was at Greenwich House that Eastman first encountered Lillian Wald, founder of the nearby Henry Street Settlement, with whom she would work closely in the American Union Against Militarism. She also met Mary White Ovington, who would cofound the National Association for the Advancement of Colored People (NAACP) in 1909. Ovington believed, as Eastman would, that "many problems attributed to race are really labor questions."[114] Greenwich House also solidified Crystal's relationship with Paul Kellogg, a lifelong mentor soon to lead the famed Pittsburgh Survey. Kellogg was a journalist and Progressive who had arrived in New York from Kalamazoo, Michigan, in 1901 to begin taking courses at Columbia. In 1902, he joined the staff of *Charities*, a journal published by the New York Charity Organization Society. By the time Crystal began at Greenwich House in 1905, the journal was merging with the in-house organ of the Chicago Commons Settlement House to become *Charities and the Commons*, naming Kellogg its managing editor. He became editor of its next iteration, the *Survey*, in 1909 and, over the next half century, lead the magazine in organizing innovative investigations of social problems that would make it one of the most eminent

Progressive journals of its time. Eastman also grew to know Kellogg's close colleague, the economist, child welfare advocate, and educator Edward T. Devine, general secretary of the New York Charity Organization Society. Devine's unofficial credo, to "attack root causes"—those "organized forces of evil . . . beyond the control of individuals whom they injure and too often destroy"—must have resonated for her.[115] He used to say "prevention is better than relief," an attitude she would mobilize and magnify in her career.[116]

Crystal's schedule during law school was packed with study, work for pay to support herself, and an active social life that intermixed organizational leadership, music and theater, men, politics, and reform. Her academic life consisted of law lectures for twelve-and-a-half hours each week, and she estimated she spent about twice that amount of time studying.[117] Now part of a community more congenial to her, she became a student leader and personality on campus. One of only sixteen women out of 156, she was elected second vice president of her class. At the class dinner right before Christmas 1906, she memorably sang a musical spoof about the faculty even while she and the other officers were seated right on the dais with them.[118] In addition to her job at Greenwich House, she earned money by tutoring, traveling to Brooklyn to work with two students in history, for five dollars a week.[119] She found time to continue her voice training, taking lessons twice a week in September,[120] then four times a week beginning in October through at least January 1907.[121] She also took Italian classes at the settlement for a time.[122] And she volunteered to conduct a glee club at Greenwich House, a venture she embraced to offset what felt to her like the strongly careerist—hence, selfish—trajectory of her study at NYU.[123]

Crystal frequently attended political dinners and talks, such as the one Charlotte Perkins Gilman gave as part of a panel on "Loneliness and Individualism" in February 1907.[124] She took in many operas, an art form on which she ran hot and cold;[125] numerous plays; and the Russian Symphony.[126] She attended some events with friends, others with the numerous men in her life at the time. Frequent invitations came from Paul Kellogg and from Vladimir Simkhovitch. Shortly after her arrival at Greenwich House, Crystal had reported to Annis, "I like Mrs. Simkhovitch better every day, and I've always loved 'Vladimir G.,' as Paul [Kellogg] calls him. He is a charmer, and its [sic] nothing against him that he likes me, of course."[127] Within a month, Simkhovitch invited her to a dinner he had organized for the Philosophical Society. Flatteringly, he seated her next to Felix Adler, whose many relevant distinctions also included a chair in political and social ethics at Columbia, her recent alma mater.[128] Throughout law school, Crystal's letters speak of many dates with male admirers: a walk in Central Park with one young man of interest, a group excursion up the Hudson including others. She went to the theater with Konrad Brandt, who was one of several suitors to fall in love with her.[129] She went on an autumn leaf-peeping outing with Max's college friend Sidney, whom Crystal liked for "his ideas and his interests and his eyes."[130] She attended football games, plays, and lectures with Rutger Green, who doted on her and, by the end of October 1906, became the first of two men that year to propose marriage.[131]

From the start, Greenwich Village suited Crystal's identity while it shaped her emerging goals. In the early twentieth century, "the Village," a five-square-mile area below Fourteenth Street in lower Manhattan, already boasted long associations with rebellion, experimentation, and creativity. Nearly 80 percent of its residents were either foreign-born or first-generation Americans; reformers like Crystal lived side by side with the Irish and Italian immigrants dwelling in tenements in the western and southern parts of the neighborhood and with upper-class families residing in a strip of refined townhouses along the northern edge of Washington Square.[132] New York's first subway opened while Crystal was enrolled at Columbia in 1904, but service would not extend into the area until 1917. As a result, a distinctive street culture prevailed in the neighborhood, while political societies, social clubs, axiomatic restaurants, and conversational "salons" emerged to further facilitate its free-spirited intellectual and social life.[133] A place apart, yet teeming, the Village, like other bohemian enclaves in America, Europe, and elsewhere, offered its residents the opportunity to cast off inherited expectations and live by their own ideas.[134]

Greenwich House and the downtown neighborhood that surrounded it reminded Crystal of Eastman family life in Elmira and Glenora. Within a month of her arrival, she reported to Annis that she had become "devoted to these people and feel[s] perfectly at home here."[135] She found much of what she had been missing and hoping for in both political and personal life since she left home. "If I can get in there and make them like me," she told Max, "I shall consider my future made as far as real living goes."[136]

Crystal's only surviving piece of writing from this time is "Charles Haag: An Immigrant Sculptor of His Kind," published during winter break from NYU in 1907. In it, she speaks of a magnificent fellowship of Progressives and radicals. She saw in Haag's sculpture the "two great spiritual forces at work in America today, both trying to solve the same problem": those that reach down from "from above" (philanthropists, charities, and organizations for social and civic betterment) with those "blindly struggling up from beneath" (workers, trade unions, and the Socialist Party). These various groups would not readily coalesce into coordinated coalitions, perhaps particularly the organizations and parties on the political left, but from the start Crystal idealized their coming together as kin. "The workingmen's interests make them brothers," she wrote; "together they must fight for a better chance for all." In Haag's art she saw an expression of her own emerging intersectional vision: "the hope and promise of the future," she wrote, lay in forging vast harmonies, in uniting groups and movements in "mutual understanding."[137]

That faith was affirmed and amplified by the music of life she found in Greenwich Village in these years. To walk out the door of the settlement was to discover what she saw as a working model of human harmonies in community. Although the freedom and equality the Villagers both created and conjured around themselves was far from perfect—black intellectuals and reformers, for example, were rarely a part of the mix—as a young woman Crystal was inspired by a new world seeming to come together as one.[138] "Everyone is out," she described to Annis. "Mothers and father and babies line the doorsteps. Girls with their beaux, standing in the shadows, or gathered in laughing groups on the corners. And children, thousands of them everywhere, little girls playing [and] singing games in the middle of the street, and boys running in and out, chasing each other, throwing balls, building fires, fighting, laughing, shouting." She became rapturous about human potential: "Oh it is wonderful,—this human nature with its infinite capacity, and unending desire, for joy. . . . Let someone only strike up a common dance tune on a wheezy street organ, and, though it be the hottest, dirtiest street, and the weariest people in the land—you'll see the eyes light up and the feet begin to go,—there'll be humming and singing here and there,—and the little ones will dance their legs off. Isn't it beautiful?"[139]

Crystal tried to explain it all to Max. "I love it so for the people that are there and the thousands of things they do and think about," she told him on the eve of his graduation from Williams in 1905. "Of course, I don't mean rich ones that drive up and down Fifth Ave., nor the very poor ones, who merely make me sad." She meant all the various people who were struggling together to change and remake things, who were trying to live greatly by her definition of it: "All the interesting between ones who really know how to live,—who are working hard at something all the time; and especially the radicals, the reformers, the students— because they are open-minded, and eager over every new movement, and because they know when it is right for them to let go and amuse themselves and because they can laugh, even at themselves."[140]

At the time, Crystal was trying to persuade Max to join her in the Village, to bring the person and the place she loved so distinctly together again in her life. He would later describe how his sister "pulled me toward the social problem; she pulled me downtown."[141] But it would not be easy. Max was apprehensive about his ability to make it in New York after college,[142] so by December 1906, Crystal was busily working to strengthen her hand. She called upon her closest contacts—Paul Kellogg and Vladimir Simkhovitch—to orchestrate employment for her brother. Kellogg instantly hired him to help with his lectures, and Simkhovich arranged an introduction to the philosopher John Dewey at Columbia, who would soon offer Max a plum lectureship. He would teach "Principles of Science," a subject in which he had neither training nor knowledge and for which he would admit he lacked the stated qualifications.[143] Max was elated by his sister's handiwork. He wrote "to say how I love you for your enthusiasm and your dependableness, and to think of all those worthies sailing forth to get *me* a place. You are a wonderful sister and I think about you half the time," he told her. He would stick right by her side, adding, "I want to live with you."[144]

When Max arrived in January 1907, Crystal quickly got him "installed in the settlement" for meals, she reported to Annis, then two days later found him a place to live.[145] It was a sizable room for three dollars a week, and best of all, it was close to her.[146] In less than three weeks, she proudly told her mother that Max was set. He had "a great appointment at Columbia,—assistant in the philosophy department. Dr. S is a wonder for influence. We are all happy over it.... It's a great start for him—small salary but very little work, and lots of time for study and tutoring if he wants to do them. It is $500 a year."[147]

At the time, Crystal was sharing an apartment with Madeleine Doty, an NYU Law alumna from the class of 1902. Doty would go on to become New York's first woman prison commissioner after infiltrating the women's prison at Auburn, New York, posing as an inmate to produce a searing account of her experiences behind bars.[148] Since October, the two women had been living in a third-floor walk-up at 12 Charles Street, about a half mile from Greenwich House and NYU. They paid thirty-six dollars a month for six rooms; Crystal paid fourteen dollars and Doty twenty-two dollars, since the latter "wanted to have room for a friend of hers who may want to come in," Crystal told Annis. If they ended up renting out the room to someone else, each would pay thirteen dollars.[149] In November, Crystal added a rented piano for four dollars a month so she could practice her singing.[150]

Vladimir Simkhovitch had introduced the two women, who would remain connected through reform, peace, and also personal channels. Doty later married Roger Baldwin, who would direct the American Civil Liberties Union (ACLU).[151] "She is a 'nice boy,' as Dr. Simkhovitz [*sic*] says—has frank gray eyes and an open smile and much the same charm as a young boy has. I shall like her," Crystal told her mother, "and there won't be any emotional strain either way."[152] From the start, their Charles Street apartment was a hub for downtown women activists, including Milholland, who shared a mutual commitment to prison reform with Doty and alumni channels with Crystal from both Vassar and NYU Law, and Ida Rauh, another NYU Law alumna who graduated in Doty's class. Before long, Max became romantically involved with both women: Inez Milholland became his first fiancée, and Ida Rauh his first wife and the mother of his only child.[153]

Max Eastman's bohemian life and political work have been well studied and are reasonably well known. Less widely acknowledged is his sister's social and emotional leadership, and her practical support, in his rise and success. Crystal introduced her brother to the whole community of Village reformers and activists, much as her father had done for her mother to enable her entry into the ministry. Beginning with Kellogg and Simkhovitch, she actively promoted Max to everyone as a promising figure, lending her contacts and local credibility to help parlay his own abilities as an orator and writer into positions and recognition of his own. In a relatively short time, he would begin thrilling audiences on the Progressive lecture circuit with his speeches on suffrage and women's rights. (His arresting good looks never hurt.) Before long, Crystal convinced Max to form the Men's League for Woman Suffrage in New York State, a move he described as humbling, but which boosted his clientele and cachet as a speaker.[154]

Even as Max gained his footing, Crystal continued to promote his career, at times transferring her own professional opportunities to him. When the high-profile muckraker William Hard, then an editor at *Everybody's* magazine, sought her out for an article on industrial accidents in 1908, for example, she set up her brother to meet with him instead.[155] She often helped Max out financially, giving him her speaking fees, for example, as gifts.[156] Later, she would put her own job as a suffrage organizer at risk to hire him on.[157] To varying degrees, it was Crystal who facilitated the connections between Max and the band of downtown artists and intellectuals who in 1912 would draft him to become editor of *The Masses*, the eclectic, irreverent, widely noted radical magazine that became both an emblem and an engine of cultural innovation and rebellion in the years prior to World War I. Although Max would later experience the magazine as something of a burden, tiring of the responsibilities of fundraising and daily management, *The Masses* developed him as a political thinker, as well as an editor and author, and ultimately would make his name. Indeed, it would make him one of the most famous radicals in American history.[158]

Crystal cherished Max's progress. She adored having her brother close to her and under her wing. "It is a joy to have him," she wrote her mother after his first meal with her at Greenwich House.[159] "Sometimes it feels unreal to have him wandering around these haunts," she reported two days later, "but it is very sweet."[160]

She embraced the project of mothering her brother, a responsibility Annis had bequeathed to her. She helped him buy a suit for work and lectures.[161] She encouraged him in his writing. "I read his essay aloud and we discussed the changes and I made a few criticisms," she told her mother in one typical report. "I think I cheered him up about it."[162] She appraised his female companions as a mother might for a son. "I suppose she is in love with Max," Crystal informed

Annis in 1907. "Poor thing! She is dear and appealing and often very pretty, but she doesn't seem to have much brains." Then she reported, looking on as a mother might, "Max has so many girls on his hands in some way or other, it's hard to keep track of them."[163]

And like her own mother, Crystal had feelings for her brother that sometimes swelled to the boundary of the romantic sublime. Like Annis, Crystal's familial love could surge into a more romantic, even sexualized, attachment.[164] Two months after Max arrived in Greenwich Village, she spontaneously wrote him a note rife with transcendent feelings similar to those Annis expressed about Morgan, her first-born son: "I thank God for you as I thank God for sun and wind, for the mountains and the sea,—for all the songs of birds, for green fields,—for moonlight and the wonderful stars; because as it is with all these,— you are very near to my soul."[165]

Effectively, Crystal and her mother collaborated in nurturing Max's launch into adulthood, with all the romantic slippage that teamwork and triangle inspired. "Yes, I am eager to have Max write and speak, and he ought to begin now," she told Annis in the early spring of 1907. "He could do a little tutoring and still have lots of time to write. Perhaps he will soon find just the job that will fit in. . . . He can certainly live on what he has if you pay the rent."[166] Then later in the same letter she semiseriously confided, "Max was the one I wanted to marry always."[167] A week later, Crystal's attitude toward Max resembled a mother happily rearing an adopted youngster. "Max and I have just had a sweet evening together. We are knowing each other better all the time. And oh what a beautiful dear, wise, faithful boy he is!" she told Annis.[168] A month after that, the siblings had attended church together, and Crystal's heightened feelings overtopped the boundary between mother figure and lover: "My mind and heart are almost distracted with vague and conflicting longings and sudden desires,—but, withal of me, poor and uncertain as I am, I know that I love you," she told Max. She went on to merge a half-joking marital trope with maternal awe at the coming man she saw before her: "When 'you left me at the church,' you stood bare-headed in the sunshine, smiling at me. I felt like saying, 'Ah, here is a *Man*! Let us live on and be glad!' "[169]

For his part, Max was drawn to his sister through mixed streams of feeling as a brother, a lover, and a son. He maintained what he would call a "passionate attachment" toward her all her life. "As a boy of ten," he would recall, "I used to announce that I would never marry any girl but my sister."[170] In fact, his desire for emotional involvement with Crystal extended through adolescence and into adulthood—and probably beyond. Her candor would always pave his way emotionally and politically; she could utter "exactly what I never quite had the courage to say, but felt," he confessed.[171] Max once said it was Crystal's unyielding social conscience that most guided and compelled him early on. "Your clear way of saying a thing is weighing on your conscience, and wanting to take it up and remove it, and never thinking that you can bend a little and let it slide off—O, it really makes me want to stand straight too!" he told her. "You have never built up a mist around yourself, and that is why you always see right and wrong, and the rest of us can't." To him, that clarion quality both distinguished and defined her. "You almost make me think there is magic in names," he said.[172]

As a twenty-one-year-old, Max wrote to Crystal, then nearly finished with her master's degree, and formulated his dependence upon her as interdependence, their spiritual destinies entwined. "I am way behind you in the battle, and get more good for our love because mine is upward, but you cannot reach down and help without strengthening yourself—so it is really upward for both of us. And if we devise together to the good, that bond will abide through all our lives' changes—won't it?"[173] The next month he imagined living by his sister's side effectively until death. "I know I will always want to be with you. When I am married, and may need a rest cure, I will come to you. That fact is, I don't intend to be married, and if your husband will only like to have me around—we won't have any absence for growing apart."[174]

Once Max arrived in the Village at the age of twenty-four, he often felt bereft without Crystal. Separations, extended or brief, triggered feelings of longing:

> When I thought I was too tired to go down to you tonight, my heart was just comfortless. . . . O, I have missed you at these two meals today—and now I am going over to dinner alone.
> O I have loved being with you so—and now everything is turned empty. I don't care about them up here.
> —But this must make you happy and not sad, because I love you and want you so much, and you will know the melancholy will be gone after a while—and we will be together often, won't we?[175]

Without her, Max could feel lost. Writing to her from uptown Columbia, he told her, "I live with my heart turned always south like a compass."[176]

The siblings would remain unusually bonded for the rest of their lives. As adults, they were probably each other's truest love. By the winter of 1907, Crystal's apartment share with Doty was falling apart; "a new girl has appeared on the scene," she reported, making her feel she was not "living *with* people but only living in the same house." She apparently wanted something more intimate. "If there is a small flat vacant in this house by Feb. 1," she told Annis, "Max and I want to take it."[177] That plan never came to pass—perhaps the small space made it too close for comfort. Crystal took the new apartment at 12 Charles Street by herself, living alone through the rest of the academic year.[178] But as soon as it was possible again, the siblings happily settled into a place together, just the two of them. "We have a wonderful house—with all the conditions wonderfully fulfilled," Max raved to their mother in September 1908. "Wide spaces—not streets—on three sides—air and sunshine—flowers blooming in the yards below us." They had "2 (segregated) bedrooms," he noted, and shared a "dandy kitchen, with laundry & refrigerator & gas stove—all for $33.00."[179] It was Crystal who arranged their new home together—as it would be time and again.

Though the emotional intensity between the siblings would rise and retreat over a lifetime, their attachment was constant, and arguments between them were rare. When they did occur, it was usually Crystal who apologized and tried to explain, quickly seeking to reestablish the connection between them.[180] But one passionate fight was different. Max, twenty-six, had announced to his sister, then twenty-eight, that he wanted to leave bohemia and move uptown. He suggested that Crystal join him, but she never could—not even for Max. She had discovered something as essential to her as he was. She tried to explain to him:

> You see, from your point of view this moving up town or staying down town is a matter of time and space and air,—known and measurable quantities that can be logically balanced until one comes to the rational conclusion. From my point of view there is another larger and altogether incalculable element, which we might call sentiment,—atmosphere. You know that if one place is <u>home</u> to a person, the other things—time, space, light and air,—don't count for very much. Well, this neighborhood is <u>home</u> to me—partly from habit, partly because my friends are here; . . . partly because Greenwich House is a center of life and interest with which I feel identified; and partly (largely) because my thoughts and hopes and ambitions in regard to work are centered here.[181]

Crystal was a woman of many sentiments, and now, nearing thirty with three degrees in hand, she was ready to claim what that meant. No single interest, or idea, or person—not even Max—could fulfill her hopes alone. Only in an atmosphere where her many facets and aspects could come together could she be herself. She would forever seek to pull her brother to her, into her element, because only in a world like that would she ever feel truly at home.

3

EMBARKING: THE PITTSBURGH SURVEY, WORKERS' COMPENSATION, AND THE FIRST BLUSH OF FAME

In June 1907, Crystal met with one of her New York University (NYU) Law professors about a job. He was starting a commission on immigration reform, an issue of legal concern in what was the peak year of US immigration between 1880 and 1920, the turn of the twentieth century. In February, President Theodore Roosevelt had signed the Immigration Act of 1907, continuing a legislative effort to limit US immigration that had effectively begun with the Chinese Exclusion Act of 1882 and would culminate with the Immigration Act of 1924.[1] Like the previous statutes, the 1907 law imposed both requirements and restrictions on immigrant groups deemed undesirable. Those groups targeted for exclusion included, particularly, the sick and disabled, but also the poor, some radicals, and those reckoned to have poor moral character. Under this latter part of the new law came an expanded definition of prostitution, which worked to limit the number of women who were allowed to enter the country.[2] It's not clear how Eastman's professor was preparing to participate in reform in the wake of the recent legislation—or indeed if the planned commission was ever formed; the 1907 act enhanced federal monitoring and control of US immigration, weakening the joint efforts of the national government and both local commissions and state boards.

The job interview was probably exploratory for Crystal anyway, or a plan B. She would long dream of a career as an attorney. But she had just completed her law degree and was preparing to take the New York State bar exam on her twenty-sixth birthday—in less than three weeks. It would be "quite an ordeal," with the "heat, and the bad air, and the long long hours of it," she said, and she would emerge uncertain. "I hope I passed, but I'm not at all sure," she told her mother. "I forgot many of the maddening little reasonless rules."[3] She would not find out

Crystal Eastman. Amy Aronson, Oxford University Press (2020).
© Oxford University Press.
DOI: 10.1093/oso/9780199948734.001.0001

until December that she had passed—1 of only 3 women out of 134 applicants to be admitted to the New York bar that time around.[4]

For now, she carried a long list of self-doubts into and out of her job interview. As she told Annis afterward, "I don't think I made much of an impression on him. I couldn't think of anything I had done, or anyone who knew me, or any reason why anyone should think I could do anything, and I told him this quite frankly." But then he had asked her why she thought she could contribute to the work of the commission, and her answer was telling. "I meditated a while," she related, "and then I said I was pretty sure I could find out the truth, and understand it when I found it out."[5] She did not get that job, but had identified a crucial intellectual quality that would help secure her another one and launch the first chapter of her public life.

Crystal urgently needed to find work. "You see, I hadn't any money to begin with," she would tell the papers about this stage in her career.[6] Then, one month after the failed interview, she was in Glenora when something woke her in the middle of the night. She got up and began wandering around the darkened house, only to find "it wasn't silent and awesome" but instead it seemed something was astir. "All the birds in the world were chirping steadily," she noticed.[7] As she followed their calls out onto the Cherith porch, she became the only witness to a partial lunar eclipse, an event that occurs when the earth moves into alignment with the sun and moon—but not perfectly. Perhaps it was a sign. The following week, she accepted a temporary job. It was not in the legal field as she had hoped but was close enough for now. At least it would draw on her sociological training, and it held out the possibility of promoting some tangible social progress, the objective that had attracted her to the law in the first place. She would be investigating accidents in the steel mills, mines, and railroad yards of western Pennsylvania as part of the new Pittsburgh Survey supervised by her Greenwich House friend Paul Kellogg. The project was slated to last two to three months. "I have thought myself out of the feeling of worry about law as my 'career,'" she would later tell her mother. "I'm going to *live*, not worry."[8]

* * *

The Pittsburgh Survey effectively began in 1905, when *Charities and the Commons*, jointly edited by Kellogg and Edward Devine, began to fulfill its charitable mission in the world: to finance, formulate, and publish original investigations of social problems. An earlier study had investigated conditions in Washington, DC, and when the results were published in a special report titled "Neglected Neighborhoods," in March 1906, readers were shocked to confront the grievous hardships of the poor in the nation's capital. After all, this was the very place that symbolized, and supposedly organized, the American vision of a democratic republic, of a shining city on a hill.[9]

At the time, Pittsburgh was the nation's industrial capital, where multitudes of immigrant workers, mainly from eastern and southern Europe, had come in search of that promise in its elemental form: jobs and an escape from poverty. Though industrialists argued that free enterprise and laissez-faire capitalism benefited laborers and owners alike, to Progressives, the city exemplified the ills of corporate industrialism unmoored from both humanitarian and republican precepts. Large corporations were dominating local governments, and "archaic social institutions," as Devine saw them, remained in place "long after the conditions to which they were adapted disappeared." The city saw a continuous influx of immigrants, he observed, who were subsisting on inadequate wages paid for virtually ceaseless toil—often in twelve-hour shifts seven days a week, an "altogether incredible amount of overwork by everybody." The gender wage gap was extreme. Men's pay rate was inadequate enough, and Devine noted it was "adjusted to the single man, not to the responsible head of a family"—the so-called family wage. But women's pay, particularly in trades where their proportion of the workforce was, as he put it, "great enough to be menacing" to men's status and control, was "one-half as much as unorganized men [earned] in the same shops and one-third as much as the men in the union." Family life was destroyed, Devine found, and "not in any imaginary mystical sense [but] by the demands of the day's work, and the very demonstrable and material method of typhoid fever and industrial accidents, both preventable."[10] Beyond all that, there were broader environmental impacts. Pittsburgh workers and their families endured inadequate nutrition, perpetual dirt, illness, and both unsafe and unsanitary conditions virtually everywhere in their lives. Kellogg argued they suffered what he termed "indirect taxation—levied in the last analysis upon every inhabitant of the city—of bad water, bad air, bad houses, bad hours."[11]

When the investigation was proposed, it quickly garnered local support from the city's mayor, George Guthrie; from Pittsburgh's Kingsley Settlement House; and from some local citizens, including $100 from Henry John Heinz of the H. J. Heinz Company, a Pittsburgh native. Nevertheless, the accumulated funding was insufficient to guarantee completion of the project. Then, in the spring of 1907, just as Crystal was finishing law school, the Pittsburgh Survey was selected for the first grant of the newly established Russell Sage Foundation. The charity had just been launched by the widow of a railroad and telegraph magnate who dedicated $35 million to the study and advancement of social welfare. With an initial grant of $7,000, the Pittsburgh work was to be completed within the three months— that was the project for which Eastman and other investigators were initially hired. Before long, Kellogg realized the potential magnitude of the project and returned to the foundation to secure another $19,500 grant to extend it for an additional year.[12]

The Pittsburgh investigation quickly promised to be the most comprehensive study of urban industrial life ever undertaken in American history. More than seventy trained researchers would produce a study published in six large volumes—four books, and two collections of essay-style reports—published between 1909 and 1914.[13] The project investigated dicey questions of equity and exploitation in an America feverish with growth and wealth: it examined wages, policies, and conditions of labor in major industries, particularly the steelworkers. One volume examined the working poor and the cost of living in typical mill town households; another, the specific conditions in trades employing women; and another, institutions and agencies for children, among other key features of working-class life.

Those involved included many prominent men—not only Kellogg and Devine, but also the University of Wisconsin labor economist John R. Commons, whose extensive research on the history of unions and leadership in the workers' compensation movement in Wisconsin would intersect with Eastman's subsequent work. Also on the team were Peter Roberts, a department secretary for the International Committee of the YMCA, and Robert A. Woods, director of the South End House settlement in Boston. Both men were strong voices in the prevailing Americanization movement, a Progressive-era education effort designed to more deliberately assimilate immigrants into the country's dominant culture. Programs through libraries and businesses, voluntary organizations and schools, taught newcomers the common skills thought necessary for American citizenship, from English language, to civic patriotism, to workplace norms, to proper dress, cookery, and child-rearing. By the 1920s, this drive to dissolve different nationalities in a great American "melting pot" began to give way to new ideas about American diversity built around pluralism and multiculturalism. Through the twentieth century and into the twenty-first, American reformers have increasingly envisioned less of a melting pot and more of a multicultural mosaic, a collective culture composed of distinct pieces that stand side by side in contributing to the pattern and beauty of American life.[14]

Other Pittsburgh researchers were men on the rise. John A. Fitch, who wrote *The Steelworkers* (1910), would continue to study the steel industry and become an important authority on it, investigating conditions in the great steel strike of 1919 and beyond. The team included the photographer Lewis Hine and the artist Joseph Stella, both of whose work visually conveyed the experiences of industrial laborers, people whose lives rarely pierced the public imagination. Hine's later photographs taken during more than a decade with the National Child Labor Committee were so arresting that they are now seen as a significant influence in changing labor law in the United States.[15]

A distinguishing feature of the Pittsburgh Survey was its embrace of women on the staff. A few, like Florence Kelley, were already trailblazing leaders whose public lives had begun in the 1890s; others, like Eastman, were part of the first generation of women to attend college in significant numbers. As these highly educated women pursued independent and public lives to an unprecedented degree, many of them successfully negotiated with traditional gender expectations by dedicating themselves to social welfare efforts on behalf of women, children, and families.[16] Elizabeth Beardsley Butler, for example, was a graduate of Barnard College and would write *Women and the Trades: Pittsburgh 1907–1908* (1909). Her study of the mechanized, dehumanizing conditions in factories in Pittsburgh, Baltimore, and Jersey City, New Jersey, is perhaps the first large survey of wage-earning women ever produced in the United States.[17] Helen Sumner, a graduate of Wellesley whose Pittsburgh research was connected to her doctoral work at Wisconsin under John Commons and another Progressive economist, Richard T. Ely, had previously coauthored a college textbook on labor problems and also worked as a field investigator in the Colorado suffrage movement. She wrote the *History of Women in Industry in the United States* (1910), published by the US Bureau of Labor Statistics, then rose to the position of chief investigator of the US Children's Bureau after joining the organization in 1913.[18] Margaret Byington, a graduate of Wellesley and then Columbia, was Crystal's housemate in Pittsburgh. She produced volume four, *Homestead: The Households of a Mill Town* (1911), a detailed survey of ninety labor households that she called a "case study of a poverty-stricken community." She became a staff member at the Russell Sage Foundation, where she wrote *What Social Workers Should Know about Their Community* (1911), a bestseller in its time.[19] Byington, like Sumner and others in this impressive cohort of women, would flourish in social welfare organizations and newly formed government agencies, some enjoying influential careers that extended into the New Deal of the 1930s.

Methodologically, the Pittsburgh Survey was an innovative experiment in collective social research. Devine and Kellogg strived "to offer a structural exhibit of the community as a whole," as they described it, by combining original field work in multiple related areas through a collaborative team effort.[20] "Individual inquiry and personal interpretation have brought us a certain distance but they cannot take us much farther," Devine argued. To advance things, the Pittsburgh Survey pursued this task force approach, coordinating an adroit team under common direction to produce comprehensive results rapidly enough to be both relevant and applicable.[21] Although this research design is not used in the academic social sciences today, in its time the project launched a public movement in social surveys that lasted through the first third of the twentieth century.[22] Spanning thousands of localities nationwide, these studies provided the general public with a social science lens, offering people ways of seeing a world that was changing as never witnessed before. This public sociology—part social inquiry, part journalistic expose, and part prologue to public policy—called new audiences, activists, and philanthropic supporters into constructive contact with the undiscovered country rising near the heart of every great American city.

Crystal's assignment in Pittsburgh was to study industrial accidents, an increasingly visible social problem in the United States at the time. The rapid pace of American industrial expansion coupled with weak safety regulations, largely unenforced in any case, resulted in higher rates of workplace accidents in cities like Pittsburgh than almost anywhere else in the world. At the same time, provisions for workers and families left destitute by injuries or death were minimal as compared with other industrializing nations.[23] Germany had established a compulsory system of workers' compensation for manufacturing, mining, and transportation as early as 1884. Similar accident insurance programs for inherently dangerous occupations had been instituted in Finland in 1895, Britain and Austria in 1897, and Norway in 1899. Yet in the United States, mandatory compensation laws, such as those passed in Maryland in 1902 and Montana in 1909, repeatedly failed constitutional challenges. In 1908, Eastman was midway through her work in Pittsburgh when Massachusetts would try to write around that legal problem by making workers' compensation voluntary—but then employers had no incentive to participate in it.[24] Ultimately, her project would seek to improve both working conditions and injury compensation for laborers and their families, while also devising an approach that might withstand any potential legal challenges.

Crystal traveled to her new job from a stay in Glenora, changing trains in Buffalo and again in Erie before heading 125 miles due south to Pittsburgh. The city sits at the nexus of the Allegheny and Monogahela Rivers, where they join to form the Ohio River. Its strategic location along these waterways, and just fifty miles from the Allegheny Mountains, made Pittsburgh a well-traveled junction for merchants and traders, as well as the military, going all the way back to the colonial era. But the completion of the Erie Canal in 1825 had virtually discontinued the flow of trade traffic through the area. The economic void had led to a rapid rise in industrial production, galvanized by vast deposits of coal for mining and, especially, for the production of iron and steel. Exactly thirty-five years before the Pittsburgh Survey began, Andrew Carnegie had constructed a massive steel plant in town, at first solely to produce steel rails for the railroad ventures he continued to pursue even after moving on from his position as a superintendent of the Pennsylvania Railroad at the end of the Civil War. Within a year, the plant was so profitable that he expanded production to include new and more advanced products—steel girders for bridges and tunnels, complete sleeping cars for railroad trains, among others—integrating his company vertically so as to own the supply chains his ever-growing business came to depend on. Carnegie revolutionized the industry in various ways, adopting technology and developing methods that vastly increased the ease and speed of production—and profits. And he made Pittsburgh a hub, attracting industrial development that broadened and accelerated around him. The inventor George Westinghouse was drawn to town for inexpensive steel and its abundance of steelworkers, and the Mellon family, already leaders in banking and finance by the early twentieth century, continued growing a range of companies and, later, philanthropic projects from their home base in the city.

When Eastman arrived in town, Carnegie was retired, having sold his Carnegie Steel Corporation, the largest of its kind in the world, to the financier J. P. Morgan and his United States Steel Corporation six years earlier. But he remained a commanding figure in Pittsburgh. Carnegie's handling of the infamous Homestead Strike, a violent confrontation between managers and workers at his plant in Homestead, Pennsylvania, in 1892, still resonated everywhere. The ferocious conflict, which ultimately succeeded in finally breaking the nation's strongest trade union at the time, had stained his reputation. A few years later, in 1899, Carnegie published "The Gospel of Wealth," an article pronouncing his philosophy, which he had already begun to put into practice, that it is the responsibility of the rich to aid the poor. Since selling his company in 1901, he had focused on expanding those philanthropic works. He had already founded the Carnegie Technical Schools (1900), a vocational institute offering training to the sons and daughters of the working class in Pittsburgh that, through mergers, would later become Carnegie-Mellon University. In 1910, he would establish the Carnegie Endowment for International Peace, gifting $10 million to advance internationalist frameworks for global peace and security. But steel, dominated by his old company now merged and grown even larger, remained a core industry in Pittsburgh. At the launch of the Pittsburgh Survey, Carnegie could be seen as an agent of what Devine called "absentee capitalism, with bad effects strikingly analogous to those of absentee landlordism."[25]

Crystal stepped off the train on September 17, 1907, to meet a distressed and bristling city. Unbridled and unregulated, it was among the most tumultuous places in the country, the very ground where the forces of the industrial revolution were playing out. Her first afternoon in town, she met Kellogg for an orientation session, and then he took her to dinner.[26] Her salary was to be one hundred dollars a month, an amount that would allow her to save quite a bit given her thrift, she thought.[27] She had arranged to live initially at Bethany, a Christian education cooperative, which charged no fee for lodgings.

The Pittsburgh Survey shared some goals and networks with the settlement house movement, and, like Greenwich House before it, the project put Eastman in contact with active, educated Progressive reformers, numbers of whom she would work with in the future. On her first full day in Pittsburgh she met Florence Kelley, who was taking her meals at a settlement house next door. "It's the Mrs. Kelley of the Consumer's League, Child Labor and Factory Inspecting fame," she told Annis, further describing a "humorous, and very wise and experienced" luminary of the investigative team.[28] When Crystal met her, Kelley was already a renowned social investigator and activist, a firebrand and national leader in the battle against inhumane sweatshop conditions and child labor. In 1892—the same year as Homestead—Kelley, then residing in Chicago's Hull House Settlement, had conducted an in-depth investigation into sweatshops and tenements in that city. She produced a comprehensive report whose recommendations led to the passage of what became known simply as the Illinois "anti-sweatshop law" in 1893. Two crucial provisions of the law limited the workday of women and children to eight hours and established the age of fourteen as the minimum at which a child could be legally employed in industry.[29] As a result of her work, Kelley had been appointed chief factory inspector for Illinois. At the time, she knew manufacturers would resist the new statute, particularly the eight-hour day. And many did. To take them on, she had enrolled in law school at Northwestern University; in 1894, she was admitted to the bar in Illinois.

In 1899, the same year Eastman entered Vassar, Kelley had relocated from Chicago to New York, residing in Lillian Wald's Henry Street Settlement in lower Manhattan. There, Kelley had cofounded and become secretary of the National Consumers League (NCL). The organization worked to foment an active consumer consciousness about the conditions of laborers who produced American goods, arousing the public—mainly women, who were predominantly responsible for shopping and family consumption—to use their purchasing power to reward those employers who ensured decent conditions and a minimum wage for their women workers. At the helm of the NCL, Kelley built sixty-four leagues across the country, spearheading multiple campaigns that were pivotal in reshaping the conditions of industrial production in the United States.[30] Shrewdly, the leagues aimed to intervene in the relentless labor conflict between owners and workers by forming alliances among women across class and income. If they could swing women consumers to the side of women workers, they would tip the balance of power decisively in favor of labor.

When Eastman met her in the fall of 1907, Kelley had recently finished amassing social scientific data for what would soon be a landmark Supreme Court case regarding protective labor legislation for women, *Muller v. Oregon* (1908), argued by the future Supreme Court justice Louis Brandeis. The case concerned a

laundry in Portland owned by Curt Muller, which required its women employees
to work more than the legal maximum of ten hours a day established by special labor legislation for women in Oregon in 1903. Muller argued that women
should be treated the same as men under law, and therefore should not be subject to the ten-hour-day statute. In February 1908, the Supreme Court handed
down a decision upholding Brandeis's argument in favor of the legal limits on
the number of hours women could work. The court reasoned that the state's
interest in protecting women's reproductive capability outweighed the right of
women workers to freely contract their labor. The ruling was a victory for Kelley
and the NCL, and enabled the passage of similar laws elsewhere.[31] Eventually,
it would lead to the Fair Labor Standards Act passed during the New Deal, a
gender-neutral law governing working hours.[32] But in Eastman's lifetime and career, the decision would raise an elemental discrepancy in Progressive labor legislation that would come to divide women's labor advocates from their former
allies in the feminist movement by the 1920s. The protective labor laws won by
women workers and their advocates like Kelley were attained on the basis of conventional gendered thinking: women workers were to be protected so they could
be healthy mothers and bear healthy children—not because they possessed the
same rights as men to contract their own terms for their work.[33]

Eastman and Kelley would find themselves on opposite sides of this debate in
the years to come. But for now the two women had much in common—in their
educational trajectories and professional experiences, their political bearings, and
their penchant, just stirring in Eastman's case, for direct action. Kelley became
one of her early supporters, while Eastman, younger by twenty-two years, viewed
Kelley more as a parent than a peer. She saw the more senior woman as a mother
figure, and since Kelley was one of a relatively few women leaders of her stature to
be an actual mother, her double maternal status, both literal and figurative, often
clung together in Crystal's mind. She instinctively compared Kelley to her own
mother, a benchmark to which no other woman would ever fully measure up.
"You are so much lovelier a person than Mrs. Kelly [sic]," she told Annis, "and yet
I admire her and like some things about her very much."[34]

The morning after she first encountered Kelley, Crystal began her active investigation. She started in the Allegheny County Health Department but soon
realized the records were too scattered and incomplete to meet her needs. She
moved to the Pittsburgh coroner's office, where she used death certificates to
record in detail the circumstances surrounding 526 workmen killed in accidents
for the twelve months ending June 30, 1907. Poring over the records, she was struck
by the ravages of working-class life, not only the number of work accidents, but
also the number of suicides and deaths in childbirth. "It's rather a gruesome business," she told her mother.[35] Her sociological training at Columbia, particularly

the statistical methods advocated by Giddings, may have served her doubly, providing the expertise necessary to compile the detailed statistical calculations, diagrams, and economic analysis in her study and also some emotional remove from the loss and suffering betokened by those records.

From there she began "the human side of my work," as she called it, interviewing the families of those laborers injured or killed, and investigating accident sites. Crystal talked to both workers and superintendents, and personally examined the heavy machinery she was investigating, from blast furnaces to great electric overhead cranes. She observed and recorded the demands in routine industrial work, appreciating the production hazards in everyday operations. Mill work for many types of tradesmen, she noted, "demands so much of eyes and nerves and muscles, and is done in such intense heat, that the men work in half-hour shifts, six hours of work during a twelve-hour day. Even so, it is only exceptional men who will attempt it."[36] She consistently recognized that hazards were structured into the very conditions of work done by industrial laborers—the risks miners took to use hazardous entrances because it saved them "a mile or two of difficult and tiresome walking at the beginning and end of a hard day's work," or the perils of storing in their homes the blasting powder they were required to provide for themselves.[37]

Crystal brought forward in evocative detail the massive machinery whose very size, speed, and function could precipitate industrial accidents. "A blast furnace is a great bulging steel shell lined with brick, about 90 feet high and 20 feet wide," she explained while detailing two explosions in which nineteen men had been killed and dozens wounded. "Inside of it, iron ore is reduced to pig iron, the first step in the process of making steel. Blasts of air heated to 1000 degrees Fahrenheit in a row of immense stoves nearby are sent through the pipes into the furnace. This ignites the coke, and creates such a heat that the whole mass melts. Fluid metal is thus always boiling at the bottom of the furnace, while solids are constantly being fed at the top." Explosions were usually caused, she related, when "the mass of coke, ore, and limestone put into the top of the furnace . . . sticks to its sides in the process of reduction. . . . Then it loosens and drops suddenly."[38]

She highlighted the daily experience of operators, often immigrant boys barely beyond adolescence, who in this setting she nevertheless called men. The "great electric overhead cranes," she observed, are "operated with levers by a man who works all day in a wooden or iron cab suspended from the crane and traveling with it. Heavy adjustable chains or ropes hang down . . . by means of which the load is carried. Sometimes the chains are fastened around the load; sometimes immense hooks are used to grasp it." Now, she urged, "think of the crane man upon whose alertness and care depend the lives of several others. His is a hot, unpleasant, lonely job. There is no one to spell him. He cannot get down from his cab for any reason. And he works *twelve hours* every day in the year except Christmas and the Fourth of July."[39]

Safety regulations were few, and, in any case, the system was rife with economic counterincentives to following them, she found. She calculated that more than two-thirds of mining deaths were due to slate or rock, loosened by frequent blasting, falling from the roof of the mine.[40] "To avert this danger," she explained, "the miner props up the roof by placing timbers at frequent intervals . . . and wedges in 'cap-pieces' on top of these posts, to cover as many square inches of roof as possible. Further, he must keep watch for cracks, sound the roof often, and take down the dangerous pieces of slate before they fall." However, she noted, "miners are paid by the ton and there can be no doubt that [the] prevailing human tendency to put off an interruption of work, is often accentuated by their eagerness to get out a big tonnage."[41] At times, she more pointedly highlighted faulty incentives built into an indifferent supervisory structure. "The way mills are run now there is no time to stop the crane," Eastman argued. "You see, there ought to be a man whose income is independent of how much steel is rolled, who has the authority to say, 'That crane has got to stand idle until a certain repair is made.' "[42]

Gaining access to these sites at times required considerable finesse. Crystal arranged to meet with "two of the 'steel magnate' variety," she quipped, and opted "to make myself charming for the sake of knowledge." She later convinced a young man to show her the Jones Laughlin Mills, where "it's almost impossible for a woman to get a permit to go." She told her mother, "He is going to help me. . . . Saturday he wants me to go driving with him, and Monday night he'll take me thro'."[43] In January 1909, she was asked by the Red Cross to investigate the Darr Mine in Jacobs Creek, just outside Pittsburgh, only weeks after a massive explosion killed 239 miners. She surveyed the site and elected to go in on her own. "I am at Jacobs Creek for the night, staying in a country hotel all by myself," she told Max. "It is strange to think of a little village in which there are almost 250 families in mourning. So quickly—even in an hour or two—it gets to be an accustomed atmosphere."[44]

Crystal also visited with the widows and children of laborers who had been killed, sometimes working with an interpreter to learn the details of how accidents happened, what economic loss had been experienced, and what compensation, if any, the family had received. She incorporated many of these original stories into her report, interjecting human faces and voices—including her own—into the otherwise faceless march of industrialization typically seen by the general public. The widow of a railroad brakeman "was left with six children, the oldest eleven. All the money she had was $500 from the Railroad Relief Association, to which her husband had belonged, $450 which the men on her husband's division raised, and $30 which his own crew gave," she reported. As was typical at the time, any workmen's injury or death benefits came from the worker's own dues to a voluntary relief association, from the kindness of an organized charity, or from informal help by other laborers and friends. Employers, in this case the Pennsylvania Railroad, were not required to help. "The company gave her $20 toward the funeral," Crystal said flatly.[45]

What helped distinguish Eastman's research was the human connection she evinced in her work, her interest and identification with the unseen lives behind the numbers her study revealed. She followed the widow's story beyond the enumeration of injustice and economic distress, exploring and explaining how this mother and her children survived. "With some of this money she rented and stocked up a little candy and notion store, using the three rooms in the back to live in. Here she tended store, cooked, and sewed, and ironed for herself and the six," she reported, then observed, she "will not have time to sit down and grieve over the death of her husband for many years to come." In this case, as in some others, Crystal intervened personally in the narrative, providing commentary that connects readers to the common humanity of workmen and their families. "The first thing brought home to me," she noted, "was that working people do not have 'the luxury of grief.' The daily tyranny of hard work in their lives, leaves little time for pondering the unanswerable 'Why?' of sorrow."[46] The combination of loss and struggle was simply a way of life. Such "unquestioning acceptance of misfortune does not often amount to either a commendable cheerfulness or a deplorable apathy," she related. "Occasionally, however, it approaches heroism."[47]

This is not to say that Eastman's professional training was eclipsed by her emotional intelligence on the page. If her sociological understanding was essential to data gathering and tabulation, and her deep humanity to her storytelling, her legal training was also vital to the work. First, it helped tremendously in interviewing men. The foremen and other managers frequently resisted both her questions and her authority as a woman to be asking them. So, when interviewing superintendents, she often cross-examined them. What's more, her legal knowledge enabled her to recognize quickly if, and how, their claims about the causes of industrial accidents were calculated to conform to current law.[48]

At the time, Eastman knew, common law standards carried over from English law turned on the relative rights and duties of the parties involved. It assigned liability in workplace accidents only in cases of employer negligence. If a worker was injured due to company negligence or "lack of due care," legally he was able to sue and recover damages. However, if the injured workman was also negligent in the incident, a factor known as "contributory negligence," he could not recover damages. Social and economic factors also favored employers over workers. The burden of proving negligence was on the plaintiff—in these cases, the worker; the burden of proving contributory negligence, on the employer. Most workers at issue were poor, and many were immigrants, groups lacking the financial and also social wherewithal to proceed with a legal case against an employer.[49]

Indeed, the legal tradition favored employers and protected their interests in a large number of respects. The principles of tort law applied to the workplace were the law of master and servant, which came to include the assumption that workers knew and accepted all the dangers of the industrial workplace when they took the job. Similarly, the law presumed they understood all the dangers potentially arising from the negligence of any fellow worker as well. In theory, a worker, knowing these dangers, could either demand higher wages for the risks he knew he was taking or decline to take a dangerous job. In practice, of course, these assumptions hardly, if ever, applied. In fact, under the law of master and servant an injured worker could recover damages only if he could prove he was injured by a danger caused by the owner, which the worker did not know about or could not reasonably have known about, and in which neither he nor any fellow worker had any demonstrable fault. Further, under this common law, no recovery of damages could occur if a worker was killed. Wrongful death statutes were passed separately by various states at various times, ostensibly opening a separate door for widows, children, and other heirs to sue for damages resulting from a worker's death.[50]

Crystal discovered that the state of Pennsylvania had passed a wrongful death statute as early as 1855, and by October 1907 she was already hopeful it could provide a basis for legal remedy to the families of felled workers. She produced an article on the logic of liability law, emphasizing its "mistaken" ideas to form a basis for reform. Published on March 7, 1908, in *Charities and the Commons*, it was excerpted in the newspapers the same week titled "Employers' Liability and Its Relation to Injured Workmen." After a detailed discussion of the history and logic of laws that stack "odds which are in favor of the employer," Eastman previewed the two options she would ultimately pursue "to make our employer's liability law fit industry as carried on today," as she put it. One was to "limit the operation of the fellow servant rule . . . taking away, one by one, the unjustifiable defenses that now protect the employer." The other was "to depart altogether from the theory of liability for negligence to take the whole matter out of the courts: to require each employer to compensate his employee injured in the course of his work according to an established uniform rate, regardless of negligence (except where the accident resulted from the wilful [*sic*] misconduct of the injured man." This plan had been in operation in England since 1897, she added, and had been adopted in some form in nearly all of the countries of Western Europe. Although a fundamental departure from present American labor law, this more radical approach was perfectly reasonable, she argued, since it offered "a just and from the point of view of society, an economic method of distributing these great vital losses of industry."[51]

Crystal adored the legal research. "I am working at the Law Library, making a report on the Law of Negligence and Master and Servant in Pennsylvania," she reported to Annis. "This work interests me so much that I am dead sure I want to stop this investigation at Xmas time and get at my profession." She discovered, however, that subsequent court decisions had held that the benefits of wrongful death statutes were extended only to US citizens, leaving out the vast majority of industrial workers at the time. She longed to use her legal training to change things. "I want to be really started with a good practice when I am thirty," she said. "There is a joy in *doing* things, fighting fights etc., that there isn't in merely finding out things so that others may do."[52]

First, however, she had to finish writing her report, which became her well-regarded book, *Work Accidents and the Law* (1910).[53] "To get this huge thing written and off my hands," she reported, she tried to establish some work-life balance in her daily routine: practice her singing "at 10:30,—and then work till lunch. After lunch I work for about an hour & then get sleepy. At that point I either take a walk, take a bath,—play tennis,—talk to somebody,—or give up & go to sleep. Then when whatever it is is over, I get to work again & work till six. I seem to be in good condition all the time," she noted. "I vary the tabulating & writing so as not to get insane over either."[54] Still, she found the research and especially the writing process to be a rather isolating experience. "I wish there were more people & doings to enliven my evenings. Sometimes I'm awfully lonely," she confessed to Max in July. "This morning was bright & beautiful when I woke up,—but my first moment of consciousness was desolate, because I knew I should be alone all day."[55]

Throughout her year with the Pittsburgh Survey, Eastman's letters describe some parties and impromptu gatherings with other investigators. She saw Paul Kellogg regularly, and sometimes had the chance to see classmates from Vassar or friends from Glenora. Through the winter of 1908, she briefly dated several men, but one after the other they proved either too bland and sapless for her taste and temperament or they were unavailable. "I went to the theater last night with a good-looking young man," she reported to Annis in January, "but alas—not interesting." Then, "I spent the day at Jacobs Creek with another—interesting quite—but nevermind [*sic*].—He thinks I am *remarkable* (!)—all the married ones do."[56]

Annis visited as often as the two could arrange it, usually staying for a week. Crystal would typically schedule times when her housemate, Margaret, was away conducting research or visiting her own family so they could spend day and night together. But together or apart, the dynamics with her mother remained her interpersonal touchstone. More than one friendship in Pittsburgh became a scenario in which Crystal assumed the role of rescuer.

She first mentioned James Forbes just weeks after her arrival in Pittsburgh.[57] The next week she related a few more details: "He is about 35 and looks ordinary; he has done a great deal of studying the underworld—tramps, criminals, pool-rooms, etc., and he seems to be big hearted and gentle and quite without pretentions."[58] Forbes was a committee chairman within the Charity Organization Society and a criminologist who became secretary and director of the National Association for the Prevention of Mendicancy in 1909. His work in Pittsburgh was published as "The Reverse Side" (1914), an analysis of "the machinery of law and order," as he described it, which would call for "exploring the possibilities for social service on the part of the police." Ultimately, Forbes would envision police work as a form of diplomatic mediation between estranged worlds, calling his concept for Progressive policing "social statesmanship."[59]

Within two months of meeting Forbes, Crystal announced to her mother that "he is going to let me in to help him."[60] Her scattered reports suggest he was struggling to organize his research, and beyond that to find "an appreciation of more things in life."[61] He was probably attracted to Crystal's warmth and natural charm. Although he was married, perhaps he was even a little in love with her. He had been quick to offer to escort her through the dangerous Homestead Steelworks.[62] The two seemed to have a connection. Once when Forbes was "shut in with a cold," Crystal took him a red rose. "It made him very happy especially because it happened to be his birthday," she told Annis. "Wasn't that a coincidence?"[63]

As for Crystal, she may have craved the sense of efficacy and value she experienced with her mother, especially in the midst of lonely work and uncertainty about who she was and where she was headed. In any case, she had a clear strategy for helping him. First, "I am going to begin by going over the plan of his report with him, to get him down to business on it," she said. Then, despite the fact that Forbes was seven years older than she, "I told him he was ridiculously young,— and that he had time to become an entirely new kind of man. He smiled and said that's what he wanted to do."[64] As uneven as this relationship might seem, Crystal clearly felt the benefits were reciprocal. "I can't tell you how relieved and rejoiced I am over this," she told Annis on New Year's Eve, 1907. "I felt him as a kind of vague, looming, problem when I wasn't sure I could get close enough to him to be any good. Now I feel him as a golden opportunity with wings to carry me to more happy and rewarding days."[65]

Through the first months of 1908, Eastman and Forbes spent a number of evenings together, apparently platonic meetings that allowed them to be pleasantly ensconced together in a family setting. "Mr. Forbes is reading *Marcus Aurelius* to me, while I sew of an evening," Crystal described. And much as she had done with Annis, she poured herself into lifting his sunken moods and outlook. "We began last night, after an hour and a half's tussle I had with him to pull him up out of a black well of resentment, anxiety and despair," she reported. "It was a marvelous triumph for the time. If only he comes back tonight in the spirit in which he left me."[66]

If Crystal now understood the abiding dynamics of her relationship with Annis—the elusive fluctuations of mood that demanded her unique dispensation—she lacked a sense of her own adequacy to supply it. She felt Forbes was "pathetically eager to get hold of something, and I am so ignorant. I know the theory and spirit of the thing, but I am totally unfamiliar with the daily precepts—the words, sentences, phrases to be used specifically as medicine for the soul. I must read and become wiser—if I am to do any good."[67] She would continue, in various relationships, to meet strife or distress by earnestly trying harder, pouring forth more and more of herself into whatever the breach.

By the spring of 1908, Crystal was herself struggling to make progress writing up her findings. In May, she rented a small house in Sewickley, Pennsylvania, then a country town thirteen miles northwest of Pittsburgh. She had contemplated returning to New York to finish her report but feared there would be too many distractions there.[68] By August, still wrestling with the work, she yearned for a familiar elixir. She left Sewickley in favor of Glenora, updating Kellogg on her progress. "I decided to tabulate the accidents of a certain group and then write what I thought I knew about the accidents of that employment, using the tables as far as I could," she told him, but admitted she had a great deal of work left to do: "about eighty miscellaneous accidents to tabulate; all the tabulating of economic cards; all the writing up of the economic side; everything else; refining process." Then she explained, "I know you'll be discouraged to find that I have started in writing about the accident part of it first just as you were over the outline—But I don't think there's any cause for alarm in that," she said. "I had to do it that way anyhow. I had to get those things out of my system first."[69]

She went on to sell Kellogg on her plan to finish the book at Cherith. "However aghast you are at this you can't be more so than I am, and yet I am calmly going along . . . cheered every now & then by the hitting off of a real idea in up to date language." She planned to work steadily, five days a week, for a solid month. "If I get a wonderful stretch of speed and devotion in the next four weeks, Paul,—I'll astonish you when you come home," she promised.[70] Crystal knew he would want to know how she was doing in a more personal sense, so she added: "I forgot to say that I'm perfectly well—go swimming every day—have learned to dive—and generally am getting a good time out of life." She had always been athletic and worked to promote the importance of exercise, especially for women. She would soon help to organize the Women's Athletic Club, an organization composed mainly of college women to help them stay physically active in the context of adult city life.[71] But work also kept her strong. "Work, bless it!" she told Kellogg. "It is good for me."[72]

Finding conditions most conducive to work was the major reason Crystal decided to retire to the country to write, rather than return to New York City to do it. Still, when she made the decision, she knew it would upset Vladimir a little bit, she carefully told her mother. "He will be disappointed—and so am I," she confessed.[73]

Crystal and Vladimir Simkhovitch had been romantically involved ever since her second year of law school. As late as December 1906, she seemed to think of him as a father figure alongside her mother, a construction of the relationship with which Annis eagerly cooperated. Crystal had made up her mind to ask Vladimir his opinion of a man she had been seeing for just over two months when a letter came from Annis suggesting just that. She wrote her mother, "He agrees with you absolutely, so I feel perfectly sure I am right. . . . [N]ow I have Dr. S's word and your re-assurance." And since both parental mentors were in sync in advising Crystal to break off the romance, she did so, without looking back. "I am going to put the whole thing out of my mind," she said. "I think I won't have to see him again, even."[74]

Vladimir and Annis had clashing reasons for recommending the same course of action, however. Sometime within the next three months, Vladimir's relationship to Crystal turned from paternal to romantic—and Annis could see it coming.

Vladimir later remembered how the affair with Crystal began. His feelings overcame him when she called him out onto Jones Street one evening to hear a Schubert serenade being sung from one of the tenement windows. All that survives of the romance are his love letters to her—which she saved. These missives, all but one delivered by hand, suggest their love affair was like a dream to him: "The world that we have thought to be gray suddenly revealed itself in all its glory and splendour!" he wrote. "And I went home, and I went to sleep, and I slept, and I woke up with the same glorious world in me. And this day is still a day of praise—And you and the world are so beautiful!"[75]

For her, the relationship epitomized the sort of magnificent connection she searched for in life, in both love and politics—and always would. "I have been feeling lately, somewhat lost and stranded," she had recently written to her mother, "as if I couldn't tell where or with what people I belonged. You know, as you go along you keep discovering weaknesses in the people, or movements, or places, that you were once altogether in sympathy with. Your thought turns from one stronghold to another, and it seems to be the same with all. On top of it, perhaps causing it all, is a sense of your own miserable inefficiency. Well after awhile [sic] you keep saying to yourself, almost subconsciously 'where,—with whom, can I cast my lot,—and feel that my whole heart and soul is in throw?' "[76]

During her first year at New York University, she had thought the pieces might come together in a relationship with Paul Kellogg. In fact, Crystal's correspondence with her mother in June 1906 strongly suggests that during the school term, he had proposed to her.[77] But by September, they spent the day together at the beach in Coney Island and "agreed on a good working basis" for their relationship.[78] "I'm not in love with Paul," she told her mother, and she was "half sorry and half glad" about it. The would-be romance with Kellogg was missing that surge of feeling she craved in love—as well as in politics. "I'd love to be in love with somebody someday, *hard* so there wouldn't be any doubt about it."[79]

Vladimir was unmistakably different—he was passionate and expressive where Paul was "a perfectly reserved man."[80] Vladimir had many sides to him. At one moment he was the picture of a European intellectual, "careless, dressed-up, blasé gentleman,—very charming,—very brilliant and witty," at another a leftist idol—"*my* Vladimir," Crystal told him—"in a gray flannel shirt, sleeves rolled up, hands in his pockets, and a pipe in his mouth, squinting a little at the sun!"[81] Plus, their feelings were forbidden. Unlike Paul, Vladimir was married—and to the head of Greenwich House.

Annis sensed something developing between her daughter and Simkhovitch just a week after Crystal revealed her longing for someone with whom to cast her whole heart and soul. "I can't help a queer feeling about Mr. Simkhovitch coming to spend the evening with you—when you live alone," she told her. "I'm sorry I didn't see more of him, for my impression was not of the pleasantest." She expressed several biases, which mixed together in her sense of predatory male sexuality. "He is *very human*, I'm pretty sure—besides he is a foreigner clear through, with Russian ideals I suppose." As Annis poured out her concerns, they intensified, along with her justifications for pressing them upon her daughter. "I must speak out these thoughts—of my heart," she continued, "or else they would spoil all my peace. I can't forget that you are young and beautiful—that he is mature and a man—and that the conventions have been good things in the past. Would you have felt perfectly happy if some Elmira friend had come in while he was there?" Annis reminded Crystal, "You are my religion. Following your ideals is very much with me what following Jesus was to the early disciples, but sometimes I am bewildered—I wonder whether you have really *thought* of all these things and decided them in your highest mood—or whether it is your innocence and fondness for charming people that leads you to swift and ill considered decisions."[82]

Annis was desperate to impress some womanly guidance upon her daughter. "I wish I knew what Mrs. Simkhovitch thinks of all these things," she wrote, persisting. "I would pin any faith to her sanity and morality rather than to his, altho' his nature and manner may be sweeter." In fact, Mary Simkhovitch betrayed no inkling of their budding romance—and never would.[83] She thought of Crystal as an energetic, delightful student—a nanny, perfect to look after their children at the family retreat in Westchester County, New York. "Mrs. Simkhovitch telephoned to me . . . asking me to come out here right away and stay over Sunday," Crystal told her mother. "She won't be out till tonight and Vladimir not until Sunday. But I have the children and the sunshine and the woods, and I am perfectly happy."[84]

Annis might have noticed, even if her daughter did not, that Crystal's only stories of the Simkhovitch children revolved around a maternal connection that also insinuated her taking Mary's place. "Last night I slept in the room with little Helena. I was as excited over it as I was the day I first fed a baby. She was in a little crib, and I in Mrs. Simkhovitch's big bed. In the morning when I finally woke up, Helena came over and played in my bed."[85] On Saturday, they took a walk in the woods. "On the way back, Stephen and I stopped in a yard to see some boys playing. A woman came out and asked me if I was the boy's mother! . . . I didn't dream that I looked sensible enough to be the mother of a five year old boy. Pretty soon her husband came out and both of them insisted that I looked more like Stephen and Helena (or they looked more like me) than their own mother."[86]

Vladimir called the love affair the "most wonderful of all God's miracles," and "a beautiful, wonderful sacred year," but it was not entirely finished when they tried to break it off as Crystal finished law school.[87] "Dearest . . . You are studying and I am singing to you and blessing you," he wrote on May 20, 1907, as she was preparing for her final exams. "I am glad the weather today is what it is—cool and fresh. I need cool air in my lungs. . . . Dearest, the days of love may be counted, but my love can not [*sic*] be measured. And great and true as my love is, so shall my friendship for you be later on."[88]

The next day, he struggled to make peace with their parting, but finally concluded, "Thank God, a great deal of you has become a part of myself. O, I am so sorry that I had nothing to give you." Then Crystal's reply, now lost, unsettled him again. That night, "after dinner":

> Dearest, I do not know whether to give you the letter I have written to you or not.—I was nearly overcome when I found your letter, your book and the 3 violets. My dearest, you are full of love in your letter, what does it mean? O, Crystal, your agony is double agony to me. Is it really love that you still have for me? I am now more confused than ever. Earlier in the day there was no ray of hope and no hope was wonted. I felt it was done, the light was out, the kingdom lost and the sole hope was—perhaps someday the kingdom of heaven within me, if I could learn to be without hope &

without desire, but patient only and good. And now your dear letter and I do not know where I am.[89]

The romance did not finally and definitively end until June 14, 1909, some two years after Eastman's graduation from NYU. As with Paul Kellogg, it ended at the ocean, romantically, in the surging waves. "Yesterday V. and I spent at Rockaway in farewell—Monday, hardly a soul there," Crystal wrote to Max. "I went barefoot in the surf—oh it was a long healthy happy day! I can't get down to earth."[90] Vladimir's last love note was inscribed "there on Rockaway." He wrote her an elegiac goodbye. "Yes, Crystal, I have changed, changed a great deal during the year and I do not know how I will repay you—I shall try to make the best of myself in memory and honor of 1906–07 and to the glory of Crystal. I am happy today, happy because there is in the world such a woman as yourself."[91]

The next morning, Crystal got herself back to reality and went to work. Since January, she had been employed by the American Association for Labor Legislation (AALL), a national labor and occupational health and safety group then in the midst of an increasingly instrumental turn under John Andrews, its new executive secretary, soon to begin editing his influential *American Labor Legislation Review* (1911–43). The founders of the AALL were well-known academics and social researchers, some of whom were already familiar to her: Richard Ely and, slightly later, John Commons; Henry W. Farnam of Yale; and Henry Seager of Columbia. They wanted to encourage and strengthen efforts around the country to develop Progressive labor legislation on the state and federal levels. Toward that end, they recruited as vice presidents well-known labor leaders, including Samuel Gompers, founder and president (for the second time) of the American Federation of Labor (AFL), and Jane Addams.

It is possible that Addams recommended Eastman to the AALL, or that Seager knew her from Columbia, or that Kelley or Kellogg suggested her, but, in any case, the academics would have been familiar with the work she had done in Pittsburgh. Excerpts of the investigations and editorials about the Pittsburgh Survey were beginning to circulate in academic journals and the popular press, particularly the investigative magazines of the muckraking era—the *Outlook, Independent, Collier's,* and the *American Magazine.* Trade journals such as *Iron Age* and *Engineering News* also covered their work. A publicity strategy designed by Kellogg had resulted in thirty-five magazine articles in the six months following completion of the project alone.[92] By whatever means Eastman came to the attention of the AALL, once she was on board, she immediately began setting up the New York branch. "We hope to have our organizing meeting the last of January," she reported to Irene Osgood, the AALL secretary, "and I have great hopes of what we may be able to accomplish in New York State."[93]

In February, Eastman became secretary-treasurer of the branch. In March, she organized a publicity campaign that highlighted a twelve-page pamphlet gleaned from her research in Pittsburgh. She titled it "Employers' Liability, a Criticism Based on Fact."[94] On the cover was a picture of Constantin Meunier's iconic statue of the industrial worker, "The Puddler," now with dollar amounts superimposed on his limbs and muscle groups to denote the value employers conferred on a worker's body. She corresponded with John Commons in Wisconsin, letting him know the pamphlet version of her study was particularly timely because a New York State commission on accident liability had been proposed, and generally, she told him, "it is in the air."[95]

In May, Eastman informed Andrews that the New York State legislature had, in fact, established a commission to inquire into the question of employers' liability and other matters under chapter 518 of the laws of 1909. It was to have fourteen members—three from the state senate, three from the assembly, and six to be appointed by the governor. Eastman quickly wrote to Commons for the names of the chairmen of similar commissions in Wisconsin, Minnesota, and any other states. The Wisconsin legislature had also created the Industrial Insurance Commission recently, part of the rising of legislative attention to industrial accidents that would yield workers' compensation statutes beginning in 1911. "I wish to be in a position to bring about some cooperation," she told Commons, "which might result in uniform legislation. It will certainly aid the passing of the bill, if similar bills are to be passed in other industrial states."[96]

Ultimately the governor's appointees included representatives of various relevant interests: George Smith of the Lackawanna Steel Company in Buffalo; Philip Titus, the resigned president of the Railway Trainmen's Association in Kingston, Ulster County; and Otto Eidlitz, governor of the Building Trades Employers Association of New York City. Senator J. Mayhew Wainwright of Westchester County became chairman; Columbia's Seager, vice chairman. Then, on the day after Crystal said a final farewell to her affair with Vladimir Simkhovitch, New York governor Charles Evans Hughes appointed her the only woman to serve on the new commission. She would in fact be named secretary and given a $1,000 budget for her expenses and salary.[97] Crystal received no official notification of her post. She arrived at the AALL offices on June 15, 1909, to "find on my desk a letter of congratulations," she told Max. "Looking in the paper—I find I am appointed on commission! Oh joy—who can expect me to work today? Oh what a clear warm loving world it is," she gushed. "I'm crazy—simply crazy."[98]

The first meeting of the Commission on Employers' Liability was held on June 22, 1909, in a rented office suite in the newly completed Metropolitan Life Insurance Company Tower on Madison Avenue in Manhattan, then the tallest building ever built. "Crystal's new office is glorious," Max told Annis, "and she is smiling and beautiful in it with a blue dress."[99] Suddenly, Crystal was sitting almost literally on top of the world.

She was now a national expert on employer liability. Newspapers picked up her profiles of workers and their families as human interest stories, tugging people's heartstrings with headlines like "The Philosophy of the Poor" and "Workers under Trial."[100] She was invited to speak to more than one state bar association, as well as to the American Academy of Political and Social Sciences and the American Economic Association (AEA). A winning speaker just like her mother, she opened her speech at the prestigious AEA with a sly nudge, making a disarming virtue of her challenging status as a female legal expert lecturing to the gathered professional men. "There is probably no one here today who would earnestly defend our way of dealing with industrial accident losses," she began. "In spite of this depressing dearth of opposition, however, I shall proceed to demolish the 'American System' with considerable enthusiasm, for the sake of certain points which it seems to me important to bring out."[101] Her public renown began to snowball. "I am asked to give two lectures on Employers Liability at the School of Philanthropy—And I'm a goin!" she wrote Annis. "It came through Mrs. Florence Kelly [sic], who read my article, and at once decided to leave all mention of that subject out of her lectures and suggest . . . that [they] ask me to give a lecture or two on the subject!"[102] Eastman's star was definitely on the rise. "Well," she quipped to her mother, "isn't it fun to be famous?"[103]

By the time *Work Accidents and the Law* came out in 1910, her work had "swept her into the main stream of social action," Max recalled.[104] Feature writers profiled her now, touting not only her labor law expertise but also "her many irons in the fire of activity."[105] From her earliest public opportunities, she displayed two characteristic qualities: a congenital candor and a drive to link ideas from multiple movements, forging a political identity at the points of connection or intersection among them. As an invited speaker at a Socialist dinner in April 1909, she "spoke a few burning truths about socialists and suffrage—social workers & suffrage etc," she told Max.[106] The following January, she connected socialism and labor legislation as a speaker at the Inter-Collegiate Socialist Society in New York, an organization of student leftists whose officers included luminaries such as Jack London and Graham Phelps Stokes. Eastman had been connected to the group since it was called to order by Upton Sinclair in 1905, when she was a grad student at Columbia.[107] Her talk, which drew three hundred Socialists from American and Russian universities, began by admitting that she was "not a hide-hardened Socialist"—although she quickly moved "to assure the Society that I am sufficiently radical."[108] In a speech to the Equal Franchise Association at the end of the year, she bridged the suffrage and labor movements by arguing that suffragists should appropriate the radical labor tactic of the strike to leverage the vote. "If I had my way . . . we would tell the men of this country we were not going to work any more [sic], we were not going to contribute or to assist them with anything until they gave us a share in the government of the country," she announced. "If this strike were possible," she asserted, "I am willing to wager that women would be given the ballot within several hours."[109]

Crystal balanced her many political commitments through combined travel scheduling, a practical tactic that also enhanced her public reputation as an emerging multimovement activist. When the Employer Liability Commission filed its influential report with the New York State legislature, she traveled to Albany with a group of three hundred suffragists on a special train organized to take them to joint hearings with the senate and assembly judiciary committees on a proposed suffrage amendment. First, she made herself heard on suffrage: "If the committee decides to go on laughing at the women," she warned state legislators, "the women will keep on working— you can count on that."[110] Then she joined her labor legislation colleagues to present the report on employer liability. Her imprint on its recommendations is clear: "The Commission is strongly of the opinion that the present legal system of employer's liability in force in this State (and practically everywhere else in the United States) in industrial employment is fundamentally wrong and unwise and needs radical change."[111]

In a previous speech at Cooper Union in lower Manhattan, Crystal had catalogued those wrongs, and with characteristic frankness lodged an indictment of the prevailing injustices in the law. Calling the legal system "vicious" when it came to labor, she explicitly enumerated why: "because it does not provide relief when it is most needed, because it lays too heavy a burden on the claimant and allows the corporation to escape liability by carrying the case from court to court, and because it encourages dishonesty on the part of the claims agent and the ambulance chaser, and because it is a wasteful system for the greater portion of the damages paid by employers goes out in attorneys' fees."[112] Eastman's solution to all this was the radical change she had called for before the legislature: to shift the logic of common law standards from liability only in cases of employer negligence toward a more collective, no-fault distribution of risk and loss shared by workers, businesses, and consumers. "As I see it," she wrote in *Charities and the Commons*, "the fundamentally important step in this reform is to establish the principle that the risks of trade, borne through all these years by the workmen alone, should in all wisdom and justice be shared by the employer."[113]

After the filing, the commission held a series of eleven evidentiary hearings throughout the state—including Albany, Rochester, Syracuse, Buffalo, and New York City. More than 120 witnesses ultimately appeared. Crystal used her detailed knowledge of working conditions in the steel mills and railroad yards of Pittsburgh to pointedly question many of them.[114] The papers noted, "When Miss Eastman argues, the woman promptly gives place to the lawyer, clear headed, clear eyed, decisive, the adversary in every word and gesture."[115] She cross-examined witnesses not only on company policies and practices but also on their political attitudes about worker rights and unionization that she knew were helping to keep those policies in place. Seizing on what one witness, a lawyer for the Lackawanna Steel Company, called the "serious evils that would follow the establishment of any system such as in England," she countered: "Could you give us any more concrete idea of what those evils would be?" When the Lackawanna lawyer spoke in generalities about cases where courts have declared social legislation unconstitutional, she pressed him: "You have nothing concrete, only the general fear of socialistic doctrines?" And through her tough questioning, she got him to admit, "There is this condition operating, in so far as the employer is concerned, to fear to a certain extent the exactions of the claims that are imposed upon him by radical unionism." As Crystal focused her gaze on him, he backtracked. He did not mean to criticize "unions properly regulated and properly run," he quickly conceded. "Only the radical end of it."[116]

By 1913, Eastman would write a research memo related to "the radical end of it" for the newly established US Commission on Industrial Relations, a nine-member body formed by an act of Congress following many years of high-profile industrial conflict—Chicago's Haymarket Square in 1886; Homestead in 1892; the nationwide Pullman strike in 1897; and bitter conflict at the coal mines in Cripple Creek, Colorado, in 1903 and at the shirtwaist factories in New York in 1909, among others.[117] More recently, the huge "Bread and Roses" strike at the textile mills in Lawrence, Massachusetts, had concluded just six months before Crystal began to write. In the frigid winter of 1912, some thirty thousand laboring men and women, some as young as fourteen, had walked off the job in response to pay cuts that would mean desperate privation to families already subsisting on starvation wages. The walkout had spread to neighboring mills, arousing a seven-week action whose power and chaos excited a barrage of retaliatory actions from employers and also the police. But the cause of the textile workers, especially the child laborers, ultimately rallied journalists and a broader middle-class public to the workers' side, helping to make it the most successful strike of the era.[118]

In the aftermath, agitation by social workers, many of them connected to Kellogg and the *Survey*, had helped push the federal government for congressional hearings, which led to the formation of the commission. Its purpose, as Kellogg described it, was to discover the underlying causes of dissatisfaction in the industrial situation.[119] He assigned Crystal to examine the legal rights of workers in times of industrial peace and in times of industrial dispute, a pivotal charge.[120] "Many of the most one-sided decisions, one way or another, are embedded in the records of the minor courts, and only such a resourceful inquiry could get them out into the open," he wrote in 1913.[121] Crystal's memo, however, would reach to go even farther than that. She attended the legal basis for the right of contract workers not only to unionize but also, in the wake of Lawrence, to strike.[122]

But for now, she continued to work on more mainstream Progressive solutions: sensible workplace regulations coupled with a program for adequate relief when the ferocity of everyday industrial production outmatched them. In May 1910, Senator Wainwright and Assemblyman Phillips introduced two workers' compensation bills to the New York legislature. Echoing the legal options Eastman delineated from her earlier legal research, one bill provided that the adoption of workers' compensation was voluntary, to be agreed on by the employer and the employee. If no agreement could be reached, an injured employee could then seek damages, but the bill changed many of the prevailing rules about that process: now the assumption of the risk of employment was restricted; contributory negligence shifted the burden of proof onto the employer; and the fellow-servant rule was largely eliminated. The second bill provided that workers' compensation was mandatory but, like the earlier English model, it was limited to the most dangerous trades.[123]

That mandate by the state to require changes to private employment contracts immediately emerged as the key point of controversy. Within the Employer Liability Commission, members debated whether New York State possessed the legal authority to impose mandatory liability on employers and to require private companies to compensate employees for injuries and deaths without regard to fault.

Eastman knew the legislature did not have such authority under current law. However, in New York, the state did possess what was called "police power," which permitted it to interfere in private business affairs when deemed necessary to ensure the public health and welfare. The creation of the two separate bills had been the commission's effort to circumvent the anticipated legal challenges to the state's authority to mandate workers' compensation—the first by making it voluntary, and the second by limiting its application only to the most dangerous trades, where under its police power, the state might have the authority to enact regulations. Both bills were signed by Governor Hughes and went into effect on September 1, 1910, making New York State the first in the nation to enact a mandatory compensation program for workers.[124] And as expected, lawsuits soon challenged the new law on constitutional grounds.

In a speech to the Employers' Liability Association the next month, Crystal began to reframe workers' compensation in larger, humanitarian terms. She asserted at the start that "the time has passed for arguing that the law of employers' liability as it exists in most of our States today is unjust. We know it is—we admitted it long ago. My task this morning is constructive," she continued. "It is to prove that the principle upon which workmen's compensation laws are based is fundamentally *just*."[125] To make her case, she used a lawyer's language—reasoned and rhetorically compelling. "It is easy enough to advocate workmen's compensation on practical grounds of economy and common sense, to show how it will reduce litigation, and lessen strife between capital and labor. But can we reconcile it with justice? With 'the rendering of everyone his due'? And can we prove it a reform important to humanity—to 'mankind collectively'? I think we can," she submitted, "and that is what I undertake to do this morning."[126]

The *New York Times* raved that Crystal was "the nearest thing to a sensation in so thoroughly businesslike a meeting."[127] A century later, legal scholars would vindicate the shift Eastman urged—from mere legal rights to broader social justice—as the appropriate purpose of relevant accident law.[128] But for now, pending lawsuits made the future of workers' compensation in New York uncertain. And then, just after Crystal made her case to the Liability Association, she received a telephone call from her father bearing horrible news. Her mother had suffered a stroke and now lay unconscious. From the Plaza Hotel in Manhattan, where the conference was held, she ran to meet Max, and together they took the midnight train to Elmira. When they got there, their mother's "body was lying on her bed fighting desperately for breath," Max would recall.[129] They watched helplessly by her bedside. At noon on October 22, 1910, Annis Ford Eastman died at age fifty-nine. The next day was Sunday, but the Park Church was dark.[130]

While Crystal was deeply in mourning, workers' compensation reached the New York Court of Appeals. The circuit court had upheld the act as within the legislative power in one initial case, but in January 1911, the case of Earl Ives, a switchman for the South Buffalo Railway Company who twisted his ankle on the job and claimed seven weeks' total disability—seventy dollars—was heard on appeal. Ives made no claim of negligence; it was just an injury due to the risk inherent in his job. Thomas C. Burke, for Ives, spoke of the inherent hazards of certain employments, against which neither employer nor employee can guard. He granted the new law was novel but argued the Constitution can be adapted to the needs of unprecedented industrial conditions. Louis Marshall, the famed constitutional lawyer said to have argued more cases before the Supreme Court than any private attorney of his era, appeared for the railroad in what was remembered as the high point in his legal career.[131] He called the legislation "both Socialistic and the product of a dangerous collectivism," language that reflected the rising fear in some quarters that workers' compensation would provide a legal beachhead for an advancing offensive on private property rights in America.[132] News coverage of the case reflected the support of liberals and social workers, who were calling it "the most beneficent legislation ever enacted in Albany." Conservatives and employers countered that the new law constituted another attack on individualism and free enterprise, and argued, as Marshall had, that the imputation of financial liability without a finding of fault deprived employers of property without due process of law.[133]

On March 24, 1911, the appeals court handed down a unanimous decision. "No word of praise could overstate the industry or intelligence of this Commission in dealing with a subject of such manifold ramifications and of such far-reaching importance to the state, to employers, and to employees," the ruling began. Nevertheless, the court agreed with Marshall, writing, "the statute judged by our common law standards is plainly revolutionary."[134] The ruling explained, "Under our form of government, the courts must regard all economic, philosophical, and moral theories, attractive and desirable though they may be, as subordinate to the primary question of whether they can be molded into statutes without infringing upon the letter or spirit of our written constitution."[135] Yet, the court reasoned, both the fellow-servant rule and the law of contributory negligence could be regulated or abolished by the legislature but had not been. And the police power, a legislative function, the court judged insufficient to interfere with the equal protection guarantees in the Fourteenth Amendment of the United States Constitution and a similar article of the State Constitution of New York. In the court's unanimous opinion, the theory advanced by the statute was "not merely new in our system of jurisprudence, but plainly antagonistic to its basic idea."[136] The act was ruled unconstitutional.[137]

The very next day, March 25, 1911, a fire broke out on three upper floors of the Asch building in lower Manhattan, just blocks from the Waverly Place apartment in Greenwich Village where Crystal and Max had made a home together since the winter of 1909. Hundreds of workers, most of them women, labored there for the Triangle Shirtwaist Company. With cloth spread across tables and remnants covering the floors, the fire spread quickly, and workers who tried to escape the blaze through exit doors found them locked. The fire escape was dilapidated and impassable. Fire engine ladders were too short to reach them so many stories up. Trapped and desperate, women workers, their clothes in flames, jumped from windows to their death. When the disaster ended, more than 140 workers had died.

The fire "sank into my soul," Crystal told Max a few days later from Glenora. "I have wanted to tell you how that tragedy has brought back vividly my thoughts our tragedy. All these days since it happened I have thought of Mamma and realized that she is dead almost every hour. And I've had the old longing to talk about her—to try to tell somebody what the loss of her means to the days of my life."[138]

The following week, Crystal traveled to Philadelphia to address the American Academy of Political and Social Science on "Three Essentials of Accident Prevention." As soon as she began, her anger and grief bubbled to the surface. "When I read in the newspaper the day after that terrible fire in Washington Place two weeks ago, that a relief fund had been started, that so and so and so and so had contributed so and so much, and the Red Cross had opened an office in the Metropolitan building to 'administer the fund,' it turned my soul sick," she told the group. "When great unforeseen disasters like the San Francisco earthquake come upon humanity by an act of God," she explained, "we can be thrilled and uplifted by the wave of generous giving which sweeps over the country—we can be comforted by contributing a little ourselves to aid the survivors." But this was different. This was the stark defeat of reasoned, humane progress against preventable agony and sorrow. And just days after the death of her mother, Crystal burned with outrage at cruel human loss, at tragedy that ought not be:

> But when the strong young body of a free man is caught up by a little projecting set-screw, whirled around a shaft and battered to death, when we know that a set-screw can be countersunk at a trivial cost, when we know that the law of the state has prohibited projecting set-screws for many years, then who wants to talk about "three years wages to the widow" and "shall it be paid in installments, or in a lump sum?" and "shall the workman contribute?" What we want is to put somebody in jail. And when the dead bodies of girls are found piled up against locked doors leading to the exits after a factory fire, when we know that locking such doors is a prevailing custom in such factories, and one that has continued in New York City since those 146 lives were lost in the Triangle Waist Company fire, who wants to hear about a great relief fund? What we want is to start a revolution.[139]

4 THE FEDERAL CASE FOR WOMEN'S SUFFRAGE

"The dye [*sic*] is cast," Crystal Eastman told Max in November 1911. The National American Woman Suffrage Association (NAWSA) had installed her as one of its rare, salaried organizers to run the high-profile state suffrage campaign in Wisconsin. "I'm working for the Political Equality League as Campaign Manager for six months at least at the rate of $2000 per year."[1] It was the same salary her mother earned at the pinnacle of her career at the Park Church.

The year 1912 was looking like a turning point for equal suffrage in America. Although twenty-five states had passed limited voting rights for women up to that point, the previous fourteen years—from 1896 to 1910—had not seen a single state approve the vote for women on the same terms as men. Suffragists struggled merely to maintain public awareness through suffrage education aimed at elite women during these years. Then, in 1910 and 1911, the states of Washington and California revived hopes by leveraging new organizational tactics and grassroots campaigning to win the vote for women. And now six more states had suffrage amendments on the ballot: Oregon, Arizona, Michigan, Ohio, Kansas, and Wisconsin.

Wisconsin was a powerful industrial battleground. Combined with Michigan and Ohio, suffragists saw this slate of states east of the Mississippi as the tipping point for the march of equal suffrage from the farms and frontiers of the West to the industrial and political centers of the East.

Locally, this was the first time in more than twenty-five years that a suffrage amendment succeeded in reaching Wisconsin voters. In 1886, women's suffrage "in any election pertaining to school matters" had passed, and that broad wording of the bill led suffragists to believe they had been inadvertently granted fuller rights to the franchise. They raised $2,000 across the state for legal fees to pursue their case in court. The circuit court judge upheld their claim, but the state

Crystal Eastman. Amy Aronson, Oxford University Press (2020).
© Oxford University Press.
DOI: 10.1093/oso/9780199948734.001.0001

supreme court overturned the lower ruling. From then on, Wisconsin suffragists mounted effort after effort, but bills were effectively delayed to death in the legislature. After three decades of arduous and dedicated activism, Wisconsin women had gained only that earlier fraction of the right to vote—school suffrage—and that only after an act of the legislature provided separate ballot boxes for women's votes in 1901.[2]

But Wisconsin now possessed some tantalizing demographic advantages that seemed to favor the women's cause this time around. It was the home state of Robert La Follette, the former crusading governor, then Progressive US senator, who was a leading equal suffrage proponent on the national stage; indeed, some believed his intention to propose a suffrage plank in the Republican Party platform was what prompted Teddy Roosevelt, a rival for Progressive support among Republicans, to come out loudly for suffrage when forming the new Progressive Party in the spring of 1912.[3]

Beyond that, the state's Socialist strongholds in several cities were seen as seedbeds of suffrage support. The Socialist Party had endorsed equal suffrage since its founding in 1901, and in the recent successful Washington State campaign, Socialists had done "excellent vigorous work and were almost fanatical in their zeal" for suffrage, according to campaigners there.[4] Wisconsin had elected Victor Berger, the first Socialist to sit in the House of Representatives, in 1910, and voters in greater Milwaukee, led by its significant labor and German populations, had elected the nation's first Socialist mayor in Emil Seidel. What's more, sizable Scandinavian populations were also "generally disposed toward suffrage," Wisconsin women found;[5] women in Norway gained the right to stand for election as of 1907, and women in Denmark and Sweden gained limited voting rights in 1908 and 1909, respectively.[6]

Wisconsin suffragists believed their time had finally come. The overall strategy was to draw local women into the center of the mobilization. "Place the responsibility of winning their own men upon their shoulders," Washington State suffragists urged their sisters in Wisconsin.[7] NAWSA president Anna Howard Shaw agreed. "Everything depends on stirring them up and making them discuss it at all sorts of gatherings, at their table and among their families. Let the men know that they want it, and make it impossible to say that their women friends never mention it and that they don't want it."[8]

All the while, the campaign would have to outmaneuver antisuffrage forces led by powerful foes in the vital brewing industry, assisted by their many political and industry allies.

Shaw saw Eastman as exceptionally well suited to organize a centralized, energized statewide campaign. "She is a live, splendid little woman who will touch some live wires and set things going," Shaw thought, "and that, as far as

I can learn, is what you need, someone with enthusiasm, youth and hope to inspire and stir other people up to doing things."[9] A bill putting the question of women's suffrage to a vote had passed both houses of the legislature in March and was signed into law by Governor Francis McGovern on June 2, 1911.[10] As a result, a referendum would appear on the ballot in the general election of 1912. Now the voters—all male of course—would go to the polls on November 5 to decide.

* * *

Eastman moved to Milwaukee for marriage, not work. The trip from New York to Wisconsin was arduous for her, physically and emotionally. She struggled with "winding-up business" in the city she loved.[11] On May 29, 1911, she had wed Wallace Benedict—intimates called him "Bennie"—an insurance agent whom she had met during a business trip to the Midwest for the American Association for Labor Legislation (AALL).[12] Crystal had received a hearty welcome from labor leaders and social democrats on that trip, including both Victor Berger and Emil Seidel, and discussed sociological and economic conditions in Milwaukee. From there she had gone to Madison, where this strapping young insurance man, whom the papers described as "well known . . . and a close student of American and foreign progress in compensation for industrial accidents," had come seeking her input.[13] Crystal was powerfully attracted to Bennie almost immediately, Max later said, "his sturdy boyish masculinity contrasting with something milk-blooded in the cerebral social worker types around her." Plus, it quickly became clear that "he was one of those rare males . . . who like to have the woman they love amount to something."[14]

She married him eleven months later—exactly fourteen days after her mother passed away. Their courtship had "pained" Annis and been a "topic of curious speculation" to family and friends alike, Max reported.[15] In the immediate aftermath of such loss, Crystal grasped at the marriage, characterizing it as an act of independence and courage amidst her grief. "It's a thing you've got to do bravely all by yourself—without looking back," she told Max on the eve of her courthouse wedding. "Your relatives and former companions and dear intimate friends—your whole past associations in fact—don't play much part." Bennie had encouraged such thinking, telling her, " 'Yes, you're a brave girl, you know what you want and you're not afraid to take it.' "[16]

Max would never quite see the match that way. He later remarked that while "a common interest in work accidents had brought them together," it had nothing to do with ideals. Her interest had "its focus in the workers, his in the insurance fees."[17] Max did not serve as a witness to his sister's marriage, even though he was around the corner in an apartment on MacDougal Street with his new wife,

Crystal's Greenwich Village friend and Women's Trade Union League organizer Ida Rauh, whom he had similarly wed in the wake of their mother's death just the day before. When Crystal and Bennie visited her father in Glenora on their way to Wisconsin, she felt dazed by recent events in her life. "I just had no mind at all, and couldn't pretend to exert it," she described. When she first arrived in Milwaukee, she spent "three days of half-sickness at Bennie's house."[18]

But Bennie showed himself to be a very supportive partner to her. From the start, he began "pulling wires" to find her a job, she disclosed to Max.[19] When Crystal applied for admission to the Wisconsin bar on September 28, 1911, she was sworn in before Judge Tarrant, on motion of Joseph E. Davies, chairman of the state Democratic committee. Both Davies and Tarrant were Bennie's frat brothers from the Delta Upsilon fraternity at the University of Wisconsin.[20] The next week "Bennie did a little press-agent work for me," she reported, generating at least one newspaper article that she clipped and sent along to Max.[21] He also introduced her to his buddy Jim Blake, an attorney. The very next night Blake accompanied her to a major Socialist protest meeting headlined by Seidel and Berger. It "made a great impression on me," she told Max. Blake "is a lawyer— very friendly and interested. He's taking charge of my career just now and I'm expecting to get the right opening very soon."[22]

Crystal's true aim at this point was a career in law, not suffrage. At age thirty, after all the acclaim she had received from her work on employer liability, she joked with the Vassar class of 1903 that she would now happily "become a 'common or garden' law clerk at $10 per [week]."[23] After only a few weeks in town, she introduced herself to Governor McGovern, who "knew all about me and I asked his advice about my legal career!" she reported to Max. The same day she had lunch with Paul Kellogg, who took her to see Commons, Crownhart, and Beck—the new industrial commissioners—afterward. She wanted them "to remember that I'm here, in case any little cases come up where they want a labor expert's legal services."[24]

On the home front too, Crystal seemed to enjoy an equally supportive part-nership with her new husband. "Bennie has fine taste—it complements mine and braces it up where its [*sic*] weak," she noted.[25] Their lifestyle might have appeared traditional, but "together we are quite untrammeled by conventions and traditions in house-trimming," she insisted to Max.[26] By the end of her first month in Milwaukee, she declared she was "feeling pretty good married."[27] A month after that, her spirits had risen further. "I'm . . . just young and glad and singing in the morning," she told him.[28] On the day she accepted her job in the suffrage campaign, she would sound quite fulfilled. "I am very well and happier than I've been in two or three years I guess."[29] "Bennie," she wanted Max to know, "is a good companion for me—in all the ways."[30]

If Crystal had been unconsciously mounting a campaign to convince her brother he had been wrong about her husband, her subsequent letters suggest she may have at least convinced herself. So compelling was her experience of marital companionship as a newlywed that she was careful to emphasize her abiding love for Max. "Don't fear that your place in my heart is any smaller or any different. It's bigger as I go on learning things," she told him.[31] Later she framed the sentiment another way, articulating the love shared among a newly constituted family of two married pairs, Max and Ida, Bennie and herself. "It's almost unbelievable that we all four like each other. And the best part of it is that it's the kind of liking that will grow as we grow instead of changing."[32] Yet Max may have remained skeptical. "By the way," she would feel the urge to add out of the blue, "Bennie is an *ideal* person to live with—you don't begin to know how funny he is—dropping into the personality of a fat German, or an old Irish woman singing a song—or something, without any warning at all—till Edith and I are roaring." She then accentuated the point. "Sometimes I can't believe my luck. Suppose I hadn't found him."[33]

All the while she was "getting a lot of fun out of the suffrage situation here," she reported. In the 1912 campaign, Wisconsin had two major suffrage organizations operating in the state. The venerable Wisconsin Woman Suffrage Association (WWSA), under the leadership of the Reverend Olympia Brown since 1885, was now joined by the Wisconsin branch of the Political Equality League (PEL), a loose network of suffrage organizations with chapters in both the United States and Canada. The newer group was composed of younger, more activist women led in Wisconsin by Ada James, the daughter of state senator David G. James, who had shepherded the current suffrage referendum through the state senate. Ada James favored new, more dramatic methods of rallying women and the electorate. Brown, though as ardent as anyone for the cause, could not see women calling attention to themselves in the streets. She believed in educating voters through boilerplate methods: organizing small gatherings to hear speakers, mainly men, explain the right of women to gain the vote. "Both sides," Crystal told Max, "are "begging for my advice and hanging on my words." The PEL was actively wooing her. "I could be Secretary of the League and run the whole campaign for a good salary," she explained, or she could be president and oversee the work without pay. "But I prefer being 'advisor' in general," she said, in case a law firm "takes me in."[34]

After more months of trying, none of them did. In these years, the legal field resisted women's entry more resolutely than any other major American profession.[35] Indeed, Eastman would never have the opportunity to work as an attorney. So, eleven months before Election Day, she moved permanently into a career in social activism when she accepted the offer of $166 a month to organize a divided suffrage movement into a coordinated statewide campaign in Wisconsin.

Crystal's marriage continued to thrive, and Bennie agreed to serve as head of the Wisconsin Men's League for Woman Suffrage.[36] The couple worked together nearly around the clock on her first major event: a rare, high-profile fundraiser featuring the English leader of the militant suffragettes, Emmeline Pankhurst.[37] "Bennie is doing it all—with lots of fun and success so far," she told Max. "It has meant long days and some long evenings of hard work and hustling for both of us—but working it out together has been a lark."[38] The banquet would not succeed from an organizational point of view; the PEL lost money because of the low turnout. Eastman suspected as much when she wrote to James to frame the upcoming event: "I think our banquet is going to be a great success, although we may be financially in the hole a little."[39] But for Crystal personally, the experience of balancing marriage and work was an uncommon victory. That day she wrote to Max, "I've just lately come to the conclusion that our combination—Bennie and me—is one of the rarely successful ones. Last summer I wasn't quite so sure of us. . . . But now I am."[40]

She was probably surprised to discover that managing the competing interests at the campaign office was a more daunting task. From the start, her assertive style rubbed many Wisconsin suffragists the wrong way. They resisted her leadership at every turn, first obstructing Shaw's wish to combine the two suffrage organizations with Eastman directing the integrated effort, then refusing to elect her to chair a central committee. "We feel that States . . . which had by quarrelling and fussing and antagonizing each other failed to get down to business by this time, would not be very successful," Shaw told James, "and it would only be a waste of money for the national to give any to it."[41] Shaw expressed more than once that she wanted Eastman, whom everyone in the movement referred to as "Mrs. Benedict," to be secretary of the central committee. The NAWSA, which everyone called simply "the national," had money at the ready to assist with her salary, Shaw repeatedly promised, as long as that happened.[42]

But when the two local organizations met, they decided to create a cooperative committee with two heads rather than allow Eastman to manage a unified effort. This "is not at all what we had in mind," Shaw shot back. "The expense of keeping up double headquarters with two sets of secretaries and so forth, is not at all in accordance with our idea of what a co-operative committee should be." She wanted one committee of seven members, three from each society and a seventh member, ideally Eastman. When another meeting was held, the new cooperative committee voted to take on a seventh member, a chair, but agreed it should be someone not actively involved with either association. Shaw was not pleased. "It seems to me that the chairman of the campaign committee should be the most active and best informed woman in regard to the suffrage movement of any woman in the State and that a figure-head chairman is not at all what is desired."[43]

Ultimately, the two organizations would not coordinate their efforts at all. Eastman's managerial authority would start and finish with the PEL. Yet within weeks new objections to her leadership emerged from within her own ranks. One veteran organizer complained, "I think C.E.B. [Crystal Eastman Benedict] will manage to antagonize us all before she has been in the office another week. She doesn't know even kindergarten methods about getting along with newspapers. She has fixed herself with our city editor so her name can't be printed again—at least until conditions change—and I've only saved the P.E.L. from going in under the taboo by an ace."[44] Other colleagues would appreciate her "unusual gifts in the way of enthusiasm that is not daunted by rebuffs" but worried about her lack of orderly oversight of financial matters.[45]

Even those in the PEL who supported Crystal had to admit she was "a little blunt [and] lacking in finesse," at least by local standards.[46] Shaw, raised in the Midwest herself, granted that her work style and intensity could be off-putting. "I can see how she would antagonize people, because she is rather brusque, and if she had any business on hand would not be apt to see anybody who was hanging around, and she has a rather short way of speaking."[47] But some key local colleagues were far less circumspect. "I'm just telling you we didn't get *on* at all, we got clear *off*," one local suffragist told James. "But really Ada dear, you better get rid of her if you can quietly," she continued. "Don't murder her in cold blood but if you can just give her enough ether to put her to sleep quietly, do it by all means." Local rivalries could be exploited, she offered, "even the Reverend Olympia . . . [who] wouldn't exactly use an axe on her, I imagine, but I can just see her smothering the aforesaid lady Benedict out of existence with a wet blanket."[48]

Later, Crystal's Wisconsin colleagues would cast doubt on her judgment, objecting to her decision to bring in Max as a paid speaker at the very top of the going rate. Eastman would consistently seek to highlight men's support for women's suffrage throughout the Wisconsin campaign, conducting outreach to many locally credible male allies—professors, clergy, leaders of organizations and associations—to the cause. And by the time she would hire Max as a speaker, he was an ascendant star on the Progressive lecture circuit, with a reputation for spellbinding speeches. His founding of the New York Men's League for Woman Suffrage in 1909 had led to a giant parade with several thousand prosuffrage men marching up Fifth Avenue in support of the vote in 1910, catapulting him to a rare prominence in the suffrage movement. Indeed, it was Max's stance on women's rights that would particularly distinguish his political career; although he became an avatar of the Left, he would never call himself a Socialist, preferring instead "hard-headed idealist"—but he would always call himself a feminist.[49] He famously called women's suffrage the lever that "will gradually bend the wishes of men toward a new age."[50] Yet through the spring of 1912, Crystal would endure multiple accusations about misspent campaign funds over the fifty-dollar fee she paid him because local lecturers generally received about half that much.[51]

Shaw would field complaints for a while, then stopped entertaining local objections and grievances. She decreed that the WWSA and the PEL would work separately but side by side to wage the campaign of 1911–12, and the territorial disputes, generational and stylistic differences, and factional rivalries were left to the women involved to resolve on their own. "We don't care anything about old or new or pioneers or modern people," Shaw finally ruled; "what we want is suffrage in Wisconsin."[52]

From the outset, the suffragists' staunchest foe was the brewing industry. The lead article in a 1912 issue of *Progress*, the trade magazine of the retail liquor dealers of Wisconsin, headlined, "Give Ballot to Women and Industry to Goes to Smash."[53]

Liquor industry men had not forgotten that women's first drive for partial suffrage in Wisconsin, in 1899, had focused exclusively on obtaining women's voting rights on matters pertaining to liquor licensing and sales. And it did not help that the WWSA membership was intermixed with many women active in the Woman's Christian Temperance Union.[54] The PEL knew from the reports of other suffragists that "it is no little thing to attack the saloon-keepers in any town," but the contest was especially formidable across Wisconsin, where the industry was responsible for countless incomes along the pipeline, from the bottlers, distributors, and bar owners to the farmers who grew the barley to the coopers who made the barrels.[55] Any business in the emerging tourism and hospitality industries—theaters and movie houses, taxi and auto companies, advertising and sales, jewelry, dry goods, hotels, and restaurants, including even the waiters—could be mobilized by brewers to defeat suffrage. Even "the habitués of saloons are a strong force," Washington suffragists warned their sisters in Wisconsin. "Politicians all want saloons because [they form] organizations thru which they get their votes."[56]

A man's whole world was at risk, according to the brewers, both his livelihood and his home. "Do you know what it means to the thousands and thousands of homes in which happiness and content now reign?" the Retail Liquor Association asked. Their answer aligned with the broad sentiments of antisuffrage agitators since the 1850s who claimed women's suffrage would corrupt women and destroy the foundation of civilization—at least as men conceived and enjoyed it. If equal suffrage passed, the brewers warned, "fair-minded women—women who think more of their homes, their babies, their husbands, and their reputation"—will be replaced by "women who lack [a] sense of motherhood, of decency and of honor."[57]

Crystal's 1912 suffrage speech, "Political Recognition of Women," addressed both sides of these claims, arguing in conversational fashion, filled with anecdotes and accessible comparisons, that women's suffrage would better support these traditional roles while properly influencing the larger modern systems of industrial manufacture and production with which family households increasingly intersected. This was a line often taken up by Progressive suffragists at the time, particularly when speaking to tentative audiences.[58] Since the domestic sphere was changing in the modern era, the vote was needed by mothers and homemakers—as separate from their husbands—to represent their business interests in the home.[59] Beyond that, Crystal reminded male listeners of the "ever-increasing number [of] wage-earning women—the millions of women who, in spite of the oft reiterated declaration that woman's place is in the home, are not in the home, but are out earning their living in competitive industry, side by side with men." To deny those women "the protection of the ballot in their struggle for a livelihood, to give them no voice in making the laws which govern their labor," she said, "is no purely theoretical injustice, it is an actual handicap to them."[60]

Eastman efficiently rebutted deep-seated arguments against women's suffrage, offering pointed observations, always delivered with finesse and often with humor. Like many other suffragists at the time, she argued that the women's vote would function as an antidote to government corruption. She referred to "the ignorant and purchasable vote," a decades-old common phrase that evoked the ward politicians whose election victories were bought and paid for, typically by Wall Street financiers.[61] But recently some pundits and popular journalists had begun revising that understanding, writing that women's suffrage would actually increase rather than redress this problem nationally. As *Life* magazine warned in 1910, "woman suffrage would increase the ignorant and purchasable vote and, in the mixed population of American cities, would prove the strongest enemy to civic reform."[62] Crystal dismissed this claim out of hand, saying it merely reflected the routine strategy of grasping at any available straw to block "every step in the emancipation of women."[63]

She then moved more substantively to quash concerns on the home front. To dispatch the powerful myth that "when women vote they will lose their feminine charm . . . they will refuse to bear children; they will neglect the home, leave the baby and let the bread burn," she first referred to empirical evidence. The very "same things were said about the higher education of women fifty years ago," she rightly observed, "and none of these terrible things have come to pass." Then she took to provocative repartee. And "seriously," she added, leveraging the candor and sarcasm that made her such a memorable speaker, "does anyone suppose that love-making has gone out of fashion in California, or marriage fallen off in Wyoming, or the birth rate decreased in Colorado as the result of woman suffrage?"[64]

On the ground, the PEL similarly mobilized to counter the claims of "the antis," as the movement called those opposed to suffrage, face to face. "We shall have to meet organized opposition, and the only way to meet it is by a better organization of our own," Eastman announced.[65] The campaign took on the task of organizing the whole state by voting precincts while also trying as best they could to evade actions that might rile up the opposition. They quietly planted seeds for a grassroots campaign, in part by feigning they already had one. If there were not enough women interested in suffrage in a particular county, the PEL outlined in an instruction sheet, suffragists were urged to form a committee and elect a chair and a secretary anyway. Then they were to announce a meeting, no matter how small, to which the PEL would send a speaker. They believed the appearance of suffrage enthusiasm by local women would become a self-fulfilling prophecy, relieving anxiety and triggering sufficient involvement for a regular organization to be formed. And in quite a few counties, they were right.[66]

The PEL organized targeted campaigns aimed at pivotal constituencies, including Germans, Catholics, and union members. In May, Eastman wrote to M. Carey Thomas at Bryn Mawr, noting "there are over 200 unions [in Milwaukee] and this is perhaps the simplest and most direct way of reaching the most intelligent class of workmen."[67] They also formed a PEL among blacks in the state.[68] Indeed, at a time when Shaw and the NAWSA were confronting charges of racial discrimination from the civil rights leader, scholar, and National Association for the Advancement of Colored People (NAACP) cofounder W. E. B. DuBois, including pointed examples of what he called the "reactionary attitude" of white suffragists at the NAWSA's annual convention in 1911, Crystal was corresponding with Mary White Ovington, the principal cofounder of the NAACP, about racial outreach efforts in the Wisconsin campaign.[69] "We just had a splendid meeting among colored people with Miss Alice Waytes as the speaker," she reported. "We took 23 names of those who are interested and a good big collection."[70]

By April, Crystal reported to Jane Addams that "we have about thirty counties in Wisconsin organized now and are in communication with the active leaders of every organization. I think we shall complete the seventy-two counties by July, and then be ready to take up the more intense district organization and house to house canvas in the big towns." She was organizing both structurally and demographically, then leveraging newspaper publicity to magnify the effects of their efforts. "I am planning how to start a German American branch of the Political Equality League and at least get it into the newspapers that there are German American women in favor of woman suffrage."[71] Two months later, she reported they had successfully established local organizations of some kind in sixty-four of seventy-two counties across Wisconsin.[72]

The women took to the stump statewide, from Beloit to Green Bay to Superior. Crystal herself gave speeches often.[73] In the larger cities, brass bands attracted crowds to processions of women shouting slogans that linked traditional ideas of women's roles in the home and the public world of politics:

> Mother mends my socks and shirts
> Mother mends my coat
> Mebbe she could mend some laws
> If she had the vote.[74]

In the summer, suffragists sold buttermilk along the march routes and oversized yellow balloons emblazoned with "Votes for Woman" in red letters.[75] A suffrage tour up the Wolf River distributed literature at landings along the way. The pilot Lincoln Beachey scattered suffrage flyers from the air.[76] When Buffalo Bill Cody brought his Wild West Show to Green Bay in July, the PEL persuaded him to carry a suffrage banner while he and his circus troupe of performing cowboys and Indians paraded down the main street.[77]

The automobile tour was their most common publicity technique throughout the campaign. In 1912, it was quite radical for women to travel alone by car. The author and later Pulitzer Prize–winning playwright Zona Gale, who would remain a friend of Crystal's from the NAWSA to the National Woman's Party to the antiwar movement, reported strong sentiment against automobile tours and street meetings, especially in the smaller towns and hamlets of her home state.[78] Crystal was undeterred. In response, she circulated detailed instructions on the way to conduct a successful automobile tour. Indeed, she urged organizers: "Get a cornet or some musical instrument to travel up and down, advertising yourselves in a thorough way"—the same "way the circus does with its parade."[79]

Through August and September, the suffragists leveraged the extensive county fair system, equipping tents in most of the seventy-five sites statewide with publicity kits that typically included 6,000 leaflets offering six different arguments; 1,300 brochures targeting specific nationalities, languages, and groups; 500 church leaflets; several dozen copies of Jane Addams's widely accessible 1910 essay from the *Ladies' Home Journal*, "Why Women Should Vote"; a box each of bangles to be given away and buttons to be sold; a dozen yellow felt pennants, a woman suffrage banner, sign, and flag; postcards of Lincoln; and membership cards in pink, white, and yellow.[80] At some fairs, they demonstrated the new "vacuum washing machine," which the PEL sold on commission to raise funds.[81] Some tents provided childcare, offering busy mothers a moment's peace to read the literature.

On Saturdays, they scheduled headline speakers, such as Belle Case La Follette, whom suffragists knew as the strength behind her husband, the senator from Wisconsin. James remembered Belle from a dinner with her father's colleagues in the Wisconsin State Senate. "At the table a hot discussion took place as to 'how La Follette could be downed,'" and "an Assemblyman brought his fist down on the table and said, 'We could down La Follette alone, but we can't down Mrs. La Follette, she has got to be reckoned with.'"[82] Belle herself told the papers "this fighting for what we believe to be right is a family affair with us." Their daughter, Flora Dodge "Fola" La Follette, another friend of Crystal's, was "as much interested as I am, and we three counsel together and all are stronger for it."[83]

When Ohio's suffrage referendum was defeated on September 3, the Wisconsin women were exhausted but refused to be debilitated by the loss. "I am cocksure that you can't kill a suffragette," James proclaimed.[84] Crystal had said six months before that Ohio was crucial because it was "bigger and further east" than Wisconsin. "If they win, it will be a great help to us and if they lose it will be a blow," she had admitted—but now she quickly regrouped to galvanize the faithful.[85] In an article entitled "Wisconsin Women Have High Hopes," published September 13, she claimed the loss "only depressed us for a day or two" because the prospects of victory in neighboring Wisconsin "never looked brighter than they do today."[86] Two weeks later, she organized a final push, hosting her friend Inez Milholland, the suffrage star, who invoked Teddy Roosevelt's 1903 speech at the New York State Agricultural Association when she addressed a packed house in Madison on why women deserved "a square deal." Roosevelt had told farmers, "We must see that each is given a square deal, because he is entitled to no more and should receive no less."[87] Milholland would always hold the same was true for women. Days later, the PEL launched a full week with Belle La Follette, who captured sizeable crowds when speaking on why Wisconsin men should support what she characterized broadly as "this great uplift movement."[88]

Behind the scenes of all this, Eastman was also dealing with the "secret underhanded mode of attack" pursued by "the big interests who fear the woman vote."[89] Antisuffrage groups were engaged in a smear campaign, circulating false claims and planting misinformation. In response, she hired a private investigator to try to trace the sources responsible so she could bring legal action. "Since the Ohio campaign, when so many crooked things were done by opponents of woman suffrage, I have felt it exceedingly important to have the services of a detective during these last weeks of the campaign in Wisconsin," she told her organizers.[90] "The only way we can prevent a universal distribution of anonymous literature in Wisconsin is to watch the proceedings of the enemy and know what they are going to do beforehand and have the district attorney intervene and stop it."[91]

Eastman had no real opportunity to pursue the investigation because she was soon confronted by a series of moves that were hostile to suffrage by the attorney general himself. In March, L. H. Bancroft informed the PEL that its work fell under Wisconsin's Corrupt Practices Act, a 1911 provision in the state constitution requiring political candidates and lobbying committees to file fundraising and expenditure reports each month. Crystal consulted legal counsel and also inquired directly to the secretary of state whether the terms of the act applied to the PEL.[92] Soon she was informed that Secretary James A. Frear and Attorney General Bancroft concurred in "holding that all organizations engaged in promoting a political issue, including the one with which you are identified, are required to file expense statements." The statute limited total PEL fundraising to $10,000 for the campaign. Still, the same requirements would also reach those who were interested in the antisuffrage movement, according to Frear.[93]

Then, in late August, the attorney general suddenly informed suffragists that the suffrage referendum must appear on a separate pink ballot on Election Day. Eastman again sought legal counsel and disputed the legality of the change directly with Bancroft. Her consulting attorney found that the suffrage amendment "should be part of the general ballot . . . and not one upon a separate ballot . . . and it seems to me this is so clear that no argument can strengthen this conclusion."[94] He advised her to institute proceedings in the state supreme court and recommended an attorney in Madison as "one of the very best lawyers in the state, if not the best" to handle it. Crystal would submit briefs from both attorneys, only to receive a reply from Bancroft saying simply, "I find nothing . . . which in any way tends to alter my former opinion."[95]

Bancroft's letter was dated September 6—sixty days before Election Day. The campaign made an all-out effort to notify voters that the suffrage referendum would now appear on pink paper. They designed a placard campaign for street cars on key routes in selected cities; they instructed speakers and trained poll workers, all to inform voters to watch for the separate rose-colored ballot. But on Election Day, "after all our work to get a favorable vote on that, the ballot was found after all to be on white paper." Suffragists believed this change "greatly operated to confuse the voter and nullify our election work." Movement leaders openly castigated "election tricks in Wisconsin," suggesting a thoroughgoing plot involving the highest levels of state government. According to one senior suffragist, it looked "very much as if it were intended to make our measure illegal, even if it had carried at the polls."[96]

In the end, the Wisconsin suffrage bid lost nearly two to one—132,000 for, 224,000 against—while three of the five states—Oregon, Kansas, and Arizona—prevailed in 1912. In "Why We Lost in Wisconsin," her speech at the NAWSA convention in Philadelphia in December, Crystal partly assigned blame to disappointing support from the Scandinavians in western Wisconsin and from Socialists and their sympathizers. She also cited the failure of Progressive Republican voters to follow the prosuffrage lead of Teddy Roosevelt and the Progressive Party. "I sometimes think the last thing a man becomes progressive about is the activities of his own wife," she commented—and not for the last time. Finally, she told the gathered suffragists, their campaign had "under-estimated the far reaching power of the great brewing industry in Wisconsin [and] the extent of its hostility to women suffrage." The brewers "put business, as, alas, most big corporations do, ahead of democracy, justice and simple human right." But "it is merely a challenge," Crystal proclaimed from the podium, and in overcoming that challenge, she intimated, suffragists would lead the way to broader justice in the world:

> "The brewers do not control the majority of the voters of Wisconsin and they cannot defeat us alone. Their power can defeat us only when it is allied with ignorance and prejudice, and it is our business to cut off these allies,—to do away with the ignorance and prejudice that still exist in Wisconsin in regard to woman suffrage. When we have done that the issue will be clear and we shall win."[97]

Privately, in the wake of the loss in what was a vicious campaign, Crystal reassessed her personal direction. She had never really felt at home in Wisconsin and struggled to put all the pieces together to create the life she wanted. Soon after she started with the PEL, she told Max she was "getting to know some fine people and some that like me. But we haven't any real companions."[98] After six months more, her letters began to contemplate staying in Milwaukee only through the end of the campaign. She told Fola La Follette, "They are a funny, funny lot out here," but vowed, "all the same, I like it and am going to stick to it, at least until we get the vote."[99] By the next month she wrote Max that "Bennie is hard at work across the dining room table—figuring how to get rich in six months and move to New York. We're pretty tired of Milwaukee."[100]

Crystal also felt there was tension between her marriage and some in the suffrage movement. Two months after she arrived in Wisconsin she told Max, "Some of my friends have dropped me since I got married."[101] After the election, some suffragists impugned her marriage so perniciously that James felt it necessary to write Belle La Follette to defend Crystal's home life against "some gossip that was repeated to me at Madison and lest it has come to you I want to say that it is absolutely false. Mrs. Benedict is the sole [sic] of honor . . . [and] she is also most charming at home. I saw a good deal of her home life and it is sweet and wholesome."[102] Crystal's descendants describe her ongoing sense of a troubled position among suffrage colleagues. She kept both weddings secret.[103] And when she tied the knot for the second time, Crystal was anguished, they say, because she did not want anyone to know she had—as she thought—betrayed the suffrage movement by getting married.[104]

At the same time, she had begun to feel stifled by the bourgeois trappings of an increasingly "successful" middle-class marriage—a setup that seemed to suit her husband just fine. He had become a partner in a new insurance firm, Topping, Benedict and Reidburg, which, at first, made him only "a more important citizen, but . . . not any richer," she told Max.[105] But the money would come soon enough, and that is what troubled her. As Bennie began to prosper, she was uncomfortable with his "grasping and unscrupulous and really crooked" partner.[106] But worse, Bennie's fast-rising income posed problems for her vision of the good life. "If we stay here," she explained to Max, "Bennie will get rich so fast it will be hard for him to pull out . . . then the first thing you know we'll be stuck out here, with expensive tastes formed and no freedom for either of us,—just regular fat Dutchmen." She feared financial success would satiate and sustain her husband, thwarting her hopes for the edgier, alternative life she craved. "You see—I can feel this deadly middle-western life with a big house and a big automobile and a comfortable home,—and no chance to raise hell if I want to,—closing in on me. I must get Bennie away *now*."[107]

With those feelings running strong, in December she attended the suffrage convention in Philadelphia, where she joined her Vassar friend Lucy Burns and Lucy's friend Alice Paul to launch the Congressional Committee of the NAWSA, the group that in 1916 became the National Woman's Party. Burns and Paul had met while studying in Europe, where both had cut their political teeth with the militant Pankhursts and the suffragettes. When Paul expressed an interest in reviving the NAWSA's moribund Congressional Committee to work for federal legislation alongside state suffrage work, Jane Addams had suggested they contact Eastman.[108]

These women were Crystal's peers—young, well educated, modern, and impatient for "rights we should have won in the nineteenth century," as she would pronounce in 1919.[109] They had concluded that nearly half a century of the exhausting, expensive state-by-state campaigning had yielded too little after too long. Addams told them they could do anything they wanted with the Congressional Committee except spend NAWSA funds; they were free to agitate for suffrage on a national level using whatever approaches they liked, but they had to raise their own money. What they wanted was a constitutional amendment granting full suffrage to all American women, all at the same time. They would utilize militant methods inspired by the English suffragettes—mass protests, rallies, marches, public spectacle, sophisticated press strategies—everything except violence, to leverage the vote. Now Crystal needed to convince her husband to give up his lucrative partnership, leave his hometown, and move back east with her to do it.

The opening gambit by the Congressional Committee was a huge suffrage parade coinciding with Woodrow Wilson's inauguration to his first term as president. More than five thousand suffrage demonstrators rallied at Washington's Columbia Theater on March 2, 1913, then marched down Pennsylvania Avenue the next day. Five mounted heralds conducted the procession, with Inez Milholland, enrobed in white, leading the way astride a stallion named Gray Dawn. The event was unprecedented for its scale and scope, although marred by Paul's repeated rebuff of black suffragists in their rightful demands for full inclusion in integrated delegations.[110] It would not be the last time she insisted on focusing the suffrage campaign very narrowly, excluding intersectional points of view she deemed extrinsic or counterproductive to the women's struggle. Eastman would battle Paul in the future over what she saw as a crushingly illiberal approach. But for now, when Paul called on her to travel to Washington to help plan the proceedings, she accelerated her schedule organizing the Wisconsin delegation and got on a train. "After we got down there and began to see all the work that was needed," Paul recalled, "we asked Crystal Eastman to come down and join us, which she did."[111]

The parade began late, and it was ended early by street violence. From the start, the huge crowd accosted marchers with jeers and sexualized epithets; but within a few blocks, things got physical—the women were grabbed, tripped, and shoved to the ground with such growing intensity that the secretary of war was called in. Ambulances carried more than a hundred marchers through the crowds to local emergency hospitals. The *Chicago Tribune* reported that Helen Keller "was so exhausted and unnerved by the experience in attempting to reach a grandstand . . . that she was unable to speak" at the postparade rally at Continental Hall.[112]

That rally became a mass meeting. Congress called for an investigation, which began almost immediately—on March 6, President Wilson's second day in office. In the end, the Washington chief of police was fired and all officers along the procession route censured for dereliction of duty. The hullabaloo, even the minor injuries, pleased militant suffragist leaders, however; they saw the chaos as a media magnet attracting national attention to their cause.

It was the first move in the seven-year struggle to win ratification of the Nineteenth Amendment. Eastman, an expert horsewoman, had been asked to ride along with Milholland as one of six "feminine Paul Reveres," draped in yellow silk and carrying a trumpet to announce the arrival of this new suffrage movement.[113] Yet she ultimately declined this high-visibility role. In fact, she skipped the parade, and the rally and the investigation that followed it. She had a boat to catch for Europe.[114] She was to speak as a NAWSA delegate at the Seventh Congress of the International Woman Suffrage Alliance (IWSA) in Budapest, but that was not until June. Her primary reason for leaving in late February was to create a second honeymoon designed to lure her husband into the life she wanted back East upon their return. "It seems a God given opportunity,—both of us young and healthy and rested, no babies, and no big piece of important work to keep me at home," she told Max. "Also, it's a scheme for getting us to N.Y. We'll work there, almost sure, when we come back."[115] When the couple received an offer of $3,500 for Bennie's share of the business, Crystal packed up the house in Milwaukee, sequestering $1,000 to get started in Greenwich Village when they returned from Europe. She told Max, "This is my last chance to get out."[116]

The Budapest congress was a clear career-builder, putting Eastman in the same league with some of the most prominent international suffrage activists in the world—among them Addams, with whom Crystal shared the podium at her session,[117] and Hungarian-born feminist and pacifist Rosika Schwimmer, whose petition to organize neutral nations to mediate the world war would help inspire the formation of the Woman's Peace Party in late 1914. Before the congress, receptions for the delegations were held in Dresden, Prague, Vienna, and elsewhere.[118] Crystal did not attend any of these ancillary events. Indeed, few of her surviving documents mention any events at the congress—not her speech on "How to Reach the Woman of Higher Education," the debate about the use of militant tactics in the suffrage quest, the principal address by IWSA president Carrie Chapman Catt, or any of the 240 delegates from twenty-two countries around the world. She would tell Max, "Budapest was worth going round the world for," but offered no further details.[119] Her contribution to *Jus Suffragii*, the official organ of the alliance, was a short dispatch that seemed to survey the congress briefly and from a distance. "If I should try to express . . . the most striking features of this great international gathering of women," she observed, one adjective "would be 'hatless,' " she observed. "Women went about with their heads bare and their hands free." The other adjective would be 'triumphant.' "[120]

Everything else she wrote conjures a trip that was "all kinds of a lark for us"— Bennie and herself.[121] From Rome, it was nothing but the sights. From Tangiers, where the couple stayed three weeks, Crystal reported, "Mr. Keram—who has a little shop and Moorish friends, has fallen in love with me, which is inconvenient."[122] She did mention meeting with the labor activist and writer Mary Heaton Vorse. Vorse had both covered and participated in the Lawrence textile strike the previous year and was already becoming a regular contributor to *The Masses*. She was also a suffragist, and like Eastman was soon to become involved in the internationalist drive for peace. She was in Europe to attend the same IWSA congress where Crystal was headed. Still, Crystal recounted the visit in personal terms. Vorse and Bennie did not get along. Some who knew Vorse would describe her as slow and self-dramatizing yet "neither brilliant nor very interesting," a combination of qualities that would irk the fizzy and jocular Bennie.[123] "Can you imagine them sitting side by side at the table?" Crystal wrote Max. "They began with mild dislike—went through a time of being interested in each other's kind of cleverness and rough talk, and ended in violent antipathy."[124] Vorse's critics would later admit that her many "errands of the heart" with striking workers conferred an admirable vitality of its own.[125] Eastman and Vorse would remain politically and socially connected through the Woman's Peace Party, the *Liberator*, and the Heterodoxy club, a downtown group of modern, active, "unorthodox" women, as the art patron and Greenwich Village salon hostess Mabel Dodge Luhan put it—"women who did things and did them openly."[126] Yet, in this context, in this moment, Crystal underlined her fidelity to her husband, remarking about Vorse, "She is awful."[127]

When the Congressional Committee arranged the first suffrage deputation to ever appear before a US president in March 1913, Crystal and Bennie had just found "a cheap old Moorish villa, now the Grand Hotel—way out on a hill" in Tangiers;[128] when Congress debated suffrage for the first time in twenty-six years that July, she and Bennie were enjoying the gondolas of Venice.[129] The couple spent through their travel budget early, making it impossible to continue on to other destinations they had hoped for—Russia, South America, or Japan. So they "decided to walk through Salzburg for a few days," go to Munich so Crystal "could sample the beer," then visit Berlin for a week, where she had quite a few friends.[130] As the trip drew to a close, Crystal extolled their "gorgeous care-free time wandering over Europe. . . . I'm perfectly happy and wouldn't have missed it for a dozen automobiles in Milwaukee."[131]

The couple returned to New York in August 1913. That fall, the escalating struggle between labor unions attempting to organize workers and management trying to prevent it, often with the support of the government, led to the formation of a new US Commission on Industrial Relations—and soon an appointment to it for Eastman. When she returned to her work with the federal suffrage campaign, she was balancing work for the commission along with her marriage; she shuttled frequently between her husband in New York and colleagues in Washington, toggling between suffrage business in the office on F Street and meetings on various issues, likely including industrial relations, on Capitol Hill. Her involvement with the constitutional suffrage amendment was clear: in October 1913, she helped develop a suffrage training school planned for December; that month, she spent two weeks teaching scores of future suffrage speakers and organizers about both methods and arguments. The next month, she met with other leading suffragists in executive session in Washington before attending a rally and reception following their meetings. Over the next few weeks, she helped make arrangements for an upcoming suffrage tour of the Midwest while also preparing to testify before the House of Representatives on the suffrage amendment.[132]

Still, Eastman was juggling so much both professionally and personally that her suffrage allies on the Congressional Committee began to wonder about her commitment and loyalty. In January 1914, she wrote to Burns that Alva Belmont, a wealthy socialite and committed New York suffragist, was a strong financing prospect for them. Belmont had shocked New York society when in 1895 she divorced William Kissam Vanderbilt, grandson of Cornelius, second son of the owner of the Grand Central Railroad, citing her husband's adultery. A year later, she became the second wife of Oliver H. P. Belmont, a banker and US congressman from New York, who died in 1908. As a widow, Alva Belmont used her multimillion-dollar divorce settlement and marital inheritance to support women's causes, including the three-month-long garment workers' strike against Triangle Shirtwaist and other New York sweatshops in 1909. That "uprising of the 20,000" followed a huge protest march by garment workers that had occurred on March 8 that year, contributing to the establishment of International Women's Day in 1910. Belmont became a major suffrage donor, both in the United States and in England. She personally financed the moving of the NAWSA headquarters from Ohio to New York City in 1909–10 and underwrote its press bureau. Around the same time, she witnessed the militant tactics of the English suffragettes on a trip to London and would try to import such measures to America—at first quite literally, by arranging to bring Emmeline Pankhurst to the United States for a speaking tour in October 1913.

Eastman met with Belmont less than three months later. She found her "quite keen" about the women and the work of the Congressional Committee, now an independent entity called the Congressional Union (CU). Belmont "wants to undermine the National—perhaps that's her chief reason for wanting to back us," she observed. Less than a week later, Paul went to see Belmont, paired, on Burns's suggestion, with Eastman. "The pairing would ease the introduction," Burns thought, "and also 'keep Crystal from being too positive.' "[133] The meeting went well; Belmont sent Paul a check for $5,000, along with a note of endorsement. It was the beginning of a pivotal relationship for the organization. Belmont became the main benefactor of the National Woman's Party, a dominating voice on its executive board, and finally its president from 1920 to 1933, after the vote was won. Meanwhile, the financing coup relieved Crystal's suffrage allies of any questions about the centrality for her of the suffrage cause. Mary Beard wrote to Paul, "I hasten to answer my own query about Crystal Eastman. . . . Her own letter to me puts her clearly with us."[134]

For the next six months, Crystal poured herself into the women's movement—in New York, in Washington, and much farther out in the field. In February, she addressed a capacity crowd at Cooper Union in lower Manhattan on the topic

"What Is Feminism?," an event billed as the first mass meeting on that topic ever held in the United States.[135] She joined a roster of twelve speakers—six men and six women, including the teachers' rights activist Henrietta Rodman; the sociologist and worker rights advocate Frances Perkins, later to become the first woman ever appointed to the US cabinet when she became secretary of labor in 1933; the journalist George Creel, later to head the US Committee on Public Information, the propaganda organization formed by the Wilson administration during World War I; the *Masses* editor and man of letters Floyd Dell; Max; and others. It was the first two such rallies organized by Marie Jenney Howe, a Unitarian minister and long-time suffrage organizer who had recently founded Heterodoxy. Since 1912, the women of Heterodoxy had been gathering in Greenwich Village on alternate Saturdays from September to June for lunch, debate, laughter, and whatever else came up.[136]

Crystal's speech at Cooper Union worked to redefine common assumptions about gender difference widely used to divide the world into separate spheres, the purportedly "separate but equal" social structure that reserves the public domain of politics and the labor market for men and the private domain of marriage and the family for women. First, she discussed census data that showed dramatic increases since 1900 in the number of women already in the "man's world" of the workplace. Then, she glided into a favorite metaphor in these years, the circus, where she conjured the thrilling sight of women trapeze performers to revise definitions of human traits typically gendered masculine—skill, endurance, "dare-devil feats of spectacular courage," strength—to apply to people, men and women alike. This image let her invoke the gender-defying mettle and flexibility it would take to fully embrace American freedom and equality. Characteristically, Crystal's speech traversed the public and private arenas, calling for a broad-based "freedom in work and freedom in play."

And, as she would argue again and again for the rest of her life, she emphasized that women's freedom must not only be won but also exercised; women must share its burdens and responsibilities, as well as its pleasures and opportunities, if they are to live as full human beings. "Now a final word about this freedom of which we talk so eagerly," she noted as she turned to close. "The hardest part of the battle is yet to come; the battle with ourselves, with our inherited instincts, with our cultivated taste for leisure, with our wrong early training, with our present physical unfitness." In the end, she declared, "we shall win this battle too." Women were strong, and ready. Equality was inevitable in America—and right on Earth, she suggested. "God meant the whole rich world of work and play and adventure for women as well as men," she proclaimed. "It is high time for us to enter into our heritage—that is my feminist faith."[137]

Then Crystal traveled to Washington, giving dramatic testimony on the federal suffrage amendment before the House Judiciary Committee as a new session of Congress began. As in her speech at Cooper Union, she deployed data, but she adopted a very different tone. She opened by displaying before the gathered congressmen a large map of the United States. Marked in white were states where women could vote, with dotted lines where they had partial suffrage, and "the black States are those where women have no right to vote whatsoever," she told them. Then she recounted the "long, laborious, and very costly way, as you gentlemen who have campaigned must know," of seeking the franchise one state at a time. Finally, she arrived at the crucial point: "we have now achieved woman suffrage in ten States. We are a political power and the time has come for us to compel this great reform by the simple, direct, American method of amending the Federal Constitution." She raised the pointed question at the heart of it all: "I ask you, then, to look at the map and consider whether you want to put yourselves in the very deliberate position of going to those 4,000,000 women voters next fall for indorsement [*sic*] and reelection after having refused even to report a woman-suffrage amendment out of committee for discussion on the floor of the House." She pressed further, warning, "If this Congress adjourns without taking action on the woman suffrage amendment . . . every woman voter will know this . . . and we have faith that the woman voter will stand by us."[138]

The papers reported that Crystal had "thrown down the gauntlet": she told them, "We are ready to go into this struggle if you force us to, but we are not eager for it. Gentlemen, why turn us into enemies. Why not keep us as friends?"[139]

The next week, she departed for the Midwest, to organize the vast states of Montana, North Dakota, Wisconsin, Wyoming, Indiana, Minnesota, Ohio, and Pennsylvania in support of "immediate favorable action" on the suffrage resolution to be presented to Congress after a huge demonstration in early May.[140] At the same time, she continued speaking on other political subjects. Crystal wrote Bennie that she would "sow a seed of truth about the Congressional Union" and also give some lectures and speeches on other topics, but on the way back "so as not to crowd the conferences for the CU."[141]

She sent reports to Burns from Pennsylvania, then Ohio—Columbus, then Dayton, then Cleveland; next was Indiana; then Wisconsin. Paul asked Eastman to cover Wyoming and Montana too, but she felt overextended. "I cannot possibly," she replied at first.[142] The next report was from Minneapolis, then St. Paul, then Fargo.[143] But three days later, Crystal had added Wyoming to her itinerary: "Fargo Sunday, Missoula Tuesday, Cheyenne Thursday, Indianapolis Sunday, Detroit Tuesday, Cleveland Wednesday."[144]

The relentless pace took a toll on her health. That spring, Crystal fell ill several times, and she was hospitalized twice.[145] She wrote her summary report from a hospital bed in Detroit in April—to Burns, who was hospitalized at the time herself. "Lucy, I heard you were sick. Are you all right now?" she asked. "What will become of the Union if we all retire to hospitals in various cities in the country?"[146]

But to Paul she emphasized the positive. "These meetings of mine—if I do say it—have seemed mighty valuable in explaining the point of Congressional Union work, making people enthusiastic over it and getting them either very friendly or completely on our side in the scrap with the National." Then she added: "There is an amazing amount of personal devotion to you out through the country," before affirming her own fealty to the group. "It makes me proud to belong."[147]

By August 1914, Crystal was healthy and back in action. After defeats in committees in both the House and Senate, the CU called a summit meeting at Belmont's Newport mansion. They decided to pursue their bold and confrontational approach for the next presidential election: organize voting women to hold the national party in power—Wilson and the Democrats—responsible for the failure of suffrage to move through Congress. Soon to be dubbed simply "Party in Power," it was modeled on the game plan of the British suffragettes and was the signature strategy of the American militants, leveraged for major goals through at least the 1920s.

That fall, the CU dispatched its hardiest and most effective speakers to the nine states that had granted full suffrage by that time—Wyoming (1890), Colorado (1893), Utah (1896), Idaho (1896), Washington State (1910), California (1911), Oregon (1912), Arizona (1912), Kansas (1912)—to convince voting women that the Democrats already had the legislative ability to enfranchise all other women nationwide, but, as Milholland would proclaim, they "have refused to put the party machinery back of the Constitutional Amendment." Women must "refuse to uphold that party that has betrayed us," she exhorted. "Let no free woman, let no woman that respects herself and womankind, lend her strength to the Democratic party that turns away its face from justice to the women of the nation."[148]

The NAWSA, by then the single largest voluntary organization of any kind in the United States, thought the CU plan both misguided and unbecoming to a woman's cause. In direct contrast to its confrontational public militancy, Carrie Catt, soon to become president of the NAWSA for a second time, advanced her own customary and more conventionally feminine campaign, relying on letter-writing and lobbying visits to the offices of individual members of Congress. Two years later, she would continue to tout this conventional approach, naming it the "Winning Plan."[149]

Crystal loved the Party in Power strategy. It was her kind of direct-action politics. She spent the week before the summit working with Paul and Burns.[150]

And she became a fierce proponent of it in the press. "Oh, the Democrats know us. We have been at them in Washington for 18 months. We have sent seven deputations to Wilson; we have made endless overtures to Congress. We'll give them a little while more," she warned, "and then we'll strike."[151] In the coming months, Crystal persistently pressed for the vote, speaking of it from every platform she had. In adapting to different venues and audiences, she expanded the case, connecting suffrage to positive outcomes in other arenas and also linking its absence to a range of social problems. Before the Commission on Industrial Relations, for example, she argued "the disenfranchisement of women as a cause of social unrest."[152]

Yet when Paul and Burns pleaded with her to go on the road to implement the plan in the fall of 1914, she refused them. "I haven't been home more than two weeks at a time since Nov. 1 last year—except for when I was sick for six weeks," she told Paul. "That doesn't make much of a family."[153]

Despite prioritizing her husband over her career and the cause, within weeks, Bennie initiated an affair with Brenda Ueland, a free-spirited young midwesterner and aspiring writer just graduated from Barnard College in 1913. Crystal was sitting right at the table in the Greenwich Village restaurant where he first made overtures to launch the liaison.[154] To coax his new love interest, Bennie said he and Crystal "might separate forever." So much of the time, he told her leadingly, "she was away."[155]

When Crystal was told about what had become a serious relationship, she cried, and resisted the breakup. She asked for two weeks to try to save her marriage. Bennie agreed, but continued seeing his new love in secret. In time Crystal began to accept that her marriage was over, but still procrastinated about filing for divorce.[156] In fact, she would not file until February 1916, when she would famously call alimony "a relic of the past."[157] "Marriage," she would say, was a partnership, a "link, not a handcuff," a "link, not a chain."[158]

Bennie and Brenda married in 1916, by then with Crystal's blessing. "Off you go, Brenda," she wrote, woman to woman. "Got the decree today. Good luck. I hope it means happiness to you. It certainly is a relief to both of us," she said.[159] Before the end of that year, a wedding announcement in the *New York Times* reported vaguely that "some time ago" Crystal too had remarried, to the English pacifist and publicist Walter Fuller.[160] Four months later, her first child was born. She also announced she would be returning to—and forever keeping—her own name.[161] In the interim, Crystal spoke often to newspapers about feminism and marriage, in articles like "Millions of Unpaid Wives."[162] She emphasized what was no doubt on her mind from her own recent conjugal experiences: the need for marriage to accommodate a wife's independence and the imperative of birth control in women's lives.

5 RADICAL PACIFIST

"We must do something besides peace talk," Crystal shouted at a rally in mid-November 1915. She was standing on the doorstep of her downtown office building at 70 Fifth Avenue, where both the Woman's Peace Party of New York City (WPP-NYC) and the American Union Against Militarism (AUAM) would do their work. "So far we have been a party of negation or at least have offset remote plans for world federation against immediate plans for preparedness," she told the crowd near Union Square. "Congress convenes December 6. It's high time we pacifists had a program."[1]

More than a year had passed since war had begun in Europe in early August 1914. It had been ignited by the assassination in Sarajevo, Bosnia, of Archduke Franz Ferdinand, heir apparent to the throne of Austria-Hungary, by the Serbian nationalist Gavrilo Princip. The plot had a deep history in Serbia's fight for independence from the Ottoman Empire, recently stirred to ire when the stormy Balkan region was annexed by Austria-Hungary in 1908. Yet the world's first global war resulted from a runaway chain reaction in international affairs that was set off almost by a fluke.

The archduke and his wife were in Sarajevo on a state visit to inspect the imperial army. It was June 28, a date memorialized by Serbian nationalists as the anniversary of a fourteenth-century battle in Kosovo that they viewed as the turning point in their loss of independence. As the archduke's motorcade wended through the streets of the city, a string of assassins waited along the route. Yet each failed to strike the target. The decisive mishap occurred when one plotter successfully threw a bomb at Ferdinand but missed: it rolled off the archduke's vehicle, wounding some spectators and an officer. Later that day, Ferdinand changed his schedule to visit those injured in the hospital, and on the way his driver took a wrong turn. Princip happened to be sitting in a cafe across the street from a place the archduke was never scheduled to be. As the chauffeur stopped to turn

Crystal Eastman. Amy Aronson, Oxford University Press (2020).
© Oxford University Press.
DOI: 10.1093/oso/9780199948734.001.0001

the car around, Princip walked across the street and fired at point-blank range. Ferdinand and his wife died within the hour.

The shooting sparked a violent reaction that quickly spread across the globe. By July 28, Austria-Hungary declared war on Serbia. From there, security agreements propelled the rapid expansion of hostilities by contractually obligating countries to enter the conflict to protect their stated allies. Combatants in two opposing alliances—the Central Powers, Austria-Hungary and Germany; and the Allies, based on the Triple Entente of 1907 that linked the Russian Empire, the French Third Republic, and the United Kingdom of England and Ireland—entered the war one after another, like dominos.[2] And when the combatants entered, they did so as empires, bringing their colonial territories with them.

For Eastman and many others in her circle, the world seemed to have rushed headlong into a reflexive global conflict. They would soon watch in horror as modern technological weaponry—more powerful cannons, machine guns, new airplane power, and the widespread use of chlorine poison gas—met the defensive strategy of trench warfare to nightmarish effect. Abetted by generals who were unprepared for such methods of war—indeed, many had dismissed the need even to consider them[3]—the conflict quickly sank into a strategic stalemate whose only real result was unprecedented destruction and human slaughter.

A conflict marked by atrocity on this scale required a nearly unprecedented publicity effort to manufacture public support. In Britain, for example, officials would soon launch a massive propaganda campaign in hopes of sustaining public fealty to a war with no clear national purpose and many early casualties. Many of England's most illustrious authors would participate in the War Propaganda Bureau, producing books and pamphlets, posters, slide shows, and films, and giving speeches in support of the Allied war effort. The government publicity campaigns highlighted German atrocities while celebrating the potency of Britain's weaponry and the bonding and brotherhood of her troops. At the same time, stories and images everywhere expressed contempt for unmanly "slackers" who dodged or demurred from what was expertly constructed as the glorious project of war. As the media campaign manufactured consent, the British government quickly expanded its powers in the name of wartime exigency.[4] That was the problem with mainstream militarism: in times deemed national emergencies, the government could use fear of invasion or attack to supersede normal democratic processes and grant itself extraordinary powers, virtually at will.

At least the United States remained a neutral nation, and therefore was in a position to remain calm and see the facts on both sides, Eastman believed. From the start, the facts from the front were gruesome and seemed to make a compelling case for peace. The opening months of the war had produced devastating losses, with more than five million casualties on all fronts in 1914, including more than one million men killed. Just a few months before Crystal exhorted the rally, the bloody stalemate on the Gallipoli peninsula in western Turkey had begun; by the time Allied forces abandoned the campaign they originally believed would crush the Ottomans, eliminating them from the war, more than 140,000 Allied troops, and upward of 250,000 Turkish and Arab soldiers, were killed or wounded there.[5] But as the world's most powerful neutral country, the United States could step in as an honest broker to mediate the conflict, ending such horrific bloodshed and loss of life by negotiating a just and lasting peace settlement. Or so the antiwar activists would continue to hope.

But when a German torpedo sunk the *Lusitania*, the British ocean liner that sailed from New York with cargo including ammunition bound for England, in May 1915, US neutrality began to be tested. More than 120 Americans were killed.[6] The incident galled many in Congress and set off blazing columns in the press to take up arms against Germany. It also prodded President Wilson toward a muscular military buildup dubbed "preparedness"—a defensive precaution, it was argued, just in case American arms were ever needed.

Crystal saw this rising clamor for militarism as the crossroads in the struggle for an American-led negotiated peace agreement and the prospect of a new world that could follow from it. Framed by her open doorway, she contended, "Two opposing fervors cannot possess a mob at the same time. America cannot be thrilled with its destiny as the inaugurator of world peace, and be caught up at the same time in the kind of fear-engendered, jingo-patriotic, pugnacious emotionalism that will vote for $500,000,000 for new battleships on the chance of German or Japanese invasion." A conscious choice now had to be made, she told the crowd. "The national genius cannot be directed to war preparation and genuine peace at the same time."[7]

Eastman and her colleagues believed the prospects for peace could be advanced—or torpedoed—by the mobilization of public demand. For peace to have a chance, the world must pursue new ways of living together, and of imagining itself. The United States must "promote preparedness for peace," the *Survey* proclaimed in January 1915; "we must put the world on a peace footing," Paul Kellogg argued, "instead of a war footing."[8] To do that, both policies and public attitudes had to change. Pragmatically, the world needed preventative mechanisms in international relations, new frameworks to resolve conflicts, and the removal of financial incentives for war. Plus, people's emotional investments had to be reshaped. Antiwar advocates felt they must rebut powerful cultural mythologies about the grandeur and glory of combat with the truth about its bloodshed, brutality, and irretrievable loss. The national genius, they believed, must be thrilled by a different destiny than was now the case: people must be taught to glory in the social and emotional rewards of peace, not war.

Their endeavor was immense. To be successful, they would need to draw together ideas, methods, and constituencies from multiple social movements—Progressive reform, labor unionism, suffrage, plus the burgeoning antiwar movement itself. And they would need to harness the emergent mass media and publicity techniques that increasingly shaped public opinion. But if they did, they could literally change the course of history. They could seed a structure for working together and solving human problems, forever securing permanent peace on earth and so much more. Ultimately, Crystal believed, this movement could change the world.

* * *

As she spoke, Eastman was standing on the threshold of a whole new era—not just in warfare but in the American peace movement as well. In her mother's generation, US peace organizations espoused a genteel brand of moral improvement inherited from even older reform traditions.[9] Led by gentlemanly officers of only local reputation, the venerable American Peace Society, for example, had mainly criticized small conflicts, and with little effect.[10] Righteous but restrained and bookish, even this leading American peace organization lacked energy and optimism. The average age of its members was sixty-three—at a time when the average life expectancy for American men was fifty. And it was out of sync with the changing global dynamics of the rising twentieth century.

As a new millennium dawned on this obsolescent movement, increasing globalization abroad and industrial conflict at home prompted a new peace rationale and approach to advocacy. Peace groups multiplied, many with names that suggested their involvement with democratic ideals—the National Peace Congress, the Universal Peace Union, the World Peace Foundation, and others; however, these groups, often founded or run by social elites and philanthropic industrialists, tended to rely on a business case for peace: war must be ended because it costs money and disrupts commerce.[11] In an era of rising American imperialism and increasing corporatization, commercial expansion soon morphed into the preferred means of maintaining order around the world. Peace projects concerned themselves with arbitration between nation-states conceived rather as business partners, aligning peace work with the values and priorities of global capitalism.[12]

Eastman and others who protested US imperialism in the years following the Spanish-American War largely rejected this capitalistic vision of peace and the nation's role in global affairs. And as calls increased for American muscle and militarism following the sinking of the *Lusitania*, a new breed of antiwar advocate coalesced from multiple quarters in her political life to respond.

They saw themselves as the "new peace movement"—a left-leaning coalition of Progressives, reformers, and citizen change agents, some from the church, education, and labor—who organized to actively confront the emergent logic of modern peacemaking.[13]

These new peace advocates broke with both the genteel reform mentality of the past and the global imperialist business model for peace they felt had rapidly ascended around them. In fact, they soon realized that in the contemporary struggle against war, they were largely fighting the same business mentality, the same mindset favoring profit-making over human needs, that they confronted in their work as Progressive reformers at home. This connection between global and local amplified the peace issue for Crystal, as it did for so many of her colleagues. There could be no progress on any social justice issue in wartime, in a militarist country, or in a world riven by nation-states competing for dominance and plunder, they believed. As a result, for Eastman and others in the new peace movement, opposition to militarism and war became bound together with their critique of the established economic and social structure, blending their quest for peace with the pursuit of a whole new world order.[14]

The resemblances they saw between the causes of violence and suffering at home and of wars around the world generated congruent solutions as well. For Crystal, the clearest vision came from Jane Addams, whose *Newer Ideals of Peace* (1907) had linked the multicultural community of the settlement house movement to the prospect of world peace through global human kinship. The time was coming, Addams had predicted, when "we shall find it as difficult to make war upon a nation at the other side of the globe as upon our next-door neighbor."[15] Eastman shared Addams's international outlook and heartfelt humanitarianism, likewise seeing in American democracy and diversity the living promise of world peace based on global interdependence and mutual respect. And while she would also object to war on more patently Socialist grounds, expressing the view that wars were fought by the poor for the benefit of the wealthy, the Socialist Party offered only critique, not a plan for preventing war or resolving conflict once it began.[16] Addams's arguments were considerably more comprehensive than that.

It was a compelling vision—and not just to Eastman. Addams, Kellogg, and numerous other leading Progressive reformers began developing new thinking about war and peace after the outbreak of violence in Europe. Through 1914 and into 1915, however, Crystal was already widely engaged elsewhere. In fact, she was reaching to bridge two major areas of her social activism—labor rights and women's equality. In May 1915, for example, she testified before the Commission on Industrial Relations as a representative of the Congressional Union. In her remarks, she promoted the National Woman's Party's (NWP's) Party in Power plan, advocating women's suffrage as a means to achieving political equality and also to resolving labor unrest.[17]

At the same time, Eastman's work on behalf of women's rights itself pursued three different avenues at once. Within the suffrage movement, she pushed for the federal amendment as an outspoken member of the Congressional Union and also participated actively in the New York State campaign. In the summer of 1915, for example, she played one of thirteen attendant goddesses in a huge street tableau, riding on a giant float drawn by four white horses that traveled to meet "Lady Liberty" as she returned from Liberty Island on a ship decorated with the yellow, blue, and white colors of the New York State drive.[18] That fall, she spoke for suffrage at a high-profile debate at Carnegie Hall.[19]

Alongside such political work, she was also leading a marketplace-oriented effort to advance women in the workplace. Earlier in the year, she accepted a position as manager of a new Women's Bureau for the Maxwell Motor Company in Los Angeles, promoting women as independent drivers and qualified saleswomen in the burgeoning and male-dominated auto industry.[20] She also joined her friends and fellow suffragists Mary Beard and Mary Simkhovich in a new League for Business Opportunities for Women in New York. "The purposes of the League," it announced, "are to explore the field of opportunity open to women and formulate methods of entrance." The group stood at the leading edge of what became a top issue on the liberal feminist agenda after the vote was won: "equal pay for equal work and equal opportunity to prepare for it."[21]

But the scope and destruction of the escalating war in Europe increasingly pulled Eastman to peace activism, just as it did Addams herself. "My temperament and habit had always kept me rather in the middle of the road; in politics as well as in social reform I had been for the 'best possible,'" Addams said in 1914, "but now I was pushed far towards the left on the subject of war."[22] Eastman already stood further to the left side of the road than Addams, and she was less circumspect by temperament. Yet both women located themselves among the new peaceniks who committed themselves to the enormous idea that the immediate motivations and machinery for international peacemaking could become the foundation of a new social and economic system worldwide.

These antiwar activists sought to redress the reasons people attack and fight: poverty and inequality, lack of democratic voice, male and class entitlement, national pride. They would organize to institute a structure and mechanisms to heal the world's divisions, facilitating a virtuous cycle that would extinguish wars forever. By ending the global cataclysm through reasoned collective agreement, they believed the terms of peace could then inaugurate a worldwide community, an interdependent federation of nations, a "United States of the World," as Crystal described it.[23] Sustained by universal democracy, committed to unity and mutual stability, world federation would end war forever by guaranteeing liberty and justice for all. With justice would come peace—and vice versa.

They came to call the concept "radical internationalism," as their ultimate goal was to end war forever by replacing competing nation-states with a single, global "country," legislated democratically, that would share the earth as one people. For Crystal, this vast and consequential struggle was a logical home. Its radical humanitarian idealism touched her elemental ardor for change, while it also organized the constellation of her political commitments and experiences to date. It brought her back in touch with her mother, who expressed the family's "ancestral interest in the affairs of peace" (in Max's words), almost as often in her letters to her daughter as she had in her lectures and sermons.[24] Beyond that, it touched every aspect of her political identity, synthesizing for that moment her public vision and posture. As a feminist, she could follow her instinct that war was a man's folly made possible in large part by the widespread disenfranchisement of women. As a Socialist, she could fight the profiteering that fueled militarism and conquest. As a reformer, she could battle to preserve the Progressive agenda that was displaced by militarism and abandoned in the prosecution of conflict. She identified with all these perspectives, a convergence of belief and feeling that anchored as it amplified her investment in the radical internationalist peace cause.

The new peace activism also gave increased license to her drive for militancy, which she had already discovered in the suffrage campaigns. The new peace movement must go "aggressively on the offensive," as one AUAM pamphlet would urge, "then concentrate by some practicable method the peace fact and argument and sentiment upon first one and then another of the bulwarks of warfare until it shall fall utterly and forever."[25] This new advocacy called for direct actions—Eastman's emergent forte. "Before the war, the peace movement was a parlor affair and 'goody-goody,'" her friend Louise Bryant quoted one activist saying, but now it promised to "reach the people in the street."[26]

Moved by so many of her deepest social and political instincts, Crystal had first organized for peace more than a year before she rallied people at her office door. In November 1914, she and her friends Madeleine Doty and Ida Rauh had organized an antiwar speech by the English suffragette Emmeline Pethick-Lawrence at New York's Carnegie Hall.[27] Pethick-Lawrence was touring the United States calling for a permanent end to warfare. She outlined four mechanisms to achieve world peace already floated in Britain by the left-wing foreign policy group the Union of Democratic Control: a federation of nations supported by "some kind of international agreement" or a "European senate" whereby law-abiding countries would protect each other if attacked; an agreement that no nation would absorb another without the consent of its native peoples; nationalization of the

munitions industries and a ban on the export of weapons; and, to ensure democratic control of foreign policy, ratification of all international treaties by popular
vote. Most distinctive was her insistence that this would be a women's peace crusade.[28] Pethick-Lawrence proposed combining the emergent campaign for neutral mediation with the international suffrage movement, asserting that women's
voices must be heard on global policy now and forever through equal suffrage
worldwide.

Pethick-Lawrence was a compelling speaker—Crystal would later say "she
has not only emotional power, but shrewd wit, great cogency, and a gift of ridicule which with her smile and essentially generous personality, is as disarming as
praise."[29] What's more, her US tour was only half of a coordinated women's effort
involving the Hungarian suffragist Rosika Schwimmer, whom Crystal knew from
the 1913 International Woman Suffrage Alliance (IWSA) congress in Budapest
before the war. With the assistance of Carrie Catt, Schwimmer would meet with
both President Wilson and William Jennings Bryan, now serving as secretary of
state, and present the two men with resolutions for a mediated peace settlement
signed by women from thirteen countries. She then followed those meetings
with a national tour urging the women of America, the most powerful neutral
nation, to pressure the president to act immediately to end the fighting.[30]

So while Schwimmer was pressing for an immediate cessation of hostilities,
Pethick-Lawrence was barnstorming for long-term policies to ensure a permanent peace after that. And what united the two women more than any particular
proposal (indeed, the two differed on several points of policy) was their belief
that this catastrophic conflict was literally man-made. Both viewed the world
war as a masculine escapade—a shocking example of "male statecraft," Pethick-
Lawrence said—with women and children as its chief victims.[31]

Charlotte Perkins Gilman had previously articulated the broad connection between masculinity and war. In *Man-Made World* (1911) she argued, "In warfare, PER
SE, we find maleness in its absurdist extremes. Here is . . . the whole gamut of basic
masculinity, from the initial instinct of combat, through every form of glorious os-
tentation with the loudest possible accompaniment of noise."[32] Gilman understood
that gender is not natural in us, but rather is socially constructed and performed
for others; her work presaged contemporary research arguing that masculinity, always insecure, must be continually proved through demonstrations of virility like
dominance and aggression, mainly for validation by other men.[33] The public sphere
generally and violent warfare in particular were male-dominated theaters where the
negative effects of this gender drama play out over and over again.

Pethick-Lawrence now argued that the world's women, the vast majority
of whom lacked a public voice, including the right to vote, bore "no responsibility whatever" for the global catastrophe. Indeed, she characterized the war as a

masculine outrage to all womanhood, a wanton destroyer of the precious human lives women bear and nurture with their own.[34] The logic and language of "maternal instinct"—"the mother half of humanity" as these peace women referred to it—has remained a premise for women's social action through the twentieth century and beyond. In Eastman's time, it would powerfully draw women across regions, nations, and political perspectives to the peace cause.[35] "Men have conflicting interests and ambitions," Pethick-Lawrence argued, but "the solidarity of the world's motherhood, potential or otherwise, underlies all cleavages of nationality. Women all the world over, speaking broadly, have one passion and one vocation, and that is the creation and preservation of human life."[36]

Crystal had met maternalist sentiment in her earlier political work but never saw it wielded as powerfully as at the very start of the war. In August 1914, a "march of mourners" was organized in New York by Fanny Garrison Villard, daughter of the eminent abolitionist William Lloyd Garrison and mother of Oswald Garrison Villard, soon to become Eastman's colleague in the AUAM. More than 1,500 women from many countries, dressed all in black, had processed down Fifth Avenue carrying banners decorated with doves and olive branches. They were silent except for the beat of muffled drums. The women marched "not as nations," the *New York Times* reported, "but as sorrowing women together."[37] As "the custodians of life for all ages," peace women would assert, women "will no longer consent to its reckless destruction."[38]

Pethick-Lawrence's speech just a few months later inspired Eastman to form a women-only peace party right in New York City, thus launching the first formal feminist peace organization in American history.[39] Under her leadership, the organization would grow quickly, boasting a membership of fifty thousand by 1916. With a relatively small group of downtown radicals at its operational core—including Doty, Margaret Lane, Freda Kirchwey, Anne Herendeen, and Marie Jenney Howe—the WPP-NYC operated a nationwide press service and organized an impressive array of demonstrations, mass meetings, and congressional hearings.

At the outset, Eastman urged Pethick-Lawrence to meet with Addams in hopes of securing her support to form a national organization.[40] When both Schwimmer and Pethick-Lawrence traveled to Chicago for the meeting, Addams was not particularly receptive to the idea of a separate women's peace movement at first.[41] She thought it contradicted the whole idea of gender equality.[42] But in this case, she told Lucia Ames Mead, a veteran peace advocate long associated with the American Peace Society, "the demand has been so universal and spontaneous over the country that it seemed to me best to take it up."[43]

Eastman experienced less dissonance than Addams did between her egalitarian gender politics and a separate women's peace movement justified by the claim of maternal instinct. Like Addams, she certainly recognized the political expediency of this widely legitimized notion of female identity in American society. Yet Crystal also responded to the authenticity she felt in the idea of a woman's instinct to nurture human life. She would continue to speak of a powerful maternal urge herself and would often peg later political positions in the feminist movement to her belief that the vast majority of women, irrespective of differences in perspective or station, shared a deep desire to be mothers. Both voices, political and personal, are audible in her correspondence with Addams about a women-only organization for peace. "It seems to me that the Woman's Peace Party, if it is going to be a real power, ought frankly to make capital out of the fact that it expresses a woman's protest," she began. Then, as she continued, she drifted somewhat from public strategy into a sense of passionate private feeling that she imputed to the women involved. "From the beginning, it seemed to me that the only reason for having a woman's peace party is that women are mothers, or potential mothers, [and] therefore have a more intimate sense of the value of human life." As a result, "there is more meaning and passion in the determination of a woman's organization to end war than in an organization of men and women with the same aim."[44]

Eastman sometimes tussled at the boundary that separates the two fundamental arguments in gender policy to this day: the claim to equal rights based on the "sameness" of men and women and the assumption of sex differences that must be born in mind. Politically, she was a passionate exponent of the "sameness" position, the defining principle of the Equal Rights Amendment. Yet privately she also felt the pull of some part of the "difference" idea, at least when it came to maternal feeling, to "women's greater regard for life, both intellectually and emotionally," as she would tell Addams.[45] On a practical level, both women were involved with the women-only WPP as well as the AUAM, whose leadership and membership included both women and men. But Eastman and Addams each operated from a somewhat different rationale and blend of emotional investments.

The national organization of the Woman's Peace Party was formally established in Washington, DC, in January 1915, just two months after the Pethick-Lawrence event in New York. More than three thousand women packed the Grand Ballroom of the New Willard Hotel for a huge founding conference. They spanned a broad political spectrum—suffragists and social workers, teachers and temperance groups, women's club members and settlement house workers, women trade unionists, and even some representatives from the conservative Daughters of the Revolution were there. Addams presided while the seventy-seven official delegates elected officers including Fanny Villard, the suffragist and Unitarian minister Anna Garlin Spencer, and Alice Thatcher Post, the wife of the assistant secretary of labor and an active Progressive reformer in her own right. They drew up an eleven-point program that Eastman would pursue unreservedly for the next three years. It included mediation of the war in Europe, the appointment of a commission of men and women to promote international peace, the nationalization of arms manufacture, democratic control of foreign policy, the removal of the economic causes of war, and women's suffrage.[46]

Several of these peace ideas carried edgy political overtones. It was only the Socialist Party that was decrying the economic incentives to war at the time, and mainly European peace groups that staked a claim for democratic control of foreign policy. The idea of mediation itself was acquiring associations with disrepute as popular speakers began labeling antiwar groups "peace-at-any-price leagues" and touting the inherent "morality" in the American right to bear arms.[47] Yet it was the suffrage plank that proved the most controversial for the WPP, sparking internal conflict that only Addams's stature and diplomatic skill could quell.

Some peace women feared the suffrage plank would reduce membership in the organization, as well as its potential for impact. To some extent, they would turn out to be right; suffrage would limit the growth of the WPP in several states.[48] Still, the organization gained membership steadily, reaching its peak in early 1916 at about forty thousand women. Tensions would persist, however, not only around the issue of suffrage itself, but also around the distinctions between different styles of suffrage-learned activism: the Congressional Union–style militancy of women like Crystal and her New York branch would clash with WPP colleagues like those in Boston, who were politically and temperamentally more conservative and connected to the more mainstream National American Woman Suffrage Association (NAWSA). These differences simmered for years but flared most definitively after the US declaration of war in April 1917.

Overall, the WPP brought collective methods and its international character to bear in its work. At the rally held on the second night of the founding conference, Carrie Catt, who, like Addams, had warmed to the idea of the organization, gave a blazing address. So did Gilman, who memorably proclaimed, "One cannot make peace all alone, any more than one can make war all alone."[49] Applying this insight, the women proposed cooperative international approaches to ending the war and to maintaining the peace, including a novel process for neutral mediation developed by one of its younger delegates. Julia Grace Wales, a University of Wisconsin instructor, had devised a plan for "Continuous Mediation without Armistice"—essentially, a diplomatic incubator where experts from neutral nations would propose ideas for a peace settlement, then circulate them to the belligerents for their responses on an ongoing basis until an agreeable resolution was found.[50] As a forum for resolving international disputes, it was not far off the central idea of the League of Nations later proposed by Woodrow Wilson as part of his historic Fourteen Points of 1918.[51]

The WPP lobbied hard and at the highest levels for neutral mediation—this version and other variations—into 1916, at which time the ill-fated "Ford Peace Ship" significantly undermined the credibility of the whole concept. In December 1915, the industrialist Henry Ford initiated and funded a grand expedition to carry citizen delegates to a people's peace conference of neutral nations to mediate an end to the war. He expected the mission to carry so many peace notables and to generate such public fanfare that it would impel a substantive convention upon its arrival in Europe. However, by the time the ship reached Oslo, Norway, the hoped-for reception by neutral nations never really materialized. Poor organization and infighting among the activists involved, accompanied by ridicule from the press, including the contingent on board, sapped the venture.[52]

Eastman had been invited to go on the Peace Ship but declined. She told Addams, who ultimately withdrew from the mission herself, that "as an enterprise of a body of individuals following a leader who believes he has a vision, I think it is rather inspiring after all." However, she noted astutely, "it is not deliberate and planned enough to be the undertaking of an organization."[53] Until the Peace Ship flop, however, neutral mediation, and cooperative mechanism to organize and advance it, was the centerpiece of the WPP program, one practical illustration of the alternatives the women would bring to the table were they given a seat.[54]

Crystal unabashedly celebrated the new perspective brought forward by the women's peace movement, calling it "unique and priceless."[55] In 1915, she covered the historic International Congress of Women at The Hague for the *Survey*. The huge gathering of peace women was organized by the Dutch feminist Aletta Jacobs in late April, just as British and French forces suddenly launched the brash and tragic campaign at Gallipoli. Eastman was not among the forty-seven delegates from the United States, but she and the WPP-NYC organized a farewell dinner in their honor the night before their ship, the *Noordam*, left New York harbor. That women-only event was attended by more than 400 supporters, whose hosts, the papers reported, told them to "check their husbands at the door."[56] Despite wartime travel dangers, interference by some governments that withheld passports, and derision from the global press, which disparaged the delegates as a "shipload of hysterical women" and the entire meeting as "folly in petticoats," more than 1,100 peace women managed to reach the Netherlands from twelve countries. The assembly included representatives from combatant nations from both sides of the war and, predominantly, the neutrals.[57]

Eastman pronounced the meeting itself a world-changing event. "The fact that warring nations met and discussed the war problems sanely and in friendship while all their male relatives were out shooting each other is to my mind a great and significant event in history—significant in the history of human progress."[58] The internationalist peace women brought an entirely new energy and attitude to peacemaking, she observed. They "do not seem to be driven by personal ambition, and yet they tackle big, unheard-of undertakings like The Hague meeting and succeed with them. Simplicity, directness, the glorious courage of children to whom everything is possible because it is untried,—these are the qualities women are bringing into the new world councils."[59]

The assembly's most novel new approach followed the conclusion of the meeting. The group organized two delegations of women to carry appeals for peace talks to leaders in both combatant and neutral nations. Addams bravely led a delegation to belligerents with American members including Emily Greene Balch, Julia Grace Wales, and the physician, medical investigator, and Hull House resident Alice Hamilton; Schwimmer, who had proposed and vigorously advocated the idea, led a group to visit the neutrals. Despite the lack of any official standing, the two delegations conferred with officials of fourteen European governments in five weeks.

Still, a women-only crusade was not enough for Eastman. By July 1915, when she stood in a drenching rain to meet Addams's ship at New York Harbor as she returned from Europe, Crystal had begun meeting with an informal collective of about three dozen social workers and liberal clergy who had formed what they referred to as a roundtable conference on the war.[60] They called themselves the Henry Street Group, taking their name from their original meeting place, the Henry Street Settlement founded by Lillian Wald. Before Eastman joined, Wald viewed the group as a very tentative exploratory committee, a place for concerned Progressives to put their heads together. "This round table is suggested as a means by which in humbleness and quiet, some of us who deal with the social fabric may come together to clarify our minds, and, if it seems wise, to act in concert," she said.[61]

Such care and circumspection were characteristic of Wald. She was the well-bred daughter of an affluent family in Rochester, New York, who had come to Manhattan to train as a nurse. Fourteen years Eastman's senior, she was a recognized spokeswoman for women's rights and child welfare, a Progressive investigator and supporter of labor women organizing, and the founder of the Visiting Nurse Service.[62] Much of this work had proceeded from Henry Street itself. The poverty and suffering she witnessed as one of the first public health nurses in the United States led her to establish the settlement, and soon to organize in-home health care with a sliding fee scale for the industrial laborers and working poor who lived in the Lower East Side tenements all around it. As Henry Street grew, providing a wide range of classes and community services typical of the settlement house movement, the health service expanded as well; it

distributed hundreds of thousands of pamphlets aimed at public health education and, by the time the European war broke out in 1914, was providing care to
more than 175,000 patients in nearly 1,700 cities and towns across the United
States and Canada.[63]

Wald was one of the most effective women reform agents of her era.[64]
Charming, politic, and determined, she was known as an astute listener who
expended her cultural capital cautiously. These qualities diverged from Eastman's
strengths at almost every turn. In 1903, the year Crystal graduated from
Vassar, for example, Wald helped to found the Women's Trade Union League
(WTUL), a group whose function was to investigate the working conditions of
women and both optimize existing trade unions and organize new ones in all
trades where women were employed.[65] Crystal became an avid member of the
WTUL, excitedly paying her membership dues two years in advance in 1912,
when she was working in Wisconsin—"the fartherest ahead paid up member
we have," the Chicago office told her.[66] By contrast, Wald, though a founder,
quietly left the organization around that same time. She had encountered fric-
tion from WTUL colleagues over what they saw as her middle-class sensibility,
and from some friends, including Florence Kelley, for her cordiality toward the
American Federation of Labor's Samuel Gompers, whose conservative attitudes
and policies many labor women decried as ill-disposed to women workers. Some
contemporaries believed that Wald withdrew from the WTUL so that she did
not alienate conservatives and businessmen who funded her nursing service and
her settlement.[67]

In electoral politics, similarly, Wald cultivated her clout quietly and deployed
it with care. From her early years at Henry Street, she worked with mayoral and
gubernatorial candidates in New York, educating several governors on the social
issues to which she was committed, then cannily letting them know the value of
her support. In 1908, she had informed the newly elected governor Charles Evans
Hughes, a Progressive and the only Republican candidate for statewide office to
win in that election year, that she had formed a League of Independent Voters at
Henry Street. Women were still nearly a decade from suffrage in New York State,
but Wald conveyed to Hughes that the group could distinctly benefit him anyway. Her group had been established "not so much for vote-getting as for interpretation," she told him, insinuating their capacity to frame and shape the public
perception of his reform agenda.[68] When the victorious Hughes later formed a
Commission on Immigration, he chose Wald as one of two women appointed
to serve.

Women like Eastman may have benefited, directly or indirectly, from the
increased sway Wald's efforts brought home to Hughes; it was in early 1909 that
he appointed her to chair the Commission on Employer Liability. But in the

presidential election of 1912, Wald had laid low, demurring from an endorsement of any national candidate in what became a divided, three-party contest. Addams and some other suffragists had decided to support Teddy Roosevelt's breakaway Progressive Party, which acquired the "Bull Moose" nickname after Roosevelt's fiery speech at the Republican convention in which he said he felt "as strong as a bull moose" as the country stood "at Armageddon and we battle for the Lord."[69] Whatever else, Roosevelt had formally endorsed suffrage, and like many reformers, Addams also saw a chance for several other Progressive aspirations to attain national focus through the Bull Moose platform. Wald—like Addams— objected to Roosevelt's militarism, and she could not support the Democrat, Wilson, because he opposed suffrage. Supporting Taft, the Republican candidate, was out of the question for her. Wald's solution was to decline public endorse- ment of any candidate, then to quietly join the New York State Convention of the National Progressive Party as a member of its permanent legislative committee.[70]

As the world war raged into a second year, the Henry Street Group evolved into an increasingly substantial organization. The mixed-gender cadre put forward a radical internationalist peace program that overlapped considerably with that of the WPP, from its drive for US-led neutral mediation to the complete demo- cratic restructuring of national self-determination and international relations. Yet the two groups diverged somewhat in tone and temperament, owing to the gender differences in their leadership, membership, and organizational rationales.

Crystal, a leader in both organizations, tried to bridge the character of the two groups. In July 1915, she wrote "To Make War Unthinkable," a letter to the editor of the *New Republic* that argued the groups' shared policy goal "to de- vise the substitute, or substitutes for war—to start the political genius of the world thinking, inventing, along this line," and then articulated a gender-attuned hope to reshape the relational reflexes of society. "Our function is to establish new values," she continued, "so that when international disputes arise, even of the most grave character—when lives have been lost, when our rights have been clearly invaded—we shall not turn to wholesale, deliberate destruction of life as the means of settling those disputes, of avenging those deaths, of asserting those rights." At the heart of the peace project lay a simple yet awesome respect for hu- manity, resonant of the maternalist voice. If they could "create an overpowering sense of the sacredness of life," she believed, war would become "unthinkable" to people worldwide.[71]

Bearing such momentous designs, the struggle for world peace and interna- tionalism would dominate Crystal's political panorama for the next several years. Her methods were relatively straightforward, involving Progressive-era logic in- creasingly enhanced by bold and sophisticated tactics of modern militancy. She combined a policy vision with public education designed to reshape America's international outlook over the long term, and used protest, magnified by publicity techniques and the media, to challenge immediately any policies that seemed to undermine progress toward that goal. In June 1915, she mobilized the New York branch of the WPP in a mass meeting at Cooper Union to "protest against the beginning of militarism in America under the guise of 'Preparedness.' "[72] In the fall, the New York branch mounted a two-week educational forum on "America's Future Foreign Policy" designed to seed the vision and values of pacifist internationalism across the country. The group scheduled high-profile speakers including William I. Hull, a Quaker and Swarthmore history professor, author of the book *The New Peace Movement* (1912); Frederic C. Howe, the commissioner of immigration of the Port of New York and husband of Eastman's suffrage colleague, the founder of Heterodoxy, Marie Jenney Howe; Inez Milholland; the eminent Columbia professor John Dewey; and Stanford University's chancellor and president emeritus, David Starr Jordan.

Also a headliner was Norman Angell, the future Labour member for Parliament and Nobel Prize winner who authored *The Great Illusion* (1909), a bestseller that argued Europe's increasing economic integration would function to prevent wars. Since conflict would be equally damaging to all parties involved, Angell contended, economic self-interest would effectively rule them out. When the book's avid audiences embraced battle just a few years later, he immediately cofounded Britain's Union of Democratic Control. His career demonstrated a number of dilemmas with which Eastman and her colleagues wrestled: that wars, like economies, can proceed on less-than-rational grounds, and that self-interest is a variable—and malleable—sociological and cultural idea. Angell's international star power helped the WPP's wide-ranging public education effort attract large crowds: afternoon sessions were attended by up to 200 people each, and the six evening sessions drew up to 2,500.[73]

In speaking of the education forum, Crystal asked, "Are we going to preserve peace by preparing to fight" or do it, she offered—channeling Addams—"by initiating some new kind of world understanding that shall make war between civilized nations impossible?" Her answer reflected her spiritual idealism blended with the empirical heft of her graduate study, her work in the settlement house movement, and her experiences in New York City every day: "I believe if we can get groups of people in different parts of the country to studying international questions and the various phases of America's foreign policy in relation to the ultimate ideal we all acknowledge of world peace, there will be some chance of America's going forth to her destiny with clear-eyed wisdom and courage." She felt even then that the country stood to usher in not just world peace, but a new multicultural order that could bring everlasting human harmony to the world: "the beginning of a kind of international enthusiasm based on a warm, real knowledge of other races and their contribution to the world's values—a delight in the culture of other nations as well as our own—and eagerness to see it survive."[74]

To nurture that possibility, radical internationalists would have to undertake campaigns to challenge a range of worldly forces and policies. In her first official weeks with the Henry Street Group, Eastman offered two pragmatic proposals. Since the sinking of the *Lusitania* had awakened martial impulses in the culture and the US Congress, she proposed dampening them with a bill to raise the income and inheritance taxes to pay for all the new armaments. She also called for an investigation of the arms industry and its lucrative government contracts in an attempt to expose a financial relationship that would much later be dubbed the "military industrial complex."[75] Wald and the executive committee voted to adopt them both.

The same week, she published her manifesto, "A Platform of Real Preparedness," in the *Survey*. True to her aims, she offered a multiplank program, which debunked the mainstays of the leading preparedness advocates and supplied internationalist alternatives. Eastman denounced blatant profiteering in the arms buildup at the heart of the preparedness strategy and excoriated America's imperialist policies as racist and hypocritical, as well as catalysts to war. The country's "incongruous possessions and entangling alliances," as she characterized them, foment international conflict, and all to maintain unjust dominion over people who by all human right are entitled to self-determination. "Many of us are out of patience with America's recent imperialist ventures," she announced, pointing to California's "oriental exclusion policy" on the Pacific coast and particularly to the controversial annexation of the Philippines after Spain ceded this long-standing territory to the United States in 1898, at the end of the Spanish-American War. "Surely there is no benefit conceivably to be gained for us, for the Filipinos, or for humanity at large, by our continued rule over those islands," she argued, "which would warrant us in entering upon an international conflict to maintain that rule." Eastman then called for Philippine independence by 1916, a full thirty years before the US government would formally recognize the island nation in 1946.

Most of all, she assailed the "possibly indefensible" Monroe Doctrine, which she called a "chief bulwark of the preparedness campaign" because prowar politicians repeatedly cited the protection of South America republics as a reason the United States must further enlarge its military. Instead, she advocated an established internationalist alternative, a pan-American federation between North and South America, which, she declared, would not only prevent imperialist wars but also "stand for the maintenance of republican ideals."[76].

Threaded through Eastman's commentary is her critique of the emotional instability she saw driving the country into a rush to take up arms. She repeatedly called for Americans to take time to think. "America can, *if her people stay in the right frame of mind*," she emphasized, "initiate some new kind of world understanding which shall make war between civilized nations unnecessary, impossible."[77]

When it came to the national mood on preparedness and war, President Wilson's fluctuating pronouncements on relevant policy did not help. He had for months been offering shifting signals on the international mechanisms for peace, first appearing to advance American neutrality and mediation, then seeming to speak at variance with that approach and that goal. While he provided reassurance of his commitment to US neutrality in multiple public statements through 1914, the gruesome process and progress of the war coupled with various entreaties to US involvement—not least the growing financial benefits and broad economic stimulus to be had in supplying the European conflict—were riling Congress and the public.

Soon some in public life, notably Teddy Roosevelt, were touting the social and cultural advantages of increased American militarism. Early in 1915, Roosevelt revived his advocacy for compulsory military training for all high school boys, arguing it would simultaneously institute discipline, increase manly vigor, and organize a desirable democratic leveling in society through universal training.[78] When the sinking of the *Lusitania* in May triggered a wave of calls for a commanding US response, the Henry Street Group stepped up plans to combat what Wald would soon characterize as "various forms of the prevailing hysteria" about the virtues of expanding militarism.[79] As she told the House Committee on Military Affairs, the antimilitarists feared "the contagious quality of war."[80]

As 1915 drew to a close, the result of such political agitation in the country was Wilson's official declaration of the US policy of preparedness. In his new National Defense Bill in December, the president proposed substantial increases in the size and capacity of both the army and navy, framing the move as a means to keep the peace. In a speech before the Manhattan Club, he announced, "The mission of America in the world is essentially a mission of peace and good will among men." The "principles we hold most dear can be achieved by the slow processes of history only in the kindly and wholesome atmosphere of peace, and not by the use of hostile force." As such, he explained, he wanted to build "an army adequate to the constant and legitimate uses of the time and of international peace."[81]

The very next day, the Henry Street Group became the Anti-Preparedness Committee. In a press release, the committee announced it had "formed to protect against the attempt to stampede this nation into a dangerous program of military and naval expansion. We believe that no danger of invasion threatens this country, and that there is no excuse for hasty ill-considered action." They protested this high-octane distraction from the pursuit of neutral mediation and Progressive welfare legislation alike. Their statement called out "the effort being made to divert the public mind from those preparations for World Peace based on International agreement which it might be America's privilege to initiate at the close of this war," as well as "the effort being made to divert public funds, sorely needed in constructive programs for National health and wellbeing, into the manufacture of engines of death."[82]

The press statement was signed by Crystal and Max Eastman, Wald, Kellogg, Florence Kelley, Zona Gale, and colleagues including the pacifist Reverend John Haynes Holmes, the physician and Socialist James Warbasse, the actress and Progressive Alice Lewisohn, the political journalist Charles T. Hallinan, and the Zionist leader and National Association for the Advancement of Colored People (NAACP) cofounder Rabbi Stephen Wise. The new group was more nimble than the sprawling WPP, with its national headquarters in Chicago and array of affiliated but independent branches. Crystal characterized the committee as a "small, active junta"—informed, connected, and capable of rapid response to relevant proposals and policy shifts as they emerged in Washington and around the country.[83]

Their strategy was to take to the corridors of power, as well as the streets. At the outset, they would use their influence with the antipreparedness minority in Congress to weaken, if not kill, the impending National Defense Bill. Toward that end, Crystal scheduled a packed trip to Washington in early 1916. She spoke at the first annual convention of the WPP on January 9–10, a sizeable affair that raised nearly $10,000. The gathering voted to adopt all four of her proposals, including not only an investigation of America's defense expenditures and the formation of a Pan-American Union but also a motion protesting the adoption of military programs in schools. She then gave an animated speech, "Limitation of Armament," in which she mocked the faulty logic of preparedness, telling an audience of peace women that it amounted to a masculine moral panic:

> Soldiers, editors, lawyers, business men are frightened. There is nothing new since Ezekiel's time in their terror and declaration that the enemy is upon us. Have you . . . seen the cartoon in which President Wilson, as a little figure, faces the great army of munition [sic] makers and cries out, "but we have no enemies!" and they retort, "Buy our guns and we will see that you have an enemy." They are saying to Congress, "Never mind the death of democracy, nor our foreign policies, whether they be just or

unjust, but prepare!" In the face of this, we say to Congress, "Gentlemen, wait; go slow. We are not afraid."[84]

Crystal called out the fact that the preparedness campaign was "built upon a lie" born of masculine thinking—the notion that a bullying display of aggressive force would make people safer. "Millions are dying in Europe to prove that is a lie," she insisted. She ended with a slogan both the WPP and AUAM would use again and again through 1916: "The road to war is paved with 'preparedness.'"

She had been saying for months that the preparedness crusade was using "loose thinking" and "bad psychology." In less gender-specific contexts, she used the metaphor of a burning rooftop to make the point that a military buildup acts as an accelerant that inevitably increases the risk of spreading a conflagration rather than reducing it. "It is a dangerous time for us—every morning we seem to face a new crisis," she warned. "A fire as big as that with only the ocean between us is bound to scorch us." Accordingly, she submitted,

> it is only by keeping cool, by playing the hose on our roofs all the time, by stowing all inflammable and combustibles out of sight, that we can keep from catching fire. To start in just now on a great program of naval expansion, to spend millions on submarines and battleships, to increase the standing army, to start military training camps, to talk, think, and act "preparation for war," is, psychologically speaking, like pouring kerosene on the roofs instead of water. Sparks are bound to fall—if they fall on cool wet roofs there is a chance of their going out. If they fall on dry roofs prepared with kerosene, what chance is there?[85]

Crystal consistently articulated her fervent belief that the sacrifice of American neutrality for nationalistic preparedness would be a fateful mistake at a consequential juncture in history. Proponents "urge it upon us although it means abandoning the brightest hope a nation ever had," she asserted as the voice of the AUAM in late 1915.[86] This moment was "America's opportunity to conceive and propose the method that shall bring the new spirit of internationalism," she repeated at the 1916 WPP convention in Washington. "If [our leaders] commit us to a 'preparedness' program, we lose the greatest opportunity a nation ever had."[87]

Simultaneous with the WPP meeting, the House and Senate committees on military affairs were beginning hearings about preparedness. Eastman conferred with Robert La Follette and Luke Lea of Tennessee, the members of the Senate Committee on Military Affairs whom she knew to be friendly to the antipreparedness position. She then testified before the House Committee on

Foreign Affairs alongside WPP colleagues including Addams, long-time peace advocate Lucia Ames Mead, and University of Chicago professor Sophonisba Breckinridge. Her remarks began with a series of everyday hypotheticals designed to debunk what she called the "false analogy" circulating in male-dominated Washington between military preparedness and homeowners' insurance or medical checkups, two commonplace means of providing a sense of security that do not, however, prevent disastrous outcomes. Once again, she unfurled the dangerous logic of escalation embedded in preparedness arguments, this time taking the role of the other countries that would be interpreting US government actions. "It is only in its own eyes that a nation arms for defense," she told the papers in late 1915.[88] Now, she elaborated, the combatants will know "in their hearts, that [Congress is] preparing us not for peace, but for war, and they believe that war is coming, and is bound to come, and that we want to have a good fight, and want the United States to be in it with flying colors and take a good part."[89]

Then Crystal seems to have gone off script, taking the opportunity to expound before Congress on WPP and AUAM policy ideas beyond the immediate problems with the National Defense Bill. She strenuously criticized the Monroe Doctrine, and outlined an internationalist world order that rejected imperialism and transcended nation-states, with all the competitive conflicts they bring. In its place she called for "unnationalism," then went rogue, promising a series of legislative proposals it appears the organization had never agreed even to mention to lawmakers.

> We would suggest that we propose this year, as a direct offset to a program of military preparedness, to bring about this Pan American Union that everybody is talking about. . . . We see in it . . . the first and most possible example of a federation of nations, . . . with emphasis on good will, on cooperation, on agreement to arbitrate all their difficulties; we see . . . a chance to put off the desperate emergency measure of greatly increased armament, and we hope to have before you before many weeks, for your consideration, well-drawn, practical bills calling for action along this line. Are there any questions, gentlemen?[90]

At that point, Addams closed off any potential questions by interjecting an apology for Crystal's policy range. "Mr. Chairman and gentlemen of the committee, I find myself a little embarrassed," she said, "because we seem to be instructing you. That is not what we intended to do at all."[91]

Two weeks later, on January 24, President Wilson announced that he would personally take a speaking tour to promote preparedness. As soon as he did, the

Anti-Preparedness Committee decided to launch a publicity counteroffensive, albeit a comparatively subdued one at first. At an executive committee meeting the same day, the committee agreed they would follow him, sending large quantities of cheap but effective literature to their allies in every city on the president's schedule. They decided to delay more elaborate plans until they could assess the effectiveness of this first line of attack.[92]

The following week, the WPP-NYC kicked off a local challenge to military training in the public schools. When the New York State legislature introduced a bill requiring compulsory military exercises in high schools, the group answered with a mass meeting at Cooper Union on January 31 to protest what they characterized as an "invasion of our public school system by military authorities and enthusiasts."[93] Beginning February 14, the group held a free week-long Training School for Speakers every afternoon from 4:30 to 6:00. Through the program, thirty to forty women learned their arguments against preparedness. After the final session, eight cars bedecked with bright blue peace flags were deployed through the streets bearing a slogan across the back: "Woman's Peace Party. America Is Safe. Preparedness Means War. Work against It."[94]

The demonstration was modeled exactly on the automobile tours Eastman had run for suffrage in Wisconsin. The vehicles met at the WPP-NYC offices, filled with speakers, then paraded up and down Fifth Avenue for an hour. Then the cars scattered to the various districts, escorting speakers to meetings. Everywhere they went they distributed literature. "Although it was a cold day," Crystal's close friend and colleague Margaret Lane reported that some cars held open-air meetings where 150 people listened for an hour to their arguments against preparedness.[95] They would follow the same model all spring. As the first of a multistate wave of pro-preparedness parades began in New York in May, the WPP-NYC countered with an antipreparedness demonstration with two truck-size floats. The first was decorated with German and French flags and carried young boys at play with baseball bats. Its streamer read, "Boys are boys in Germany and France." The second carried American boys bearing rifles and delivered the message "Boys are now soldiers in New York State."[96]

Eastman and the WPP-NYC had hired Walter Fuller to help with their citywide antipreparedness events. Fuller had first come to the United States from England in 1912 as an impresario and business manager for the Fuller Sisters, a singing group composed of three of his four sisters: Dorothy, the eldest; Rosalind, who later became a celebrated actress of stage, radio, and screen; and Cynthia. Costumed in nineteenth-century dresses, the three siblings performed folk songs, their harmonies recalling an era of simplicity that, if it ever existed, was now vanishing into modernity. Walter, a budding PR man before the profession really existed as such, promoted them; folk songs, he claimed, "are a voice from secret places, from silent people and from old times dear, and as such they stir us in a strangely intimate fashion."[97] The group caught on.

When the war broke out, the Fuller Sisters had just finished a successful concert tour and were back in England. But they returned to the United States in November 1914 for a string of East Coast bookings. Their songs, some traditional English folk tunes and some original pieces written by Walter for his sisters, now helped advance the age-old linkage between folk music and antiwar sentiment that still resonates more than a century later. "There are any number of old English and Scottish songs which prove that the humble people have always been against war," the Fullers told the press.[98] Before long, the trio came to the notice of rising American peace groups, including the main Chicago branch of the WPP. In her memoir, *Twenty Years at Hull House* (1910), Jane Addams recalled one of the group's original numbers, Walter Fuller's masterpiece called "Five Souls," saying it "poignantly expressed what many of us felt in those first months of the war."[99]

By June 1915, Walter was shifting from concert impresario to peace campaigner, using his creative talent and promotional skills to develop pageants and other interactive events designed to educate and arouse the public in the antiwar cause. That is how he met Crystal in September. He was taken with her virtually on sight, appreciating her looks, dauntlessness, and political breadth. "She is a very striking, attractive person," he wrote to his baby sister Riss. "She is very American—in the New York sense of the word—no respecter of persons—no sentimentality—no Europeanized refinements. She's rather a smart dresser—though she's a little daring in the matter of colours. She's a fierce Suffragette, and whenever she isn't working for the Peace Party she is speaking at street corners for suffrage, I'm told."[100]

The two were compatible in crucial ways: "she enjoys my fancy, my wit and humor and suggestiveness," Walter said, "and I encourage her strength of mind and purpose, and her activity."[101] They had an almost immediate meeting of the minds. "I was talking with her, and urging my old idea about the need for Pacifists to go out in the highways and hedges, and educate the people there," he told Riss.[102] Crystal too believed in hitting the streets to change people's minds, in talking to people "in a language that is familiar to them, and one which they can understand," as Walter put it.[103] And they shared a sophisticated ambition to engage people's understanding—their emotional lives as much as their rational minds—and an instinctive sense that by incorporating emergent electronic media, such as photography and film, they could both amplify and deepen their effectiveness.

In fact, when they first met, the pair quickly decided to make a movie together. Crystal had conceived a satirical script about a German invasion of the United States based on an article by Ray Stannard Baker, the muckraking *American*

Magazine cofounder and author of an early book on American race relations, *Following the Color Line* (1908). Walter saw the potential immediately, and as they talked over the idea, he told Riss, they "began to see such vast opportunities that we arranged to collaborate in the writing of a scenario (as moving-picture plots are called)."[104] Over the next few weeks, Walter and Crystal worked on their treatment as often as they could, sometimes spending two mornings a week together at a time when Crystal, particularly, was in high gear at both the WPP and the AUAM. Then the pair began socializing with Max and mutual friends outside their work on the film. Before long, Walter announced he would skip a touring date with the Fuller Sisters to stay in New York with his various peace projects and Crystal. Walter's enthusiasm for what had become their baby was brimming over: "the German Invasion play is going to be simply wonderful!" he exulted. "It's worth a special run up in London—yes, indeed. Simply wonderful. And so full of new ideas and methods. Incredibly beautiful, and altogether convincing."[105]

In the fall of 1915, Walter and Crystal excitedly hoped to get their screenplay in front of D. W. Griffith.[106] At the time, film was emerging as the most powerful propaganda tool available, soon to be touted for its ability to forge an intimate bond between filmmaker and audience,[107] and Griffith was the most-talked-about filmmaker in history—a self-proclaimed cinema artiste whose innovations in storytelling, from close-ups to angles to cross-cuts to dissolves, would define the silent film era. Griffith positioned his motion pictures in the service of remaking public awareness, culminating in the claim in 1915 that above all his work strived to make people understand the world differently.[108]

Shamefully, the vision he impressed on viewers was the toxic racism of his film, *The Birth of a Nation*, which not only takes the side of the South in the Civil War but also traffics in virulent images of savage black freedmen during Reconstruction, justifying the rise and actions of the Ku Klux Klan in what is portrayed as the South's righteous retaliation. Griffith considered himself a pacifist and became an anti-interventionist by 1916. His next film, *Intolerance* (1916), more consciously attempted to convey such sentiments.[109] Even *Birth of a Nation* has since been acknowledged to carry some antiwar undertones, with its battle scenes accompanied by title cards concluding "war claims its bitter, useless sacrifice."[110] But its role in fertilizing racist hate groups in America was seen clearly by some at the time and by many more since. Yet in their starry-eyed eagerness to seek out the country's leading filmmaker, Crystal and Walter remained shockingly blind to the malignant racism of the film—even while intense protests organized by the five-year-old NAACP raged in cities from New York to Boston to Los Angeles after its release in April, just a few months earlier.

Meanwhile, the antipreparedness literature assault following Wilson around the country continued. In an attempt to correct misinformation, the

Anti-Preparedness Committee circulated pamphlets such as *Seven Congressmen on Preparedness*, which publicized antipreparedness speeches given on the floor of the US Congress that had been all but ignored by the mainstream press.[111] But the fever for militarism did not break. Thousands of people continued gathering enthusiastically, and for hours at a time, at preparedness rallies around the country.[112] When the American Legion polled its attendees about preparedness at the Panama-Pacific Medal Winners Exposition in late February, a larger standing army and navy was favored by more than ten to one—army: 17,490 to 1,463; navy: 17,740 to 1,463.[113]

More assertive tactics were needed, both inside Washington and across the country. Crystal proposed reorganizing their Washington office in the Munsey Building and hiring a full-time lobbyist to work on Capitol Hill. She argued for adding an office space in New York. And she proposed a much stronger response to Wilson. First, she wanted people—not pamphlets—to argue their side of the debate, and she wanted to hold mass meetings to gather crowds and reporters to publicize their message. "I would recommend that we undertake immediately a tour covering all the cities where President Wilson speaks . . . and that we engage a first class advance agent to start immediately organizing the meetings for this."[114]

Directly on the heels of these proposals, on March 1, 1916, the Anti-Preparedness Committee hired her full time as executive secretary for $300 a month. In April, it changed its name to the American Union Against Militarism. Over the next six weeks, the group organized its answer to Wilson and preparedness: an extensive "Truth about Preparedness" campaign, which included demonstrations, debates, and mass meetings. Its centerpiece was a large, interactive "War against War" exhibition that Walter had been working on with Crystal—and which he had been "pegging away at" for considerably longer, since at least September 1915.[115]

Crystal organized logistics for the campaign, which launched with a mass rally in Carnegie Hall on April 6, 1916, then opened in Brooklyn a week later. After two weeks, it moved to Manhattan, where it began its multicity tour—Buffalo, Cleveland, Detroit, Chicago, Minneapolis, Des Moines, Kansas City, St. Louis, Cincinnati, and Pittsburgh. The estimated cost was $4,700—a hefty sum in 1916.[116] But Crystal rightly believed contributions from local sympathizers and collections at the meetings would more than cover the cost.[117] In the end, the whole traveling pageant was seen by more than 170,000 people and was so successful that the AUAM grew to twenty-two branches nationwide.

The goal for the exhibition, as for the campaign overall, was to fight fire with fire—to make propaganda of their own to critique and counteract the mythologies being used to stoke the zeal for war. "U.S. newspapers," Walter commented, "still give too much of war's exciting 'heroic' sporting side." In response, the AUAM planned to write, speak, and visualize, and to surround audiences with the counterarguments, using the latest approaches. "Why not use the cinematograph? . . . This idea is specially [*sic*] urgent over here just now, because half the theaters in New York—moving picture-theaters and the other kind—are all about war, and most of them rather glorifying it—and all preaching the lesson that America must aim to be armed to the teeth, so as to be prepared to fight whoever wins in Europe, in case the victor there should become drunk with victory and attack America!"[118] Like Crystal, Walter understood that the latest visual media could cultivate feelings and desires, changing the conditions, both individual and cultural, in which opinion formation and decision-making occur. "If there had been started some ten or fifteen years ago in both England and Germany an active imaginative campaign amongst the people in the principal cities in both countries declaring graphically, pictorially, dramatically and always attractively the truth about both countries," Walter perceived, "there would have been no war today."[119]

Walter's initial "Scheme for an Exhibition of Peace and War" was an elaborate multilanguage, pan-historical event. He proposed plays, exhibits, paintings, photos, giant maps and graphics, music, live speeches and debates, and more—an extravaganza of public entertainments that would pack a political punch. He brainstormed concepts including "the effect of war on Science—especially on medicine"; a show about "the perfect Athlete—so that the human body may be seen as something too beautiful, too noble to be destroyed by machinery for any purpose whatsoever"; "a chamber of horrors, to which only adults would be admitted, showing some actual war horrors"; "a terrific indictment of *Secret Diplomacy*—photos of men who 'represent' nations in the different capitals." He also suggested a section of the exhibition about the changing information environment itself: one about modern war journalism and its cultivation of prejudices among people of different countries, and another an indictment of censorship.[120]

The point was for people to have an immersive experience that first deconstructed the military ideal they had been sold and then moved them—both physically and emotionally—toward constructive alternatives. It was an amplified, updated rendition of Progressive-era print strategies like those used in connection with the Pittsburgh Survey and Crystal's *Work Accidents and the Law*: make the problem accessible, logically and viscerally—visualize and humanize it, mount the critique to the status quo, and trigger people's deepest emotional responses to foment their own desire for a new way of doing things.

The exhibition ultimately produced was considerably smaller in scale than Walter originally planned. Indeed, when even this scaled-back version was proposed, the national WPP decided not to mount it, citing its $2,000 price tag. But Crystal and the AUAM stepped in to do it, hiring Walter at $50 a month, plus relevant expenses, for his ongoing services. She spearheaded fundraising to keep him employed there and raised private donations to cover the broader costs of producing, mounting, and transporting the exhibition around the country.[121] The reduced program remained impressive, including a gigantic relief map, material in multiple languages, and silent films with footage of the conflict interspersed with text commentary.[122]

There were also lunch-hour lectures, and theme days—a Political Day, a Physicians' Day, a Mothers' and Suffrage Day—targeting particular constituencies, just as Crystal and others had done in suffrage and other modern political campaigns. Memorably, the exhibition opened in each host city with a gleaming, golden, seventeen-foot papier-mâché dinosaur named Jingo that was paraded through the streets on a horse-drawn platform bearing the cheeky tag line "All armor plates and no brains. This animal believed in 'Preparedness' and is now extinct." In many cities, the procession also included an eight-foot-tall figure of Uncle Sam carrying all the latest weapons and wearing a gas mask. The antipreparedness message he carried: "All dressed up and no place to go."

The campaign culminated in a meeting with Wilson on May 8, 1916, which Crystal arranged to brief the president on the mass meetings that the AUAM had held in eleven cities over the previous two weeks.[123] Fuller and Kellogg led in drafting the AUAM's position paper; the Eastman siblings revised and edited it.[124] The delegation, led by Wald and including Kellogg, Pinchot, the Eastmans, and others, decided to push for "sane and reasonable preparedness" in the pending bill, as Max recalled, "rather than a plea to stop the war."[125]

Wilson entertained their concerns, but as the *New York Times* reported on its front page, the president "expressed his fundamental disagreement with the anti-preparedness advocates."[126] He told them he "never dreamed for a moment that America as a whole, its rank and file, had got any military enthusiasm or militaristic spirit." The issue he faced as president, Wilson said, was the practical challenge of determining the appropriate size for the US Army. Much to the chagrin of the antimilitarists, his decision-making seemed centered on the notion that might makes right—in public opinion just as in war: "the peace of society is obtained by force, and when action comes it comes by opinion, but back of the opinion is the ultimate application of force. The greater body of opinion says to the lesser body of opinion, 'We may be wrong but you have to live under direction for the time being until you are more numerous than we are.' That is what I understand it amounts to," the president concluded.[127]

Immediately following the meeting, the group returned to the Munsey Building to prepare a press release regarding the president's reply.[128] On May 9, Wilson issued a statement saying he believed "the heart of America is too sound ever to permit militarism." The AUAM's reply came swiftly, as usual. "We enjoyed our interview with the President, but we were unconvinced."[129]

Three weeks later, on June 3, President Wilson signed the National Defense Act into law, dealing the antimilitarists a significant defeat. It doubled the size of the regular army, integrated the National Guard into the federal defense program, and increased the National Guard's strength considerably. The Naval Appropriations Act called for ten battleships, fifty destroyers, fifteen fleet submarines, seventy-five coast submarines, and six battle cruisers to be built in the next three years. Crystal denounced it as the "largest naval appropriation bill . . . in the peace history of any country."[130] Plus, a conscription clause had been slipped into the act without most members of Congress even realizing it. The only consolation to antimilitarists was the Hensley Amendment to the Navy Act, which authorized the president to invite all the great governments of the world to send representatives to a conference to consider the question of disarmament at the conclusion of the war.[131]

The AUAM's immediate response was a plan to wield a huge publicity campaign to press the president to act on the Hensley provision.[132] If they could accomplish that, Charles "Charlie" Hallinan told Crystal, it would render the entire Naval Appropriations Act "so much waste paper."[133] Then, quite suddenly, world events gave them a high-stakes chance to convince the president, the Congress, and the public that their calls for a mediated peace—still the foundation for all their larger hopes—could actually work in the real world.

On June 21, a series of engagements between the US military and Mexican forces following the revolutionary leader Francisco "Pancho" Villa resulted in a confrontation in the village of Carrizal, just south of the Texas border. For two hours American cavalry, moving through Mexican territory, fought against a superior Mexican force that barred their way. The papers reported that at least ten American soldiers were killed, nine others wounded, and twenty-two captured.[134] A revolution had begun in Mexico in 1910, launching a bloody, tortured saga that would repeatedly challenge the foreign policy designs of the Wilson administration. American newspapers wrote of a country in near anarchy in 1914 and headlined vicious battles in 1915.[135] Between the revolutionary dynamics still unfolding in 1916 and American investment stakes in Mexico, what was first referred to as the "Carrizal incident" soon became the "battle of Carrizal." On the morning of June 22, 1916, the *New York Tribune* screamed, "American Troops Ambushed; 40 Slain, Mexicans Report" on the top of page one.[136] "The stories that followed," Wald later recalled, "accentuated rather than minimized the headlines. With the world at such tension, this interpretation of the episode to the American people—as an unprovoked attack by troops of the regular Mexican army—inevitably meant war."[137]

Eastman got on the phone to Wald the moment she heard what had happened. An emergency meeting was called at 4:30 p.m. the same day, June 21, to decide what, if anything, could be done to prevent a war with Mexico. It did not conclude until 2:30 in the morning. They focused on two main issues: first, how to counter the war propaganda and wild reports on the Carrizal events dominating American headlines; second, how to impress upon the US government, as well as potential mediating countries—Argentina, Chile, Brazil—that many Americans citizens opposed a war with their neighbor. The AUAM voted unanimously to wire a strong protest against war to the president and urgent pleas to relevant powers in Washington to use their influence to stave off hostilities. Then, that night, they cabled "an 800-word story—at our expense—to three papers in Mexico City and to two influential papers in Havana, Cuba—papers which we were told had a good deal of influence in Latin-American affairs."[138] They aimed to convince the Mexican public directly that many American citizens were not in favor of intervention.

As the clamor for military action grew, the *New York Times* reported an "eleventh hour decision to try for mediation in Mexico."[139] The strategic action was Crystal's brainchild. She proposed to organize a citizens' committee to mediate between the countries—a democratic effort, a people's effort in citizens' diplomacy, to resolve the international conflict directly, bypassing officialdom on both sides. She helped prepare a press statement: "The American Union Against Militarism, believing that the people of the United States and the people of Mexico are deeply opposed to war, is asking three representative Americans to confer unofficially at El Paso, Texas, with three representative Mexicans in an immediate effort to prevent war by delaying hostilities, promoting mediation and relieving conditions on the border."[140] Soon after, the WPP-NYC followed with a telegram to the women of Mexico via the editor of *La Mujer Mexicana*, the leading women's magazine, emphasizing the need for women's solidarity across nations to promote international agreements—rather than military actions—to ensure peace.[141]

"Let our plan be the beginning of a practical internationalism," Crystal declared.[142] The executive committee selected as the Mexico leaders Modesto Rolland, an engineer and former consul general currently living in New York; Dr. Atl, the nom de plume of the Mexican revolutionary painter Gerardo Murillo Cornado; and Luis Manuel Rojas, director of the Biblioteca Nacional in Mexico City. The Americans selected were William Jennings Bryan; Frank P. Walsh, still chairman of the Commission on Industrial Relations since the time Crystal briefly worked for him there; and Stanford's David Starr Jordan.[143] "Miss Crystal Eastman deserves the credit," AUAM leaders announced, "not only for originating the idea but for convincing the members of the conference that it was feasible and that nothing short of some such scheme would save the situation."[144]

Bryan and Walsh were slow to reply, and ultimately declined.[145] But Jordan, who was on a speaking tour when he read of the invitation in a newspaper, agreed immediately. "Waiving all ceremonies, he wired his acceptance, left the train, turned his back on a string of engagements, and started straight for El Paso," the AUAM recorded, "straight for unconcealed local hostility and the cheap jibes of the press of the entire country."[146] Jordan had "nothing of epaulets or spurs or in between to suggest the warrior," Paul Kellogg recalled. He "was a tall, gaunt man in later life—the kind that ate seaweed wafers at lunch for the sake of his digestion." Nevertheless, he was "a compact of sheer nerve and lean insurgence that would stave off a mob—and might—as it turned out, stop armies in their tracks."[147]

At the same time, the probability of war with Mexico continued to escalate. The House passed a joint resolution—by a vote of 332 to 2—authorizing Wilson to call up the National Guard into military service and declaring that an emergency now existed sufficient to justify the draft.[148] Jordan arrived in El Paso, the sole representative of the AUAM, for a conference scheduled for June 26. Only Modesto Rolland was able to be there for the Mexican delegation. The two men were forced to leave El Paso; "it wasn't practicable to continue in a border town," the AUAM reported, but they continued to confer and signed a statement at an alternate site, Albuquerque, New Mexico.[149] "There is no rational cause for war between the American people and the people of Mexico," they agreed. "If it be true that the de facto government of Mexico has not suppressed bandits along the border, it is equally true that the Government of the United States has not apprehended conspirators along the same border, currently believed to be in collusion with these bandits."[150]

Meanwhile, in Washington, an American officer, Captain Lewis Morey, one of those wounded at Carrizal, reported there had been no entrapment of American soldiers leading up to the battle. The AUAM obtained a copy of the report, which was not publicized by the government or accurately reported in the papers. Eastman met with Wald, Villard, and others, and they decided they must try to cut through all the misinformation and misleading reporting. They agreed they must show the public that the Carrizal engagement "was not by any means an unprovoked attack upon American troops, and could not constitute a just cause for war."[151] Their half-page ad, "Shall We Have War With Mexico?," put forward their case in the *New York Times* and *New York World*. "The invasion of Mexico, or any form of military intervention would mean the perpetuation of a tragedy as great as that of Belgium," they argued. "It is the present duty of every patriotic citizen of the United States to prevent such a catastrophe so terrible and disgraceful."[152]

On July 6, Crystal issued a pamphlet for the AUAM announcing the formation of a new Mexican-American League, a citizen-led diplomatic effort to promote common understanding and "help bring about a new and constructive era of friendliness between Mexico and the United States." The AUAM explained the clash between the United States and its much poorer neighbor as an imperialist iteration of the same fundamental power dynamics that had sparked the French Revolution. Positioning US interests among the forces of privilege—of global commerce, not democracy—they attributed the conflict to the overwhelming ambitions of international capital colliding with the rights of the Mexican people.[153] The AUAM's radically democratic intervention sought to balance the powers of both sides, allowing countries to speak on equal terms and focus on the same basic human interests each had at stake.

Wilson almost certainly entertained different explanations of what happened and why, but in September he appointed a Joint High Commission on Mexico to mediate the dispute. The president did employ an internationalized approach involving Argentina, Brazil, and Chile, the same countries the AUAM had informally engaged, to sustain the official arbitration and reach a successful resolution. Kellogg proudly recalled a simple, rational solution to what was an escalating international conflagration: "they worked out a formula; our own forces were withdrawn from Mexican soil," he said.[154] War was averted.

Crystal had led the way to a radical internationalist scheme that demonstrated that citizen diplomacy can successfully prevent war. The triumph through direct democracy, Max later said, made "a little less fantastic her effort, by similar means, to stop Woodrow Wilson from going to war with Germany."[155] Crystal herself saw it the same way at the time. "We must make the most of our Mexican experience," she urged the AUAM. "We must make it known to everybody that people acting directly—not through their governments or diplomats or armies—stopped that war, and can stop all wars if enough of them will act together and act quickly."[156]

By the end of the year, Crystal proclaimed in an article entitled "War and Peace" that "the moment of achievement seems to be at hand." It was 1916, a presidential election year, and the world war was the defining issue of the campaign. She believed the radical internationalists had demonstrated a diplomatic breakthrough that could end the world's fighting and address the inciting causes at last. A mediated resolution ushered by the people, and the whole vision of democratic world federation and permanent peace that could follow from it, now seemed within reach. For "the radical peace movement, barely two years old," she announced, this victory carried them to the brink of their greatest hopes. Now, she urged, was "the supreme moment for action."[157]

6 | AGONIZING DILEMMAS AND THE MARCH TOWARD WAR

Two weeks before the events at Carrizal, on June 5, 1916, Eastman was the keynote speaker at a rousing "Suffrage First" luncheon in Chicago. Her speech kicked off the annual convention of what was about to become the National Woman's Party (NWP)—the first women's political party in the world. Independent of all other parties, the NWP would campaign on a single plank: immediate passage of the federal suffrage amendment.

The meeting coordinated nicely with the Republican National Convention, also in Chicago, which began right on its heels on June 7. Eastman's colleagues from both the major movements with which she was involved—the suffragists and the pacifists—were on hand to lobby the convention. From June 5 to 7, she toggled between the two groups. After she gave her suffrage speech at the Blackstone Theater, she traveled up to Addams's office on Astor Street in advance of the "War against War" exhibition arriving that day from New York for a one-week run while Republican delegates were in town.[1] Then, that evening, she joined NWP colleagues Inez Milholland and Alva Belmont, as well as Helen Keller and Sara Bard Field, a suffrage leader in the Nevada, Oregon, and California campaigns, to strategize a lobbying effort aimed at two goals: getting a GOP endorsement of the federal suffrage amendment and adding an equal suffrage plank to the party platform.[2]

Once the convention began, however, Crystal seems mainly to have worked with her American Union Against Militarism (AUAM) colleagues to press for peace policies in the GOP. She had arranged for the AUAM leadership to meet with the eventual nominee, former New York governor and now Supreme Court Justice Charles Evans Hughes, on July 20. Hughes was not a pacifist, but Crystal knew him personally from her work on the Employer Liability Commission and had told Wald she thought they would get a fair hearing from him.[3]

Crystal Eastman. Amy Aronson, Oxford University Press (2020).
© Oxford University Press.
DOI: 10.1093/oso/9780199948734.001.0001

The following week, the suffragists would lobby the Democrats in force, but Crystal skipped the Democratic convention altogether. She and her antiwar colleagues knew the incumbent Democrat, President Wilson, had been running on a pledge of American neutrality and peace. After all, his campaign slogan for re-election was, bluntly, "He Kept Us Out of War."

She returned to New York on June 10, arriving in time to confront an expected but foreboding sight. While the Democratic convention proceeded in St. Louis, Wilson marched at the head of a great preparedness parade down Fifth Avenue on June 14. Wearing dapper white flannel trousers, he sported an American flag draped across his chest. He issued a proclamation declaring that day "Flag Day." The Woman's Peace Party of New York City (WPP-NYC) was ready with a response. They answered the president's display of nationalistic preparedness by draping a thirty-foot banner outside their store on lower Fifth Avenue, just across the street from the grandstand. It read: "To the Marchers: There are only 10,000 of you. You are not the only patriots. Two million farmers, half a million mine workers and organized American laborers are against what you and Wall Street are marching for. Are you sure you're right?"[4] But afterward, Crystal probably wondered the same thing about her trust in Wilson's promises about America's unique role in shaping internationalism and peace and protecting the voice of democracies worldwide.

The presidential race of 1916 was one of the closest ever in American history. Victory seesawed back and forth all through election night, and finally turned on a single swing state where an official recount found a margin of victory so slim it took sixteen days for the loser to concede. The two candidates were divided by their different stands on the pre-eminent issues of Eastman's political life. Wilson staunchly opposed suffrage but campaigned as the candidate for peace. Hughes endorsed suffrage but opposed peace negotiations and American neutrality. In fact, his platform advocated greater military mobilization, and by the final days of the campaign, some pro-Wilson newspapers claimed that Hughes was planning to take America into the war if he won the presidency.

For Crystal and her allies in the internationalist peace movement, this was the moment when the greatest opportunity a nation ever had could be achieved—or lost. At the same time, for Crystal and her allies in the suffrage movement, this was the moment they had chosen to press for their birthright as Americans, the moment they felt they had labored, pleaded, and battled for since the nineteenth century—the moment when they would deploy the Party in Power strategy, leveraging the bloc of "suffrage states" where women could now vote, as a third party in a tight presidential race.

For the first time, two of Crystal's deepest political commitments could not be balanced or aligned. She would have to choose. Most in the press seemed to think she would throw herself behind suffrage. In July, the papers reported she would tour the twelve suffrage states speaking for the NWP.[5] But instead she prioritized the personal over the political. Later that summer, she was in Glenora introducing Walter to her father. They were now formally a couple.

In August, after Hughes suddenly came out in favor of the federal suffrage amendment (although his Republican Party, like the Democrats, maintained a states'-rights stance in the official platform), the press again reported Crystal would be campaigning with the NWP. Her name was released on a list of suffragists slated for the western campaign organized by her friend Doris Stevens.[6] That would not happen either.

At the end of the month, Eastman did join her suffrage colleagues for a consequential meeting at Belmont's mansion. She raised her hand high in a unanimous vote to use the Party in Power strategy to push through a resolution, then in Congress, that embodied the Susan B. Anthony Suffrage Amendment granting full suffrage to women nationwide.[7] Yet following through on that direction would entail opposing the peace-promising Wilson and instead marching with Hughes and the GOP, possibly into the catastrophe of a world war.

Crystal faced a cruel dilemma: Where should she stand? For suffrage or for peace?

* * *

Woodrow Wilson faced an uphill battle for re-election in 1916. Once Teddy Roosevelt turned down the chance to run again as the candidate of the Progressive Party, Republicans could coalesce around their nominee. And the GOP had cultivated strong ties to the banking and financial sectors in the Northeast, giving Hughes a deep war chest with which to battle in this highly competitive race.

Long before women had the vote, Crystal began situating herself in presidential politics. At Vassar, she had been in the minority of students to support William Jennings Bryan, the populist, anti-imperialist candidate, over William McKinley, joining about twenty-five to thirty Bryanites who confronted a hundred Republicans for McKinley in the Main Hall in 1900.[8] In 1912, when William Howard Taft's nomination by the GOP had prompted Roosevelt to create the Progressive "Bull Moose" Party, Crystal had gone to hear Wilson speak in Wisconsin. She liked him well enough, although he "never even touched the surface of any of the big problems" from her perspective and seemed "too much of a scholar and a gentleman for a real big political fight." She predicted Roosevelt would win. "Nothing can stop that muddled, brash, egotistical, *popular* man," she said. "Honestly, I don't think any of them is much good for the job. Wilson might be if he could get it—but he never can."[9]

Her prediction about Wilson's electability in 1912 was off, but perhaps not her assessment of his inclinations when it came to the policy battles she believed he should prosecute without reserve. After the party conventions of 1916, a similarly equivocal attitude about Wilson prevailed among Eastman's peace colleagues. The president had earned it. In the months before Election Day, he had actively courted their support, but he was fitful and inconsistent in affirming their policy agenda.

In his nomination acceptance speech on September 2, for example, Wilson had strayed from a firm stand on American neutrality, raising doubts among the antimilitarists. "No nation should be forced to take sides in any quarrel in which its own honor and integrity and the fortunes of its own people are not involved," he began, then turned, "but no nation can any longer remain neutral as against any wilful [*sic*] disturbance of the peace of the world." Then he continued down that path of greater military involvement: "The effects of war can no longer be confined to the areas of battle. No nation stands wholly apart in interest when the life and interests of all nations are thrown into confusion and peril." And now secure as the Democratic nominee for re-election, the president seemed to be moving toward taking a side in the Great War. In fact, he implied that the nation's leadership role in the world now depended on intervention, not neutrality. "We can no longer indulge our traditional provincialism. We are to play a leading part in the world drama whether we wish it or not," Wilson declared. "We shall lend, not borrow; act for ourselves, not imitate or follow; organize and initiate, not peep about merely to see where we may get in."[10]

Just five days later, on September 7, Wald reported she had been approached a number of times by the Democratic campaign managers asking her to endorse Wilson's re-election, but she had so far refused.[11] Then on September 30, the president addressed the Young Men's Democratic Club, flatly stating that "a vote for Wilson would mean peace, a vote for Hughes would be war."[12]

However uncertain they may have remained, shortly after that speech both Wald and Addams came out for Wilson. Most of Crystal's antiwar colleagues did too. Kellogg publicly praised the Democrats as the only party committed to neutrality and an internationalist outlook. Amos Pinchot, the anti-imperialist son of a wealthy businessman whom Crystal had recruited to the AUAM earlier in 1916, organized Wilson volunteers to conduct a campaign tour through New York State.[13] Crystal herself began to deliver speeches endorsing Wilson in October, as did Max. Of the AUAM leadership, only Villard would refuse to endorse the president, saying he did not have "a principle on earth that he would not bargain away."[14]

At the same time, the NWP commenced Alice Paul's orchestrated gambit against Wilson and the Democrats. So with every endorsement of the president,

Crystal seemed to be defying her political roots, countering suffrage allies such as Lucy Burns and Inez Milholland—women who were like family to her. Milholland, for one, seemed to publicly rebuke Eastman in one of the last speeches of her life, given shortly before she collapsed at a California suffrage rally on October 22, 1916. "Do not let anyone convince you that there is any more important issue in the country today than votes for women," she thundered. "There are people who honestly believe—HONESTLY BELIEVE!... that there are more important issues before the country than suffrage, and that it would be very becoming on our part . . . to retire at this time." Milholland expressed the resentment that had simmered among many suffragists for more than forty-five years, since the passage of the Fifteenth Amendment had granted voting rights irrespective of race, color, or previous condition of servitude—but not irrespective of sex. She expressed outrage at once again being told other issues were more important, that the women must wait their turn. "Now I do not know what you feel about such a point of view," she announced, "but it makes me mad. . . . We must say, 'Women First.'"[15]

To suffragists, Crystal's apparent abandonment of "Suffrage First" at this critical time must have been difficult to fathom. True, she had thrown herself into antipreparedness throughout the momentous previous year. Moreover, those who knew her best probably perceived that she was temperamentally drawn toward encompassing, intersectional political schemas—more to the comprehensive than to the targeted. On the ground, the Wilson campaign had managed to woo prominent supporters from the labor and Socialist movements—Jack London, Mother Jones, Upton Sinclair, Helen Keller—incorporating an unusually left-wing and class-conscious contingent to help expand his narrow path to re-election.[16] Her suffrage colleagues probably knew she would be powerfully drawn to such a constellation of allied organizations and movements. What's more, the radical internationalist vision incorporated the demand for women's suffrage—worldwide. For suffragists active beyond the organizational perimeter of the NWP—pre-eminent world leaders like Jane Addams among them—the internationalist peace movement was a means to fill two needs with one deed. And then some.

But beyond all that, Milholland and other suffrage colleagues may not have known about another potential factor in Crystal's decision-making: by the time she decided to cast her lot with world peace over women's suffrage, she was secretly pregnant with her first child. Crystal had finally filed for divorce from her first husband, Bennie, four months after she and Walter first met on business at New York's Belmont Hotel in October 1915.[17] Seven months later, just as she began campaigning actively for Wilson, the couple were married. Samuel

Eastman had quietly performed the ceremony in Glenora on September 11, 1916.[18] Six months after the wedding, their son, Jeffrey, was born.

* * *

After Wilson narrowly won re-election, Crystal immediately took steps to affirm her alliances in both the peace and suffrage movements. Margaret Lane shared the "good news about Crystal" with peace colleagues, adding "she is such a wonder that she deserves all the happiness there is."[19] Eastman herself shared news of her nuptials with Addams, noting on November 14, "You knew Walter Fuller and I were married? We both send our love to you—."[20] Soon after, she was back in action with the WPP-NYC, organizing a peace gathering at Washington Square Arch on New Year's Eve designed to foster unity across the country. In coordinated events in Chicago, Denver, San Francisco, and lower Manhattan, peace women joined hands and sang together: "Ring out the old war, ring in world peace."[21]

Crystal made even more heartfelt overtures to the NWP. Inez Milholland had passed away on November 25, and her death while fighting for suffrage had immediately imbued the organization with even greater group commitment and resolve. From that time forward, Milholland was historically situated as a suffragist above all. Crystal organized a huge memorial service for her at Cooper Union in New York on December 21, four days prior to the historic service held in the rotunda of the Capitol on Christmas Day 1916. In her remarks, she shaped a healing vision of likeness with her friend, summoning a Milholland who lived in multiple movements, not just one. "How can her spirit at once express for the socialist-trade unionist-prison reformer-feminist-suffragist-pacifist the hope that sustains us? How can it be?" she asked. Her answer: "Because my friends—all our great movements at which the dull world laughs—are one at heart—they are phases of the struggle for liberty."[22] She invoked Milholland's memory as a call to cross-movement solidarity among activist women. "Here we are today, the representatives of so many great movements," she observed, "and we all claim Inez Milholland. This is very wonderful to me," she testified, because it affirmed her fundamental bond with her lost friend, a woman whose "whole aspiration," she emphasized, "was for fuller liberty"—just like her own.[23]

After the Washington ceremony, the NWP passed memorial resolutions, which three hundred women took to the newly re-elected president when he finally agreed to see them in January 1917. At that meeting, they asked Wilson to use the power of his office to end what they called "this wasteful struggle of women." When Wilson sharply refused and walked out on the delegation, his disregard ignited a three-year blitz of banners, picketing at the White House, and other high-octane protests the militant movement used to finally secure votes for women. Their actions in 1916–17, adamant and tenacious, would result in imprisonment and then hunger strikes by NWP leaders. They were "peaceful means," as Mabel Vernon, the organization's first national suffrage organizer and one of the first to be arrested for picketing, would say, used tactically "to achieve a violent reaction" from the president.[24]

Eastman did not participate in these historic actions. However, she applauded her suffrage sisters heartily from the sidelines, and particularly when the campaign intersected other social justice movements with which she saw universal suffrage allied. When a Russian diplomatic mission met with President Wilson six months later, on June 20, 1917, the event was closely watched by suffragists. One of the first reforms put in place at the dawn of the Russian Revolution was to give women the vote. That afternoon, the NWP displayed a controversial "Russian banner" at the White House, unfurling an argument so risky it had to be carefully vetted by Lucy Burns's brother, an attorney.[25] The banner screamed in capital letters:

WE, THE WOMEN OF AMERICA, TELL YOU THAT AMERICA IS NOT A DEMOCRACY. TWENTY MILLION AMERICAN WOMEN ARE DENIED THE RIGHT TO VOTE. PRESIDENT WILSON IS THE CHIEF OPPONENT OF THEIR NATIONAL ENFRANCHISEMENT. HELP US MAKE THIS NATION REALLY FREE. TELL OUR GOVERNMENT IT MUST LIBERATE THE PEOPLE BEFORE IT CAN CLAIM FREE RUSSIA AS AN ALLY.

Crystal, joined by Max, quickly sent an enthusiastic cable to Burns and the NWP. It conveyed their "endless admiration" for the Russian banner action.[26]

While the NWP was confronting Wilson and the Democrats as the adversaries of their political interests, the president was behaving as a far better friend to the peace movement—at least initially. On January 3—one week before the suffrage picketing began at the White House—Eastman attended a private dinner at the Hotel Astor given by George Foster Peabody, the purpose of which, she told the papers, was "to place the American people on record as squarely and unreservedly behind President Wilson in his move for peace in Europe."[27] Then, on January 22, Wilson thrilled the antiwar movement with a speech to the US Senate that seemed like the moment of achievement Crystal had declared was at hand. The president called for "peace without victory," announcing the United States would participate in "a universal covenant," acting to guarantee a just and permanent peace without dictating any peace terms to either side. The speech mirrored the politics the internationalist peace movement had advocated since

1914. It guaranteed the right of every country to govern itself and enjoy freedom of trade on the high seas. It called for armed forces only large enough to police order, not attack neighbors. And it envisioned a "League of Peace," which nations would join to enforce these internationalist principles.

However gripping the notion of neutral "peace without victory" was to Eastman and her colleagues, the belligerent countries, almost two and a half years into the ferocious conflict, were unreceptive to an end to the fighting with nothing to show for their sacrifices. Nine days after Wilson's speech, on January 31, the German foreign ambassador escalated tensions by announcing that his government would commence unrestricted submarine warfare. The antiwar movement knew the action could provoke the United States to enter the war.

The very next day, twenty-six leading voices of the AUAM, including Crystal and Max, telegraphed Wilson that the United States "should refuse to allow herself to be dragooned into the war at the very end by acts of desperation committed by any of the belligerents." They urged the president to stand strong for American neutrality: "The men and women of this country who elected you," they said, "will back you in the most extreme measures for keeping the country clear of any ignominious eleventh-hour participation in a struggle for mastery which is not their own."[28] The day after that, February 2, a group of well-known peace women, including Fanny Villard and Emily Greene Balch, formed the Emergency Peace Federation to help coordinate a rapid response program of urgent preventive measures. They organized a huge rally in Madison Square Garden headlined by William Jennings Bryan. Balch's prominence in this increasingly desperate peace work would soon cost her her job; in light of her influential involvement with the International Congress of Women at The Hague, the postcongress delegation to European leaders, and her considerable antipreparedness campaigning, Wellesley College dismissed her from the faculty.

Nevertheless, on February 3, President Wilson severed diplomatic relations with Germany. The peace movement recognized this as a decisive step in the march to war. They intensified their commitment to rapid response tactics. The AUAM called an emergency session at the McAlpin Hotel in New York on February 5. Wald presided as twenty additional members traveled from the Philadelphia branch in time for the 5:00 p.m. meeting.

Crystal presented an initial action offered by Walter: a scheme for conducting an unofficial referendum on war and peace using postal cards. After a long discussion, the postcard referendum drive was adopted, and a subcommittee appointed to draft the questions.[29] Then the AUAM led a mass meeting at Carnegie Hall to protest American entry into the war and demand a national vote before Congress acts.[30] At 6:37 the following morning, Lane wired an update from the New York WPP to Addams at the national headquarters in Chicago: "conducting hundred thousand post card referendum on war. Many cities favor demanding Congressmen to conduct referendum before declaring war even in case of overt act." She added: "We are warned from Washington that Army General Staff is pushing press censorship. Most dangerous to Democracy. Bring Pressure on Congress against censorship."[31]

The idea of a public vote on a declaration of war was not new in American politics, but it had never seen the high-level attention it attained in 1917. Not only the antimilitarists but also Bryan, Senator La Follette, and the Socialist Party of America proposed or endorsed such a measure. Over the next two weeks, numerous referendum bills were introduced in Congress. At 3:13 a.m. on February 9, Lane wired the WPP headquarters in Chicago that "new bill providing for peoples [*sic*] advisory referendum vote will be introduced in Congress shortly. Will wire names of sponsors later. Bill provides referendum to be conducted by Census Bureau through post offices taking twenty five days."[32]

None of these bills even made it to the House floor, but the AUAM's unofficial referendum went forward as planned. The result was "a heavy vote for peace. . . . The average spread was six to one," Crystal reported, with "the lowest vote in any district four to one, and the highest, eleven to one."[33] Nevertheless, many in Congress and around the country had begun to voice their unquestioning support for the president should the United States enter the war. On the same day Wilson severed diplomatic relations with Germany, Carrie Catt led the National American Woman Suffrage Association (NAWSA) in offering the services of its two million women in the event of US intervention. She and NAWSA quickly organized a mass meeting in Washington to affirm that suffragists would always stand by their country—just another indication, Catt would say, that American women deserved full citizenship through the vote.

Eastman and other militant suffragists committed to the antiwar effort were furious at the move. "New York suffragists indignant at being handed over by officers to government for war work are making strenuous protest," Lane reported to the national WPP.[34] Crystal herself resigned from the New York Suffrage League over the issue.[35] She strenuously objected to Catt's claim that a woman's war support validated her claim to citizenship. Shortly thereafter, the WPP of New York would "accidentally" drop Catt's name as honorary vice chair as Crystal began publicly contesting Catt's action from multiple relevant aspects of her political identity. As a pacifist, she pointed out in the *New York Times* that she had "signed onto platform of 'suffrage only' and they should stick to that now."[36] As a suffragist, she told a New York suffrage society, "I believe a great many suffragists, who are not pacifists, felt decidedly aggrieved that their services had been so lightly pledged to a government which has denied to them for forty years a fundamental democratic right."[37]

The national WPP insisted that Eastman apologize to Catt, and she did—sort of. "I need not tell you how eager we are to keep you," she wrote, adding, "if you are still in sympathy with the position of the Woman's Peace Party." If so, Crystal asked, "Could you possibly give us a statement which would show you are in substantial accord with the position taken in these various resolutions? It would mean great strength and power to the peace movement just now if you could take a strong public stand on our side."[38]

Catt never rejoined the WPP, while her reasoning that support for the war equaled patriotic citizenship became a pervasive national trope. Peace demonstrations in Washington and New York were beginning to look to some like acts of disloyalty. Even some peace activists began to wonder if they could continue to press their opposition. At the February 9 meeting of the AUAM, Rabbi Stephen Wise, an original member of the Anti-Preparedness Committee, was the first of Crystal's close colleagues to wrestle with the feeling he could no longer identify with the group. Indeed, he told the AUAM he felt German militarism had to be eradicated, and war seemed the only way to accomplish that. He was willing to support American intervention as the lesser of two great evils. Eastman, Wald, Balch, and Kellogg urged that war could not stamp out any evil. Pinchot argued the issue was militarism—not "Germanism." The debate was the "most gripping experience I have ever been through," Kellogg told Addams, as Villard too grew uncertain as to his position. Wise left the meeting "shaken," he recalled, and he needed time to think. After struggling for four months, he finally resigned from the AUAM, never to return.[39]

Four days after that meeting, on February 14, Congress passed the Threats against the President Act, establishing criminal penalties for anyone who "knowingly and willfully" made statements, written or spoken, seen to threaten the life of or bodily harm to President Wilson. It was seen as a first step to criminalizing free speech.[40] Congress was also considering bills specifically to censor antiwar speech as disloyal to the country. The peace movement's dilemma was becoming clearer: should its members maintain their opposition to war and risk being branded and punished as traitors, or surrender their principles?

AUAM leaders met the day the act passed. Crystal urged they stay the course: she pushed for a meeting with the president to discuss the practical possibility of a national referendum and an international league to enforce neutrality as an alternative to war. Since at least February 5, the AUAM had been promoting Bryan's outline for a joint official conference of neutral nations to consider safeguarding common rights at sea. The concept received additional promotion in an article by a fellow New York antimilitarist published in the *Survey*.[41] Now the AUAM rallied influential supporters of mediation, such as Mrs. Malcolm Forbes, urging them to wire the president, senators, and congressmen to endorse such a league.[42] Eastman's only concession to the changing political climate was to encourage "a dignified national campaign of publicity" for the idea.[43]

However, desperation was setting in. Less than a week later, Crystal and Walter were grasping for new approaches, even at the cost of questionable neutrality. On February 20, they pitched a "non-intercourse" plan modeled on the ideas of Norman Angell, of the Union of Democratic Control, and J. A. Hobson, another leading British antimilitarist. It was a sanctions package that would prohibit postal, telegraph, and wireless communications, as well as trade and passenger traffic with Germany, and cancel payments of all debts due to German citizens and companies.[44] The AUAM agreed it might be effective in some ways but voted not to adopt it. Eastman then made a motion for Wald to call Joseph Tumulty, Wilson's chief of staff, "on the long distance" to try to expedite a meeting with the administration. Then, just before they adjourned, came word that the Senate had passed the espionage bill, which would suspend such civil liberties as free speech and assembly in the name of national security.[45]

By the next afternoon, the national WPP executive board and delegates from state and local branches were gathering for their own emergency meeting. They called for arbitration between the United States and Germany and argued it was the duty of every patriotic American citizen to keep clear of hazardous war zones. But the New Yorkers went much further. They urged a law that would forbid the United States from entering the war zones and deny clearance to ships carrying contraband. They also advocated a popular referendum on US participation in the war. Whereas the national WPP policy called for the United States to refrain from allying with any belligerents, the New York branch condemned the US break in relations with Germany and, in the next issue of its magazine *Four Lights*, publicly suggested the president's policy to protect freedom of the seas was merely a commercial gambit to maintain lucrative international trade.[46]

Then, on February 25, an intercepted telegram transformed the national debate. President Wilson received word from the British that they had intercepted a message from the German foreign minister proposing an alliance between Germany and Mexico in the event the United States joined the war on the side of the Allies. The now-infamous "Zimmerman telegram" offered that Germany would help Mexico recover territory lost to the United States in the 1840s. Wilson spoke before a joint session of Congress on February 26 and asked for the authority to arm merchant vessels to protect ships and people in legitimate and peaceful pursuits on the high seas. His policy, called "armed neutrality," was based on a principle of neutral rights in use since the late eighteenth century in Europe. It met with praise from almost every political quarter in the country, including most antimilitarists, who claimed a hand in publicizing it.

The AUAM immediately voted to officially endorse the policy as a practical alternative to war. Crystal expressed reservations, however, and reminded her colleagues of their earlier support for a collective league of neutrals to enforce rightful freedoms at sea. The real hope of success in the armed neutrality idea, she argued, lay in "internationalizing" its execution. "In these days of cables and newspapers, when the whole nation can become a rioting mob over night" [*sic*], she explained, a dispassionate league of armed neutrals was the more effective and constructive policy to achieve their goals.[47] Although proposals to substitute a league of neutral nations for armed neutrality continued to circulate in some liberal papers at the time, including Villard's *New York Evening Post*, Eastman's comment was merely noted; the AUAM took no action.[48]

The following day, February 28, President Wilson met with pacifists including Addams, Wald, Kellogg, and Pinchot at the White House. Crystal, now eight months pregnant, was not among them, but Max was there. The AUAM urged the president to reassert America's friendliness to both sets of belligerents, oppose conscription and compulsory military training as undemocratic, and endorse the principle of referendum for war.[49] Max pushed for a league of neutral nations, advancing his sister's argument from the day before by saying it would serve as "a step toward Peace without Victory and a League of Nations, rather than a step toward our alliance with England in victory and an imperial domination of the globe that will certify the continuation of world wars into the future."[50]

Nevertheless, the delegation left that meeting believing war was inevitable. The president had decided he would be in a stronger position to effect the peace if the United States participated in the war, Addams would recall. As a belligerent, proved in the brotherhood of battle, he could command "a seat at the Peace Table," Wilson told them. But as the head of a neutral nation, even the head of all the neutral nations, he would be diminished or unmanned, forced to—Addams remembered the phrase very well—"call through a crack in the door."[51]

7

FROM PROTEST TO DISSENT:
WARTIME ACTIVISM AND
THE FOUNDING OF THE ACLU

When President Wilson presented the Declaration of War to Congress on April 2, 1917, he made it clear that protest would no longer be tolerated. "If there should be disloyalty," he warned, "it will be dealt with a firm hand of stern repression."[1]

Within a week, the administration formed the Committee on Public Information (CPI), launching an unprecedented government propaganda campaign to both cultivate and control the US narrative about the war. The agency's more than thirty-five departments would include divisions for both news and pictorial publicity. By the war's end, the CPI would produce government news through some 75 million copies of pamphlets and an *Official Bulletin* with a daily circulation of 118,000, virtually all of it communicating the importance of American participation and national loyalty in a time of war.[2]

George Creel, an investigative newspaperman and strong Wilson backer in both 1912 and 1916, was in charge of the whole operation. At the start of the war, he told the president in a memo that "*expression*, not *suppression*, was the real need." Thereafter, the agency fed the country a daily diet of material designed to arouse national ardor for the war effort.[3] But the CPI also maintained a censorship board, which issued a voluntary censorship code under which editors agreed not to print material that might aid the enemy—that is, by compromising or contradicting the desired narrative of the US government. In the end, Creel would aptly characterize the work of the CPI as "a plain publicity proposition, a vast enterprise in salesmanship, the world's greatest adventure in advertising."[4]

One week after the declaration of war, Crystal and her New York City colleagues in the Woman's Peace Party organized a public demand that the government explain what the United States was fighting for and delineate the country's peace terms.[5] Two days later, American

Crystal Eastman. Amy Aronson, Oxford University Press (2020).
© Oxford University Press.
DOI: 10.1093/oso/9780199948734.001.0001

Union Against Militarism (AUAM) leaders also organized a message to Wilson, spearheading an open letter that asked him to remind officials in Washington and across the country "to uphold in every way our constitutional rights and liberties."[6] The president's reply was tactful but evasive; he suggested his sensitivity to their concerns while at the same time pursuing legislation to censor the press.[7]

Not two months later, on June 15, 1917, Congress passed the Espionage Act, suspending free speech and assembly in the name of national security. That law was supplemented by the Sedition Act of 1918, which set prison terms for anyone convicted of obstructing the war effort, including by expressing antiwar opinions. The president justified the censorship as essential to public safety in a time of national emergency, telling Max the "wholly exceptional" moment made it "legitimate to regard things which would in ordinary circumstances be innocent as very dangerous to the public welfare."[8] To Crystal and her colleagues, these laws were blatantly antidemocratic, and, like wartime censorship laws passed so quickly in Britain in 1914, they seemed clearly calculated to control domestic opposition to whatever the government saw fit to do.[9] Nevertheless, the coordinated assault on political debate and dissent was readily accepted by pundits and the public as necessary in the American mobilization to join the war on the side of the Allies.

The friendly neighborhood US Post Office Department became a leading force for the suppression of dissent. The day after the Espionage Act was passed, Postmaster General Albert Burleson alerted post offices nationwide to keep tabs on any publication that could either embarrass or impede the government in conducting the war.[10] The few mainstream pacifist journals after 1914— primarily *The Nation*, William Jennings Bryan's *Commoner* (1901–23), and *La Follette's Magazine* (1909–29)—faced intense scrutiny and, within weeks, experienced suppression as antiwar publications across the political spectrum from mainstream liberal magazines to the Socialist press were seized or blocked from the mail. In all, forty-four US newspapers and magazines would run afoul of the new laws suppressing publication during 1917 alone, and another thirty maintained themselves only by agreeing to print nothing about the war. In less than the four years between the passage of the Espionage Act and 1921, the federal government would commence more than two thousand prosecutions to punish anyone whose words or deeds were seen as intentionally interfering with military operations.[11]

Many ordinary Americans involved themselves in the national campaign to enforce patriotism. Just after the United States severed diplomatic relations with Germany on February 3, a Chicago advertising executive named Albert "A. M." Briggs visited the US Justice Department with a proposal to organize the nation's businessmen into a clandestine force of volunteer surveillance agents. Their purpose was to watch fellow citizens and make reports of suspected disloyalty. With the declaration of war in April, the idea won rapid approval, and by the summer of 1917, A. Bruce Bielaski, head of the nascent Federal Bureau of Investigation (FBI), had introduced Briggs to special agents in field offices around the country, enabling the launch of the American Protective League (APL). This national network, headquartered in Washington, DC, was a secret service through which thousands of Americans from every industry and profession would volunteer to work with federal law enforcement, conducting surveillance to identify suspected German sympathizers or other groups now labeled as enemies of the people.[12] The APL grew rapidly, counting 250,000 citizen spies in six hundred cities by the end of its first year.[13] And its many members pursued people largely on the basis of their own suspicions and initiative. Frequently, they fomented violence; mobs at times tarred and feathered, even lynched, those seen as or suspected to be war critics.[14] Although members were ordinary volunteers, the league effectively functioned as an arm of the US government: its citizen operatives carried membership cards and identification badges from the Department of Justice.[15]

The climate of wartime repression affected every movement with which Eastman identified. Socialists, the picketing suffragists, birth control advocates, and antiwar internationalists all battled verbal, legal, and sometimes physical assaults from government officials and members of the public, all because they attempted to speak freely or assemble publicly. Indeed, from the very moment the Espionage Act was passed, it hit Crystal very close to home. That same day, an issue of the *Four Lights*, the WPP-NYC's magazine, was seized from the mail. It was not a surprising target. The outspoken *Lights* had taken its name from Ferdinand Magellan, who, its tagline explained, "showed four lights when he wished to set full sail" in circumnavigating the globe. From the first issue, it promised to speak for "the young, uncompromising women's peace movement, whose voice is daring and immediate," an intention that troubled even some in the WPP.[16] When the magazine appeared on January 27, 1917, Alice Thatcher Post, WPP vice chair, had written to Jane Addams asking her to halt its publication. Post feared its bold stands would cast suspicion—or worse—on the national organization or even the entire women's peace movement. When Addams contacted Eastman about it, Crystal had replied politely but firmly: she reminded the WPP chair that the party was organized with independent state branches so the New Yorkers were not required to seek approval for their activities from anyone except their own members.[17]

Two weeks after the *Lights* was suppressed, *The Masses* was similarly declared unmailable. Max Eastman's magazine had weathered disputes over free expression twice before. In 1913, the Associated Press (AP) had accused it of criminal libel because of an article Max had written charging that an AP employee had suppressed information about a violent confrontation between labor and capital at a coal mine in Katawa County, West Virginia. Art Young had drawn an accompanying cartoon that pictured a reservoir contaminated at its source by a dark figure labeled the Associated Press. More than two thousand people had flocked to a rally at Cooper Union to hear Lincoln Steffens, Morris Hillquit, and Amos Pinchot defend the editors and freedom of the press.[18] Soon after, the AP dropped the case. Then, in 1916, a more commercial assault came from the distribution company Ward and Gow. The company operated all the newsstands in the New York City subway system and ousted *The Masses* from its shelves over two offending items: a cartoon satirizing the capitalist interests of the press, and a poem comparing the Virgin Mary with an unwed mother. Again, prominent voices spoke in support of *The Masses* and a free press—John Dewey, Walter Lippmann, *New Republic* editor Herbert Croly, and the publisher Charles Scribner among them. But Ward and Gow would not reverse its decision. Other distribution channels had then followed suit. *The Masses* was rejected by the United News Company of Philadelphia and the Magazine Distributing Company in Boston, and it also disappeared from college reading rooms across the country after Columbia and Harvard ceremoniously canceled their subscriptions. These moves drastically reduced circulation, but *The Masses* survived.

Now, under the Espionage Act, the magazine's outspoken content again came under fire, this time from the US government. The August 1917 issue contained four articles and four cartoons that the government would only later identify as in violation of the new wartime laws. Some of the offending material seems quite tame, if not innocuous, today: a cartoon of a crumbing Liberty Bell, and another entitled "War Planes," which mocked the military-industrial complex by picturing a group of businessmen examining plans in a congressional office while the representatives themselves looked on asking, "Where do we come in?"[19] Although the editors were given no specific reasons delineating what was illegal about this and other content, the government charged Max and several of his colleagues with criminal obstruction of military service and prosecuted them—twice—for sedition. When their trial opened on April 15, 1918, it was the country's first major test case of free speech in wartime.[20]

After Max's arrest, Crystal took up the job of raising bail money—$20,000 for her brother and $10,000 for each of the other editors.[21] Within weeks, she published a pamphlet, "Our War Record: A Plea for Tolerance," through the WPP-NYC. In it, she ingeniously suggested her organization's antiwar arguments were politically neutral by supporting them with policy statements by officials from both sides of the conflict. The WPP-NYC called for a fulsome discussion of America's war aims—a policy supported by Britain's Marquis of Lansdowne, Crystal noted. The organization advocated the "simple, generous practical peace formula pronounced by Revolutionary Russia"—a formula largely endorsed by the German Reichstag. And when the end of hostilities should finally come, the group asked for "the obvious essentials of an enduring peace," much of which they had been pursuing now for months: a treaty that included free markets, free seas, a League of Nations, and universal disarmament negotiated with the direct representation of the people of all countries—including women—at the conference table. "We hold that there is nothing treasonous or unpatriotic or even emotional about this," she concluded. "On the basis of that record we ask protection from the government for our propaganda," adding wryly, "no matter how popular it may become"[22]

Crystal had been publicly emphasizing the democratic legitimacy of their continued activism ever since the United States entered the war.[23] But she and her antiwar colleagues were facing the most powerful propaganda buildup ever seen in American history. A climate of compulsory patriotism—largely defined as complete fealty to US policy and the president—was reshaping public opinion that only weeks before had been divided in its attitude toward intervention. Suddenly, the established mission of the AUAM and WPP seemed dangerously untenable, even to some in the leadership of the peace movement. When someone scrawled "Treason's Twilight Zone," a cryptic yet incriminating phrase, in the lobby at 70 Fifth Avenue, Crystal called an emergency meeting of the executive committee.[24] She pressed for a defensible agenda that refused to compromise their mission and their goals, a "logical, courageous and at the same time law-abiding" stance for the radical internationalist peace movement now.[25]

*　*　*

On April 16, 1917, ten days after the declaration of war, the AUAM executive board wired President Wilson to register its deep concern over "the breaking down of immemorial rights and privileges" that had so quickly begun to occur. "Halls have been refused for public discussion; meetings have been broken up; speakers have been arrested and censorship exercised," they protested, and "not to prevent the transmission of information to enemy countries, but to prevent free discussion by American citizens of our own problems and politics." They warned of profound long-term consequences to the very spirit and soul of democracy. "It is possible," they told Wilson, "that the moral damage to our democracy in this war may become more serious than the physical or national losses incurred."[26]

They met the next day. Emotions were running high, and internal frictions began to surface as their established political agenda, as well as their methods of presentation and protest in pursuing it, was becoming illegal. Ever the militant idealist, Crystal urged that they continue the work they had started. After heated discussion, she essentially got her way. In "The Wartime Agenda of the American Union Against Militarism," the AUAM articulated a six-point program, now evenly divided into two distinct themes. The latter three points concerned their enduring long-term goal of a negotiated peace and just settlement, keeping "the ideal of internationalism alive and growing in the minds of the American people to the end that this nation may stand firm for world federation." The first three points stood for the more immediate work to safeguard democracy during wartime: they would oppose "all legislation tending to fasten upon the United States . . . compulsory military training and service" and vowed to fight for the complete maintenance of the right to speak, assemble, and protest while the country was at war. The two issues seemed inherently interconnected: "America's entry into the World War makes more necessary than ever all efforts to maintain democratic liberty . . . to build toward world federation and the ultimate abolition of war."[27]

Having agreed to continue pursuing their prewar goals, the AUAM then designed strategies to test new wartime laws—and to protect citizens' rights to do so. They began with point number one of their wartime program, campaigning to prevent Congress from enacting compulsory military service through a draft. Eastman always opposed conscription, and from more than one political point of view. As a Socialist, she denounced it as a "demand stimulated by the self-interest of corporations, imperialists and war traders."[28] And from a peace perspective, she regarded it as an extreme example of the antidemocratic impulses and consequences of militarism. In 1917, she and the rest of the AUAM leadership reviled the draft as a gross violation of democratic principles, indeed of the most fundamental human rights. Oswald Villard likened conscription to slavery, arguing in an AUAM pamphlet, "The truth is that men of noble spirit are in every land crushed by the whole system of compulsory military labor precisely as compulsory servitude deadens men's souls everywhere."[29]

By the end of April, the AUAM voted to take action on points number two and three. They agreed to establish a Legal Defense League whose main function was to prevent prosecution of critics of the administration and its war policies.[30] At the same time, they also contemplated an innovative possibility for combatting involuntary servitude through the draft. They discussed extending the accepted claim of religious objection to war. Crystal and others in the AUAM leadership argued that the language of the conscription bill opened the door to a new brand of exemption on the basis of "conscience."[31] She told Amos Pinchot she felt confident the president would respect the liberty of conscience, a core principle of Protestantism, as a basis for dispensation from military combat. Pinchot disagreed, citing what he saw as the president's emotional pique at those who challenged his wartime authority: "the knot over . . . all who would oppose the temporary little fatherhood which [Wilson] is assuming in order to discourage autocracies in other climes." But most of the executive committee eventually concurred that Wilson's deepest principles, both religious and political, would prevail; he would not want "conscription of the unwilling."[32]

When Congress passed the Selective Service Act on May 18, the AUAM swung into action, establishing a new bureau on May 19 to provide information to those who sought exemption from the draft on the basis of conscience. They also planned to form an oversight committee of civic leaders and an advisory committee composed of representatives from interested national and local agencies.[33]

As the June 5 draft registration deadline approached, inquiries from young men of conscription age flooded the AUAM office. The group produced an informational pamphlet, "Conscription and the Conscientious Objector—Facts Regarding Military Service under the Conscription Act," which explained the proposed new category.[34] At the outset, many in the AUAM leadership felt confident that discreet advocacy with administration officials would enable them to successfully arrange such exemptions for young men who sought them. So, on May 23, they issued a statement on conscientious objectors (COs), advising all eligible men to obey the law and register for the draft.[35]

By June 1, Crystal was pushing for the AUAM to go further. She argued that a committee of lawyers should be added to press the case for COs in American courts.[36] Within a month, "legal complaint" bureaus, staffed by volunteer attorneys, opened in large cities across the United States.[37] Among the lawyers who offered their services free of charge were Morris Hillquit and Eastman herself. Further, she proposed a more comprehensive strategy to secure the exemption through the judicial system: she wanted to design actions that were certain to elicit repression so they could spotlight the denial of civil liberties.[38] "It is high time that all honest liberals in this country, whether for or against the war, realize that all that is real in American democracy is in danger today," she told the *New York Times*.[39] By provoking legal cases, she argued, either the AUAM would see free speech and assembly rights upheld or they would produce a strong test case for an appeal in the higher courts.[40]

Despite its unanimous opposition to conscription, the AUAM was divided over this confrontational approach, fearing it would appear to oppose government policy and obstruct the prosecution of the war. Crystal did not share these doubts. Indeed, she continued to feel conscientious objection to war fell well within respected American traditions—traditions supported by President

Wilson. As the executive committee struggled with the appearance of opposing government policy and the new wartime laws, she argued that their efforts might in fact boost their prestige with lawmakers. In a letter to Wald the same day the AUAM announced this new political category for exemption, she questioned, "Shall we really be [seen as] an opposition party in our fight for liberty of conscience, after all?"[41]

The AUAM called a "Free Press Luncheon" in July. "Seventeen radical publications have been suppressed since June 15 by postal authorities under the Espionage Act," Crystal announced. The meeting drew nearly one hundred editors, journalists, magazine writers, and other public-spirited citizens to protest that.[42] Working with representatives from some of the other suppressed publications, the gathered group elected a committee of four high-profile attorneys—Clarence Darrow, Frank Walsh, Seymour Stedman, and Morris Hillquit—to go to Washington and talk with administration officials. Wilson refused to see them, but he did promise a thorough investigation. The delegation was able to see Postmaster General Burleson, who wielded wide discretion on what constituted permissible material under the Espionage Act, but he divulged nothing about the standards he was using to exclude information from the mail.[43]

To some in the AUAM leadership, this action too seemed like a challenge to government authority, and it touched off divisions within the organization that by now had been simmering for months. Just as the legal complaint bureaus for COs were formally launching across the country, Crystal received letters of resignation from both Lillian Wald and Paul Kellogg. The resignations presented a major crisis to the AUAM, and, in different ways, to Crystal herself. To lose Wald, the group's well-respected chair, and Kellogg, one of the best-known social welfare reformers in the country, was to sacrifice not only their insight and guidance but also their credibility, qualities that had only become more essential to the organization since the declaration of war.

Moreover, there were personal dimensions involved. Kellogg was Eastman's first champion at the Pittsburgh Survey and remained among her most trusted mentors and friends. As for Wald, her disaffection from the AUAM was connected to Crystal personally; she would speak publicly about Eastman's role in her growing estrangement from the organization. Wald criticized what she saw as Crystal's "impulsive radicalism" and told the *New York Times* that "much as I like [her] personally, she is more than I can manage single handed."[44] She later remarked that Crystal's exceptional "fire and imagination" was "often impatient of more sober councils."[45] As she had before, Wald concluded that to ally herself with such controversial people and policies would threaten the status she needed to pursue her broader reform agenda. Like Kellogg, she was a social worker, dependent on respect and largesse to accomplish her social goals. "There are so many things that I must plead for," she would tell Addams. "I cannot throw away any part of my reputation for good judgment."[46]

But Crystal could not abandon what had always been the AUAM's world-changing mission, now dependent on its wartime agenda to maintain democratic freedoms in full. In an effort to save both the goals she venerated and the liberties she believed were indispensable to achieving them, she began an internal lobbying campaign to mediate the conflict that was tearing the AUAM apart. In a memo sent to Wald, Kellogg, Balch, and other influential leaders, she essentially prosecuted a legal case in pursuit of the outcome she maintained was right not only for the organization but also for the country and the world.[47]

Wald felt the AUAM's work depended on friendly relations with the powers that be and was perturbed by protests that situated the group as a party of opposition to the government. To answer this concern, Crystal again pressed what she saw as the political benefit to the president of the AUAM's work with COs. By providing a means to ensure the Wilson administration was protecting democracy by not forcing any American man into the army against the dictates of his conscience, their work might really help, not hinder, the White House, she argued.[48]

As for Kellogg, he wondered about cross-purposes, or at least mixed messaging, in the two lines of the AUAM's current work. The internationalist effort might even be destroyed, he felt, if the group became "so hopelessly identified in the public mind with 'anti-war' agitation as to make it impossible for us to lead the liberal sentiment for peace." In response, Crystal pressed her continued belief that democratic liberties and world peace through international federation were interdependent—"the two go hand-in-hand," she insisted. In fact, she argued, only by using civil liberties such as freedom of speech and assembly to mobilize people and shape public opinion could the AUAM accomplish its internationalist goals. She believed they needed the untrammeled ability to reach other citizens directly—to "enlist the rank and file of the people, who make for progressivism the country over, in a movement for a civil solution to this world-wide conflict and fire them with a vision of the beginning of the U.S. of the World."[49]

Crystal then proposed an eleventh-hour solution: create a single legal bureau for the maintenance of fundamental rights in wartime—free press, free speech, freedom of assembly, and liberty of conscience. All the civil liberties work would continue but be moved into a separate entity, to be located in the same building at 70 Fifth Avenue and to function as a collaborating group. The internationalist effort would go on through the AUAM, aided by the work of the new bureau to protect its methods to do so. It was a structural solution to an elemental problem that was threatening to rupture the organization from the inside.[50] With her proposal, those members of the AUAM who wanted to emphasize internationalist peacemaking were satisfied that the civil liberties work would not damage their interests and credibility, while those who emphasized the need to challenge government propaganda and the suppression of dissent would now have a formal—and formidable—organization through which to do it.

Characteristically, Crystal herself wanted both. And in an era of government repression coming just one year after her triumphant test case with citizen diplomacy in Mexico, she would never think more decisively about how crucially connected they were. If citizens acting together were going to be able to bring about world peace and world federation, she knew they were going to have to call upon some kind of natural right to a democratic voice that could supersede national policies, supersede national governments. Indeed, in the midst of the wartime laws, she could see quite clearly that they must secure fundamental safeguards to protect democratic citizens from the government's power to quash their efforts in the interest of its own authority.[51] "I believe a thorough-going movement for a democratic peace, for world organization, for universal democracy must rest on a clear understanding of each nation's problem in guarding its own democracy," she explained in her memo. She believed "an unequivocal avowal" of this equation was therefore crucial to the goals of the AUAM; without the absolute guarantee of the democratic means to their internationalist ends, their mission would become impossible. The "movement will lack reality," she warned, "valiant people will lose faith in it, and it will go the way of all peace societies."[52] The separation seemed the only way to keep both lines of work alive—and thus for her vision of the postwar world to survive.

Kellogg described Crystal's "strong memorandum" as a master stroke, telling Jane Addams it resolved all debate.[53] On June 15, 1917, the executive committee voted overwhelmingly to approve the separation as she had proposed it. Whether they were voting for the vision Eastman maintained or to maintain the leadership of the organization as it was is unclear. All we know is the leadership emphatically followed Crystal's lead in deciding to create the Civil Liberties Bureau (CLB) of the AUAM. In October 1917, it was named the National Civil Liberties Bureau (NCLB) and gained an executive committee and staff of its own. In 1920, the bureau was renamed the American Civil Liberties Union (ACLU).

Crystal immediately drafted a press release defending the AUAM's civil liberties work in wartime. She wanted to clarify immediately that "we are not a party of opposition." In fact, it was a "democracy first" movement, she explained, in which the people's right to speak was paramount. Crucially, to her, the people's democratic voice transcended everything—national governments, national treaties, national borders. Eastman acknowledged that once the war was "a fact," she wanted the United States to win, although what she meant by winning was the advancement of the internationalist vision for peace they had been seeking all along. And recently that settled platform had acquired a radical association: the essential planks had been voiced by the Bolshevik forces who were nearly halfway to victory in the Russian Revolution. That connection certainly did not alter Eastman's commitment to it, or her continued conviction that a people's path to peace and world order was the right one for the world. Quite the contrary. "We want [America] to win by joining hands with the awakened peoples of the most liberal republics among her allies in their growing determination to secure an early negotiated general peace ... in harmony with the principles outlined by the revolutionary government of Russia," she announced.[54]

But a pivotal minority within the AUAM leadership did not agree, or, at least, did not want to call attention to the enhanced radicalism now imputed to their long-standing internationalism. The proposed statement was never released. Two weeks later, the AUAM put out a different statement to the press, one that conveyed a distinctly patriotic message. Now the purpose of the new Civil Liberties Bureau was cast in more nationalistic terms: "to combat this tendency [of wartime militarism] where it threatens free speech, free press, freedom of assembly and freedom of conscience—the essentials of liberty and the heritage of all past wars worth fighting."[55] The bureau's rationale was now grounded not in international alliances with the awakened people of the most liberal republics of the world, but right here at home, in American heritage and on domestic soil. "To maintain something over here that will be worth coming back to when the weary war is over—that is what our Civil Liberties Bureau is for," the statement said. When the AUAM soon released a pamphlet to explain the mission of the CLB, it amplified this all-American message. The booklet was entitled "Announcing the Civil Liberties Bureau of the American Union Against Militarism." On the cover was a Boardman Robinson drawing of Yankee Doodle, and the tag line read: "The Spirit of '76—Under Fire."[56]

As the AUAM quieted its policy connections to revolutionary Russia, the CLB offset prewar internationalism with a new display of nationalistic imagery and appeal. The political ground had shifted dramatically with the onset of the Russian Revolution and the US declaration of war just weeks later—but Crystal's stance did not. In that summer of 1917, she joined with many others who tilted to the radical wing of the antiwar movement in organizing the People's Council of America for Democracy and Peace. She and Max both attended the founding convention, held at the Holland House in lower Manhattan, on May 30–31. Her husband, Walter, was on the organizing committee, along with Emily Greene

Balch, Morris Hillquit, and Norman Thomas, the Presbyterian minister who became a six-time presidential nominee of the Socialist Party beginning in 1928. Members included Eastman's suffrage colleagues Fola La Follette and Mary Ware Dennett; the Columbia-trained anthropologist and folklorist Elsie Clews Parsons; and David Starr Jordan, who the papers would report was elected to national office as treasurer, despite hisassertions that he had never agreed to run or to serve.[57] Walter became editor of the *People's Council Bulletin*, first published in August.[58]

The group's resolutions maintained the pre-1917 internationalism that Crystal had written as point number one in her abortive press release—"democracy first." Their familiar planks included an international organization for the maintenance of world peace and the democratization of diplomacy. Unlike the AUAM, the People's Council did not downplay its internationalist call for a quick and universal peace in harmony with the principles outlined by revolutionary Russia. Neither did it brook any discreet bargaining about the draft; the council opposed it outright. And it simultaneously insisted on the maintenance of free speech, press, and assembly in wartime. In contrast to the reservations and divergent interests simmering within the AUAM, the council's program wholeheartedly embraced the connection between democratic civil liberties and radical internationalism, accepting the two as interdependent forces in the project of world peace and beyond.[59]

This large and uncompromising agenda resonated among many on the left. A network of councils quickly formed across the country, and hundreds of radical organizations affiliated with them—Socialist locals, trade unions, and single tax groups among them. In rapid succession, conferences on "Democracy and Terms of Peace" were held in Chicago, Philadelphia, Los Angeles, San Francisco, Salt Lake City, and Seattle.[60]

The rapid growth of the People's Council made the group an almost immediate target of both official repression and private vigilantes. In early September, Crystal, Max, Walter, and others tried to organize a meeting in Minneapolis to draw up a constitution, but they were driven out of town by an angry mob, aided by law enforcement. They moved to Chicago, to a factory outside of town, after the mayor offered to protect them. But as they began the meeting, the governor of Illinois called out the state police to shut them down. At that point, Max and Walter returned to New York, but Crystal stayed behind; she convened a group of women in a hotel in nearby Lake Geneva, Wisconsin, using the name American Liberty League. The papers reported the women "resolved to go to Washington, D.C., to picket the celebration of conscription day there, September 5. Picketing would consist of a display of banners after the fashion of the suffragists."[61] If that protest ever took place, the newspapers failed to cover it. What did appear were articles characterizing the People's Council as an internal threat and labeling antiwar groups, including the AUAM, as conspirators and traitors, as "enemies within."[62]

Back in New York, the general assembly of the People's Council had aroused conflict within the AUAM from the start. Crystal had proposed the organization send delegates and, on a motion by Paul Kellogg, they had voted to do so.[63] That vote, however, finally pushed Wald to her limit. To her, Crystal and her allies both represented and orchestrated links to an internationalist agenda not just radical but now revolutionary in its hues. On August 24, Wald once again threatened to resign. Crystal tried twice to convince her to stay, but as Wald would confide to Addams, she now had "no confidence in Crystal's judgment."[64] Finally, at Wald's request, the AUAM executive committee met to discuss her ultimatum: essentially, it was Crystal and the People's Council or Wald and the AUAM as they knew it—but not both. "I am aware that this may result in the resignation of the Chairman or the Executive Secretary, but it would be lacking in sincerity for us not to be perfectly frank with each other," Wald told Eastman flatly.[65]

The matter came to a vote. Ultimately, seventeen members sided with Eastman, electing to send a delegation to the People's Council constituent assembly, while five—including Kellogg, Villard, and Wald herself—voted against it.[66]

Less than two weeks later, the civil liberties debate re-emerged for the AUAM, reigniting conflicts the formation of the separate Civil Liberties Bureau had been designed to quell. The AUAM was investigated by the post office in September, and two of its pamphlets about conscientious objectors were seized. Wald, still nominally the chair, believed the pamphlets were innocent and wrote the post-master that the AUAM had never done anything to obstruct or embarrass the government. She offered to withdraw the pamphlets to prove the organization's "good intentions."[67] Eastman and several others disagreed with what they saw as Wald's accommodationist stance. The language of the new law was vague, they thought, and neither the post office nor the Justice Department had been quick to respond to their requests for clarification. Crystal was among those who felt the pamphlets did not violate the law and advocated that the AUAM sue the post office.[68]

After four months, they did go to court, and the Justice Department ruled the pamphlets legal, but the ruling was too late to resolve the political rifts now irreversibly severing the organization. Crystal had already written to Wald to assure her that there were no official ties between the AUAM and the People's Council, and had emphasized that she refused to accept any per-manent office on any committee so there would be no question or appearance of interlocking directorates.[69] Later, she also proposed stepping down from the AUAM herself, offering her resignation to distance the organization from some of its more radical colors.[70] She urged Wald not to leave, expressing her "profound hope that an effective, liberal, constructive, antimilitaristic program might be maintained at this time of dire need."[71] But that same day, September 13, Wald submitted her resignation as chair of the AUAM. In the end, Crystal expressed the view of the majority when she avowed that if keeping Wald meant abandoning the civil liberties work, then she must oppose it. The program of the AUAM, she said, "would not have much hold on the country" without that work in wartime.[72]

Shortly following these events, Crystal drafted another announcement to the press. On September 24, she proposed the American Union Against Militarism change its name to the Civil Liberty Defense League. "It takes an exceedingly large-minded liberal to fight for the right of another man to say exactly what he himself does not want said," the announcement explained. And the AUAM—or was Crystal thinking of the new Civil Liberties Bureau?—now took as its mandate "to prevent in this country those extreme manifestations of militarism . . . [which] in a war avowedly fought for the sake of democracy, are a tragic mistake."[73]

Her proposed announcement positioned the civil liberties work at the fulcrum of present and future; it sat at the crux, as she saw it, of the AUAM's "stake in war." And as she shifted from a more fluid concept of antimilitarism toward a more grounded call for universal disarmament, she only accentuated the right to speak, assemble, and protest as indispensable powers for the achievement of any humanistic and transnational goal. Without civil liberties, no genuine democratic pressure—let alone the radical citizen diplomacy she so valued after the international triumph between the United States and Mexico—could be brought to bear. These mechanisms were the engine of the whole virtuous cycle between peace and internationalism she had been working for since 1915. Crystal had long regarded civil liberties as a natural right of democratic citizens—not a set of legal affordances provided by any country or national constitution. "Free speech," she now declared, was "not an empty legal right,—but the living essence of democracy."[74]

In September 1917, her proposed announcement sought to reclaim the civil liberties fight for the larger cause of radical internationalism once more. While Crystal acknowledged the recent establishment of the CLB, her announcement essentially articulated the rationale for reabsorbing its work into the AUAM, its parent organization—*her* organization. She always wanted to be on the front lines of the most active political fight. Besides, she thought from the beginning that civil liberties were inseparable from the internationalist project of the

AUAM.[75] With Wald and others now irretrievably gone, she wanted to rescind the compromises and again integrate the civil liberties fight with the AUAM's larger democratic struggle for world peace and world federation—and back under her operational control.

Crystal polled the leadership about the prospect of reunifying the AUAM with the CLB the very next day. In effect, she wanted to recommit the organization to its original wartime agenda, which, after all, had been announced just three months before. Contacting at least a dozen key leaders including Addams, Starr Jordan, Balch, and Thomas, she asked: should the current board remain in place, leaving the AUAM "to those who would work very quietly in wartime and take no stand on the issue of Civil Liberty," or should those who cannot remain if the civil liberties work continues "resign and let their places be filled by others who do enthusiastically support that work?" In so many ways, the organization was split right down the middle. "It must be borne in mind," she noted, "we have now 3400 contributing members, scattered all over the country . . . [and] about half . . . have joined since we undertook the Civil Liberties fight."[76]

Most who responded saw the AUAM as a permanent institution—the one that needed to be there "to fight the big fight" against the "root causes of the whole evil," as Wald put it.[77] Indeed, several key figures saw the CLB as only a temporary organization that would naturally pass away with the end of the war. Given the choice, the majority preferred to reunify as one organization—the AUAM—once again. With the significant exception of Addams, who preferred the option to work "quietly," as she said, most others believed that to abandon that work for civil liberties would prove fatal to the organization.[78] Some criticized the continued separation as disruptive to the entire fabric of the work, discrediting both organizations and much of the membership.[79] Norman Thomas said "sorrowfully" that he thought those who could not be connected to the civil liberties fight should be replaced. Like Crystal, he felt the CLB "would be hard pressed to stay out of the ground staked off for the AUAM," and the AUAM "would have very little appeal without civil liberties work in wartime."[80]

Despite the thinking of the majority, the reunification was not to be. Although the CLB had only been officially formed in July, and this was late September, the bureau had grown up fast, becoming considerably more independent than that timeline would suggest. Its director, the social worker Roger Baldwin, was an exceptionally tireless presence from the start. He had first come to the notice of the AUAM at a meeting in February 1917. He had written from his office in St. Louis to urge mass mobilization of the antiwar sentiment of men, as distinct from men and women. The AUAM had decided this approach would require a separate organization, which was simply not feasible given the crisis of impending US intervention. But Kellogg suggested they stay in touch with Baldwin. Eastman was directed to wire, urging him to organize protest meetings where he was.[81]

Baldwin would organize against the war in St. Louis, but just four days later, on February 14, he again contacted the AUAM, this time corresponding with Eastman directly. "The time is rapidly coming now when I feel that I can no longer carry on this local work," he told her. "If war is actually declared," he continued, "I should cut loose at once from this local work."[82]

Crystal was nearly eight months pregnant at the time. On March 5, she asked the executive committee for permission to begin searching for someone to assist her during her maternity leave. To maintain her leadership and authority in the organization, she wanted to pay the new assistant out of her own salary. "Under this arrangement, I should like to continue in general charge of the work," she told them.[83]

By March 13, Crystal's doctor ordered her to stop working altogether.[84] She asked Wald for two months maternity leave and proposed two specific people to cover her most basic duties until her return—her WPP-NYC colleague Polly Angell to handle local organization and edit publications, and Joy Young, a part-time office secretary. There is no extant response to her proposal, but eight days later, she again received a letter from Baldwin, this time offering to relinquish his $5,000-a-year paid position with the Civic League of St. Louis and volunteer his services to the AUAM free of charge. He told her he had saved enough money to work without salary for a time. "How and where in your judgment could you best use me?" he asked.[85]

Despite his multiple overtures directly to Eastman, by the next year Baldwin would recall being invited to join the AUAM by Wald.[86] Whatever or whoever finally prompted him to move from Missouri to New York to join the organization, he and Crystal were very different people. By "tradition and temperament," as he put it, Baldwin was more like Wald and the other social workers in the leadership. He described himself as a practical reformer and service provider, whereas Eastman was an activist, radical, and firebrand. Baldwin would later recall that the war and the AUAM forced him "to grapple with new and troublesome issues: problems of nation-states, capitalist rivalries, and the morality of warfare as a means to good ends"—questions Crystal eagerly sought to engage and confront.[87] She was a radical internationalist whose vision was to transcend what she would call "capitalist nationalism," creating world democracy and transnational structures to replace it.[88] To Baldwin, such grand designs were less intelligible, and perhaps less desirable as well; affluent, Harvard educated, a renegade but a businessman's son and Mayflower descendant,[89] he later admitted he found Crystal's perspective "obscure."[90] And "while we never openly clashed," Baldwin disclosed, "the alliance was uneasy."[91]

Eastman and Baldwin did share a zealous commitment to the civil liberties fight—so much so that some colleagues blamed the pair jointly for the attitudes and actions that divided the organization. "To tell the honest truth," Villard said, the AUAM "was wrecked because of loss of faith in the judgment of Crystal Eastman and Roger Baldwin."[92] Still, the two justified the civil liberties agenda differently, and pursued it with a different endgame in mind.

No professional conflict appears to have ever erupted between them, however. Eastman's private life had intervened. Baldwin first formally volunteered himself to the AUAM in a letter dated March 20, 1917.[93] On March 19, she had given birth to her first child.

It had been a difficult pregnancy. Four days before the birth, Crystal had had convulsions and was rushed to a hospital on the Upper West Side of Manhattan. She underwent surgery, likely a cesarean section, and delivered what her sister-in-law described as a "very puny, weak child."[94] And she was very ill afterward. It was not until a week later that Margaret Lane could circulate news to their WPP-NYC colleagues that she was out of danger.[95] Crystal's lifelong poor health had forced her to bed rest before the birth and a long, isolating recovery postpartum. She complained that her doctors were keeping her endlessly, all because of her persistently high blood pressure. She wrote to Max: "I am appealing to you from the tower where I am kept—to save me from this dragon and his mysterious blood pressure. I have begun to sleep and I haven't an ache or a pain. He himself admits I am well enough to begin to get up if it weren't for the B.P. That, he says, does not go down yet. Every morning he comes in and measures it, shakes his head and goes off."[96] She told Wald she was trying "to forget it all and *get well*. But it is hard to leave this work for so long. I didn't figure on such complete separation for more than three weeks!"[97] More than a month after delivery she wrote to Kellogg, "Your spring flowers stayed steady beside me for days—Bless you for remembering me."[98]

With Eastman sidelined for three months, Baldwin had enjoyed unusual latitude, and at a moment of enormous exigency. He had arrived in New York in time to attend a meeting of the executive committee on April 2, and two days later was given charge of the emerging legal defense work for conscientious objectors, the major crucible of the civil liberties fight. He was awarded the title of associate director that same day.[99]

Crystal had responded to these events by writing urgently from Atlantic City, New Jersey, where she was confined to her bed. "I felt that I must have a little conference with you about the AUAM," she wrote Wald, "but now that I'm down here—that along with my other responsibilities seems very far away." But "one thing I do want to ask—very earnestly," she entreated. "That is, that no new arrangements be made with anyone until I get back or until I can be consulted. I mean no new contracts or understandings to extend beyond June 1."[100] She was almost certainly referring to an employment contract for Baldwin.

Soon after, she again wrote to Wald, this time to specifically quarrel with the direction Baldwin was taking with the burgeoning civil liberties work. He had proposed "a constitution and program . . . which in a great many respects I don't approve of," she said. Organizationally, she felt he was proceeding too quickly in her absence. "I don't think we need such elaborate formal organization just yet," she told Wald, and, particularly, "in the statement of objects etc., I do want to have a hand, if possible."[101] As days became weeks, Crystal confessed, "I am crazy to get back on the job. . . . I'm so afraid it will be over—the fight lost." She told Amos Pinchot, "I fear there will be nothing left for me to do" when she returned.[102]

She was able to resume work on June 1 as she had hoped and took her immediate stand, together with Baldwin, for a committee of lawyers to press the case for COs in court. She then spent the summer and early fall taking care of her newborn, promoting the People's Council, and avidly advancing the civil liberties agenda. She had quickly put forward her recommendation "that we undertake the actual testing of the right of free speech in the districts and localities where it had been specifically denied." Ever a lawyer at heart, she emphasized the virtues of the test-case approach, which became a signature strategy of the early ACLU. "This could be done in an extremely dignified and effective way and, I believe, would do more to restore the right of free speech than almost anything we could do," she insisted.[103] In August, Eastman organized AUAM member fundraising campaigns to finance CLB operations, signed a letter to Wilson protesting the brutal treatment of COs, and mobilized AUAM locals and affiliates for civil liberties actions.[104] Her September proposal to reunite the two ostensibly separate organizations as the Civil Liberties League reflected the fact that the civil liberties fight was the only live, pressing, active work with which she and the AUAM had been involved for months.

But by October 9, as the AUAM accepted Wald's resignation "with deep regret," the CLB became the National Civil Liberties Bureau and established an executive committee structure.[105] Baldwin had already been listed as director on AUAM letterhead. It firmly belonged to him—and clearly bore his political imprint. He had arrived in the midst of exceptional hostility to the antiwar movement, as well as intensifying political divisions within the AUAM itself. Buffered by complex tensions both within and without, he had been the one to shape the patriotic connections to the American Constitution, separating civil liberties from their English heredity[106] and broader internationalist involvements alike.[107] Capitalizing on the prevailing nationalism rather than challenging it the way Eastman consistently did, Baldwin would successfully build the new organization and also make it his own.[108]

At the same October 1917 meeting, Crystal regrouped. Hoping to revitalize the depleted AUAM, she proposed another name change, arguing that it should stand *for* something, not just against militarism. "It should be a winning name, suggesting our real goal: internationalism and disarmament," she urged.[109] League for a Democratic Peace, League for International Democracy, and League for a Just Peace were all possibilities.[110] In a press release in early November, she announced it was now the American Union for a Democratic Peace. The group would advocate "for" a democratic and enduring peace at war's end in terms consistent with Eastman's internationalist hopes. Pivotally, these included a peace settlement "without acquisition of territory by any belligerent, and without punitive damages, and without an aftermath of economic hostilities." The new name indicated "no change in fundamental beliefs or in the objects, only a change in emphasis," she said.[111]

But so much more than that had changed for the organization, and indeed for Crystal herself. The previous week she had made numerous proposals for new actions, especially around the need for the AUAM to have a voice at the Paris Peace Conference when hostilities finally ended. All were either postponed or voted down.[112] She had also written to Addams, entreating her to remain on the executive committee of the newly renamed group. "I have great, new hope for the organization," she told her.[113] But in mid-November, Addams too resigned, just weeks after Wald.[114]

Less than two weeks later, Crystal herself resigned. At that same meeting, the AUAM voted to disband altogether and to fold itself into the ongoing work of the National Civil Liberties Bureau—not, as so many leaders polled in September had forecast, the other way around.[115] Although the AUAM would subsequently revive itself under new leadership, focusing first on opposition to compulsory military training, then in 1919 against the punitive elements of the Treaty of Versailles and "the whole flourishing of American imperialism" witnessed in the peace process and beyond, it never again gained political traction or public influence.[116] The organization finally disbanded in February 1922.

Only the National Civil Liberties Bureau would live on, thriving illustriously as the ACLU. Now deeply imprinted with Baldwin's emphasis, the civil liberties fight developed a distinctly American bearing. While the organization stands today as a shining hallmark of national philosophy and character, its mission became increasingly dissociated from internationalist campaigns for global democracy and world peace, struggles Crystal had always dreamed could march forward together in the postwar world, arm in arm.

Eastman's parents were each unconventional. Her mother, Annis Ford Eastman, a Congregational minister and the first woman ever ordained in New York State, became both the economic and emotional engine of the family. *Courtesy of Anne and Cordelia Fuller and Rebecca and Charles Young*

Max Eastman was apprehensive about making it in New York after college, but Crystal orchestrated a plum lectureship with the philosopher John Dewey at Columbia beginning in 1907. The siblings remained unusually bonded as adults, as emotionally attached as any couple. *Bain News Service, Library of Congress, https://www.loc.gov/item/2014685763*

Samuel Eastman was a man whose radical "generosity," as Crystal described his elemental empathy for others, led him to treat his wife and daughter as equals to himself and his sons. *Courtesy of Anne and Cordelia Fuller and Rebecca and Charles Young*

Eastman (seated, third from left) attended the Granger Place School, a finishing school for young ladies outside Canandaigua. Crystal's cousin, Adra Ash (standing, first from left), who lived with the Eastmans beginning as a teenager, graduated the following year. *Ontario County Historical Society*

Always an athlete, Eastman was an excellent swimmer and refused to wear the bulky, binding swimming costume still dictated for women at the turn of the twentieth century. *Eastman, Mann, Wingard Genealogical Collection*

A popular member of the Vassar class of 1903, Eastman (far right) was elected class historian. Seen here studying circa 1901, she distinguished herself as a singer and actor, as well as a political leader, while in college. *Vassar College Archives and Special Collections*

Backstage at a policy conference on industrial accidents and workers' compensation in June 1910, Eastman offset her fierce attitude with silk gloves and a floral hat. *Chicago Daily News negatives collection, DN0055962, Chicago History Museum*

Following her groundbreaking appointment to chair New York's Commission on Employer Liability in 1909, Eastman was amused to read about herself in a newspaper profile touting her work. *Eastman, Mann, Wingard Genealogical Collection*

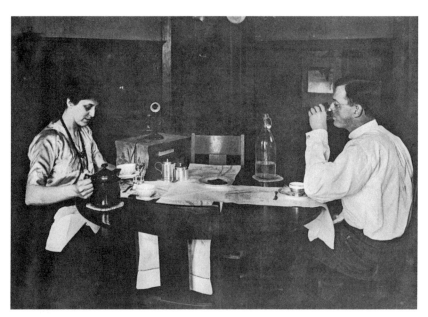

As campaign manager of the Wisconsin suffrage drive in 1911–12, Eastman had to negotiate between her New York feminism and the traditional expectations of a middle-class marriage with her first husband, Wallace "Bennie" Benedict. *Eastman, Mann, Wingard Genealogical Collection*

Eastman addressed the Seventh Congress of the International Woman Suffrage Alliance (IWSA) in Budapest in 1913. She is talking with the journalist Joe O'Brien in front of the Redonte Building where the congress was held. *Schwimmer-Lloyd Collection, Manuscripts and Archives Division, New York Public Library*

On the advice of Jane Addams (seated with arms crossed at right), Eastman was the first person Alice Paul and Lucy Burns contacted to help organize the drive for a constitutional suffrage amendment. At the annual National American Woman Suffrage Association convention in Philadelphia in December 1912, Eastman and Burns were tasked to convince Dr. Anna Howard Shaw (presiding). Eastman stage-managed from the sidelines at the far left but was cropped out of the shot when it was circulated to the papers. *National American Woman's Suffrage Association Convention, ca. 1912–13, Records of the National Woman's Party, Library of Congress*

From the War Against War Exhibit

Send to American Union Against Militarism, Munsey Bldg., Washington, D. C., for this poster in colors (size 3 ft. by 5 ft.) 25 cents. Complete exhibit (30 posters, all different), $8.

From the War Against War Exhibit

Send to American Union Against Militarism, Munsey Bldg., Washington, D. C., for this poster in colors (size 3 ft. by 5 ft.) 25 cents. Complete exhibit (30 posters, all different), $8.

From the War Against War Exhibit

Send to American Union Against Militarism, Munsey Bldg., Washington, D. C., for this poster in colors (size 3 ft. x 5 ft.) 25 cents. Complete exhibit (30 posters, all different), $8.

From the War Against War Exhibit

Send to American Union Against Militarism, Munsey Bldg., Washington, D. C., for this poster in colors (size 3 ft. by 5 ft.) 25 cents. Complete exhibit (30 posters, all different), $8.

In April 1916, Eastman organized a campaign to combat the US military buildup. Its centerpiece was an interactive "War against War" exhibit, which included striking visuals such as these oversized cartoons designed by her husband, Walter Fuller. *American Union against Militarism Records (DG 004), Swarthmore College Peace Collection*

In 1915 and 1916, Eastman's Woman's Peace Party of New York mounted large-scale demonstrations to advocate for world federation—"a U.S. of the world," as Eastman described it. (Crystal is fourth from left in the first photo. The second depicts a protest of legislative proposals for compulsory military training in New York's public schools.) *Woman's Peace Party Papers (DG043), Swarthmore College Peace Collection*

Eastman attended the Republican National Convention in Chicago in 1916 representing both the National Woman's Party and the American Union Against Militarism. With the well-known reformer Amos Pinchot, she lobbied the GOP nominee to maintain American neutrality in the Great War. *Underwood and Underwood, Vintage News Service*

Eastman always longed to become a mother, and when she gave birth to her first child, Jeffrey, just three weeks before the US declaration of war, it forever changed her life—and career. *Courtesy of Anne and Cordelia Fuller and Rebecca and Charles Young*

In April 1918, Max Eastman and several other editors and writers of *The Masses* stood trial for sedition under the wartime Espionage Act. Crystal raised the bail money—$20,000 for her brother and $10,000 for each of the other defendants (from left: Crystal, Art Young, Max, their attorney Morris Hillquit, Merrill Rogers, and Floyd Dell). *National Archives, photo 165-WW-164B-4*

Around the time she and Max launched the *Liberator* magazine, Eastman attends a community spaghetti dinner at Grace Godwin's garret, a second-floor tea room on the south side of Washington Square Park. Eastman adored Greenwich Village because, she said, people were "open-minded, and eager over every new movement, and . . . know when it is right for them to let go and amuse themselves and because they can laugh, even at themselves." *Jessie Tarbox Beals Photograph Collection (PR004), New York Historical Society*

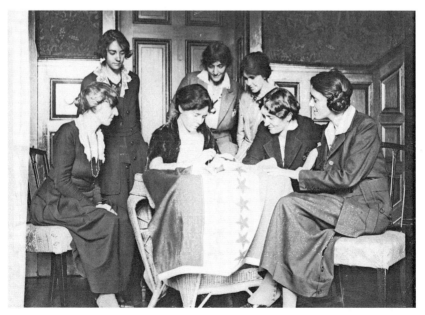

As the suffrage amendment neared ratification in 1920, Eastman (rear, center) joined other National Woman's Party activists at their headquarters in Washington, DC, to watch Alice Paul sew another state's star onto their ratification flag. *Records of the National Woman's Party, Library of Congress, http://hdl.loc.gov/loc.mss/mnwp.160073*

Eastman's husband, Walter Fuller, an intuitive pacifist and publicist gifted with a creative conscience, struggled to maintain a sense of independence and volition alongside the couple's egalitarian ideal of shared responsibility for children. *Courtesy of Anne and Cordelia Fuller and Rebecca and Charles Young*

Eastman may have made Virginia Woolf's acquaintance through the feminist journal *Time and Tide*, which published both women's work in the 1920s, or via Walter's connections to the Bloomsbury group. She and her two-year-old daughter met Leonard Woolf, the noted socialist and publisher, in 1924. *Courtesy of Anne and Cordelia Fuller and Rebecca and Charles Young*

Beginning in the fall of 1922, Crystal and the children shuttled between England and America at various intervals, living mainly in northwest London while Walter boarded with mutual friends nearby. *Courtesy of Anne and Cordelia Fuller and Rebecca and Charles Young*

Since the children lived with Eastman in London and New York, in most respects she functioned as a single parent, both breadwinner and homemaker. Metaphorically and literally, she stood always at an intersection (Bournemouth, England, 1925). *Courtesy of Anne and Cordelia Fuller and Rebecca and Charles Young*

8 REGROUPING: THE *LIBERATOR* YEARS

On the day before Thanksgiving in 1917, Crystal wrote to Jane Addams. She wanted some time with her for "quiet, uninterrupted talk" to explain her resignation from the American Union Against Militarism (AUAM) the day before. "My whole philosophy about the way to get things done has undergone a change in the last two or three weeks," she confided.[1]

It had been a tumultuous year. The joyous onset of motherhood in her private life had coincided with world events that dramatically altered her political outlook as well. Just as her first child was born, the Russian Revolution had begun. Although the revolution is often regarded as a single event, it was actually a pair of revolutions, one that dismantled the Russian autocracy and a second, led by the Bolsheviks, that ushered in the Soviet Union. Just days before Jeffrey Fuller was born, Tsar Nicholas II had been overthrown in the February Revolution—March 7–16 on the Western calendar—and a provisional government established under Alexander Kerensky in Petrograd, today's Saint Petersburg. Three months later, large numbers of Russian soldiers, starving and angry at their conditions as the Great War wore on, mutinied or deserted the Imperial Russian Army, leading to a wholesale collapse and defeat on the Eastern Front. At the time, Leon Trotsky forecast that the Bolshevik faction, a radical group of workers and soldiers under the leadership of Vladimir Lenin, would overthrow the Kerensky regime and negotiate for peace with Germany. Both predictions would come to pass by year's end.

The promise of peace was as significant to Eastman's support for the revolution as was the people's republic the Bolsheviks promised to usher in. US intervention in World War I had made plain to her the failure of what she called "polite petitions and private delegations" to bring about a mediated settlement.[2] Months earlier, she had finally given up on Wilson's intermittent evocations of peace without victory, telling Addams he had been "faithless" to the antiwar movement. "I

Crystal Eastman. Amy Aronson, Oxford University Press (2020).
© Oxford University Press.
DOI: 10.1093/oso/9780199948734.001.0001

didn't mean that Wilson had not been moved by any of our efforts or appeals. . . .
I didn't mean that he had not been intellectually moved," she explained. "It is
because I think he has been, again and again, convinced in his mind, by you and
others, that we were right in our principles and in what we were asking him to do,
and yet he has not acted on that conviction."[3]

Crystal had also tried to embrace the arguments of some antiwar Progressives,
including some in the AUAM, who had come to accept the war as a prelude to a
structural program of social reform that they believed could be instituted in its
wake. Although these liberal reformers anticipated the threat to civil liberties,
they saw those dangers as less consequential than the opportunity a wartime
economy would provide to permanently nationalize infrastructure industries and
advance greater economic equality.[4] Crystal had met with such prowar liberals
on November 16, just hours after the Bolsheviks secured their triumph by forcing
Kerensky to flee the city and soon the country, eventually to arrive in France.
She found she simply could not support a zealous war effort; it offended her
"common sense [and] regard for human life."[5]

Disappointed by her realization that the American people could not be
moved to action when presented with credible and compelling information, and
even more by an elected government she saw as indifferent to the people's will,
Crystal now believed that prewar strategies of citizen mobilization were fruit-
less. Effectively, she was withdrawing her earlier faith in evolutionary Socialism,
which had promised that her socialistic goals—human equality and mutual prosperity, as well as internationalism and peace—could be achieved through existing
democratic measures. She mourned what she now saw as "the ineffectiveness of
propaganda carried on by an organization like the American Union at a time like
this." She felt their trust in American democracy and its first principles had been
betrayed, lamenting, "the American Union Committee can do very little in an
organized public way, in the present state of public feeling and under existing limi-
tations upon freedom of discussion."[6] Still holding onto her original goals of world
peace and world federation, she reasoned that revolution was required. "The only
great movement against war must be the radical movement," she concluded.[7]

* * *

American radicals had been unsure of the prospects of a people's republic after
the initial overthrow of the tsar in the February Revolution, but after Lenin's
October Revolution (November 7–8 on the Western calendar), they were struck
by the realization that it was possible for the masses to seize government power.
And when they did, mechanisms to promote other forms of equality quickly
seemed to follow. Crystal must have been struck by the early moves to promote

gender equality. The provisional government had granted full suffrage to women in July, and then the Bolsheviks went further: they supported reproductive rights and relaxed laws pertaining to divorce while establishing public services to reduce domestic burdens and enable women's entry into the workforce.[8] She and many other American radicals began to hope the Bolshevik triumph could usher in a European or even worldwide revolution. When peace negotiations between Russia and Germany began in early December at Brest-Litovsk, utopian hopes for world democracy and internationalism—vast aspirations Eastman had championed for years—seemed a dawning reality.

There were many differences among US radicals when it came to applying the lessons of the Russian Revolution to the American case, but at the outset there was near-complete concurrence—a rare event for this set—on a single stand: support the Bolsheviks. The country's leading Socialists emphatically spoke out: Morris Hillquit, Victor Berger, and Eugene V. Debs, the Industrial Workers of the World (IWW) founding member and five-time presidential candidate of the Socialist Party (his fifth run was to come in 1920), from his prison cell where he was serving a ten-year sentence under the Sedition Act for castigating the war. The Bolsheviks promised a solution to inequality comprehensive enough to appeal to radicals of every stripe—not least the boundary-bridging Eastman: Jewish Socialists cheered the downfall of capitalist land and property owners; black Socialists imagined an end to racial oppression and violence.[9] It was a euphoric moment for Crystal and her political kin. The Woman's Peace Party of New York (WPP-NY), now a statewide branch, embraced the Bolshevik revolt, as Freda Kirchwey and Madeleine Doty put it in the *Four Lights*, "with mad, glad joy!"[10]

John "Jack" Reed witnessed the Russian Revolution firsthand. And when he cabled Max directly, telling him "this afternoon I was present at the opening of the all-Russian assembly of Soviets," he knew he had to do something with the story.[11] At the time, Max saw Reed as the most highly regarded war correspondent in the country, a distinction he himself claimed a hand in making. Reed had published his first breakthrough reportage, on the silk workers' strike in Patterson, New Jersey, in *The Masses* in 1913. That work, amplified by the huge public pageant Reed organized in New York's Madison Square Garden to publicize the strike and raise money for the workers, raised his profile as a radical journalist. Although the pageant ultimately lost money and the strike would end in defeat, Reed's efforts resulted in an offer from the *Metropolitan* magazine, a left-leaning political monthly, to cover the revolt in Mexico led by Pancho Villa and Emiliano Zapata.[12] That assignment vaulted him to star status. He spent four months embedded with Villa's troops, and the experience reporting from inside a live, unfolding revolutionary conflict inspired the most incisive journalism Reed had produced to date.

Upon his return, Reed's dynamic reporting of the Mexican Revolution brought him to the level of a policy expert; President Wilson and Secretary of State Bryan soon consulted with him on Mexican-American relations.[13] And as a journalist, he became what is now called a "media brand." That is, he maintained a distinct public image. Reed was a daring writer-hero, the firebrand of his generation, the journalistic Byron of Bohemia.[14]

Max felt that way about him as much as anyone, even though Reed's fortunes had fallen a bit between the time of his breakthrough reporting on the Mexican Revolution and his cable from the Russian assembly in Moscow. In September 1914, the *Metropolitan* had sent him to cover the outbreak of the war in Europe, and it did not go well. Reed spent weeks searching the Western Front for stories that captured him the way his encounters in Mexico had. An antiwar Socialist, he saw the European conflict as a collaboration between capitalists and imperialists, and, like Max, Crystal, and so many others in their orbit, he advocated that the United States maintain neutrality. For that and other reasons perhaps, the European war reporting Reed produced fell well short of his editor's expectations, as well as his own.[15]

A second trip to Europe in 1915 took him to the Eastern Front, but this time as a freelancer without an advance contract from any magazine. Reed arranged to work with Boardman Robinson, *The Masses* artist and illustrator, and met him at Bucharest for their joint journalistic expedition. Their three-month trip extended to more than double that long, but the project never really found its heart or its focus. When it was published as *The War in Eastern Europe* (1916), Reed tried to package its deficits as a benefit, saying they had "tried to give our impressions [of] the many human qualities [that] are covered up which come to the surface in a sharp crisis."[16] But the book did not sell well.[17]

So by the time Reed gave Max Eastman exclusive access to his dispatches from Russia in 1917, he was searching to reclaim a connection to potent political feeling, and he also had something to prove. He had sailed for Europe, this time with his wife, Louise Bryant, in August. Before he left, he and Max had devised a rough code so he could smuggle the inside story of the October Revolution—the Bolshevik story—past any censors. The Eastman siblings had already been talking about starting a magazine together, and now Reed's matchless news story belonged only to Max.[18] Reed's venture and Max's were joined.

Crystal's resignation from the AUAM became official on January 31, 1918, and by Lincoln's Birthday, she and Max had launched the *Liberator: The Journal of Revolutionary Progress*.[19] Its namesake was William Lloyd Garrison's fiery nineteenth-century journal, a vehicle of radical politics for its day: Garrison's *Liberator* (1831–65) advocated abolition and supported women's suffrage. The Eastmans' *Liberator* was a sequel in two senses: it likewise promoted a radical remaking of the world and also picked up where *The Masses*, already silenced by the Espionage Act even though the first trial would not begin until April, had left off.

Max felt he needed Crystal for the new venture. He had never really wanted to edit a magazine in the first place, and he had learned from *The Masses* that he was ill-suited to fundraising and everyday management. Everyone in journalism knew it. "Business is not Eastman's line by any means," noted the newspaper publisher E. W. Scripps in 1916.[20] At the *Liberator*, Max saw Crystal as the perfect choice for a job he described as "co-editor and manager and money-raiser."[21] Indeed, she rapidly raised $30,000 in start-up funds for the magazine. She was to oversee day-to-day operations for a salary of $90 a week; Floyd Dell, the literary critic, author, playwright, and former managing editor of *The Masses*, became their associate editor at $75 a week; and Max, "to justify and encourage [his] truancy," he remarked, was paid $60.[22]

The *Liberator* quickly became the paper of record for revolutionary movements worldwide. Like *The Masses* before it, the magazine boasted an array of vanguard writers, some of the most important of the modern era: Sherwood Anderson, John Dos Passos, Amy Lowell, e.e. cummings, William Carlos Williams, Djuna Barnes, Jean Toomer, Claude McKay, Edmund Wilson, Vachel Lindsay, Carl Sandburg, Dorothy Day, and Edna St. Vincent Millay among them. Drawings and lithographs by leading-edge contemporary artists appeared regularly, particularly by representatives of the Ash Can School—candid, documentary-style illustrations of immigrant and urban life—including Boardman Robinson and John Sloan, who functioned as editors; George Bellows; and the school's unofficial leader, Robert Henri. The magazine published caricatures by Al Frueh and George Grosz and illustrations by the sculptor Jo Davidson and the modern artist and portraitist Randall Davey. Even Pablo Picasso turned up in its pages. With the Eastman siblings working together, the *Liberator* would double the circulation of *The Masses* in its first month, and it reached sixty thousand subscribers in its first year—three and a half times the seventeen thousand *The Masses* hit at its height.[23] It differed from its predecessor in one other respect as well: the *Liberator* "abandoned the pretense of being a co-operative," as Max put it; Crystal and Max co-owned the magazine.[24]

The *Liberator* plainly supported Bolshevism, protesting policies and political actions the editors saw as threatening to the stability of the new Soviet republic. Early on, it denounced the exclusion of Russia from the League of Nations. The United States had been the first country to recognize the provisional government established after the February Revolution, but once the war ended in Europe with the defeat of the Central powers, the Allies instead supported anti-Bolshevik forces.[25] In an unsigned editorial in February 1919, the *Liberator* blasted the exclusion, saying that without recognition of the Soviets, "the League will be a compact of tyranny."[26] In June, the magazine published "The Allied Intervention in Russia and Hungary," an editorial upbraiding both the Allies' blockade against Russia and the material support—manpower, money, and supplies—by Allied governments for counterrevolutionary actions throughout its territory.[27] And throughout Max and Crystal's tenure, the magazine covered international revolutionary leaders and uprisings in Hungary, Austria, Germany, and France; it discussed party politics pertaining to radical movements; and it regularly reported on the important political trials of the day in the United States and elsewhere.

The Eastmans also saw the magazine as a watchdog for propaganda and misinformation concerning revolutionary revolts. From the moment Russia agreed to the peace treaty with Germany, a move that discontinued the commitments made by Imperial Russia to the Triple Entente alliance and freed the Central Powers to concentrate on the Western Front, American newspapers began blitzing the Bolsheviks, publishing horror stories designed to demolish their international credibility.[28] The peace agreement forced enormous sacrifices on Russia, terms both Trotsky and Lenin bitterly fought. Nevertheless, their ultimate assent to it, however desperate and resigned it may have been, helped to fuel a rising "Red Scare" in the United States and elsewhere. Since the Allied blockade also closed off most means of communication—telegraph, telephone, and mail—opportunities for false information in the press were nearly boundless. "Bolshevism was so fabulously lied about in the American press, pulpit, barroom, and drawing room, in Congress and on the lecture platform," Max recalled, "that truth itself seemed to be crying for help."[29]

Publicly, the Eastman siblings pronounced their intention to speak freely and truthfully about revolution. "Never was the moment more auspicious to issue a great magazine of liberty," they declared, as "the world is entering upon the experiment of industrial and real democracy." Yet internally, they were acutely aware of the risks in confrontation with wartime laws, hazards that only increased as their persistent calls for peace now merged with the official foreign policy of a new, ex-combatant Russian state. The Eastmans agreed they should be more "temper[ed] to the taste of the Postmaster General." [30]

The magazine was more moderate in tone than *The Masses* was, supporting some of Wilson's policies, particularly the League of Nations. The siblings called the *Liberator* a "historic necessity," and even though their friends told them "that we would 'go down with our colors flying,' " Max recalled, they felt they "ought to sacrifice the glory of such a going-down for a chance to serve, in whatever less beautiful way, the new society coming into being in Russia."[31]

Indeed, whatever the concessions, Max and Crystal found the attraction to starting a new magazine irresistible: they had Reed as their exclusive asset; plus, they had "the subscription list, and the fame—and yet more, the infamy—of the old *Masses*," as Max observed.[32] Together, they had the opportunity to serve as parents to what they saw as "the unbounded dream hopes of a new world coming to birth."[33]

For Crystal, the magazine facilitated a parallel new world coming to birth as well. She was now a working mother, and the *Liberator* became the anchor for communal living arrangements she engineered to support her pioneering effort to balance work and family. She organized what Max called a "delightful halfway family" with friends in Greenwich Village: on the first floor of a house on Waverly Place was Ruth Pickering, their dear hometown friend and WPP-NY ally, who would soon marry the millionaire reformer and AUAM colleague Amos Pinchot; the second floor was occupied by Eugen Boissevain, a dashing Dutch importer, the widower of Inez Milholland, who would soon marry the poet Edna St. Vincent Millay; and on the top floor, in two rooms with slanted ceilings, was Max, who frequently entertained the silent film starlet Florence Deshon, with whom he was passionately, if precariously, in love. Crystal, "the prime mover in the whole arrangement, ended up living down the street," Max said.[34] At the time, Walter was working as editorial secretary for the Christian Socialist and pacifist magazine *World Tomorrow*, doing much of the actual editing work for the named editor, Norman Thomas.[35] Crystal and Walter set up quarters for their young family right nearby and had dinners with the group. Crystal sat at the head of the table, as "a sort of general manager and Queen Mother."[36]

Crystal wanted to be economical and enjoy the group, but she probably also wanted to establish the supportive community it takes to raise a child while also launching a magazine. The group shared a collective kitchen and courtyard, and together hired a cook named Geneva who also kept house. When they were not in Manhattan, Crystal enjoyed a similar coterie around her in her home in Croton-on-Hudson, albeit with only informal collective support from her surrounding friends. Her clapboard cottage was situated among fellow travelers including Reed and Bryant; Boardman Robinson; Floyd Dell; her National Woman's Party and WPP colleague Doris Stevens and her husband, the activist and suffrage attorney Dudley Field Malone; and her WPP-NY colleague Margaret and her husband, Winthrop "Dan" Lane, all of whom bought or rented homes in the same enclave.[37] In Croton, it was Max who lived just up the street.

The *Liberator* structured and sustained Crystal's next chapter in life. It supplied the supportive habitat she needed to achieve work-life balance: an extended group of friends who felt like kin, and a secure job in a propitious venue, owned and shared with her beloved brother, to define and express her voice.

* * *

From 1918 through mid-1919, Crystal was all-in for the Bolsheviks. A week before the *Liberator* appeared, she called a closed meeting of the WPP-NY at the Breslin Hotel in New York. There, the gathered members passed a resolution to join with Russia in their peace proposal. They called on President Wilson to recognize the Bolshevik government and to join the peace negotiations between Russia and Germany then in progress at Brest-Litovsk.[38]

Over the coming weeks, the Bolsheviks were buffeted by both the harsh peace terms from Germany—the loss of its Baltic, Polish, and Ukrainian regions, more than a million square miles of territory and roughly one-third of its population—and by counterrevolutionary forces within Russia. Crystal's support grew even more impassioned in response. As the *Liberator* published Lenin's apology and explanation for the peace concessions,[39] she penned an open letter to the president of the All-Russian Congress of Peasants' Soviets, the peasant group most supportive of the Bolsheviks, and published it in the Socialist daily, the *New York Call*. "Please express to the Bolshevik government our firm belief in their courage and wisdom and ultimate triumph and our horror at the brutal demands of the German autocracy," she wrote. "Be assured that we will use all our strength toward bringing about official recognition of the Bolshevik government by our own."[40]

Then, in April, she and Max embarked on a speaking tour, joining British Socialists and other radicals in the "Hands Off Russia" campaign designed to protest Allied military and counterrevolutionary activities in the new Soviet state. Crystal threw herself fiercely into the campaign, embracing the struggle to defend revolutionary Russia from what she saw as pernicious forces threatening to destroy it. She was fearless. Max described one stop on the lecture tour, in Cleveland, when the siblings were surrounded "by a gang called 'vigilantes'—American fascists in embryo—with the purpose of kidnapping us after the meeting." Some of their allies from within the trade union helped Max and Crystal hide in a small supply closet where protest banners were normally stored. The siblings, huddled together, could hear the vigilantes hunting them throughout the building, storming through rooms, tearing open doors. Finally, one of the gang rattled the doorknob of the locked closet; it must have twisted just inches from Max's gut. The "thump of my heartbeats was drowned by the drawling voice of the union's secretary," who was leading the search for them, he remembered. Max "listened to Crystal's heartbeats" to sustain himself. They "were steadier than mine."[41]

As ever, Crystal proceeded from her belief that theirs was a righteous and liberating cause. At the first anniversary celebration for the *Liberator* at the Yorkville Casino in March 1919, she likened the supporters of the Bolsheviks to the volunteers who responded to Abraham Lincoln's call to replenish the ranks of the Union army in the summer of 1862, singing, "We Are Coming, Father Abraham, 300,000 More." As a trained contralto, her voice must have filled the hall:

> If you look across the hilltops that meet the northern sky,
> Long moving lines of rising dust your vision may descry;
> And now the wind, an instant, tears the cloudy veil aside,
> And floats aloft our spangled flag in glory and in pride;
> And bayonets in the sunlight gleam, and bands brave music pour,
> We are coming, father Abr'am, three hundred thousand more![42]

She told the crowd, "I have hope in my heart that America will be the second Socialist republic." Then she exhorted them to join this new fight to save the sould of the nation: "How many weeks will it be that we can call to Lenin, 'we're coming Comrade Nicholas, 100,000,000 strong?'"[43]

At the same time, Crystal's early *Liberator* articles tended to be less dramatic and effectual than were such vocal utterances. Her contributions, overall just fourteen in number in her three years at the magazine, retained the extemporaneous energy and wit that helped make her such a compelling public speaker, yet they generally lacked either the emotional punch of her spoken voice or the authoritative analysis for which the *Liberator* was gaining attention. Her first contributions were also very short. Her "Impressions of the A.F. of L. Convention," published in August 1918, consists mainly of a quick, biting jab at the labor organization for its report ignoring the "radical developments" in its own mission while instead following "an informal conversation with King George and Queen Mary."[44] Three subsequent contributions—"Aeroplanes and Jails" in November and "Signs of the Times" and "The Socialist Vote," both in December—are essentially news briefs, each of which deserts reportable facts in favor of Crystal's thoughts on more expansive questions, usually about the nature or progress of the radical movement overall.

"The Socialist Vote," for example, is a four-paragraph piece about the November 5, 1918, midterm election. Crystal began by briefly acknowledging the defeat of four Socialist candidates for office—Meyer London, Morris Hillquit, Scott Nearing, and Algernon Lee—in what was a divisive campaign marked by interparty conflict and voting irregularities. But she soon turned away from that analysis in favor of a more soulful message she found in the returns. Increasing vote totals in "hopeful" districts, she assessed, "demonstrate once more that the Socialist party is only incidentally a political institution; it is something politicians cannot understand, a deep-rooted faith and a thoroughly understood intellectual conception which must grow because it satisfies the vital desires of real human beings."[45] She was interested less in reporting on political scores and more in communicating the spiritual vitality she felt in the Socialist idea.

Her first full-length article, "The Mooney Congress," published in March 1919, set out to assess the "stormy congress of 1,200 labor delegates which voted to organize a general strike" if Thomas J. Mooney was not released. Mooney was one of two militant trade unionists believed to have been framed for a 1916 bombing at a San Francisco preparedness parade that killed nine people and wounded about forty more. Crystal opened the piece by identifying the tactical focus of the congress: whether to "strike for the release of all political and class-war prisoners, or . . . strike for feeling our power [so] we can use it for anything we want afterwards?" Yet the article quickly turned from union tactics to her personal interest in radical organization and action.

Irrespective of the particulars of the assignment, Crystal went after what she saw as the trouble with the American labor movement: the machine-produced "conservatives," as she called them, generated by the American Federation of Labor (AFL) and its president, Samuel Gompers.[46] Gompers was an antiwar unionist who turned preparedness advocate and supporter of the Allies by the end of 1915. Long a controversial figure among Progressives, he had more recently incurred the wrath of radicals by supporting US interventionist policies against Soviet Russia. Crystal's piece focused on how to organize the union movement to avoid or resist the rise of figures like Gompers going forward. She had always wondered how to prevent the development of the machine coalitions within democratic organizations, how to maintain what she saw as the essential and definitive energies of radical groups without sacrificing a structure capable of wielding their collective power. Crystal consistently presented this question through her own involvement in activist organizations: how to create a democratic structure that would encourage organic majorities to form and refrain from quelling the minority voices and nonconformists, all without dissolving into perpetual process, dissension, or disarray that would render them incapable of action.

She clearly identified with the problem she singled out at the congress. Crystal included herself in the "we" of participants, interjecting her voice at will on the page: her questions, her assessments, even authorial explanations of her narrative choices appear intermittently in the first person. She candidly followed her interests, wherever they led. Whatever the value of her own search for answers, and whatever insider intimacy the piece may have imparted to readers, the article also roams with the writer through the crowd, roving from thought to thought, speaker to speaker, reportage to critique to commentary, offering less narrative direction and information value for readers than the magazine typically offered. It is raw, and radically underdeveloped as writing or reportage.

If Crystal's early contributions seemed somewhat extemporaneous, they were also searching and came from the heart. If they were distracted or disorganized, it partly had to do with the multiple jobs she was juggling in her life at the time. She was now the mother of an active toddler, and alongside the *Liberator* was also continuing to head the WPP-NY, the only branch to persist in its activities after the declaration of war. Indeed, the New York branch was busy in the first months of the *Liberator*'s life. In March 1918, Crystal published a broadside, "A Program for Voting Women," which aimed to bring together suffrage politics and the world peace movement. She urged new female voters in New York State to use their votes to elect candidates who supported the WPP's policy positions to eradicate war.[47] The New York branch then organized a training school for speakers on "The Fundamental Principles of a League of Nations," in which Crystal also served as an instructor.[48] All the while, the branch was rebranding itself as the "Women's International League"—the name had been Crystal's suggestion—a move they believed would help evade the wartime censors who were stalking their correspondence and activities while at the same time signaling to the public their forward-looking interest in securing internationalist peace terms at the war's end.

Intensifying the workload was the tension such efforts exacerbated within the WPP. Nearly simultaneous with her "Program for Voting Women," Crystal's "Our War Record" (1918) was republished in the *Advocate of Peace*, the official organ of the New York Peace Society. Her piece was positioned in debate with a column by Lucia Ames Mead, the American Peace Society veteran and now national secretary of the WPP. Mead had never really accepted Eastman as a peace colleague, and in fact had made moves very early on to isolate or expel her. Just three months after the WPP was founded, she had written to Addams to report she had "consulted with various people" and was "convinced that while she is an able, good and enthusiastic woman, she has given very little study to this question." Mead quickly labeled Crystal an outsider, characterizing her as "an extreme socialist"—in 1915— before concluding she "cannot greatly help the movement."[49]

Mead was a former piano teacher from Boston whose widely circulated American Peace Society pamphlet, *A Primer for the Peace Movement* (1905), had launched a decade of sundry involvements within the peace movement, culminating at that time in her senior position with the WPP. Her column opposite Crystal's shared identical policy goals, but Mead rejected militancy, categorically asserting their "divergence of methods" was a definitive difference between the two women.[50] Mead was also a longtime member of the National American Woman Suffrage Association (NAWSA) and a former president of the Massachusetts Woman Suffrage Association; as a suffragist, she had similarly criticized what she felt were extremist methods by the English suffragettes, censuring them in traditionally gendered terms for "throwing away our womanhood."[51] By the mid-1920s, Mead herself would face censorship as a "Red," as associations between radicalism and international peace work itself spread for years, particularly in the American South and Southeast.[52] But in 1919, a time when the interconnections between the Great War and the Russian Revolution were fresh and visible, even if misunderstood by many Americans misinformed by newspaper representations, such tensions tended to flare between leftist militants like Eastman and the New York branch and more conservative peace women at other state branches, especially Mead's Boston WPP.

But then, beginning in the fall of 1919, Crystal's *Liberator* articles appreciably improved. "British Labor Is Moving," published in September, covers the British Labor Party Convention of June 1919. It begins by announcing a two-to-one vote "overwhelmingly in favor of industrial action to stop the Allied butchery and torture of Soviet Russia," and proceeds to unfold the debates that both drove that vote and connected to the larger questions Crystal cared about: the extent of the party's radical attitude and militant methods, as measured, particularly at this time, by its willingness to support the Bolsheviks. "The Trades Unionist movement can either become direct actionist now or be left behind," she quoted one forceful convention participant. "Don't let us apologize about the Bolsheviki," she skillfully quoted another. "They are our comrades."[53] The next month, her "The Workers of the Clyde" detailed a July rally where three thousand Clyde workers had gathered to welcome William Gallacher, whom she described in punchy prose as "the chief hero of the 40-hour strike after his three months in Edinburgh jail." With a new eloquence in her storytelling, Crystal's lead expertly set the scene:

> And there on the front row of the platform sat the beaming hero—a trim, square-shouldered young lightweight, with a red rose in his button-hole, healthy, rosy-cheeked and smiling, like a boy home from school. Through six long speeches of tribute he sat with downcast eyes, quietly blushing, and never looked up. It may be an annual performance but Gallacher isn't used to it. Surrounding him were the chief figures in the great strike, behind him a socialist chorus, girls all in white, below him rows upon rows of hard-headed Scotch machinists, munition makers and shipbuilders, all in their working clothes with caps on, typical Clyde workers, the sort of men that kept Glasgow, despite all government blandishments, an antiwar city throughout the five years.[54]

Then came the point of the article, a clear-eyed yet evocative single-sentence paragraph: "This meeting was the final chapter of the story of the first general strike in Scotland."[55] From there, the article proceeds to chronicle the deep history of Scottish labor actions and attitudes in poised and nuanced prose.

These 1919 articles succeeded at what "The Mooney Congress" had intended but failed to do. Both narrate from complex, dynamic meetings, yet both evince a clear analytical focus and more sophisticated organization and narrative skill than the earlier article, published just six months before. Crystal's next major feature article, the "Socialist Party Convention," again shows narrative fluency and finesse. It narrates the path from liberal Progressivism to revolutionary Socialism taken by Eastman and many of her closest friends and colleagues following US intervention in the war. While balancing a tone of impatience with the party, the piece adroitly analyzes Crystal's enduring interest in the "two possible attitudes . . . toward the decaying institutions of political democracy"—the reformers versus the radicals.[56]

Chances are, her improvements on the page resulted partly from her accumulating experience, both as a journalist and as a working mother. In both work and family, she was finding her legs. But her articles probably also benefited from editorial intervention by Max or, more substantially, by Walter. By this time, Walter's work at *The World Tomorrow* had established him as a gifted rewrite man.[57] And, beginning in 1918, Walter and Crystal's relationship across the various arenas in their lives—work, marriage, and parenting—made their partnership as close, balanced, and happy as it would ever be.

By 1918, Walter and Crystal had put together what they both felt they needed for a successful two-career family life: both were gainfully employed; they lived in Croton among friends, commuting to the city as needed; both enjoyed some flexibility, including the option to work at home; and they were assisted by Annie, their "colored girl," who looked after Jeffrey and also cooked.[58] Their son, born with minor physical problems, was now flourishing. "Jeff is able to stand alone now, and timidly take one or two steps," Walter told his mother. "He can't talk yet, but is very bright and intelligent."[59]

Crystal and Walter enjoyed equal measures of time together as a family, time as a couple, time with mutual friends, and, importantly, time in their independent lives. When Crystal took a two-week trip to Glenora in August 1918, for example, Walter, assisted by Annie, stayed in Croton with Jeff. "I don't think I'll take any holiday this summer," he told his mother.[60] Instead, he enjoyed the friendships they had built together and also took time to focus on his own work. "Sunday morning here in Croton—a little after 12 o'clock noon," he reported to Crystal as he recounted the big event of the day: Margaret Lane and her family were joining their little colony in Croton.

Voices and calls for me (I being upstairs writing home to my mother—yes really). I came downstairs to find Margaret + Dan Lane + Polly Angell + her brother all very much excited because 30 dollars had just changed hands across the road. The talk was all about the glorious news, and what friends David + Jeffrey would be, and when should Walter Nelles come up to put everything in apple-pie order. They had all walked over from Hartsdale to Irvington, and were going to walk a good part of the way back. I gave them some bread and butter + cheese and an onion or two, (washed down with unlimited water) for lunch—they stayed only half an hour.[61]

The next day Walter wrote her, "All's going on very well here—Annie is very friendly + happy. The August *World Tomorrow* is going through the mails all right, and is making a great hit."[62]

With work, money, friends, marriage, and family in balance, Crystal and Walter were together even when apart. "Gee I wish you were here tonight— but don't hurry back.— Have a good time," Walter wrote her. Their relationship thrived. "You are everybody's dearest you are, but you are mine—and I am yours— first and best of all," he told her. "Dearest I *do* love you—love you dearly—I have such hopes & dreams for a glorious happy future."[63]

Still, there were two hazards on the horizon, one at home and the other at work. On the home front, an accumulating body of family debt was becoming a difficult issue to avoid. While Crystal was away, Walter had a chance encounter with Edward Filene of Boston, the founder of a successful department store chain. Filene was a pioneer in prolabor policies including credit unions, profit sharing, paid vacations, a minimum wage for women, and the Filene Cooperative Association, perhaps the earliest American company union. Although they undoubtedly traveled in the same circles, Crystal and Walter disagreed with Filene about American intervention and they also owed him money. "There was no escape for me," Walter reported. "I had to face him out and a pretty sickening 15 minutes I had of it—mostly about the war. . . . I got away at last.—(He brightened up at the mention of your name every time—I'll say that for him.)" Two days later, Filene informed Walter they owed him $16.38, presumably for goods purchased on credit. The couple assigned separate responsibility even for shared expenses, splitting the family bills fifty-fifty. "Will you please pay it, and I'll go halves with you," Walter asked Crystal, "and will give you my eight dollars when you return."[64]

Back at the magazine, an even more substantial crisis was emerging. That summer, Reed turned up at Max's door one evening to announce he was leaving the *Liberator*. "I cannot in these times bring myself to share editorial responsibility for a magazine which exists upon the sufferance of Mr. Burleson," the postmaster general, he explained. However, "In the happy day when we can again call a spade a spade without tying bunting on it," he said, "you will find me, as you have in the past."[65]

The news struck Max "like a gunshot," he recalled, and he could not talk about it that night. But he too, in his own ways, had been struggling to live with the compromises the *Liberator* was asking of him. In September, Max published Reed's resignation letter along with his own reply. In it, he clearly identified with Reed's epic vision of the Russian Revolution and conveyed a simmering resentment at the daily, thankless duty required to parent a new world coming to birth. He admitted how much he envied Reed's "power to cast loose when not only a good deal of the dramatic beauty, but also the glamour of abstract moral principle, is gone out of the venture, and it remains for us merely the most effective and therefore the right thing to do."[66]

Although they may have begun the *Liberator* adventure as partners in the project of revolutionary progress, the two men quickly developed very different relationships to the magazine. Reed remained a free agent—a bachelor—maintaining the prerogative to leave if he did not like the way things were going. Max felt married to the magazine, day in, day out, and he had pledged his fidelity to his sister—the only woman from whom he had never been able to walk away.

To Max, Reed's departure took with it all the irresistible adventure, all the masculine heroism of the revolutionary idea and enterprise with him, leaving little more than obligation, self-sacrifice, and ongoing responsibility behind. Given the dynamics of familial dependency entwined with the magazine from the start, Max might well have attached his growing resentment to his sister anyway, but then, as it turned out, Reed blamed her for his discontent as well. Although there are no extant documents detailing the exact points of contention, Crystal's surviving letter to Reed suggests she was directly implicated in his decision to leave. "I think it's a crime for you to resign from the *Liberator* just because you don't like me as an editor," she wrote him urgently in July 1918. "That's the advantage in having two editors,—if you don't like one you can deal with the other. And we could make a special arrangement that all your dealings should be with him and not with me."[67]

Crystal understood all that Reed signified to the magazine, not to mention to Max. She tried desperately to dissuade him, probably sensing the freighted feelings his departure would bring to the surface for her brother. "You're awfully necessary to the success of the *Liberator*—more so I suppose than I am," she told him. "Isn't it chiefly personal feeling, and can't you get rid of it if you don't have any editorial dealings with me?" she asked.[68]

Apparently, their differences were irreconcilable. In the November 1918 issue, Reed's name no longer appeared on the *Liberator* masthead. If Crystal's editorial direction was the conciliatory bunting Reed could not abide, it was uncharacteristic of her up to now. But the ongoing operation of the magazine was crucial to her—materially as much as politically. She depended on its secure salary and flexible assignments to maintain both her career and her family.

Yet politically too, Crystal was discovering differences in perspective that would put her at odds with Reed. By mid-1919, she would confront a profound ambivalence about revolution as a means of change, even when she believed wholeheartedly in its ends. Unlike Reed—and, ultimately, Max as well—abstract principles could confound each other, and anyway they were cold comfort in the face of actual violence, bloodshed, and war.

* * *

Crystal's most important work for the *Liberator* was her on-the-ground reporting from inside the new Hungarian Soviet Republic, the first by any American reporter, published in July and August 1919. She had wanted to meet the revolutionary leader Bela Kun, Communist Russia's first ally, and, as Reed had done, she wanted to see a Communist state firsthand. Her journey to Hungary was arduous and dangerous, but she was familiar with the region, having traveled there with Bennie in 1913. And when she arrived, she was welcomed by the revolutionary leadership, who invited her to stay at the Hotel Hungaria, the same place the young commissars lived.

Crystal's reporting from Hungary mixed travelogue with reportage and moments of memoir, a conversational combination that brought out the best in her voice as a writer. She revealed the new world she was seeing through her own eyes and in markedly human terms. The Marxist philosopher Georg Lukacs, whom she may have met in 1913 when he chaired two panels at the International Woman Suffrage Alliance (IWSA) congress in Budapest on what men could do to support suffrage, was now the Hungarian commissar of education.[69] She described him familiarly as "a slender, fair-haired, studious Jew with blue eyes, and spectacles." The housing commissar looked "like a college hero—big, brown, handsome, and built like an athlete." Kun himself was "a young man (they are all young)," she wrote. "He is stocky and powerful in physical build, not very tall, with a big bulging bullet head, shaved close. His wide face with small eyes, heavy jaws and thick lips is startling when you first see it close . . . but his smile is sunny and winning, and he looks resolute and powerful."[70]

Crystal candidly related "the exact process by which private capital was abolished" in Hungary, just as it was disclosed to her. There were three levels of wages assigned to workers, all higher than they were before; she discussed the banks and the farms, "which the Soviet State has taken possession of . . . exactly as it has taken factories. The Soviet steps into the place of shareholders, and hires the employees," she explained. She particularly detailed the changes in housing, and the conditions for families and children. "I shall never go into a big, comfortable house again, whether it is the house of a Socialist professor or a railroad president, without quietly figuring up the number of rooms and the number of people, to determine if the family will be allowed to continue in possession of the whole house when communism comes," she wrote. In Hungary, "The housing room thus gained is being used as rapidly as possible to relieve the overcrowding of the poor. Of course, it is not simple," she noted. "Kitchens have to be put in. But it is being done."[71] Beyond that, Crystal observed,

> the summer villas on the mountain are turned into homes for convalescent children. I saw one, a great white palace of twenty-eight rooms, which had been occupied by one man during two or three months in the summer. It is transformed into a gay and spacious getting-well place for thirty children, light tuberculosis cases, with doctor and nurses employed by the State. I did not see many people who looked happy in Buda-Pesth [*sic*], but those children did. They were lying out on a big stone balcony in sea chairs, wrapped each one in a red blanket, talking and laughing together.[72]

As she traveled through Budapest, Crystal unveiled not only what she witnessed but also how profoundly those observations resonated for her. "I remember when I first caught sight of big photographs of Lenin decorating a newsstand," she wrote. "It was the same friendly, quizzical, half-smiling picture we had on our January cover, and it suddenly peered out at me through the musky dimness of a country railroad station, where our train stopped for an hour on the all night trip from Buchs to Buda-Pesth [*sic*]. I must have been a little lonesome," she confessed, "because I felt like crying when I saw Lenin's face, and I said to myself, 'Lenin is my father, and I am coming home.' "[73]

Crystal celebrated the possibility that revolution would soon extend around the world, even reaching her home in the United States. When she addressed the Central Council of the new Hungarian Soviet Republic—the first American to do so—she denounced the prosecution of Debs and other radical leaders and also proclaimed her hope that the victory for democracy, for the people, "will spread to all the other countries of the world and likewise will lead to the liberation of the American proletariat." As she stood before this new republic, she called it "the most beautiful moment of [my] life."[74]

Those remarks were published in July. Yet by the time she wrote her article for the August issue, she could not celebrate the revolution unequivocally. Engaging emotionally and wholly as she typically did, what Crystal witnessed in revolutionary Hungary seemed more complicated than what Reed, and Max, saw as a clear abstract moral principle at work. Even if the ends looked beautiful, the means were hideous to her. "There is no use having any illusions about the revolution," she confided to her readers. "It was born in starvation, and its first business is war."[75]

Most Hungarians, as she had indicated in her July article, were not happy; many were subjugated, even if in defense of possible new freedoms. All were subject to widespread violence from within and without. "Cherished dreams of scientists, educators, artists, engineers, who were waiting for a free society, must be set aside," she explained, "while the whole proletariat organizes in desperate haste to check the invading hosts of the enemy. And war means recruiting propaganda, conscription, military discipline, the death penalty, the whole damnable business of organized dying and killing," she wrote. Revolutionary violence, she concluded, betrayed its righteous cause. "Max Eastman said in Madison Square Garden two years ago, 'When our own war comes you'll know it, because it won't be necessary to conscript the workers to fight in it.' I thought he spoke a profound truth," she had told *Liberator* readers. "I do not think so now," she declared. "Now I know there can be no such thing as a democratic army. People don't want to die."[76]

At the time Crystal wrote those words, departing from the consensus of both Max and the magazine, the most celebrated account of revolutionary insurgency in Europe to reach the American public was Reed's *Ten Days That Shook the World*, which also appeared in 1919. Reed's book was prominently connected to the *Liberator*'s identity; full-page ads offering a free copy with new subscriptions ran at the front of the magazine, before the masthead, in the same issue Crystal's first article from Budapest appeared.[77] Like her, Reed made no attempt to be neutral; he admitted, even advertised, his political sympathies. In graphic prose, flush with zealous immediacy, he celebrated the Bolsheviks, characterizing counterrevolutionary forces as arch-enemies. But unlike Crystal, he evaded ambiguities and questions, overlooking the humanitarian particulars in favor of the stunning sweep of a people's triumph. When she wrote of revolutionary Hungary, she could not disregard the lived human experiences of revolution she witnessed all around her. She praised the abolition of private property, but also counted the cost of violence and repression under the revolutionary government. A pacifist and feminist, as well as a radical, she could not ignore the intersectional dilemmas these realities presented. And she could not resolve them. "I hope there is some pacifist revolutionary with an answer to that," she wrote. "I have none."[78]

Crystal would struggle with the problem of the pacifist revolutionary for years—perhaps for the rest of her life. She searched repeatedly for some workable accord between the two elemental goals, once aligned in her radical internationalism, which now appeared to be competing claims: justice or peace? In an era of revolutionary victory, she found herself facing a dilemma that could rupture her political location and stance. How could she, how should we, make sense of violence perpetrated to achieve the equality and justice she had long believed was the only recipe for permanent peace around the world?

Crystal had carried this problem to fellow delegates to the International Congress of Women after the War held in Zurich in May 1919. The WPP had been planning to convene a women's meeting simultaneous with the official postwar peace conference ever since women met at The Hague four years before. But when the time came, Paris was closed to women of defeated countries, so they convened in Switzerland, with delegations from both the Allies and Central Powers in attendance.

Crystal almost certainly expected to attend the congress as part of the American delegation. A total of up to thirty women were to represent each country, with groups determined by a process beginning with two representatives, who then selected an additional three; then each "committee of five" organized their full country contingent. However, for weeks, internal conflict had besieged the WPP executive board, the US committee of five, over Crystal's inclusion, even in an overall delegation of this size. Her name appeared on list after list of potential delegates as a decision was deferred from one meeting to the next. As late as December 1918, her name remained on the list, but was marked with neither the "X" used for "no" nor a check for "yes," but a dash, gone over and over, then circled many times, indicating the indecision of whoever was holding the pen, probably Jane Addams.[79]

Some members, such as Lucia Ames Mead, held that Crystal's radical associations disqualified her, arguing her presence would undermine the women's political legitimacy. Critics also cited Crystal's outspoken positions on birth control and equality within marriage as dicey challenges to dominant conventions. And concerns about the propriety of her own sex life also emerged. Like some in her generation, particularly those in her Greenwich Village cohort, Crystal lived as a free woman and she had never been shy about claiming women's right to sexual desire. She believed the time had come to do away with dated patriarchal conventions that dictated women's private lives just as much as their public choices, and she openly encouraged women to simply live as they chose to do— and let the culture catch up.[80] To some members of the committee, that attitude, underscored by two moves that exemplified it in Crystal's personal life, threatened the reputation of the entire congress. To them, her divorce from Bennie was a scandal in itself, and the disrepute had been magnified rather than rectified by her remarriage to Walter within an unclear number of months before the birth of their child.

The private lives of public women acquired increased cultural significance in Eastman's lifetime, and perhaps particularly within women's organizations. The early twentieth century witnessed the rise of the sexual revolution in America as discussions of divorce, birth control, and family planning recognized various degrees of sexual agency by women. With this dawning recognition of women as sexual beings came increasing concern about age-old questions of female respectability, especially since women were increasingly entering the professions and the public sphere beyond the home. What's more, consciousness of women's sexuality also raised the possibility, however dimly at first for many Americans, of homosexuality, a specter that seemed remarkably well quartered in the workplace intimacy and female partnerships formed in women-only organizations.

With these perils rising, scrutiny of female behavior and character increased, not only from the wider culture that had always proscribed and policed women's sexual conduct, but also from women's groups themselves. Indeed, in Crystal's experience, the sexual revolution brought increased inspection of her choices as much from the other women with whom she worked as from the men. An overtly heterosexual woman like Crystal was sometimes perceived as overly involved with men, which was a political affront within the culture of some feminist groups.[81] At the same time, the visibility of her heterosexuality could trigger questioning of sexual identity and lesbianism among the women working closely together in women's organizations, posing a threat to group identity, membership, and cohesion.[82] And all the while, any display of female sexual agency continued to imperil traditional claims to women's respectability, jeopardizing the main form of cultural capital most women colleagues still exercised in a man's world. As a result, women like Crystal came in for magnified criticism. These concerns suffused feminist groups and internationalist women's organizations at this time.[83] And the WPP was both.

Whether as a proxy for her politics or an exacerbating accompaniment to it, Crystal may have been openly snubbed, even shunned, by some colleagues for controversial activities in her private life at least as much as in public affairs.[84] Some spread the censure covertly. Within the WPP executive board, for example, Vice Chairman Alice Thatcher Post deemed it "rather amusing" that Crystal had finally become "Mrs. Somebody" when she married Walter. Post's remark circulated among colleagues, reaching all the way up to Addams on March 14, three days before Crystal's emergency cesarean section and the birth of her son.[85] The sentiment apparently persisted in women's peace circles, even reaching Zurich, and at a high level there as well. At the congress itself, Alice Hamilton, recently employed at what became the Harvard School of Public Health, the woman who had coauthored *Women at the Hague* (1915) with Addams and Balch and whose long work in occupational health had overlapped with Crystal's in the rise of workers' compensation, wrote to Ethel Snowden, the British viscountess and wife of a prominent Labour politician and future chancellor of the exchequer. In her note, Hamilton took a moment to pointedly remark, "Crystal Eastman is here as Mrs. Walter Fuller. For once she has found husbands valuable."[86]

Eastman did, in fact, attend the Zurich congress, the event where the Women's International League for Peace and Freedom (WILPF) was officially founded and the WPP designated its US branch. She traveled under her husband's name. Wed to Walter since 1916, Crystal used her British passport after the US State Department, which had begun surveillance of her activities, stalled her application. Yet she did not really choose to travel as her husband's wife; a British passport was the only way she could have legally gone abroad at the time. In 1919, US law held that American women who married foreign nationals lost their citizenship and automatically acquired the nationality of their husbands. It was not until the mid-1920s that political pressure from an unusually united coalition of women's groups forced reform.[87]

Perhaps aware that she was under scrutiny, perhaps scorned by some women of the WILPF, Crystal appeared in only a single photograph in the congress proceedings. Unnamed and with her eyes askance, she is pictured as one of "an international group of women."[88] But she was an active, vocal presence throughout the meeting. She endorsed or directly participated in the major resolutions passed at the congress—including its call for an end to the blockade of Germany, total disarmament, and universal free trade. Even more significant, the women at the congress were the first group to publicly denounce the terms proposed by world leaders at the formal peace conference at Versailles. Crystal was tenacious in calling for the women to press their own, better ideas.

The Paris Peace Conference had been meeting since January, convening statesmen representing twenty-six countries. The dominant players, however, were Britain, France, and the United States—the "big three" Allied victors—who led the gathering of leaders to lay sole moral responsibility for the war on Germany. With its "war guilt clause," the Treaty of Versailles then called for the surrender of large swaths of German land and payment of more than 260 billion gold marks to compensate the Allied and associated governments for the damage done. It was a punishing debt that the country, then staggering and nearing the threshold of starvation, would not finally discharge until 2010, close to a century after the end of the war.[89] The men representing the Allied victors argued that these and other terms of peace would repair losses while repressing rivalries and reducing the likelihood of militarization, thereby preventing future wars. In fact, the terms of peace would have the opposite effect. The human suffering that followed, coupled with the deep sense of grievance in defeated countries, helped drive the rise of the Third Reich. In September 1939, World War II, unprecedented in its scope and carnage, began.[90]

The women at Zurich forecast this outcome twenty years before it happened. By a unanimous vote, they agreed, prophetically, that the peace terms elaborated at Versailles were so punitive, so likely to worsen hunger and deprivation, so likely to breed humiliation and rage, that another war with Germany was all but inevitable. The terms "so seriously violate the principles upon which alone a just and lasting peace can be secured, and which the democracies of the world had come to accept," they warned, that they "create all over Europe discords and animosities, which can lead only to future wars."[91]

More than two years earlier, immediately following American intervention in the Great War, Crystal had pegged this destructive mentality as the prime mover behind the war itself, arguing internally to the AUAM that the United States should refuse to cooperate "with the spirit of revenge and lust for conquest which inspire some of the old world governments with which she is allied."[92] Now, at Zurich, she was avid in her rebuke of the continued application of such thinking in the official terms of peace, as well as to the League of Nations covenant contained within the treaty negotiated in Paris. "There is the same difference between the League of Nations that we want and the one proposed at Versailles that there is between our idea of a possible peace treaty and that now put forward," she argued. "If this morning we most energetically repudiated the peace terms and telegraphed our view to Paris, we ought to have the courage now to repudiate the League of Nations too." Some prominent delegates, notably Florence Kelley, successfully argued for a compromise position: support the idea of the league, but publicly denounce its undemocratic elements. Eastman, characteristically, urged her colleagues to hold fast to their vision: "We are not here to compromise. We are here to work. We ought to make out a plan for a League of Nations as we want it, and stand for that and work for that."[93]

The next day, Crystal was appointed to one of the political drafting committees, where she added a significant caveat to the League of Nations compact: that "under no circumstances should the terms of the Covenant be enforced by military means or by cutting off a population from the necessities of life."[94] The resolution was passed.

That afternoon, she put forward a controversial—and convoluted—resolution all her own. It essentially asked peace women to join with her in confronting the problem of the pacifist revolutionary, proposing the congress "recognize the fundamentally just demand underlying most of these revolutionary movements." That the subsequent resolution is so rhetorically awkward, and seems patched together piecemeal, speaks to the difficulties inherent in bringing together peace and revolutionary change at all. "We declare our sympathy with the purpose of the workers who are rising up everywhere to make an end of exploitation and to claim their world," she began. "Nevertheless, we re-assert our belief in the methods of peace, and we feel that it is our special part in this revolutionary age, to counsel against violence and above all to prepare the wealthy and privileged classes to give up their wealth and yield their special privileges without struggle, so that the change from a competitive system of production for private profit to some cooperative system of production for human happiness, may be made with as little bloodshed as possible." While "only workers can bring about revolution," she continued, elaborating, "a group like ours, in counseling against violence, must recognize that the only way in which violence can be avoided is for the possessing classes to give up their possessions and consent to the new order without resistance. I suggest that the chief function of women like ourselves is to prepare the minds of the wealthy and possessing classes, to persuade them to yield without hesitation, and thus save bloodshed," she concluded.[95]

For all its tensions and rhetorical turns, Crystal's resolution met with opposition on the grounds that it was too simplistic in its substance. The English suffragette Kathleen Courtney charged it was "very simple to say that if one side yields everything there will be no bloodshed. That does not solve the question however."[96]

The congress quickly agreed to postpone further debate. But that afternoon, Crystal persisted, presenting an amended version that attempted to reframe, but did not remove, its far-reaching objective. If her original version asked the congress to reach beyond its defined antiwar work by connecting its efforts to the class struggle, her second try took a gentler tack. Now she rhetorically alluded to the basic parallel between the international class struggle and the demand for equality and democracy also articulated in the drive for women's suffrage. The congress should "declare our sympathy with the purpose of workers who are rising up everywhere," she wrote, "to claim their world."[97]

This time, considerable debate ensued. Characteristically, Crystal built further analogies between movements; she pushed to persuade delegates to adopt her resolution by making the connection between imperialist aggression, which the peace women opposed, and the class exploitation targeted by the Russian Revolution. "It is illogical to be unanimously against the oppression of a small country by a large one," she argued, "and at the same time to admit the oppression of a part of the people within a nation."[98] After more debate, another American delegate insisted on a clearer and narrower focus for the organization and its work. "The main thing is to keep alive our belief in pacifism and internationalism," she argued from the floor. This group "must avoid questions among ourselves" as to other things, she said, like the radical restructuring and "economic questions" that Crystal's resolution was attempting to embrace.[99]

In the end, the resolution was adopted, by a sixty-to-fifty-five vote, the tightest of the congress. But it passed only in significantly limited form. The new resolution, proposed by the same American delegate, was stripped of its pacifist-revolutionary complications, stopping at the simple assertion that the special part of women pacifists is to "counsel against violence on both sides."[100]

For Crystal, nothing had really been resolved. She had been wrestling with the intersection of world peace and the radical restructuring of society necessary to ensure it for many months. Back in the previous March, she had asked a labor source at the "Mooney Congress" to weigh in on this dilemma, and his response seems to have modeled her resolution, months later, at Zurich: "I suggest that the chief function of women like yourselves," he had told her, perhaps more dismissively than she knew, "is to prepare the minds of the wealthy and possessing classes, to persuade them to yield without hesitation, and thus save bloodshed."[101] In Hungary, she had asked Kun himself "whether it will be possible for the Hungarian government to establish communism without violence except against invading armies." He replied, "not completely," a fraction of an answer she let speak for itself.[102]

But she could not let it go. She put the question out to the wider community of radical internationalists. After Zurich, an anonymous article appeared in the *Bulletin of the People's Council of America* in which reconciling revolutionary change with pacifist convictions became, inaccurately, the predominant concern of the congress. The lead claimed, "taking the social Revolution as a foregone conclusion," the delegates "fixed their attention on how that revolution could be brought about in a bloodless way."[103] Walter was editor of the *Bulletin* at the time and spent that summer after Zurich with Crystal in London. The article, with its fixation on the problem of the pacifist revolutionary, was likely hers.[104]

Crystal contemplated this dilemma for years afterward. At some point, she asked Vladimir Simkhovitch to help translate a poem from Russian that wrestled with the dilemma of violence in the cause of justice. She kept a copy of the poem written in her own hand. It began:

> The sword of justice, for ruling and
> Avenging, I will give to the mob,
> Now blind with passion, in
> Whose hands it shall flash and
> Strike like lightening [*sic*].[105]

In its final stanza, like Crystal's own meditations on the subject, the poet became trapped by the cycle of violence, reproducing itself without end:

And who so drank of this terrible
Poison of vengeance, what shall
He now become, but the
Hangman or his victim?[106]

Crystal had pursued radical internationalist peace as far as she could go, to its limits and its logical ends. Yet she found herself at an impasse. She had tried to bridge the movement she had come to believe carried the best hope for achieving global justice with the one pursuing international peace, but she could not make them cohere. Through politics, protest, collective process, and now poetry, she had tried and failed to resolve or escape the problem of violence perpetrated in pursuit of the equality and justice that she had long believed was the only formula for world peace. She could go no further. After Hungary and Zurich, she would turn away from active peace work, never to return to it again.

* * *

Crystal returned to London, where she and Walter worked together all summer organizing the British side of an Anglo-American Tradition of Liberty Conference, a transnational event tackling another political combination of enduring importance to her: connecting "the restoration of civil liberties" with the development of a "foundation of enlightened and democratic internationalism."[107]

In September, she received a wire from Max asking her to return to the office in New York. He wanted to travel to California to spend time with Deshon and felt angry and frustrated that he had already had to delay his trip to tend the magazine without her. Exasperated with holding down the fort, he told Deshon he was trusting Crystal would "be here in time for the December number. . . . But if she doesn't—well . . . I'll come back if I absolutely have to." But, he said, "I want to stay with you. I don't want to come back."[108]

Max did not seem to know that while he was alone with the magazine, special agents of the Federal Bureau of Investigation (FBI) had infiltrated its office at 34 Union Square East. On July 10, a small reconnaissance team sketched the floor plan for the purpose of wiretapping the editors and writers at work.[109] That summer of 1919 saw the launch of the postwar Red Scare in New York. It began with police raids of the Russian Bureau and the Rand School of Social Science in June under the auspices of the Joint Legislative Committee to Legislate Seditious Activities of the New York State Legislature, informally called the "Lusk Committee" after its chairman, state senator Clayton R. Lusk. Then, in August, US attorney general A. Mitchell Palmer inaugurated the General Intelligence Division, or "radical division," of the FBI and began collecting files on "left-wing agitators"—more than two hundred thousand files in the first year—under the strategic supervision of a twenty-four-year-old law school graduate and former Library of Congress cataloguer, J. Edgar Hoover. The FBI would watch a large number of pacifists, internationalists, Socialists, feminists, and other radicals—Addams, Wald, Kelley, Villard, Baldwin, Max, and many of the *Liberator* writers among them. Crystal herself was under surveillance by three agencies: the Secret Service and military intelligence, as well as the emergent FBI. She was also placed on a watch list of "doubtful speakers" by the Daughters of the American Revolution.[110]

When she returned from London to New York on the *Rotterdam*, arriving on October 20, 1919, Crystal seemed unaware of the government surveillance of her as a "Red." Perhaps she was just unruffled by it. In any case, her public utterances grew only more barefaced despite her arrival on the eve of the infamous "Palmer raids." As federal officials were preparing to crack down on meetinghouses in New York and several other cities in raids that would produce hundreds of arrests, Crystal and Walter sailed back into New York harbor with three-year-old Jeffrey. Only eight days after the Justice Department raided the Russian Seaman's Union in lower Manhattan, Crystal spoke at a luncheon of the League of Free Nations at Manhattan's Hotel des Artistes just five miles uptown; she charged that the economic blockade by the US government had "prevented the safe and orderly working out of socialist theories in Communist Hungary," adding provocatively, "Bela Kun's dictatorship seems less extreme than Woodrow Wilson's."[111] The next week, a citizen spy reported to the FBI that she made similar statements in a talk for the Intercollegiate Socialist Society at the Civic Club in lower Manhattan. "The Kun dictatorship is no different than the U.S.," she reportedly said, "as far as the International is concerned."[112]

In the same talk, Crystal freely wisecracked that she "made a lot of trouble with the State Department" to get her passport to go abroad to Hungary and Zurich. In fact, the department had worked assiduously to determine how she had managed to travel to Europe, never apparently realizing she had outsmarted them simply by following the government's own sexist laws. After a multiagency correspondence, one operative reported she might be traveling under the alias "Kathryn Fuller" or "Kathryn Fullerton" but made no connection to her married name.[113] Six weeks later, after federal officials raided radical organizations across thirty-three US cities, Crystal was again observed by surveillance bragging, this time before a banquet in Chicago, that she had outfoxed the State Department in obtaining travel documents to go abroad.[114]

As the Palmer raids continued into the winter and early spring of 1920, the Lusk Committee submitted its final four-volume report to the New York State Senate. It did not specifically mention Crystal—or that many women radicals at all, compared to men—but it did mention Max, the magazine, and many people in their orbit. Twelve days later, on May 5, she responded by filing a 114-page lawsuit in Northern California on behalf of the *Liberator*. In it, she alleged that the police in both San Francisco and Oakland had conspired to suppress the magazine not through the mail but through the marketplace.

According to the complaint, the officers had gone much further to close off market access to the *Liberator* than Ward and Gow had when they removed *The Masses* from newsstands in the New York City subways. Crystal charged they had used the power of the state to choke off circulation by threatening booksellers with fines, imprisonment, or both if they carried or displayed the magazine. Their actions had diminished sales of the *Liberator* not only in San Francisco and Los Angeles but also Oakland and even Seattle, resulting in a rapid circulation drop of some fifteen thousand copies.[115]

The suit alleged collusion among numerous agents of the State of California to commercially crush the magazine out of existence. All "these matters and things done by said defendants, their agents and servants, individually and collectively and . . . by such other persons whose names are unknown . . . were done with intent," the pleading asserted, "willfully, wantonly and maliciously to injure and have injured your orator, and to render unsalable its magazine, THE LIBERATOR."[116] The publishers sought an injunction to stop these authorities from carrying out such "unlawful, oppressive and coercive acts," describing their actions as a "journalistic lynching" that denied their constitutional rights—as guaranteed by the United States and the State of California—by blacklisting its authors.[117] They also argued that their rights under copyright—their right to vend—had been infringed.[118]

It was the only lawsuit Crystal would ever file.[119] Immediately afterward, she withdrew from the spotlight and the magazine. She spent the summer in Croton with Jeffrey, while Walter, now both editor-in-chief and managing editor of the left-libertarian magazine *The Freeman*, came up from Manhattan on weekends. It remained a happy time for the three of them. Crystal sent a picture of her three-year-old to her sister-in-law, Cynthia Fuller, reporting that Jeffrey was "so charming now that Walter and I can hardly tear ourselves away from him to go to work. The measles and influenza, through which we passed last winter, are just a dim black memory now," she said. "Jeffrey and I are both blooming."[120] Focused on private rather than political life, she saw only sunny skies ahead: "I think it's going to be a happy summer. Walter's work is going magnificently. Everybody is very proud of him and very dependent on him. . . . [H]e will be ready to ask for more money in the fall."[121]

When fall came, it brought considerable turmoil to Crystal's social, professional, and geographic vicinity. The indictment for robbery and murder of the

Italian-born Nicola Sacco and Bartolomeo Vanzetti on September 11, 1920, quickly became a cause célèbre among radicals who saw the men's immigrant roots and anarchist politics as the true reason for their arrest. The *Liberator* covered the case extensively, and also organized a defense committee to raise funds and public support for the two men they understood as martyrs to political repression.[122] Then, just five days later, on September 16, a bombing in the heart of New York's financial district was seen by authorities as an act of domestic terrorism, and later connected to a call by Vanzetti to avenge the men's arrest, eventual conviction, and execution.[123] With all this agitation swirling around her, Crystal stayed ensconced in conventional—she might have said "bourgeois"—domestic concerns. She was renovating a house she had purchased at 90 MacDougal Street in Greenwich Village; Margaret Lane, now the *Liberator* business manager, lived at 78 MacDougal, "so we'll have a big yard for our two children to play in."[124] Crystal's political struggle was juggling work and family. October was "a terribly complicated month," she told Cynthia, "trying to get the workmen to finish the house, taking care of Jeffrey and paying a little attention to the *Liberator*."[125]

It seems, however, she managed too little sustained attention to the magazine to satisfy Max. For months, he had been feeling dissatisfied with her contribution. "Crystal is barely walking around the room, and even when she is well she seems to have lost all her zeal for action," he observed. He found fault with her "low physical stamina," one of several symptoms that might be explained by the exhaustion of work-family balance, her fickle health, or both.[126] Max, fed up with the demands of the magazine when he wanted to return to his own writing and join Deshon in Hollywood, belittled his sister, citing Crystal's "frail ego" as the root of the problem. A bit backhandedly, he explained, Crystal "had her own eminence, and her own pride in it, but she was not primarily a writer—not at all a poetic or a humorous writer—and on such a magazine all the wages of praise and appreciation went to the artists and writers." He lamented to Deshon, "I can never leave the *Liberator* in her hands. . . . It isn't sufficiently *hers*, and never can be."[127]

Max's chagrin and his strong desire to abandon their magazine would have been painful for Crystal. To everybody, Max and Crystal had always been "the Eastmans," a pair, a unit, as emotionally attached as any couple—indeed, perhaps more so. Two early psychoanalysts diagnosed a "Freudian Oedipal situation" stemming from Max's intense love for his mother and a strong, related "sisterly investment" that held the siblings together while also disquieting their bond.[128] The year Max turned twenty-one, Annis had told Crystal that she and her brother belonged together, like it or not. "You are his ideal—and I'm afraid *he* is yours," she said.[129]

Part mother, part sibling, part paragon, part wife, Crystal had been deeply entwined with Max—socially, interpersonally, professionally—since young adulthood. For his part, Max, the self-proclaimed "mama's boy," may have felt the need to separate himself from his sister, to alienate her or to flee, but he had never been able to do so, at least not for long. But now Deshon was beckoning from across the country, so Max found his sister to be "a great problem to me." There is no extant evidence that he ever discussed these matters with Crystal, whether it was their differing personal investments in the magazine, their expectations of one another as co-owners of their joint venture, or anything else. He seems only to have expressed his grounds to Deshon, while speaking of his sister in distancing, passive-aggressive terms. "It was a great mistake her coming on the *Liberator* with me," he said, because "it puts her in a position of fixed and public inferiority."[130]

Whatever misgivings Max had about leaving the magazine in Crystal's hands, he resigned in January 1921, making her its sole editor. Almost immediately thereafter, she too detached from the magazine, returning to her original political home in suffrage work, where a new era was stirring after the passage of the Nineteenth Amendment. By March, she would formally resign, citing health problems; an editorial said she intended to devote more time to the labor movement and revolutionary women's activity.[131] Neither plan would come to pass.

In the coming months, a financial scandal further strained the relationship between the Eastmans and the magazine. From its launch, the *Liberator* had been denied second-class mailing privileges, a continuation of repressive tactics by the US Post Office imposed on *The Masses* before it. Then, suddenly, in May 1921, as Crystal moved to a figurehead role on the *Liberator* board of directors, mail censorship finally ended. Warren Harding had become president, and Will Hays, later known for developing Hollywood's movie production code, was appointed the new postmaster general. The editors got word that the magazine, along with many other radical publications, could now be mailed second-class, and the *Liberator* was refunded $11,277, the difference in cost since the day they had launched. The magazine was suddenly flush. It could pay its debts and upgrade its operations, including perhaps the cheap paper they had been forced to use—paper so thin that few copies survive intact today. Beyond all that, the magazine would have a cushion, insurance against a rainy day, an actual cash reserve.

The rainy day came quickly, and it pelted Max and Crystal hard. By December, the *Liberator* was forced to announce its impending bankruptcy when its bookkeeper and ad manager, E. F. Mylius, absconded with the magazine's $4,000 reserve. He took "a fling on Wall Street," he wrote to Max, and "unfortunately,

I lost." What's worse, after Mylius was arrested, he published a letter to the editor of the *New York Times* saying he had not really stolen the money but had borrowed it—following the example of Max and Crystal. He announced that they too had taken money from the magazine "for personal and private uses at a time when, like myself, they were in financial difficulties."[132]

Max replied immediately that the magazine had in fact lent money to its editors, but on the books—and it had always been promptly repaid.[133] Max admitted he borrowed $500 and Crystal $200 in June 1921, after both siblings had stepped down. The Eastmans had lived on an exacting budget all their lives, but at that moment Crystal faced a significant new expense. In May, she had become pregnant again. Her second child, a daughter, Annis, was born in December, more than two months premature.

On September 22, 1921, a California judge found in favor of the *Liberator* in Crystal's only lawsuit against the San Francisco and Oakland police. The magazine survived, eventually merging with two Workers' Party publications to become the *Workers' Monthly* in 1924. But the *Liberator* era was over for her. Just weeks after the Mylius incident came to light, Max decamped for the USSR, where he married, and continued to live for the next five years. Crystal stayed in New York. She had another baby coming and a husband growing restless now, and she had to begin searching for a job to somehow replace the only anchored venue for her life and her work that she would ever have.

9 PASSAGES: FEMINISM, JOURNALISM, AND THE TRANSATLANTIC TWENTIES

In her opening address to the Woman's Freedom Congress, held in New York in March 1919, Crystal began to look past war and peace to call for the next chapter in the global quest for equality. "For two years the whole Western world has been talking about freedom and democracy," she began. "Now that the war is over and it is possible to think calmly once more, we must examine the popular abstractions, and consider (especially here in the America where the boasting has been the loudest)—how much freedom and democracy we actually have."[1]

The freedom congress embraced multiple movements, but the fundamental logic of her opening address echoed the tactical attitude of the National Woman's Party (NWP). Like Crystal's Woman's Peace Party of New York (WPP-NY), the NWP had dared to pursue its case even in wartime, neither suspending its suffrage activities nor participating in war work. And like Crystal's address at the freedom congress now, the NWP aimed to shame the US government into action. After all, the party's "silent sentinels" compared President Wilson's political rhetoric about democracy with the political reality of disenfranchisement for the majority of American women.

The eventual arrest and workhouse imprisonment of NWP members, followed by prison hunger strikes beginning with Lucy Burns and ending with Alice Paul, finally helped leverage Wilson's support. By June 1919, the Senate would finally follow the House of Representatives in passing the Susan B. Anthony Suffrage Amendment. It would take another fourteen-month campaign to achieve ratification by three-fourths of the states. Eastman's old stomping ground of Wisconsin was the first state to ratify the amendment, in June 1919. However, it was not until August 26, 1920, when the Tennessee legislature became the thirty-eighth state to pass the amendment, that the US Constitution finally guaranteed national equal suffrage for women and men.

Crystal Eastman. Amy Aronson, Oxford University Press (2020).
© Oxford University Press.
DOI: 10.1093/oso/9780199948734.001.0001

But in the early spring of 1919, Crystal felt the long battle for the ballot had already been won. Her freedom congress marked a new chapter and issued a new call to action. More than six hundred participants gathered in New York for panels spanning all the great themes of her political life: "Labor Legislation for Women," "Women in Revolutionary Countries," "The Future of the Colored Woman," "The Cooperative Movement and the High Cost of Living," "Birth Control and the Illegitimate Child," among them. Jane Addams was asked to give the keynote dinner speech but declined.[2] Still, the congress assembled numerous women leaders from across social issues and movements—Elizabeth Gurley Flynn of the Industrial Workers of the World (IWW); Rose Schneiderman of the Women's Trade Union League; Minnie Brown from the National Association for the Advancement of Colored People (NAACP); Mary Ware Dennett and Crystal's law school classmate Elinor Byrns, both members of the NWP, WPP, and Heterodoxy; and of course Crystal herself.[3]

Publicity materials billed Crystal's address as "Women and Direct Action," but her actual speech was ultimately entitled "Feminism." Not surprisingly, she assumed a powerful, natural connection between the two topics. She took stock of statistics showing women's second-class status in American democracy, laying bare not just the political and economic factors that handicap women, but also cultural expectations and stereotypes that kept them down—forces, she knew, that were beyond the reach of the vote. "Women in America today not only share the wholesale denial of civil liberty which came with the war and remains to bless our victory, but carry a special burden of restrictive legislation and repressive social custom," she declared. This exhaustive burden, which was "not in any way relieved by the war for freedom nor affected by the two years' crusade of democratic eloquence," she hastened to add, "halts them in almost every field of endeavor, and effectually marks them as an inferior class."[4] Now that the war was over, Crystal imagined women acting together in a "spirit of humane and intelligent self-interest" to change all that. Positioning women's liberation as the meeting ground of her politics, her freedom congress now envisioned a broad-based coalition and intersectional agenda that would finally and fully bring women equal rights.

To many in New York's recently renamed WPP branch, now the Women's International League (WIL), the congress was a pronounced failure. Some said it included too many radical women; others complained it had drifted far afield from the WPP's original goal, defining protest against war. Everyone agreed the event ran over budget. The freedom congress had only increased the debt Crystal's administration accumulated by continuing to mount political actions despite vastly decreased public support after the US declaration of war. There was a move to fire her, but instead she resigned. Crystal and Walter were already planning to go to London in April, the pivot point for her trips to Budapest and Zurich. Agnes Brown Leach, WIL treasurer and a philanthropist and activist long involved with suffrage, peace, and civil liberties, stepped in to cover the debts; she had helped Crystal before—and would again. Once Eastman departed, the WIL became mired in infighting without her. Many of its most prominent members resigned by the fall.[5] The organization would formally fold in November 1919, when the national Woman's Peace Party officially became the US section of the Women's International League for Peace and Freedom (WILPF).

By that time, the Nineteenth Amendment was progressing toward ratification. When Crystal got an assignment for the *Liberator* to cover the annual convention of the Labor Party in January 1920, she quickly turned it into "Practical Feminism," the first of three important articles she would write about the women's movement after the vote. Her assignment was the Labor Party's announcement of a new equal representation requirement for men and women on its national executive board, but the article focused on the feminist concern she saw captured by the party's move: "After all these centuries of retirement women need more than an 'equal opportunity' to show what's in them," she asserted. "They need a generous shove into positions of responsibility."[6] For the rest of the short piece, she discussed the NWP ratification drive, never looking back at the Labor Party or its convention again.

By September 10, 1920, three weeks after ratification was achieved, Eastman attended a meeting of the executive board of the NWP. She joined Lucy Burns, Doris Stevens, the NWP's legislative chair, and suffrage leaders including Harriot Stanton Blatch, Florence Kelley, and Charlotte Perkins Gilman at Alva Belmont's newest estate on the north fork of Long Island. Now that the vote was won, the group assembled to discuss whether the organization should continue to operate.[7] After the ballot, what, if anything, was next?

After considerable discussion, the gathered insiders agreed they must press on. To become full and equal citizens, women needed a political organization to develop and advocate policy on their own behalf—a feminist lobby, essentially, to politick their interests into law and society. Belmont, the group's chief financier and longtime strategist, ascended as president. Gilman invoked the NWP's post-suffrage identity: an independent feminist pressure group pursuing equality using guts, savvy, and brains.

Yet the specifics of their program remained a very open question. Burns commented that the party's grand designs would "take until eternity to translate into fact."[8] She withdrew from organizing at that point. But other members of the inner circle continued to meet through the fall of 1920 to develop resolutions to be presented at a large convention in February 1921. In November, the NWP polled members about their vision for voting women going forward. Now "with immense power in their hands," had women just won the first battle in what Crystal would call "this hundred-year war for equality," or had they completed the war and legitimated women's interests in American public life?[9]

In her article "What Next?" Crystal decisively cast her lot with the ongoing struggle for equal rights. She took up the mantle of what was dubbed "equalitarian" feminism—the political pursuit by women, for women, of complete gender equality with men. In so doing, she aligned herself with the NWP, as distinct from the National American Woman Suffrage Association (NAWSA), soon to become the League of Women Voters. Indeed, she began her piece with an immediate refutation of NAWSA president Carrie Catt, who had argued that suffragists should now be seen "not primarily as women but as joint members of the human family" working to promote broad humanitarian reforms. "If the [feminist] program is to be drawn on large humanitarian lines, including all the more popular human betterment proposals," Crystal retorted, "why is it a woman's program? Have women a corner on progress? Must they jealously guard their right to improve the world?" No, she reasoned, the goal for women now was to break down gender disparities and all the separate set of rules that disadvantaged women as compared to men. "The object of feminism," she asserted, "is not to separate the activities of men and women but to unite them."[10]

Yet to accomplish that vast and transformative goal, she pointed out, "the vote is not our only weapon, or even our chief weapon."[11] Single-issue campaigns like the one recently waged for suffrage would not be sufficient to secure complete gender equality, she believed; indeed, the complete feminist program she wanted was "at most but one-third political."[12] Another third was the economic arena of wages and the workplace, and the final third was the crucial private domain of love, marriage, and the family.

Again, Eastman wanted it all. She would continue to press this broad, tripartite architecture for the feminist project—politics, economics, private life— for as long as she lived. "What we are really after," she wrote soon after the big meeting on Long Island, was a comprehensive program designed to give women the freedom "to exercise their infinitely varied gifts in infinitely varied ways."[13] Toward that end, no single movement, not political suffragism, not social reformism, not Socialism or Communism, would be sufficient by itself:

> Women's freedom, in the feminist sense, can be fought for and conceivably won before the gates open into industrial democracy. On the other hand, woman's freedom, in the feminist sense, is not inherent in the communist ideal. All feminists are familiar with the revolutionary leader who "can't see" the woman's movement. . . . "My wife's all right," he says. And his wife, one usually finds, is raising his children in a Bronx flat or a

dreary suburb, to which he returns occasionally for food and sleep when all possible excitement and stimulus have been wrung from the fight. If we should graduate into communism tomorrow this man's attitude to his wife would not be changed.[14]

By the time the NWP held its postratification convention, Crystal had discussed her vision of a "fairly complete feminist program" with Alice Paul. Her proposals echoed the agenda of her own Woman's Freedom Congress, which itself was influenced by ideas circulating in the international women's movement at the time. The Zurich congress had held sessions on ending sexual double standards and the economic dependence of wives and mothers, for example, and voted to adopt resolutions on equal parental rights, the economic recognition of mothers, the responsibility of fathers for illegitimate children, women's access to information about birth control, and the national rights of married women. The International Woman Suffrage Alliance also studied questions that bridged the public-private divide; in a two-year transnational survey of member countries, the group examined such questions as the financial support of motherhood, the nationality of married women, and "moral questions" surrounding women's sexuality.[15]

Eastman told Paul she hoped American feminism would battle women's subordinate status from as many angles. She outlined her agenda encompassing economic and political opportunity and the modification of laws governing inheritance, marriage and divorce, the guardianship of children. She included the removal of laws denying women access to birth control information. And she further advocated feminist resolutions about disarmament, "to give expression to the overwhelming pacifist sentiment at the Convention," and a "resolution of protest against the disenfranchisement of Negro women" since she found NWP members "almost unanimous in [their] indignation on that subject."[16] To her, the first NWP convention after the vote was the right place to transform successful but single-issue suffragism into an ambitious, extensive, class- and race-conscious, transnationally minded feminism.[17]

Crystal also felt it was the right time. The 1920s opened a surprisingly difficult era for the American women's movement. While the decade began with victory in the suffrage cause, the achievement of that goal, pursued for generations, had a paradoxical effect. It sapped the sense of purpose, and, for some, the feelings of female superiority, that had long fired women's public participation. Many other suffrage leaders were retiring from activism, and the movement itself began splintering along lines of class, race, and region, signaling an oncoming struggle for solidarity and direction that would challenge policy and organizing for decades. Culturally, the future was looking doubtful as well; younger women were turning toward personal fulfillment as a measure of empowerment while the rising mass media and culture of consumerism were reformulating the very notion of public engagement.[18] The world war and the Russian Revolution, followed by the red scare and an economic recession, all raised reactionary attitudes that would hinder women's progress. These combined forces threatened to turn the next generation away from systematic political action in general and the women's movement in particular.

Yet this was the very moment Crystal was returning to the feminist fray, and with full force. At the convention itself, she led a group of allies who saw themselves advancing an invigorating new chapter in women's activism and progress now that the vote was won. They offered a minority resolution composed of six points. Notably, five of them concentrated on laws or customs pertaining to private life, questions of animating concern to younger women. While the press played up her attention-grabbing stands on birth control and women's economic independence within marriage, Crystal saw her positions on sexuality and the whole province of family life as nothing more or less than obvious, necessary, and unifying; she saw herself simply getting to the root of problems that affect the real lives of the vast majority of women across the lines of class, race, educational background, and nationality.

Feminism must offer "a program that works not just for women judges and women lawyers alone," she argued. "It is the great masses of women of this country who are still in slavery that we must rouse—the women who have to ask their husbands for a new hat, and cannot say whether they will have children or not, or when."[19] Eastman felt next-wave feminism must find a site of solidarity where college women, career women, women laborers, and unpaid homemakers could meet. In the years to come, the absence of some shared terrain for the women's struggle would divide feminists along many fault lines through the 1920s, and indeed into today.[20]

But Alice Paul did not see things the same way. While Eastman wanted to talk about a vision for the next phase of the movement—"the nature of our subjection and . . . the terms of our freedom," as she put it—Paul was laser focused on establishing a single objective. And in marked contrast to Eastman's idea of a grassroots democratic process at the convention, Paul wanted to use the gathering to inaugurate that pragmatic goal. "Never endorse anything that your organization isn't ready to fight for," she told Crystal. "I am not interested in writing a fine program," she continued. "I am interested in getting something done."[21]

Paul proposed a narrow policy seeking "the removal of the legal disabilities of women."[22] The papers delighted in characterizing the debate between the two female leaders as a cat fight, covering it sensationally as a "feud which rages all day."[23] Crystal believed any large meeting like this was designed to air different ideas, and criticized what she saw as Paul's controlling, illiberal approach. She also scorned her game plan as dated and ultimately unworkable. Clunky and inhibited, limited to only the law, and dictated through a double negative—"removal" of "disabilities"—Paul's idea would never speak to the younger women of the day, she thought. "Nobody that has a thread of modern feminism will care a rap" for the NWP, Crystal contended from the convention floor, if it adopts what she saw as Paul's constricted and distinctly "old-fashioned" aim.[24]

The conflict reflected more than a difference in philosophy and policy; it was also a struggle over organizational identity and territory. Eastman had returned to the fold bearing a program that embraced issues and ideas from her "outside" experience—both in other social movements and her own private life; Paul's plan marched forward from inside the organization to the next single-issue campaign. While both women put "feminism first"—their shared objective was the achievement of gender equality—Crystal called for a coalition vision for feminism that dreamed of bringing women together from all walks of life and from wherever they lived. To Paul, she was coloring well outside the lines. And she was doing so after crossing other lines, battle lines, in the recent past—favoring peace over suffrage, Wilson's re-election over Paul's signature Party in Power strategy, in what became a defining moment for the NWP.

Paul was not present at the convention when the competing proposals came to a vote. Crystal complained that debate was shunted to a few hours at the very end of the three-day meeting—"hardly enough time to determine the future of a high school dramatic society!" she remarked—and even then it was effectively shut down: "the time limit and a very efficient steamroller disposed of it before the discussion had fairly started," she maintained.[25] When the votes were counted, her minority proposal lost decisively, two to one, to what she saw as Paul's more machine-produced plan, backed by a methodical majority. The *New York Tribune* headline proclaimed, "Miss Paul wins triumph."[26]

Just over a month later, Crystal published her account of what had happened in the *Liberator*, her home turf. In "Alice Paul's Convention," she publicly speculated about "the motives and intentions of a shrewd and able leader who keeps [her] own counsels." Her conclusions were sharp, sketching Paul as a cool, strategic commander, focused on the discrete moves of each battle to the exclusion of the hearts and minds of her people, and the soul of what the struggle is all about. "Alice Paul is a leader of action, not of thought. She is a general, a supreme tactician, not an abstract thinker. Her joy is in the fight itself, in each specific drawn battle," she wrote, "not in debating with five hundred delegates the fundamental nature of the fight." It was particularly galling that Paul expected an assembly of militant feminists to acquiesce to whatever an authority figure told them to do. Crystal let loose on this point, imagining on the page Paul's interior calculation for autocratic rule:

> The Executive Committee have provided a good enough phrase—To re-move all the remaining forms of the subjection of women. Let the delegates with the least possible debate adopt this phrase to serve for purpose, pro-gram and constitution. Of course she said nothing. But that, I believe, was Alice Paul's notion of what the Convention's actions should be. I will let you know what the first step is to be, how to act, and when. Go home now and don't worry. These words were not printed in the program, but they seemed to be written between the lines.[27]

Years later, Paul gave her own account in an oral history. She cast Eastman not only as an outsider but also as someone whose marginality rightly re-flected her ambiguous fealty to the cause. Although the international feminist movement was considering similarly expansive proposals, she remembered Crystal as a leftist, not a feminist. And although she was not alone in her hopes for broader discussion, a broader base of issues and constituencies, or her criticisms of the NWP's new party line, Paul cast only Eastman as a rene-gade turncoat, tacitly stripping her of legitimacy as a bona fide member of the group, as "one of us." She recalled the minority proposal as "embracing eve-rything that Russia was doing" and Crystal herself as an interloper "taking in all kinds of things that we didn't expect to take in at all." Betraying little sense of their shared history in the organization or Eastman's stake in the American women's rights movement, Paul remarked, "We didn't give a second thought to it."[28]

* * *

Less than a month after the NWP convention, Crystal stepped down from the *Liberator*. Without the peace work, the magazine, or an immediate role in the postsuffrage NWP, she felt worried and unmoored. She wrote to Kellogg, asking him to help her sublet her house on MacDougal Street, her only source of income. "I see my whole summer's income melting away & I'm scared," she confided.[29]

By that summer of 1921, Crystal was pregnant with her second child and living more or less alone with Jeffrey in Croton. Walter was less and less present in the family. In August, she wired him from Provincetown, Massachusetts, where she and Jeff had accompanied friends who had formed a loose collective of radical artists who called themselves the Provincetown Players.[30] "NO LETTER FROM YOU SINCE FRIDAY I AM DESOLATE IF I HAVE DONE ANYTHING

BAD PLEASE FORGIVE ME AND WIRE AT ONCE." It was time-stamped 3:24 a.m.[31]

Once their second child was born in December, Walter began making plans to return to England alone. In March 1922, he wrote his parents from the office, on letterhead from *The Freeman*, "I simply can't tell you how eagerly I am longing for a sight of you both and of the dear girls," his beloved sisters.[32] The next day, Crystal made sure to let Walter's sister Cynthia know that the young family was "very hard up." She explained, "We're in a terrible hole what with babies and hospitals and all." She blamed the patriarchal family model, with its single bread-winner, not Walter himself. "And how this town is too expensive. No one man can be expected to keep a family going."[33]

Crystal began putting out feelers for a new job but found few opportunities. Her fickle health and need for flexibility must have narrowed her options. Plus, she would later learn that her political activities had also seriously damaged her employability. Even in the twenties, Kellogg would tell her, "we still have a lot of beating up of bugaboos" that would touch her in any public work.[34] As the month of March progressed, Walter's impending departure made Crystal desperate for something, anything. "After ten months of domesticity varied by illness I am out on the war path," she wrote Cynthia. "I must have money and I don't care much how I get it. All ways are hard I believe. This time I am trying to do it in some way that won't interfere too drastically with the business of being a mother. Some business. Isn't it?"[35]

Two weeks later, Walter sailed off to England, arriving on April 9, 1922. On April 14, while his ship was still at sea, Crystal wrote to him. "I am so lonely it makes a little sick feeling in my solar plexus. I am not made of stern enough stuff to live alone," she told him. "I hope you will come back here." She then related that she had found a job for him in New York. It was with Kellogg, as an editor with his new venture, the *Survey Graphic*, an illustrated social research magazine initially published as a supplement to the *Survey*.[36] The starting salary was $4,500, moving toward $5,000, almost certainly more than Walter had received at *The Freeman*, a start-up. "They have the money to run the *Survey Graphic* for three years—just as long as you like a job to last!" she enthused. "With you on it, I think the magazine could be wonderful. And it already has a real circulation, so it would be a chance to work on something growing." She wrote "to urge you to look favorably on the offer if you get it. You see, darling, I am still a very dependent wife. I've rented the apartment in New York to save the day!"[37]

There was no word from Walter until a month later, when he wired to refuse the job, saying only, "Deeply appreciative but cannot accept."[38] At that point, Crystal admitted she was in the dark about Walter. "I am crazy to have him take the job," she told Kellogg, "but I always think it unwise to urge people to decisions, especially husbands." Still, she said she wanted to make one attempt to convince him to accept the position and return to the family in New York. "I am writing today, setting forth the case calmly, suggesting that the thing is still open, and asking for a cable reply."[39] Kellogg promised to hold things open a reasonable time for word from him.[40]

In the meantime, Crystal had taken a low-paying job handling publicity for the National Labor Alliance for Trade Relations with and Recognition of Russia, an affiliation that was noted in her surveillance file by the Federal Bureau of Investigation (FBI).[41] It was inadequate to her needs, both as a breadwinner and as a parent. "I leave Croton at 12—back after supper 5 days a week—for $5 a week!" she reported to her father. It was considerably less than she had earned at the American Union Against Militarism (AUAM)—when she had no children— or at the *Liberator*, which additionally offered her both flexibility and relative job security. "We'll pull out of debt after an eon or two," she told him, barely joking.[42]

Less than two weeks later, she again wrote to Walter in London. "Don't worry about harsh words, etc. Have I said any?" she asked, perhaps coyly. "If I have they certainly can be forgotten now." She hoped they could get back on track somehow. "I know you had to run away," she told him. "That you couldn't even send me a line to say so or say you were sorry will forever be incomprehensible to me. Four-fifths of you is a closed book to me and 4/5 of me is a closed book to you—and yet we love each other a great deal," she wrote. "Don't we?"[43]

Shortly thereafter, Crystal got a bit more information about Walter's activities. Upon his arrival in England, he had begun networking, making contact with the journalist Frazier Hunt and the novelist Sinclair Lewis, who then introduced Walter to the novelist Hugh Walpole.[44] Walter had sent Crystal some money in April, which must have come from the new business prospects these relationships had bred in the short time he had been back on his home soil.

Almost immediately upon receiving this lifeline, she began to suggest that the family might reunite in London. As she pressed Walter for details on his finances, she unfurled a fairly detailed arrangement for the shared support of their household and children: she could rent her house in Croton for a year and get "enough to pay interest on the debts, taxes, repairs and have 50 or 75 a month left over . . . to pay for rent in London," she offered. He could pay for "servants, food, fun and clothes." Part of the time she might leave the children with one of Walter's sisters and "take my rent money to travel on the continent. Perhaps you could come too!" she joked. But, in all seriousness, she refused to "book plans to come to England with the children . . . if we are going to start out by being in debt. Please be honest about it," she said. If it was going to work, "the first thing is to get out of debt here—and then start clear over there."[45]

Walter's most promising business prospect at the time was the Transatlantic Literary Agency, which he started with his old friend, the writer and soon-to-be publisher Stanley Nott, and Charlie Hallinan, from the AUAM, now an expatriate living with his wife, Hazel Hunkins, and their children in London. Their business strategy was to place the work of British writers with American book publishers and periodicals. They had some contacts and a promising start: between March 1923 and March 1924, the agency handled work by Bertrand Russell, George Bernard Shaw, and H. G. Wells.[46] Walter sought to build relationships with the linguist and writer C. K. Ogden and T. S. Eliot at this time as well.[47]

Still, gaining clients for the new venture was difficult, and publication fees, even for well-known writers, were modest. With a small percentage as a commission, it would take a large number of clients and placements for Walter to earn a living even for himself alone. Crystal did what she could to advance his prospects. Sometime that summer, she brokered a business arrangement for him with her old Greenwich House friend and American Association for Labor Legislation (AALL) colleague, Paul Kennaday, now a cofounder with Arthur Livingston and Ernest Poole of the rising Foreign Press Service. She had learned that Kennaday was unhappy with his London agent, so she arranged a fifty-fifty agreement for a six-month trial: he would place all things in England through Walter, and Walter would place all things in the United States through Kennaday's office, splitting commissions in both directions.[48] "It seems it would be a good thing," Crystal told Walter. "You see [Kennaday] has sold 4 successful plays—handles all of Ibanez—and has sold the movie rights for *The Four Horsemen*." She told Walter, "the next move for you is to write him a grand type-written letter, stating your business, and making it sound as important as possible."[49]

Walter may never have written that letter. In early September, Kellogg suggested Crystal take steps herself to try to seal the deal. "With all due respect to Robin Hood's barn and knowing the gentleman concerned," he told her, "I think it might very well pay for you to see Kennaday again now . . . and ask him to take the matter up from this end."[50]

With only spotty communication from Walter, Crystal was uncertain where anything stood. She'd heard through a mutual friend that he was enjoying what was essentially a bachelor's life.[51] Almost immediately upon his arrival in England, he had embarked on a series of adventures, mainly road trips with male friends, old and new.[52] Crystal tried to engage her husband's apparent effort to turn back the clock, to go home again in the way nobody ever can. "Would you rather live that way—free and irresponsible?" she asked him finally. "I suppose if that's really what you want you wouldn't be happy with me, even in London. But I don't think we ought to conclude that without trying it. Do you?"[53]

Two weeks later, she received some sort of a reply in the form of a huge $600 check from him. "Mt. Airy was so excited. Everybody so happy for me!" she wrote Walter. "Now it will be just a few weeks & we can talk everything over." But she began talking in the very next paragraph, jotting down a list of parental tasks for Walter to begin in preparation for the family's arrival: "look into a modern all-day school, with lunch, for Jeffrey and see if we can't make some cooperative plan at eating dinners. I don't want to keep house (except for the children) if I can *possibly* help it," she told him.[54] Apparently, Walter did not make much progress on these practical assignments, but he did mention to his mother and father that his family was arriving soon. Ten days later, it was the eve of their departure, and Crystal became definitive about what she wanted. "Walter dear," she began, then put her foot down about any plans to see his parents right off the bat. "I'm going straight to London—find a place to lay our heads, find a school for Jeffrey, find a nurse,—and then start out on my articles," she told him. "I am crazy for work & cities & shows. I'm through with the country & the futile domestic life. I've had six months of it now. . . . Anyhow, with a baby, I can't make any stops anywhere. So please be firm with your family. It's sweet of them to suggest it—but *I won't go*! We can go visiting on weekends—after I'm settled."[55]

She would have to take charge of the family's transatlantic move—the first of several relocations back and forth between London and New York—all on her own. Sometime after September 15, 1922, Crystal set sail with five-year-old Jeffrey and nine-month-old Annis for England. As it happened, on September 22, President Harding signed the Cable Act, giving most American women a pathway to retain their US nationality when they married a foreign husband. But Britain, where Crystal was headed, did not offer a reciprocal right. She told the papers the bill was signed while she was "on the high seas, on an American ship," but when she landed ten days later at Tilbury docks in England, "was I then a subject of King George again?" Adrift between worlds, Crystal protested, "I'm a woman without a country."[56]

She was also a working mother without a job. Her most feasible career choice at the start was freelance journalism. It was not really what she wanted to do. But as an expat and an ex-publisher, it made the most immediate sense. And if her prior political moves stymied her in some respects, her activities also gave her contacts in many organizations and networks valuable in journalism.

Crystal was now a head of household paid by the word. As a result, she started early on to use the same basic material to produce parallel versions of her articles for different outlets, typically one for English and one for American audiences. Her first publication in London was "Rome, May 14, 1923," a news report about the International Woman Suffrage Alliance congress, for the *London Daily Herald*.[57] Then in June she published a feature treatment of the meeting,

"Suffragists Ten Years After," in the *New Republic*. The next month, Crystal published "Personalities and Powers: Alice Paul," in the English feminist journal *Time and Tide*, followed in August by a reframed version for publication in the NWP's magazine, now called *Equal Rights*. This practical strategy proved doubly profitable: it duplicated fees without duplicating the work, and also helped forge a distinctive transatlantic perspective in her feminist journalism.

When she began working in England, Crystal highlighted her own broad-based feminist program, particularly when writing for a general audience. In her early article in the *New Republic*, for example, she explained, "Feminism, ten years ago, demanded of its leaders eloquence and passion, of its followers devotion and hard work. . . . Today when there is no longer a single, simple aim and a solitary barrier to break down," she continued, "there are a hundred difficult questions of civil law, problems of education, of moral and social custom to be solved, before women can come wholly into their inheritance of freedom."[58] However, as her career became increasingly dependent on publishing with the feminist press, her journalism focused more intensively on the issues and cross-currents of the trans-atlantic women's movement. For her, this meant heated, heartfelt discussion of the growing ideological divide between the equalitarian feminist project of the militant wing and the humanitarian mindset of more conservative suffragists and the Progressive reformers. In what was a rocky suffrage landscape—American women won the vote in 1920, but British women attained only partial suffrage in 1918, continuing to battle for the full franchise until 1928—Crystal worked hard to position herself as a leading expert on both sides of the Atlantic.

Toward that end, she first had to mend fences with Paul and the NWP. Almost immediately, she published "1848–1923," a remembrance on the seventy-fifth anniversary of Seneca Falls that proclaimed the NWP to be the single, simple, direct heir of the American women's suffrage movement.[59] Perhaps more impor-tant, she also put out a much more complimentary profile of Paul than the one she had published as her last feature article in the *Liberator*. Crystal's new piece, published in both Britain and America, asserted her belief in the positive value of "feuds" like the one she had triggered at the NWP convention two years before. "The [suffrage] movement grew and grew from the mighty dissention in their ranks," she wrote, and Alice Paul she now celebrated as the single-minded leader essential to this "glorious fight worthy of our best mettle."[60]

Crystal expressed her long-standing faith in the value of dissent to galva-nize self-discovery and growth in organizations and movements. She seemed to refer to dynamics both inside and outside the NWP when she ventured to say, "Indifference is harder to fight than hostility, and there is nothing that kills an agitation like having everybody admit that it is fundamentally right." Rather, "if you can so frame your issue or so choose your method of attack as to precipitate discussion and difference of opinion among honest men, so that all your followers become passionate explainers, you have put life into a movement."[61] Such claims did much more than justify her actions at the NWP convention and repair her sins of the past with Paul. They also rescued internal conflict as natural and ultimately constructive, rebutting the sexist "cat fight" frame while creating a positive context for the sharp schisms in the women's movement her journalism was conveying to women and the world.

Through the rest of the decade, the issue that most divided feminists was protective labor legislation for women—special workplace health and safety regulations, won before suffrage, that continued to be instituted in industrial workplaces in the United States and in Britain.[62] Crystal called this question "an acid test for suffragists": "whether women with their newly-won political equality are going to countenance any industrial inequality even when offered in the guise of a benefit."[63]

The debate detonated in 1923, Crystal's first year in England, when the Equal Rights Amendment (ERA) was introduced to the US Congress in December. The ERA was devised by Paul and the NWP, certainly with Crystal's support and perhaps her concrete coauthorship.[64] It emerged after the NWP had invested two long years in intensive state lobbying to remove individual, sex-specific discriminations and yet had achieved only very modest results. The amendment was its strategic policy response. After several drafts, it articulated their new "Great Demand": "Equality of rights under the law shall not be denied or abridged by the United States or any state on account of sex." In its all-encompassing simplicity, the ERA appeared to solve the problem of how a single-issue campaign could raise the hundred difficult matters that created and reinforced gender inequality.

Elegant as this solution may have seemed inside the NWP, the ERA splintered coalitions in the women's movement, alienating the organization from a whole network of political groups with which they were once either partly or largely aligned. Its reasoning not only reasserted the schism between the NWP militants and the NAWSA reformers but also divided NWP feminists from labor women and Progressives who saw the amendment as a threat to social welfare legislation they had struggled for two decades to see enacted. For years, labor women had successfully championed protective legislation to keep women legally barred from the most dangerous industrial jobs, to guarantee them distinctive contract conditions such as a forty-eight-hour work week, and to eradicate child labor. When the logic of the ERA was soon appropriated to invalidate the minimum-wage laws covering women, the NWP became all but anathema to women of the labor movement.[65]

Florence Kelley denounced the amendment, saying it was "as dangerous as anything can possibly be" in the hands of the courts.[66] Before long, even Kellogg, while keeping an open mind, had to remind Crystal how much "the Woman's Party crowd has done to kill the 48-hour bill here in New York." He raised the class privilege of many women of the NWP, reminding her that labor women "have their feet actually on the ground and know what they are talking about when they say that there are definite excruciating evils which they want to guard against by minimum wage and night work legislation." He wondered "whether the professional woman, the feminists, and Women's Party really have taken the trouble to find out about things and have any other solution to offer."[67] Many other social reformers went further, including some in the women's movement.[68] The director of the Women's Bureau of the Department of Labor vowed to do everything in her power to defeat the ERA, and later denounced it as the "so-called Equal Rights Amendment."[69] Workers' advocates, including representatives of the American Federation of Labor (AFL) and several international unions, joined numerous women's organizations to voice fierce opposition to the proposed amendment and so to the NWP.[70]

But as Crystal saw it, feminists advocating the ERA were not opposed to laws improving the labor conditions; they merely claimed they should apply to men and women alike.[71] She and the NWP were equalitarian feminists: they believed men and women should be treated exactly the same under the law. Any sex-based laws were ultimately a threat to all women, in all areas of their lives, they believed; as long as women could be the objects of special legislation along any line, they argued, women could be targeted for special restriction along any other. Thus, the amendment was essential for women's equality. "There is a lot more in the Woman's Party position than, for example, Mrs. Kelley would credit," Crystal replied to Kellogg. "Perhaps there is a new approach along health lines which would accomplish the realistic ends of protective labor legislation," she suggested, but it must "at the same time be consistent with the principles of feminism."[72]

Unfortunately, no such reuniting approach was forthcoming. In "Equality or Protection?" Crystal framed the increasingly bitter divide as a "battle royal" embodied by Florence Kelley versus Alice Paul, its "two lionhearts [sic] on opposite sides of the issue." At the outset, she acknowledged "all the so-called protective legislation for women is not so indefensible. . . . It is no idle rhetorical question . . . but a very real question indeed." Therefore, "to answer it with courage and consistency and yet with sympathy and sound practical human judgment may well be the major concern of feminists for the next decade."[73]

Her projected timeline was close to correct. Initially, Crystal's articles explained the stakes on both sides of the debate, but, increasingly, she became a vocal partisan for the ERA in the press. More than fifteen years earlier she had pushed for legislation to ensure safe conditions for all workers, men and women alike. Plus, she and other equalitarians knew that the more strenuous and risky jobs from which women were protected were also the ones that offered higher pay, a badly needed boost for laboring women who still struggled against a significant gender wage gap across all industries. And down the road, gender wage discrimination would only worsen in an environment shaped by protective labor laws: since this legislation intrinsically opposed the concept of equal work for men and women, it made it more difficult to advance the call for equal pay. But most of all, from the beating heart of her feminism, Crystal believed women must be treated as free individuals, as equal independent actors, in both the home and the world. In their choices, about their labor as in every other area of their lives, public and private, she held that it must be up to women themselves to determine their own equations about pursuits and priorities, risks and rewards.

By the mid-1920s, Crystal readily identified herself with the logic of unconditional equality embodied in the ERA. In "English Feminists and Special Labor Laws for Women," published in *Equal Rights*, she placed herself with the unanimous stand recently taken by all three national feminist organizations in Britain: the argument that workers should be protected from dangerous conditions not on the basis of sex but on the nature of the occupation.[74] Dangerous work was dangerous for everybody—not just women, she insisted. As if in dialogue with Kellogg, she soon refuted his veiled accusation that the equalitarian position was classist, reflecting the ignorance of industrial conditions shared by privileged professional women. In "Protective Legislation in England," she supplied an in-depth interview with the union leader Mary Bell-Richards. Bell-Richards boasted "a more genuinely proletarian background" than almost any woman in the country, Crystal maintained—and she supported the equalitarian view. "If you demand equality," Bell-Richards said pointedly, "you must accept equality."[75]

Crystal persistently highlighted the threat posed to women's progress by the logic of laws grounded in the age-old patriarchal ideas of female protection. In a system where legal reasoning proceeded from precedent and legislation from popular assumptions and opinion, she argued, these laws would proliferate and expand, maintaining women workers in a subservient status across the workforce. She admonished a recent decision by the International Labor Office (ILO) of the League of Nations as a case in point. The ILO had recently adopted the "Washington Conventions," which not only incorporated protective rules in the industrial legislation of Great Britain and other nations affiliated with the league but also extended them to cover agriculture. Crystal warned that there was nothing to prevent the further extension of the rules to include knowledge workers as well.[76]

She went all-in on the equalitarian stand. To her mind, it was an essentially intersectional position from which all women stood to gain. In June 1924, she returned to the United States for a job with the NWP, her first paid position with the organization since she helped get it started in late 1912. In September, she launched its Women for Congress Campaign (WCC), a program "to elect women nominees, irrespective of their political affiliations," the party announced, which is the spiritual forebear of the modern-day Emily's List. The idea was that electing more women to the US Congress would naturally generate support for the Equal Rights Amendment and a general feminist program.[77]

As it turned out, the job demanded even more than organizational and logistical work. Crystal also faced a strategic communication challenge to define and defend the politics of what quickly became a controversial campaign. On October 30, she penned a letter to the editor of the *Nation*, which was published under the headline "Feminists Must Fight." It was the first of several attempts to explain a campaign to mobilize women as candidates against the rising criticism, even from the Progressive Left, that it made better sense as publicity than as politics on the ground. A *Nation* article had asked whether the WCC sought to elect women because they were women, or because they were ERA-supporting feminists, a particular political stripe of woman. And even more fundamentally, the magazine went on to question the whole underlying idea of the NWP that gave rise to the WCC initiative, and which still resonates today: would women hold together as a voting block? Would women vote as women, rather than on the basis of other identifiers and interests? The *Nation* columnist thought not. "Now that women [are] voters, economic and class interests [will] prove stronger than sex interests," the writer asserted. Ultimately, he believed gender would not trump party. "For every political office, for every legal change in the direction of equality, women will have to fight as women. But the lines will be drawn inside party lines, not across them."[78]

Crystal thought otherwise. In general, she conceded that women would indeed have to vote along party lines. "If women want to be in politics they must be politicians," she granted. "They must choose their party and play the political game from the ground up." But that would only take them so far, she continued. "It seems to me most emphatically not true that the battle for 'equal rights' must be fought within party lines. It can never be won there." That battle—for equal status as a person under the law and in society—preceded party affiliation and therefore transcended party lines.

Crystal advocated a social movement model that could press the case inside, across, and beyond party politics. And she believed the rallying point for women was their common experience of the gender double standard, which suffused every aspect of American life. Only an independent coalition of political women could mount effective challenges to inequality so insidious and so widespread. The fight for equality "must be fought and it will be fought by a free-handed, nonpartisan minority of energetic feminists to whom politics in general, even 'reform' politics, will continue to be a matter of indifference so long as women are classed with children and minors in industrial legislation, so long as even in our most advanced States a woman can be penalized by the loss of her job when she marries." The "principle of the Equal Rights Amendment is supremely important," she believed, not least because it threw down the gauntlet from a common rallying place—the second-class status that all women shared.

Eastman did not acknowledge that some women suffered lower status than others, although she surely recognized it. She tried instead to call for solidarity among all women as a class in their inferior position as compared to all men. It may seem dated now, with our critical recognition of the way differences among women shape very different experiences and perspectives, but at the time it was a radical play. Crystal believed this was the true basis for common cause. It would help all women to some extent or other, and would situate them to march forward together for more. It was the inclusive battle of the decade. "To blot out of every law book in the land, to sweep out of every dusty courtroom, to erase from every judge's mind that centuries-old precedent as to woman's inferiority and dependence and need for protection, to substitute for it at one blow the simple new precedent of equality," she proclaimed, "that is a fight worth making if it takes ten years."[79]

Of course, it is taking many more years than that. Indeed, the question of how to properly take account of our different identities, and the unequal freedom and justice these differences tend to predict, confronts women's organizing and broader social change activism on the American left to this day. For the rest of her life, however, Crystal never ceased believing this fundamental position all women could share was the right place to make their stand and win. She immediately returned to the original question about the particular breed of woman candidate the WCC would support and clarified her answer. The day after she wrote her letter to the *Nation*—but nearly two weeks before it appeared—the *New York Telegram* ran a profile of her bearing the headline: "Feminist for Equality, Not 'Women as Women': Crystal Eastman Explains She Favors Election of Congressional Candidates on Account of Their Principles, Not Their Sex."[80] A week later, she wrote a second letter to the editor, this time to the *New Republic*, in which she specified a political litmus test for the candidates the WCC intended to promote. It was "feminism first" women candidates—now defined as those "who will put the Equal Rights Amendment ahead of everything else."[81]

Whatever unifying hopes Crystal invested in an independent women's lobby like the NWP, the WCC struggled amidst the whole contested rationale for the ERA, in the women's movement and the wider culture. Only a single woman candidate backed by the WCC prevailed in the election of 1924.[82] By the time

Crystal's letter to the *Nation* appeared eight days after the election, she had left the NWP job. "For three weeks I tried to raise money for this Campaign with no results," she told Walter. "What I did was to raise enough to pay my salary and then quit."[83] She felt defeated and alone. "I am wildly homesick for you, darling," she added, and she was struggling financially to support the household: "I need money pretty desperately so I hope it is double amount this week to make up for last."[84]

It was the final political action job of her career. As she left, Crystal resigned herself to a future not in activism, but in journalism. "In this wandering life I seem destined to lead there is no other way for me to make a living than to be a writer," she conceded. Essentially a single working mother now, struggling and lonely in both her literal and her political home, she felt exhausted from the fight for the first time in her life. Now forty-three, she admitted to Walter, "this little experience with a 'cause' convinced me that I am too old and tired and disillusioned to work up other people for causes."[85]

Crystal returned to England on January 3, 1925. Living in the same city but in a separate residence from Walter, she took primary care of their two young children and worked from home. Over the next two years, she wrote regular articles as a feminist journalist. Reaching to reconnect with her roots and her youthful hopes of practicing law, she produced several articles about the criminal justice system. In "Justice for the Prostitute," she boldly discussed a new bill by Lady Astor, the first woman to take her seat in Britain's Parliament, highlighting in stark terms the sexual double standard embedded in the existing criminal law. "No more astounding relic of the subjection of women survives in western civilization than the status of the prostitute," she asserted at the outset. In England, "as everywhere else it is a *one-sided* crime; i.e., it takes two to commit it but only one is penalized." In what other illegal transaction, she pressed, "is the seller alone penalized, and not the buyer?" Further, she fumed, "the man who bought what she offered to sell, not only goes scot free and escapes all publicity, but has the money he paid to the prostitute refunded by the State."[86] In "London Letter: The Married Teacher," Crystal denounced the patently sexist laws that forced women to retire from the teaching profession upon marriage, blasting a recent appeals court decision that affirmed a married woman should attend to her domestic duties full time. Never before had she felt more certain, she said, "that women in all Anglo-Saxon countries need a *bill of rights*."[87]

Still, as the 1920s drew to a close, her main beat remained the continuing transatlantic debate about equality versus protection. She consistently detailed the arguments and counterarguments, the allies, enemies, and personalities, of the ongoing political dispute. She repeatedly explained cross-currents of the English side to American readers and vice versa.[88] By the winter of 1927, she summarized where things stood. "Here is the question Feminists must agree on, before they go far in their campaign for industrial equality. Are they going to level up or level down? Are they going to insist that men workers be brought under the safety and health regulations that now apply only to women? Or are they going to insist that women be taken out from under those regulations?"[89] It was not far from where the controversy began more than four years before.[90]

With progress stymied by divisions, the NWP turned to circumvent the stalemate by taking up a resolution that had passed at the 1921 convention, before the ERA and its associated debates began. Beginning in 1926, Alice Paul began meeting with allies in Europe and elsewhere about forming a group of international advisory committees to campaign for equal rights provisions in international treaties.[91] The party would increasingly pursue international directions into the next decade. In 1938, Paul established the World Woman's Party, which operated until 1958.

Crystal blessed a new beginning, especially one that touched on her long-unfulfilled internationalist hopes. She celebrated this as the start of what could become a global equal rights organization. To the press, the NWP's multicountry network was "an international feminist lobby." But to a self-described "Woman's Party exile" like Crystal, it was both a homecoming and a place to go. To see Alice Paul in London, "this wonder-worker—so quiet, so indefatigable, so sure—once more beginning to move mountains," Crystal breathed, "revives ones [sic] faith in the future."[92]

10 "MARRIAGE UNDER TWO ROOFS": FEMINISM AND FAMILY LIFE

In "Modern Adventures in Maternity," an unpublished article written sometime in the mid-1920s, Crystal divulged her profound longing for motherhood. "When I was about twenty-six years old I began to wonder if I would get married in time to have children," she confessed. "I was in the midst of a busy professional career, which was not without its fun and fame," yet having a family "always remained the central dream of my waking hours. . . . Whatever else I was," she revealed, "I would be a mother." At first, she professed an equal desire for work and family: "I could not bear the thought of being a woman without children any more than I could bear the thought of being a woman without a job," she explained. But then she recalibrated the work-family equation, admitting, "That is hardly a fair setting forth of the state of my mind. I wanted children more than anything else life could bring, more than love or fame or fortune, and more than all together."[1]

As Crystal revised the article with the hope of publication, she excised the last comment, letting stand her statement of equal desire for children and meaningful work outside the home.[2] And from then on, she explored this feminist dilemma persistently—indeed, sometimes obsessively—in her writing through the twenties. While few of her movement colleagues emphasized these issues, sometimes the questions she confronted were so perseverant that they infiltrated or even overtook her articles about other subjects. More than half a century before second-wave feminists coined the phrase "the personal is political," Eastman was pushing to bring her feminist politics into her family life, to integrate her deep desire for motherhood with the equalitarian values she experienced as similarly essential to who she was. It would be as daunting a challenge as any she had confronted before.

Crystal Eastman. Amy Aronson, Oxford University Press (2020).
© Oxford University Press.
DOI: 10.1093/oso/9780199948734.001.0001

The movement was not especially helpful to her on this one. The private sphere of the home—women's supposed turf—was very thorny terrain for feminists. Generations of thinkers and activists through the nineteenth century had examined it, only to expose myriad fallacies and false promises residing there. They had unmasked marriage, the culturally accepted source of women's social legitimacy and financial support, for instead sustaining women's subordination and economic dependency. While they at times acknowledged motherhood as a source of distinctive strengths and values, mothering was also seen as a self-sacrificing responsibility, often at odds with a woman's intellectual life and individual autonomy. Well before Eastman's time, feminists denounced the whole concept of a world divided into separate spheres—with the public as men's domain and the private as women's—not merely as unjust but as a patriarchal fable. Both realms were controlled by male interests. A man's home was *his* castle—not his wife's. In 1925, Crystal would quote approvingly when her younger colleague, the English writer Rebecca West, summed up this sentiment by declaring, "Home is a symbol of a state of resignation to the male will."[3]

By the early twentieth century, the ambivalence (at best) of many feminists toward the private sphere of domestic relations spurred policy innovations designed to revolutionize the home and family life. In *The Home, Its Work and Influence* (1903), Charlotte Perkins Gilman had proposed collectivizing and professionalizing housework and childcare to effectively liberate the average woman from the private realm almost entirely. Over the next decade or so, some downtown New York feminists, many of them Crystal's friends, had attempted to directly apply Gilman's ideas. In 1906, they formed a communal housing venture called the A Club at 3 Fifth Avenue in lower Manhattan, just a short distance from where the American Union Against Militarism (AUAM) and Woman's Peace Party of New York (WPP-NY) later had offices. A group of eighteen people, most of them reformers, writers, or settlement house workers, lived there. The group included married couples (among them Mary Heaton Vorse and her husband) and singles, both men and women.[4] Later, Henrietta Rodman attempted to form a cooperative apartment building on Washington Square in Greenwich Village, complete with a professional staff of cooks and childcare workers. Despite being ridiculed in the mainstream press, she and others commissioned architectural plans and had selected a building site; only a lack of financing ended the project.[5]

Crystal's own model for collective living was the compact she experienced in Glenora, where her mother had informally pulled off the crux of these feminist goals—but with one central difference. At Glenora, mothers were at the heart of it all. When *The Home* was first published, Crystal seemed to agree with its structural reorganization of domestic chores but may have resisted its ambition to supplant mothering. In 1903, Annis wrote her daughter, then a Vassar senior, to say, "I love your ideas about home. . . . I wonder whether the cookstove and the washtub are essential parts of the home. Mrs. Gilman says not—very convincingly. Max is delighted with her book—but I am bracing myself to hear that you do not like her at all—that if the new ideas make such women you'll have none of them!"[6]

Before the vote was won, Crystal's feminist colleagues did begin calling for legal changes that, while emphasizing a woman's independence, directly pertained to the private domain. The National Woman's Party (NWP) sought a married woman's right to retain her birth name, equal rights of child guardianship, and the right of a woman to establish her own domicile, for example. Crystal not only supported such measures but also experienced the need for all of them in the course of her life. Yet by the time she was a mother of two in the early 1920s, there had been little progress on such policy initiatives in any state legislature in the country. One consequence of such underwhelming results was a renewed emphasis on a single wellspring source of liberation—and one more decidedly divorced from the home. Economic power, individual financial control, emerged as an indispensable instrument for women's equality.[7] Liberation was to be reached by kicking open the doors of industry to women. That logical sequence—paid work outside the home producing economic independence producing emancipation—became a dominant proposition in both British and American feminist thought at the time.[8]

Eastman, who straddled British and American equalitarian feminism, endorsed economic independence through work outside the home as a crucial plank of women's empowerment. Indeed, like her mother before her, she saw work as a fulfilling and essential enterprise and a blessing as part of a woman's life. However, it still represented only one part of a more comprehensive and complicated vision. She believed millions of women like herself experienced acute feminist concerns not merely in the battle for economic opportunity and remuneration in the workforce but also from conflicts between their desire for the economic and personal value of a job or career and for the rewards of motherhood and family as well.

Once again, many activist women with whom Crystal agreed on so much did not seem to go far enough. The majority of women worldwide, she believed, searched not just for economic independence but for balance between independence and interdependence, emancipation and devotion. And while her equalitarian colleagues in the NWP and elsewhere were known to avow that women could have it all, both a job and a marriage with children, through the 1920s the feminist movement undertook little sustained examination of the intricate difficulties in combining work with family for its own sake.[9]

Crystal vigorously pursued that missing policy and analysis. Politically, she believed the quest for equality across public and private affairs would drive the next wave of American feminism. "This to me is the central fact of feminism," she believed. "Until women learn to want economic independence, i.e., the ability to earn their own living independently of husbands, fathers, brothers or lovers,—and until they work out a way to get this independence without denying themselves the joys of love and motherhood, it seems to me feminism has no roots. . . . Its manifestations are often delightful and stimulating but they are sporadic, they effect no lasting change."[10] For her, work-family balance represented the place where the vast majority of women, irrespective of other affiliations and differences, could readily come together. "Ninety-nine out of every hundred women want children," she pronounced in 1920.[11] And the issues at the heart of this debate—sex, love, marriage, family—blended contemporary questions of personal fulfillment with feminist politics, holding the power to draw younger women, from many backgrounds and walks of life, back to the barricades. Without such a galvanizing issue to revive and unite the movement, the feminist revolution would stall, half-finished, or even fail, she warned. "If the feminist program goes to pieces at the arrival of the first baby," Crystal said pointedly, "it is false and useless."[12]

As an equalitarian feminist, breadwinner, wife, and working mother, Eastman personally experienced the challenges of feminism and family as neither politically peripheral nor possible to ignore. She resolutely confronted them in her journalism and her life, insisting that for feminism to truly change the world, it must transform the family—the place where gender inequality is not just experienced, not just exercised, but also born and raised. A number of these articles remained unpublished, never finding a venue or an audience in her lifetime. But the issues, haunting and implacable, persisted for her. "How to reconcile a woman's natural desire for love and home and children with her equally natural desire for work of her own for which she is paid, for some normal work-contact with the world at large, this is not an easy question to solve," she wrote in the penultimate publication of her life. "But it is the very essence of feminism."[13]

* * *

Crystal mapped out what she called her "bill of particulars" for the modern feminist project in "Now We Can Begin," published at the cusp of universal suffrage in January 1920. Since the goal of "break[ing] down the barriers to the professions" was already on the movement agenda, she focused on what was not as well addressed—law and customs affecting women's status in the home and family, policies on which, she repeatedly argued, the achievement of economic independence ineluctably depended.[14]

First on her list was access to birth control. In 1918, she discussed "Birth Control in the Feminist Program" in Margaret Sanger's *Birth Control Review*. The term "birth control" was coined by Sanger herself in 1914, "to get a name for contraception which would convey to the public the social and personal significance of the idea."[15] At the time, several methods for preventing pregnancy were available—including condoms, spermicidal jellies and powders, and the rhythm method—but Sanger, a visiting nurse, found that her patients in New York's Lower East Side tenements lacked basic information about them. Indeed, most had no idea how the reproductive process really worked. Yet even as they pleaded for her help in avoiding pregnancy, she could not advise them because providing information about contraception was against the law—even for medical practitioners.

Such basic sex education information had been deemed obscene decades earlier. In 1873, Congress passed a set of so-called chastity laws drafted by antiobscenity crusader Anthony Comstock. The statutes defined contraceptives as both obscene and illicit, and made it a federal offense to disseminate information about birth control through the mail or across state lines. When Sanger published two vehicles for contraceptive information in 1914—her pamphlet *Family Limitation* and a short-lived eight-page magazine, the *Woman Rebel*—the papers labeled her a "vile menace" who was "determined to explode dynamite under the American home."[16] Comstock, who was by then in the midst of his forty-year career as US Post Office inspector and America's leading moral censor, immediately confiscated her magazine.

Sanger was arrested on nine felony counts of publishing indecent material, charges that carried a potential sentence of forty-five years in prison. She fled to Europe the following year, leaving her husband and three young children behind in New York. Returning a year later, she garnered public supporters, including many in Crystal's circle, Alva Belmont, Harriot Stanton Blatch, and H. G. Wells among them. In time, government prosecutors dropped the charges. Shortly thereafter, in October 1916, Sanger established America's first birth control clinic in Brooklyn, New York. Within days, she was arrested, again under the Comstock laws. She served thirty days in jail, but in a later court proceeding on the case, the presiding judge issued a ruling that allowed licensed doctors to prescribe contraceptives. It would take more than twenty additional years, but the decision helped pave the way to the legalization and public acceptance of birth control.[17]

Three months after her release, in February 1917, Sanger founded the *Birth Control Review*. By the time Eastman came to publish her article there the following year, she had known Sanger for nearly a decade—ever since she came to Greenwich Village from Corning, New York, in 1910, and began circulating with the crowd at *The Masses*. But Crystal's birth control advocacy was most directly connected with Mary Ware Dennett, who founded the National Birth Control League (NBCL) in New York in 1915, six years before Sanger's American Birth Control League (ABCL), the earliest predecessor of the Planned Parenthood Federation.[18]

Dennett was an outspoken suffrage, antiwar, and Heterodoxy friend who became a divorcee and the sole breadwinner for her two children. Eastman and Dennett had worked together virtually their entire careers, beginning in the National American Woman Suffrage Association while Crystal led the campaign in Wisconsin, extending into the Congressional Union and National Woman's Party, then in the WPP and the AUAM, where Dennett became a field secretary in 1916, and on into the People's Council of America. Eastman had also joined Dennett in the establishment of the Twilight Sleep Association, an organization that weighed in on a rising transatlantic controversy between feminist women and medical practitioners about the health advantages—to both babies and mothers—of using painkillers in childbirth. Among those on the executive committee were the *Suffragist* editor and labor advocate Rheta Childe Dorr and Heterodoxy founder Marie Jenney Howe. Also at the first meeting was Mrs. J. P. Morgan.[19]

Like Sanger, Dennett's advocacy for sex education and contraception put her at odds with the Comstock laws, and she too would see a ruling in her legal case contribute to the eventual legalization of contraceptive information. But where Sanger entered this fray as a consequence of her professional experiences as a nurse, Dennett was initially motivated by her personal experiences as a mother. In the absence of any kind of sex education for the general public, she wrote an informative pamphlet, *The Sex Side of Life*, as a primer for her sons. She covered topics in sexual health from masturbation to menstruation to sexually transmitted infections (STIs) in such a candid and factual way that parents, teachers, and also medical practitioners made use of it. It went into seven editions.

In 1922, the postmaster general told Dennett the pamphlet violated obscenity laws and would be confiscated from the mail. She responded by organizing for "full repeal" of the Comstock laws. After her progress was stymied, she tried working discreetly with the post office to relax the censorship. But in 1929, she was tried for violation of the Comstock Act and found guilty. A year later, her appeal was heard in the US Circuit Court of Appeals in New York and her conviction overturned. That ruling became part of the series of legal decisions that exempted contraception information from obscenity statutes, at least when the guidance was provided by physicians.[20]

Though less widely than with Dennett, Eastman shared important political commitments with Sanger, particularly to Socialism. Sanger's first published work, a defiant column titled "What Every Girl Should Know," was published between November 1912 and June 1913 in the Socialist *New York Call*. Her *Woman Rebel* set out in no uncertain terms to be "red and flaming."[21] Indeed, in its second issue, Sanger exposed what she saw as the cynical interests of capitalism at work in blocking access to birth control information: she charged that business owners relied on poor women to produce big families of poor children who would then supply labor for their sweatshops.[22] In *Family Limitation*, Sanger similarly made the case that working-class women were constantly at war with the "boss class" for control of the pivotal resource of their own bodies.[23]

"A woman's body belongs to herself alone," she declared in the *Woman Rebel*.[24] Although this assertion carried strong feminist implications then just as it does now, Sanger had a contentious relationship with the women's movement, even the militant wing with which Crystal identified. She took issue with its emphasis on professional councils and semi-professional women, with what she saw as the trifling concerns of the affluent and upper-class.[25] Eastman shared Sanger's cognizance of class and other forms of privilege operating within the women's movement, writing in *Birth Control Review*:

> I don't believe there is one woman within the confines of this state who does not believe in birth control. I never met one. That is, I never met one who thought that she should be kept in ignorance of contraceptive methods. Many I have met who valued the knowledge they possessed, but thought there were certain other classes who would be better kept in ignorance. The old would protect the young. The rich would keep the poor in ignorance. The good would keep their knowledge from the bad, the strong from the weak, and so on.[26]

However, unlike Sanger, Crystal saw the feminist movement—as least her own idea of it—as part of the solution, not the problem. In her article for Sanger's magazine, she introduced an uncommon perspective that helped her modulate class tensions while forging a distinctive feminist stance.

To advocate for birth control, Crystal spoke from her lived desire for motherhood. By exposing the practical dilemmas afflicting ordinary women as mothers, she could simultaneously represent the great masses of women, as she had argued to the NWP, and also those with greater social and economic privilege—women who were not necessarily exploited by their fertility and aspired or acceded to capable mothering.

Her emphasis on the experiential proved both radical and remarkably traditional. On the one hand, Crystal revealed the living connection between pregnancy and women's sexual desire, an unorthodox dimension rarely argued by birth control advocates. "Feminists are not nuns," she flatly observed, "that first must be established." Then she explained: "We want to love and be loved, and most of us want children, one or two at least. But we want our love to be joyous and free—not clouded with ignorance and fear." At the same time, she recognized, and accentuated, what she experienced as women's longing for motherhood and deep devotion to it. "We want our children to be deliberately, eagerly called into being when we are at our best, not crowded upon us in times of poverty and weakness."[27] Positioning birth control in the service of radical female heterosexual desire, as well as traditional dedicated mothering, Eastman's arguments reached toward opposite ends of the spectrum of women's sexual politics at the time.

Crystal's emphasis on child-rearing within the discussion of women's exercise of new freedoms also diverged from the prevailing sentiment expressed by the movement. For many of her colleagues, motherhood seemed a deterrent to living a free and fulfilled life of one's own, not a component—and certainly not a pillar—of it. Yet to her, as she observed in *Birth Control Review*, the desire for children "seemed so obvious to me that I was astonished the other day to come upon a group of distinguished feminists who discussed for an hour what could be done with the woman's vote in New York State and did not once mention birth control."[28] In contrast to so much mainstream thinking in both the feminist and birth control movements at the time, Crystal advocated contraception less strictly in terms of pregnancy prevention and more in the context of family planning. Indeed, she repeatedly reminded her feminist colleagues that work outside the home—and the emancipation they argued would depend on it—could never be managed without first unfettering access to birth control.

Eastman emphasized that any woman who wanted a career already faced enormous obstacles from direct sexism and gender discrimination in the workplace. On that, she and her feminist colleagues agreed. But once a working woman became a working mother, Crystal continued, she was disadvantaged by an added burden: a man, even a father with children at home, could function and think of himself as an unencumbered individual at his job; a working mother, on the other hand, would wear both hats in both spheres of her life. Working mothers "must make up their minds to be a sort of supermen," she thought, if they are to manage all that family life "seems inexorably to demand of the mother." Family planning was the ounce of prevention and control that made the feminist ambition of life-long work outside the home feasible at all. "If we add to this handicap complete uncertainty as to when children may come, how often they come or how many there shall be," she explained, "the thing becomes impossible."[29]

Next in Crystal's bill of particulars was the transformation in education she began calling for in "What Next?" in 1919. If feminists wanted an equalitarian society not divided by gender into spheres or hierarchies, she contended, "we must somehow even up this business of home-making. . . . Girls as well as boys must be trained for self-support, not as a matter of bitter and regrettable necessity, but as a natural fulfillment of their powers."[30] Eastman had grasped in her teenage years that gender categories must be flexible, expanded, so fluid they would yield to shared cultural universals about the human behavior of *adults*. She continued to assert that fundamental precept in her later thinking and writing. "It must be womanly as well as manly to earn your own living, to stand on your own feet. And it must be manly as well as womanly to know how to cook and sew and clean and take care of yourself in the ordinary exigencies of life," she wrote in 1920.[31] "Girls, *as well as boys*, must be brought up as a matter of course to earn their own living," she asserted again in 1924. "Boys, *as well as girls*, must be taught, as a matter of course, the rudiments of home-making."[32] Nothing short of a revolution would do. Society and culture had to be transformed from the bottom up and across the board. Both sexes had to be raised to understand each other—and themselves— as individuals, free to pursue their own paths and preferences, and simultaneously as partners, parents, and friends, capable in caretaking and responsible in relationships. She called for a complete overhaul of the gendered division of labor and power in private life that has only now begun. And the engine of that transformation was a radical concept in mothering. "We must bring up feminist sons," she proclaimed.[33]

Crystal again supported her vanguard assertions with evidence from her personal family experience, first as a child, then as a mother. "Many, many years ago I remember announcing to my mother that I would not make my bed unless my two brothers had to make theirs," she wrote in "Bed-Makers and Bosses," published in 1923. Then she linked her own upbringing to a "conversation with my six-year-old son, who has chosen a sailor's career." Jeffrey had told her he would bring his wife along on his journey, but when Crystal asked him what his wife would do on the ship, he had replied, "Oh, make the beds, I suppose." Crystal gently protested, trying to shift the winds in more equalitarian directions. " 'Why not a sailor like you? Why not the captain? Or why not have her be the wireless operator and then she would have a little office at the top of the ship where you could come and visit her?' " she suggested. "This last won a sparkle of enthusiasm from the brown eyes," she said, although she quickly conceded, "I feel sure he will revert to his original plan." Gender messages about male dominance and separate spheres were so pervasive they seemed natural to people, masking their true social and cultural sources. "How can I expect to counteract the steady insistent suggestion of school, story, song and game that girls are weak and boys are strong," she wondered out loud, "that a proper heroine looks forward to a life concerned with 'keeping house,' while a hero has the world to choose from?"[34]

Some answers emerged when her article turned into an ad hoc book review. She gave her recommended volume a rave. "Never before, have I felt so well fortified against the fast-accumulating masculine assumptions of my son," she wrote, as when she read what became a classic work in feminist sociology, written by Mathilde and Mathias Vaerting, a Weimar husband and wife team.[35] Like Gilman before them, the authors understood that gender inequality does not rightly arise from natural differences like men's physical strength or women's reproductive capacities. Rather, the idea of innate and consequential gender differences is devised in the culture, then pressed into the service of a prior demand for women to be subordinate to men. While our patriarchal society rationalizes gender discrimination based on the claim of natural difference, the truth is the other way around: difference is largely created and magnified to justify gender inequality.[36]

Following on the analysis of the Vaertings, Crystal pressed for a bloodless revolution. She did not see solutions emerging from role reversals or reprisals, from any battle of the sexes where one "side" or the other would win. "The most militant of us has no desire to see the race revert to a period of feminine dominance," she wrote.[37] What was needed was succession, fundamental change achieved by a society ready to move beyond the old order. Like the Vaertings, she concluded by saying, "All we ask is that 'humanity should find ways and means for the permanent realisation [sic] of sex-equality.'"[38]

Finding those ways and means was the driving question for any equalitarian feminist, but Crystal was open to some less-traveled lanes. In pursuing her comprehensive democratic vision for equality, she expressed greater comfort with full-time homemaking than did many of her peers. Her dominant concern as a feminist was that women should be in a position to make real choices about their lives—freely, honestly, and with full and fair economic empowerment whatever they did. Accordingly, she attended—as a feminist—to some homemakers' concerns. She showed sincere interest in the professional field of domestic science, for example, which for decades had popularized the idea of homemaking as a skilled trade, mainly through its close ties to women's magazines. In an article in *Equal Rights*, she approvingly quoted Caroline Haslett, a feminist who formed the first professional engineering association for women in Britain, suggesting that professional women, even those who broke into traditionally male-dominated fields, might direct their expertise back into the home. "Home making is the oldest industry in the world . . . but it has never had good tools," Haslett told Eastman. "During the war women got a chance to see how differently industry is organized, how the whole emphasis is on eliminating drudgery, eliminating fatigue. . . . Women engineers, while I want them to go into all lines of work, will perhaps, make their first big contribution by bringing this emphasis into the work of the home."[39]

Traditional women's magazines had long presumed that domestic labor, whether by paid maids or unpaid homemakers, was exclusively a woman's field. Crystal brought an equalitarian feminist angle to bear on that assumption. She argued that both men and women should be educated equally in all domestic skills, so individual life and labor choices could always be freely made, irrespective of gender. "Why not welcome the idea of a compulsory course in Domestic Science but insist that it be general,—for boys and girls alike?" she asked in 1924. "Those who like it, of either sex," she noted, "can take it up as a trade."[40] By letting loose people's individual predilections on a level playing field of equal training, she looked to improve the equalitarian character of the professionalized domestic workforce that Gilman advocated to emancipate women from customary household toil. Crystal's suggestion promised to reduce sex segregation in this field by bringing more gender equality to the labor pool.

However, when it came to the management of emotional labor in the home and family, Crystal's vision of gender-equal training led to a very different model than Gilman had proposed. Rather than outsourcing motherhood to trained professionals, her plan was to facilitate a relational model of shared childcare by bringing both mothers and fathers into the home. In contrast to the dominant discourse of many of her colleagues, Crystal had no desire to see women fully liberated from motherhood and child-rearing; she wanted women to be allowed to choose family life—or not—and to share all associated labors and opportunity costs equally with men. As a result, she shifted the gender equality conversation from debates about women, work, and mothering to discussions of sharing, balance, and parenting.

It was a rare position to take. Around that time, only a relatively few feminists in either Britain or the United States similarly suggested that men might contribute to domestic labor, and they mostly did so in the years following Eastman's first expression of the idea.[41] One of the American feminists who argued for shared responsibilities in the home and family was her friend Mary Ware Dennett, who suggested that full partnership in work and family would not only help liberate women but also elevate the character of men. Men would then become "complete human beings instead of mere males," she remarked.[42] Crystal surely agreed. She saw nothing but progress in the idea of shared breadwinning and shared parenting. It was "impossible to exaggerate the importance of such common training in freeing the women of the generations to come," she declared.[43]

That was the big picture, the long-term strategy. More immediately, other interventions were available and needed. Crystal endorsed the idea of motherhood endowment—essentially, today's European-style paid family leave—as one policy that could support women as mothers while also equalizing their position as workers alongside men. Ideas about some kind of maternity endowment had been circulating among feminists internationally for years by the time she came to endorse it, first in "Birth Control in the Feminist Program" in 1918, then at the Woman's Freedom Congress in 1919, and again in the *Liberator* in 1920. However, the policy grew increasingly controversial through the 1920s, dividing political women with whom she worked on both sides of the Atlantic.

As early as 1912, feminists in British, American, and international contexts saw a government subsidy for mothers as variously empowering to women. For decades, some feminists on both sides of the Atlantic had likened women's positions in the patriarchal family to enforced prostitution, where wives effectively bartered their sexual services in exchange for financial support. Direct payments to mothers would be a powerful means to disrupt such systematic exploitation. At the same time, many feminists applauded the potential of state maternity support to quash the "family wage," that long-standing practice that justified the gender wage gap on the presumption that men did, or would, support a wife and children. Socialist women further praised the collective cost sharing baked into the concept of motherhood endowment: since mothering was a form of labor that benefited everyone in society, they reasoned, everyone should contribute to its support. And by 1918, some American feminists, notably Harriot Stanton Blatch, were characterizing maternity endowment as an appropriate subsidy for women as disadvantaged workers in the labor force.[44]

In time, however, this consensus began to fray. By the 1920s, some feminists moved forward on an increasing interest in questions of sexual difference, particularly when it came to maternity and birth control. These "new feminists," as they called themselves, began celebrating motherhood endowment for its recognition of essentialist differences between the sexes, of women's special physical and emotional needs.[45] While Crystal's colleagues were pressing the case for the identical treatment of women and men in public policy, new feminists advocated government support for mothers based on an assertion of women's unique characteristics—gender distinctions in legislation the equalitarians thought dangerous.

Complicating this growing feminist divide, the idea of government maternity support gained popularity among more traditionalist women who believed the workplace was an unsuitable environment for mothers at all. Julia Lathrop, head of the US Children's Bureau from 1912 to 1922, supported payments by the state to help mothers escape what she saw as the bitter necessity of work outside the home.[46] Mainstream US women's groups, such as the Woman's Christian Temperance Union and General Federation of Women's Clubs, as well as bestselling women's magazines of the day, including *Good Housekeeping* and

The Delineator, threw their considerable clout behind maternity endowment, and did so using language that recalled antisuffrage activism and the eighteenth-century notion of republican motherhood: they portrayed the policy as a means of sustaining motherhood as a distinctive calling and full-time job.[47]

Eastman's equalitarian allies grew to counter the alignments they saw emerging, attacking the implications of new feminism for its too-close camara-derie with age-old patriarchy. They now feared that payments to mothers could actually return women to the home. They argued it might undermine women as workers, shunting them into a "mother category"—today's "mommy track"—in the eyes of employers and policymakers. At the same time, they worried it might tempt women to abandon the whole struggle for equality, with all its risks and difficulties, in favor of the familiarity of feminine tradition in marriage and family, now bankrolled by the federal government.[48]

Eastman was a resolute equalitarian, yet she had always contended her team's agenda was too narrowly focused, particularly where motherhood was concerned. She continued to support maternity endowment through the entire arc of the debate, but as it peaked in the mid- to late 1920s, she redrew the boundaries of strict equalitarianism, carving out a distinctive space for motherhood and for herself. She classified motherhood endowment, along with birth control, as "border-line issues." In a letter to the English feminist magazine *Time and Tide* in 1927, she acknowledged such policies could not "be stated literally in terms of equality"—that is, in the argument for the identical treatment of men and women in law and public policy. However, she asserted, "in the minds of many clear-thinking feminists," maternity endowment "bears as directly and as vitally upon the problem of equalizing the status of men and women as any other feminist issues."[49]

When it came to motherhood, Crystal had long argued for a little latitude in the NWP parameters, a little leeway at the borderlines. From the start, she had argued essentially as a Socialist feminist, asserting in 1920, "It seems that the only way we can keep mothers free, at least in a capitalist society, is by the estab-lishment of a principle that the occupation of raising children is peculiarly and directly a service to society and the mother upon whom the necessity and privi-lege of performing this service naturally falls is entitled to an adequate economic reward from the political government." Then she added, as if signaling her equal-itarian colleagues, "It is idle to talk of real economic independence for women unless this principle is accepted."[50]

The fact that Eastman saw motherhood as much more than an exploited form of gendered labor seeps through in her language. To her, motherhood was both a "peculiar" and a "direct" service to society, and both a "necessity" and a "privilege" for women themselves. She would always support policies to promote equality around maternity, seeking to free women from the discriminatory burdens of their reproductive difference. However, she backed such policies not merely to free women *from* discrimination, but also to free women *to* embrace motherhood at will in their lives. She pushed to cultivate and institute equality while accommodating the fullest range of options for women, including full-time motherhood and homemaking. She believed women should neither "be destined by the accident of their sex to one field of activity—housework and child-raising [nor] if and when they choose housework and child-raising . . . to be dependent on some man."[51] To her, guaranteed support by the government promised women "real economic independence," as she put it—that is, freedom not merely from traditional patriarchal husbands but also from the capitalist employers now touted as the source of the feminist solution in wage-earning work outside the home. The endowment of motherhood would enable women to independently follow their own maternal feelings and preferences, to devise their own life equations and plans. Carving out a distinctive position that opened new ground at the boundary between equalitarianism and difference, Eastman challenged feminism to champion the right to live a woman's life on her own terms—whatever she felt those terms to be.

* * *

As a feminist, Crystal wanted that choice for all women and for herself. Through the twenties, she experimented and innovated, trying to develop some scenario that would sustain her feminist identity and economic independence while also sustaining her marriage and family.

From the beginning, Walter had been ambivalent about committing to it all. Given Crystal's vocal advocacy of birth control, her unplanned pregnancy may have surprised him, to say the least. Perhaps it all seemed to happen too quickly, although Crystal, then thirty-six, noted that her biological clock had been actively ticking in her ears for at least ten years by then.[52] But for Walter, no such design for life had emerged, and he may well have felt trapped by Crystal's, especially since both marriage and family arrived at nearly the same time.[53] Later, when he discussed the marriage with his own family, he would characterize it as provisional, improvisational, and nonbinding. When Jeff was three months old, Walter told his sister, the actress Rosalind Fuller, that her own prospective marriage "could be just like Crystal's and mine—a bare legal contract with the personal & private agreement and understanding to live together—to give the marriage a chance—for three years."[54]

At first, with only one child, both parents employed full time, and some hired help, Crystal and Walter lived comfortably as a dual-career couple. However, with the birth of their second child, the balance of so much in their lives shifted—the responsibilities doubled at the same time as the *Liberator* years ended, and the postwar political climate made employment more difficult for them to come by. Crystal was thrilled beyond words to have a second child, especially a daughter, while the armistice opened up transatlantic travel again for Walter to return to his native country and to his parents and sisters. For several reasons perhaps, the trial period Walter had described to his sister ended. It lasted four years, not three.

Crystal persisted in efforts to keep Walter involved in the family, at least to some degree. She developed a series of two-household arrangements, designed to restore independence to both partners while keeping them connected and mutually engaged in child support. Her first scenario was a coordinated, cross-European effort in Berlin and London in 1922. She thought the low cost of living in Germany would allow her to take full-time care of their new daughter for a while, and the distance to England would make family visits feasible. To finance her part of the arrangements, she rented out her house in Croton. "There is no doubt we can live on the rent money with a little help from you in one of those cheap foreign countries—Italy, Germany and Austria," she had told Walter as she hatched the plan. "We can see each other once in a while—& perhaps I can help a little too. But I'm not going to do anything that would take me away from this littlest charmer of ours. You don't want me to, do you?"[55]

But by the spring of 1923, Crystal and the children were back in the United States, where she attended the NWP convention and the seventy-fifth anniversary celebration of Seneca Falls that summer. Come September, she returned to Europe, this time to London. She asked her sister-in-law Cynthia, rather than Walter, for the logistical help she always needed: "be on the lookout for a good nurse and a school for Jeff, all day school with lunch—very free and modern. These I must have," she told her. "And I hope to find a way of living where I won't have to keep house. I hate planning meals and don't want to do it for at least a year. But I do want to live with my children." The family finances would depend principally on her as the breadwinner: "I will have $100/month from my house in New York and expect to get a contract for at least one feminist article a month at $100. That's what we'll live on. If Walter can contribute something that will go for him. I'm not depending on his business prospects for bread & butter—or a roof," she stressed. "I know too little about them."[56]

Within a year, Crystal found she couldn't earn enough money in London and decided to return to New York again. In fact, she would never earn more than fifty dollars for an article through the twenties, and often earned considerably less than that. The search for some workable work-family balance was on in force. London "is certainly a place where you have to work hard," she told Cynthia. Still, "I love the country much more than I thought I did." Nevertheless, "I think I'll stay in America until the children grow up," she reflected. "How's that for a promise? Will I keep it?" She was wondering out loud.[57]

She didn't—or couldn't. After a six-month stint initially organized around her job with the Women for Congress Campaign, she wanted to reunite the family again—somehow. She was separated from the children all week while she worked in Manhattan and they stayed in Croton. Two weeks before Christmas, 1924, she wrote to Walter. "To be alone in a hotel room in New York, with you in London and the children sixty miles away—and then try to write. The loneliest kind of work!!" Her feelings brought home to her how he "must have suffered when I took the children away. Never again!" she announced. "Let's stick together—rich or poor—England or America."[58]

Within weeks, in January 1925, Crystal returned with the children to England again, settling more decidedly into a dual-residence arrangement refined through her previous experiments. Both children lived with her in a rented house in northwest London at 6 Upper Park Road. Walter rented a room from their mutual AUAM friends, Hazel and Charlie Hallinan, who lived with their three children not far away.

Crystal had described their unconventional domestic arrangements in a confessional article, "Marriage under Two Roofs," published in *Cosmopolitan*, then a "smart set" lifestyle monthly. It appeared in December 1923, the same month the ERA was introduced into Congress. The piece had caused a stir, and since she was paid the fifty-dollar fee that would top her rate scale, it had set her hopes high that she had finally found a genre that capitalized on her unconventional life and made the most of her conversational writing style. "They say my 'Marriage Under Two Roofs' started a fashion for Confessions," she told Walter, "and that you can sell anything in the shape of a confession." The realization left her brimming with ideas. "I also hope to get some people to stake me for this month while I try to write something worthwhile on Equality versus Protection for Women. Another plan of mine is to do a publicity story for the United States Lines on the new Student's Third Class and get a free passage. A final plan is to make all but final arrangements to do a weekly London letter for somebody."[59]

In the piece, Crystal highlighted the feminist qualities of her two-roof arrangement—its personal independence and economic equality—as the foundations of its success. Burnished for publication though it may have been, she presented her experience as one paradigm for feminist families. Its combination of greater individual autonomy, voluntary participation, and shared financial responsibility for children, she argued, facilitated the absolute equality envisioned by the ERA while also fostering stronger marriages and happier families, crucial areas of women's lives that lay mostly beyond the amendment's purview.

Crystal suggested her two-roof arrangement delivered a truly companionate partnership while simultaneously sparking a more authentic experience of romantic love. Early in their relationship, Walter had described his uneven compatibility with Crystal: "in some things we are very much alike—both natural-born radicals for instance—in some things we are as unlike as chalk and cheese."[60] Virtually from the start, he told his sister, "I can imagine a lively restless unsettled working partnership between Crystal Eastman and me."[61] Those tensions of course asserted themselves in their subsequent marriage. But "now that we live under two roofs there are no storms, no quarrels, no tears," Crystal wrote. "Our differences of opinion are not passionate and unbearable. They have an almost rational quality. Criticisms and suggestions are made with the gentleness and reserve that is common between friends." At the same time, separate residences brought back the freedom and spontaneity "of sweetheart days," she said. "Every morning, like lovers, we telephone to exchange the day's greetings and make plans for the evening." At the end of an evening they might be "going home together like married lovers or parting on the street corner and going off in the night alone to our separate beds. And because neither course is inexorably forced upon us, either one is a bit of a lark."[62]

The arrangement raised the subject of marital fidelity, she admitted, but on that concern too, Crystal argued two roofs fared well—and might even be better than one. "In most conventional marriage there must be considerable area of confidence as to the technical faithfulness of the parties. In marriage under two roofs, you deliberately extend that area of confidence, that is all," she explained. "And as all wise women know, increasing the confidence usually lessens the risk."[63]

Crystal advocated two roofs as a feasible response to a number of key considerations in feminist family life. But it was far from a complete solution. Indeed, the arrangement better attended to problems in their marriage than it did the broader concerns of balancing family needs with a woman's independence and work outside the home. It seemed to specifically recognize Walter's feelings of entrapment or suffocation. "Most women tend to own and manage their husbands too much, and I am not free from that vice," Crystal admitted. "Often when we lived under the same roof he must have said to himself, 'I love her but can't stand her. She is too much for me.' Now I know he never feels that."[64]

Whatever the arrangement did to relieve pressures within the marriage, it was less serviceable when it came to shared childcare and the distribution of domestic and emotional labor in the household. Indeed, it raised, rather than resolved, tensions between two visions of feminist family: one an egalitarian sharing of both work and family responsibilities; the other a woman-centered configuration of mother and children, with the male element peripheral, provisional, and largely voluntary. While Crystal advocated the former in most of her writing on the subject, she partly wanted, and certainly got, the latter in her own life.

Marriage under two roofs is not the same as children under two roofs. Since the family lived under Crystal's roof, in most respects she functioned as a single parent. She was head of household, the main support of the family, and also responsible for the cooking, cleaning, child health, school and education decisions, home maintenance and management, and more, all by herself. Walter probably contributed to family finances at his discretion, and at this time seems not to have earned enough, regularly enough, to have contributed child support consistently or to have made hired help an option. His rent and board were chronically in arrears.[65] Crystal faced inescapable pressures, and it was not easy. It was also hard on her children, who would carry into their adult lives and pass onto their own children the feeling that she had largely abandoned them, whether for work or her own needs.[66] At the time, she struggled desperately with the pressure to take care of everyone and everything, including herself. "This job of mine and looking after home and children week-end and trying not to go back in health but to keep going forward a little stretches me, brain and body, to the limit," she expressed to Cynthia. "And it is a job in which everything depends on me."[67]

The limits Crystal was experiencing in her two-roof solution probably piqued the persistent questions about equality inside the home that kept cropping up in her journalism. Back in 1920, she had already noted the phenomenon that would only much later be termed "the second shift"—where women employed full time are also responsible for the care of the home and family after the workday is done.[68] She knew very well that women's participation in the workforce had been expanding since at least her mother's generation in the 1890s, not merely, as she described, the "whole towns full of wives who are forced by the bitterest necessity to spend the same hours at the factory that their husbands spend," but also the educated, professional working women like herself. Yet regardless of class or occupation, these "breadwinning wives," she wryly remarked, "have not yet developed home-making husbands." Even in the households of more privileged professional women who hired help, the responsibility was still hers. "She may be, like her husband, a busy executive at her office all day, but unlike him, she is also an executive in a small way every night and morning at home."[69]

Through the twenties, the problem of gender inequality in domestic relations was an insistent theme in Crystal's writing. In June 1925 she published "Is Woman's Place the Home?," which pointedly discussed a debate between a conservative member of Parliament and the novelist and critic Rebecca West about the dynamics of power in the domestic realm.[70] The next month, "Anna Wickham: A Poet without a Wife" appeared in *Equal Rights*, a reprint of an earlier version she had published in *Time and Tide*. The earlier article seemed to align with Virginia Woolf's contemplation of the "uncircumscribed spirit" from her essay "Modern Fiction" (1919) and to presage her meditation about the woman writer and the free and undivided mind in *A Room of One's Own* (1929).[71] Eastman, who was friendly with Leonard Woolf and published in one of the same magazines as his wife, Virginia, noted Wickham's "revolt . . . not against her economic handicap alone, but against herself."[72] Crystal's second version of the Wickham article, however, reframed the piece, headlining the problem of male resistance to sharing responsibility for household labor. "Who ever heard of a male poet who had to keep house for a family?" she quoted Wickham. "Sometimes I think that the reason why women have not distinguished themselves more in creative art is not because they bear children, but because they keep house."[73]

Crystal had long ago noted a male "privilege of helplessness" that shields men from household participation. "With shrewd, instinctive wisdom he cherishes and cultivates . . . an imperious helplessness with regard to the details of food, clothing and shelter," she observed, "which acts as a sort of protective colouring to his genius."[74] Years later, she continued to be provoked by this crafty exercise of male entitlement inside the home. In "Lady Rhondda Contends That Women of Leisure Are a 'Menace,'" she covered a debate between the writer, orator, and lay theologian G. K. Chesterton and Lady Margaret Mackworth Rhondda, the Welsh peeress, businesswoman, equalitarian feminist, and founder of *Time and Tide*. The question related to the feminist critique of separate spheres, asking whether "idle women of the upper class" undercut prevailing equalitarian arguments about emancipation arising from women's participation in the labor force. In that connection, Chesterton asserted it was a fallacy for women to think they were serving themselves by working outside the home. "Home is the only place where there is any liberty left," he contended, "any chance for creative imagination, any room for the development of personality." In response, Eastman— not Rhondda—replied. In fact, Crystal effectively took over the discussion, asking her reading audience, "Has it ever occurred to Chesterton, or to any other man, I wonder, that for women there is no such thing as home in this sense?" Probably not, she assumed. "The feminist does not want to abolish the home," she explained. What she wants is "to find a man who will share the burden and joy of home-making as she would like to share the burden and joy of earning a living." She drove the point home in her catchy conclusion to the piece: "'Home is for women too' might be the new feminist slogan."[75]

Essentially, she had been campaigning for feminism to take up such a slogan for nearly a decade. She followed that idea in various journalistic directions. An initial move was to seek out the stories of unseen women whose work and talents, hidden from view in the home, nevertheless fueled the advance of famous men. Crystal particularly noted unsung mothers, publishing "Lindbergh's Mother" in *Time and Tide* on May 27, 1927. Just as Virginia Woolf would ask about Shakespeare's sister in *A Room of One's Own* (1929), Crystal questioned how and why women's lives remained so cramped, distorted, and almost completely contingent upon men's.

She pursued the question further in an interview with Dora Black, a feminist author and Socialist campaigner, like Eastman a noted experimentalist in balancing women's comparable desires for personal independence, sexual autonomy, and maternity. Black had chosen a symbolic dependence on her husband by electing to call herself "Mrs. Bertrand Russell" on the cover of her forthcoming book, *The Right to Be Happy* (1927). Although both women were active proponents of keeping their own names, Crystal declined to apply "the Lucy Stone Challenge," the tag she used in reference to the early suffrage pioneer who had publicly refused to take her husband's name in 1855. She would not make this the litmus test of a feminist. "I don't feel like walking out of a woman's house over it," she told readers at the outset.[76] Rather, with so many other social and political commitments in common, she wanted to understand the reasons and go from there.

Crystal quickly discovered two things. First, she herself was "the world's worst interviewer" in the journalistic sense. She inevitably abandoned her "sincere intention of sitting quietly, pencil in hand," instead diving into a "free-for-all discussion [and] search for essential truth and justice." Second, she found she had much in common with Dora Russell, not least in the belief that feminism must pertain to both private and public life. "Unfortunately we fall in love," Russell told her, "and Feminism must take that into consideration."[77] The two women became friends.

Several months later, Crystal returned to profile Dora's husband, the analytic philosopher, mathematician, and leftist social critic Bertrand Russell. She wanted to ask a man of both science and letters, and the author of a new book on early childhood education, about family life. "This, surely, is a task above all others for thinkers," she observed. Her top priority was to solicit his views on what she called her "favorite educational reform, i.e., that both boys and girls should be taught the rudiments of the household arts as a matter of course, as part of the essential preparation for life." She reported his answer with delight. "To this, Mr. Russell had no masculine objection to offer. Rather, he made a valuable suggestion. 'The time to teach those things,' he said, 'is when they are very young.'"[78] She had long ago made that point in print herself.

Despite these high-profile sources, Crystal's many contacts from across movements, and her growing track record as a transatlantic journalist, some of her articles never saw the light of day in her lifetime. These unpublished pieces share something in common: they all concerned feminism and family life. In one such piece, she applied a feminist analysis to the position of stay-at-home wives and mothers, women who may not have considered themselves feminists at all.

In "Are Wives Partners or Dependents?" Crystal denounced the conception that a traditional wife and mother was the legal dependent of her husband, entitled only to bed and board in return for her services and nothing more. Notably, she did not contemplate the analogy between prostitution and marriage that troubled some of her colleagues; rather, she defined relevant "services" as homemaking and childcare, the whole quotidian complex of invisible labor that was conventionally required in exchange for a married woman's support. Legally, she explained, traditional women's work had no acknowledged value. Despite putting in "about eight hours a day cooking, cleaning, washing, sewing, marketing—trying with all your patience and strength to make [a husband's salary] go as far as possible despite high prices," she fumed, the entirety of a man's 'family wage' belonged to him because he "earned it." And here was another equality problem that lay beyond the reach of the ballot. "Suffrage has made no difference in this situation," she observed. "A married woman can cast her vote, but if her husband is mean enough he can make her beg for a nickel to pay her carfare to the polls!"[79]

Crystal envisioned an altered paradigm that would recognize both child-rearing and housekeeping as occupational labor. Indeed, she elevated traditional women's work to equal status with that performed by men or women outside the home. Gleefully placing "a little dynamite under the rock" of patriarchy, a phrase the papers had used to vilify Margaret Sanger's aims with birth control, Eastman argued, essentially, for wages for wives. She called for full-time homemakers to exercise equal authority and equal pride of ownership over what she redefined as mutually-produced resources: "The home-keeping, child-rearing wife," she wrote, deserves a "working-partner's claim on the family income that her household labor helped make possible."[80]

It was a pioneering yet attainable proposal, expansive in its vision of feminism and women's lives. By acknowledging the option for women to remain employed as full-time homemakers if they chose to do so, Crystal widened the pathway to economic equality while continuing to affirm the importance of women's work. However, the unpublished article, traditionalist in its gender formulations and socialistic in its sharing of costs and benefits, did not insist or depend on a woman's participation in the marketplace economy outside the home.

Crystal's most radical inquiry about the feminist reorganization of the family was "Modern Adventures in Maternity," which also failed to find an outlet despite two extant manuscripts showing at least three rounds of revision. The piece explored what she characterized as the next "rather astounding phase of feminism": the small but growing cadre of women Eastman knew who were becoming single mothers by choice. Near the outset of her earliest extant draft, she admitted she felt "tremendously curious about a new type of woman I meet both in England and America who is determined to have a child whether she is married or not." The piece maintained a confessional quality. Deep down, she divulged, "I understand that girl so well because she might almost be me."[81]

These were women "who would have children tomorrow if they were allowed, without social opprobrium, not to marry," she wrote.[82] At the time, cultural narratives about unwed mothers were shifting, reframing the long-standing stigma yet hardly devitalizing it. Evangelical reformers in the nineteenth century had offered narratives of unwed mothers as abandoned victims of seduction. With the increasing professionalization of social work in the early twentieth century, including its links to the new science of Freudian psychology, came calls for a more scientific evaluation of unmarried mothers, as well as a plan for intervention. No longer seen as unfortunate victims forever fallen from virtue, unwed mothers were increasingly understood as deviant or delinquent, and their collective impact a social problem that necessitated public redress. The most immediate cure was to "normalize" conditions for the child. As a result, social agencies began the long-lived push for single mothers to give up their children for adoption.[83]

At one point, Crystal had contemplated a subversive scheme loosely compatible with this new orthodoxy for herself. When her biological clock began to impress its timetable upon her, she confessed that "I began to get anxious—not anxious to get married (I was having too much fun) but anxious to be sure of my children.—Now I am not the type to waste away under anxiety. I always have a plan," she hastened to say. "To secure myself against this risk of defeated maternity, I decided that if I was not married by the time I was twenty-nine, I would have a child anyway. I would save up enough money to go to Italy for six months and come back with an 'adopted baby,' let people think what they liked."[84]

Crystal's breezy attitude reflected her comfort with modern ideas about sexuality, but for an increasing array of women, the 1920s brought a very new visibility to the sexual revolution of the era, and not just to cosmopolitan feminists like Eastman who kept their own names and embraced the battle for legal birth control or other educated urbanites who were familiar with Freud's legitimation of libido as natural. A wider public began to come into contact with images and suggestions of sexual satisfaction in the mass media and ordinary contemporary life. In novels, films, advertising, and magazines, not to mention some city streets, "flappers"— plucky, middle-class, young moderns who smoked, sported bobbed haircuts, and drank liquor despite US prohibition—insinuated a new female insouciance into mainstream venues. Moreover, a flurry of sex and marriage manuals were appearing in Britain, mass-market self-help books that not only offered readers factual information about the physical side of the marital bond but also admitted such forbidden topics as desire and pleasure into the context of the routine.[85]

Crystal acknowledged as much, noting in an early draft, "heroines of popular fiction are coming home with adopted babies every other day and most of us know in real life at least one proud and smiling unmarried mother."[86] The sexual landscape was changing in the twenties, and with it the various planks of patriarchal family structure were coming apart, or at least coming in for more discrete cultural questioning.

When it came to family formation, some women were beginning to wonder whether men were necessary at all. Both extant drafts relate the story of a group of educated Australian women who had written to an eminent American biologist to inquire, effectively, about artificial insemination. The group "begged him to tell them if science had advanced so that women might become mothers through exogenesis, the male cell to be transferred by a scientist, instead of deposited by a male mate in the usual fashion." These women wanted to become mothers, a source told Crystal. "What they do not want is to contract for lifelong association with a husband," she said.[87]

In "plotting to get the initiative in motherhood," as Crystal put it, these pioneers exemplified the independence contemporary feminism prized for women. On principle, they were deconstructing "the old forced responsibility of the father for both wife and child," opening up the new sexual autonomy into various life options for themselves.[88] Since patriarchy had always defined the family by the relationship of mothers and children to fathers, these single mothers by choice anticipated by many decades a radical redefinition that would construe the family as an institution designated by the bond between mother and child.[89] "I believe a child belongs to its mother," one single mother told Crystal. "I don't believe in Equal Guardianship laws." Not even shared financial responsibility seemed right to her; she did not want to feel obliged by it to include the father in any decisions about her child. Moreover, a father's economic support would corrode the financial foundation of the new single-mother family by acclimating its members to a scale of living beyond the capability of its single female breadwinner to maintain. Most of all, this single mother wanted her partner to love her and her child freely and without compulsion—or not at all. As she told Crystal, "I don't want him to feel bound . . . by any tie except his love for us."[90]

The principled displacement of male-centeredness in the family produced three models of paternal involvement among the single mothers Crystal interviewed. A man could be an "involuntary father," biologically involved but with no knowledge of the child's life at all. Or, he could be a romantic partner who remained a lover only, accepting the fact of a child or children but not loving or caring for them. Finally, he could fill only the "psychological" role of father, acting as a parental guide "without the corresponding economic and social responsibility."[91]

This third type was strictly a father figure; he need not have any intimate relationship with the mother or biological relationship to the child at all.

In each scenario, Crystal found herself thinking about the practical complications that might upend such well-laid plans. "'Wait till you are sick, or the baby is sick, or you lose your job!' some tired devil in me whispered. But I did not say it out loud," she confessed. "Why discourage this invincible Amazon who has never laid off for a day since her baby was six months old?"[92] Most of all, she kept wondering if these alternatives really would work psychologically, developmentally, for the children. "I have told the story from the standpoint of the mother," she wrote halfway through both extant versions of the piece. "Now let us think about the child." Her thoughts unfurled mainly as questions:

> Suppose the unmarried mother can keep her job and her health and her courage, how about the baby? Admitting that the woman has a right to choose an heroic destiny for herself, to stand against the world for a principle she believes in, has she the right to determine the destiny for an unborn child? The finest qualities are not always inherited. The child may not be of the heroic type. Life may be too much for him. . . . In short, a woman may have a right to a child. But has not the child a right to two parents? Isn't life hard enough without having to begin at seven explaining to your contemporaries that you have no father?[93]

These concerns were heightened by Crystal's observation of one daughter of a single mother who began imagining a fantasy father. The child would "stand by the window, singing to herself, 'Daddy, you must come—Daddy, you must come—,'" Crystal reported. She warbled to herself, "'My Daddy lets me have cookies.'—'My Daddy doesn't make me do up my own buttons,' etc. etc." When her mother soon consulted the best psychoanalyst she could find, she was instructed to secure a father at once, lest the child's natural development be disrupted. Crystal translated the doctor's orders using the mainstream psychoanalytic language that was rapidly popularizing both in Britain and the United States at the time. "The chances are she won't be able to fall in love," she detailed. "She won't be able to transfer her love and affection from her father to another love object because her father only existed in fantasy."[94]

With such dire consequences for her child at stake, the mother contacted an old lover who had previously been devoted to her but had been unable to accept her unconventional, feminist ways. As a result, the couple had split up and pursued their different paths in life and love. "Making no appeal of any kind for herself, she told him how desperately she needed a 'father,'" Eastman recounted, "and he said he would try." Almost immediately, he "turned out to be a natural born father," and his visits became more and more frequent. "Now it looks as though Kate's great experiment might end as the fairy tales do," Crystal announced.[95] The family that began radically, with the single mother and her child, would reproduce the traditional model in the end, living happily ever after.

Yet was that progress? Between Crystal's investments in dedicated mothering and the patriarchal prescriptions embedded in the new psychological science established and dominated by men, where, now, did her feminism fit in? In a revised draft, she confessed, "I search my mind and heart in vain for any final wisdom." She ended in speculation, half in passive voice, that at least feminist consciousness was rising when it came to the quandaries of family life: "women are taking more and more conscious control of themselves . . . and little by little some wide change in the family relations of men and women is being forecaste [sic]."[96] In the end, she left wide open many of her questions about gender equality in the family—economic resources and support, division of housekeeping labor, distribution of authority in child-rearing decisions, balancing autonomy and responsibility—the very issues that had piqued her interest in single motherhood by choice in the first place.

Indeed, they were the same issues Crystal wrestled with in her own marriage and family life every day. If her unusual arrangements with Walter were any guide, answers would remain elusive. In her experience, an à la carte menu of family participation for men often amounted to a daily buffet requiring women to shop, plan, cook, and clean up. And what might drop off the menu entirely in many women's lives—sex, love, and companionship among them—were key components of individuality and self-expression. The trade-offs felt confounding. If single motherhood by choice could supplant the traditional family with a woman-centered, woman-directed one, it simultaneously threatened to counter those gains by augmenting a woman's maternal identity and daily life. If it offered mothers new authority in the lives of their children and themselves, it also replaced adult sexuality with childcare and its maternal affections. If it promised women greater personal autonomy and control than the patriarchal family did, it also offset those gains with increased isolation and a higher demand for personal selflessness since at the end of the day, the single mother, and her children, had to rely on her and her alone.

In Crystal's own life, single motherhood was not ideal. She eventually realized the quest to rewrite the rules and roles of family life would be an ongoing venture that required the collective thinking of the millions of women involved. At some point in the twenties, she tried to turn this search into a collective project and rewarding journalism job. She twice pitched "Pandora's Box—or What's Your Trouble?," a regular column designed, essentially, to confront "the problem that has no name"—decades before Betty Friedan formulated it in *The Feminine Mystique* (1963). "This is not a column of advice to young women about their love affairs," she explained in her proposal. "It is an attempt to meet the growing need of the distinctly modern woman . . . who is not altogether satisfied with love, marriage and a purely domestic career. She wants money of her own or she wants work of her own perhaps. . . . She may feel herself a misfit as a housekeeper and long for some other field in which to exercise her abilities and satisfy her personal ambition. But she has a husband, home and children, too." The driving question was: "Can these two desires be reconciled in real life?"[97]

To Crystal, these concerns had been visible—indeed, pivotal—for many years, and she knew she was not alone. Yet her proposal went nowhere. It lacked issue appeal to her main publication venues in these years, the NWP's *Equal Rights* and *Time and Tide*, the political weekly founded by Lady Rhondda, which were the leading organs of equalitarian feminism in the United States and Britain, respectively. Both journals were agenda setters for the more vanguard edge of the feminist movement and focused their editorial attention on the new worlds women could now enter—and conquer. With newly enfranchised women facing opportunities and obstacles aplenty, their editors seldom saw the need to expend critical attention and column inches on such richly criticized, well-trodden ground. The challenges arising from marriage and the family were, in a sense, settled law, and the newsworthy frontiers of feminism lay elsewhere. Even Crystal's edgy explorations at the intersections and borderlines of the private sphere seemed backward or beside the point—anything but the way forward for feminism.

Her proposal also failed to resonate with the commercial editors she knew. She sought feedback from knowledgeable quarters and revised the column as "Women at the Cross-Roads," perhaps to serve a more general-interest audience. Dora Russell shepherded it to Andy Heath, cofounder of A. M. Heath, already one of the leading literary agencies in London. But its sexual politics and feminist interests were too pronounced for the popular women's magazines of the day. Her idea did not fit, he explained, in women's service journalism as generally understood and structured in the industry.[98] It remained unpublished.

Crystal settled for "What Shall We Do with the Woman's Page?," an article in *Time and Tide* that made the case for rethinking what women's service journalism was all about. "Modern women need a forum, a clearing-house for the exchange of ideas, a meeting-place where they can learn from each other's experiments and benefit by each others [*sic*] conclusions," she argued. She described multiple timely themes, making the far-sighted case that women's pages—like feminism itself—must speak to a diverse group of stakeholders, including that seemingly inescapable interest group: men. "No one is so bewildered by this modern woman's revolution as the average husband," Crystal submitted. "If he could turn once a week to the Woman's Page and find there women stirred by the same unnatural discontent that seemed to be threatening his own home comfort, he would certainly be intrigued," she ventured. Better yet, he might even become an ally. "He might even begin to understand."[99]

11 COMING HOME

"I've been doing quite a lot of writing for *Equal Rights* this last year, fifteen or twenty articles," Crystal wrote Paul Kellogg from London in February 1926. "And I think I do it better than I used to." Yet, she told him, "I'm just hungry for a good piece of work to do." For years now she had been living as the freelance journalist she never wanted to be, pitching article after article to conservative or capricious editors. She was exhausted from childcare and homemaking, frustrated by declining health, and almost always behind on her bills. She longed for a return to more substantial and sustaining work. "I could come home if I got a line on something," she said. "I really do care more what I am working at than where I live. The domestic method of justifying my existence destroys me as it does all women of my type."[1]

Kellogg's characteristically honest reply probably helped Crystal clarify where she wanted to go. "I have read your English letters from *Equal Rights*" and found them "tremendously interesting . . . but darn partisan," he said. "You are not a reporter in this situation," he continued. "You are an ardent believer in the cause; and where that cause, feminism, overlaps movements equally vital, that have had their roots, say, in industry, you carry the flag of feminism over the whole of the overlapped territory." Kellogg may not have understood her vision of equalitarian feminism as a cross-movement position, but he certainly knew the bind she was in given the history of her status within the movement. "If in reporting a meeting you brought out pretty vividly the discomfiture of the crowd you are against, they would charge you, of course, with bias. And on the other hand, if the feminist bunch pulled a bone, and you set it forth the way an independent journalist would, they would not stand for it and you would lose your job; for tolerance is not their thickest virtue," he said. But they both knew the issue also had to do with *her*, with who she was at heart. "I think . . . you have a lot of the scientist and industrial investigator under your skin," Kellogg ventured, "but none the less, it seems to me after reading these letters, that you cannot function in both ways at once."[2]

Crystal Eastman. Amy Aronson, Oxford University Press (2020).
© Oxford University Press.
DOI: 10.1093/oso/9780199948734.001.0001

When it came to her politics, Crystal could never be neutral. When she had a stake, she took a stand. She was an American activist, not an ex-pat journalist, and at age forty-five, after years of struggle to fit herself into a different kind of life, she craved a return to her turf and to herself. Crystal had been keeping her hand in with the international women's movement to the extent she could. In 1926, she traveled to France for the summer, arranging to provide a vacation for her children bookended by assignments for *Equal Rights*. In September, she concluded the trip in Marseilles, where she covered the International Conference of Socialist Women at Chateau des Fleurs.[3] Her swing had begun in Paris, the site of what turned out to be a momentous International Woman Suffrage Alliance (IWSA) congress from May 30 to June 5. She produced an extensive three-part account of the congress, focusing almost exclusively on the organizational maneuvers behind the IWSA's decision to deny an application for membership by the National Woman's Party (NWP).

"The Great Rejection," as Crystal called it, reflected the still-smoldering schism in the women's movement between the NWP militants and the former National American Woman Suffrage Association (NAWSA) suffragists, now evolved into an international divide between equalitarians and reformers. Crystal, naturally, took a side. In fact, she was a leader in Paris in the attack by equalitarians against protective legislation. "We have a new international tyranny growing fast upon us," she told the papers. "The International Labor Office of the League of Nations is all the more dangerous because its designs are benevolent and more to be feared because it is a super government organized and financed for the good of the whole world. When the International Labor Office presumes to say that women must not work nights," she declared, "I say an enemy is at our gates."[4]

In her articles about the NWP, Crystal claimed her loyalty from her first sentence: "I am almost ashamed of my good luck as a member of the Woman's Party," she announced, because "the rejection of our application . . . by a vote of 123 to 49, like so many defeats, has turned over night into a victory." Although she promised to tell the story as clearly and accurately as possible—"as though I were drafting an affidavit," she said—in fact she published some of her most partisan pieces in years.[5]

She drew heavily from her own participation behind the scenes. Crystal and other suffragists in Britain had been invited to a meeting at the Sorbonne on May 22, eight days before the congress began. During these precongress meetings, four feminists led by Lady Rhondda founded the Open Door Council, a political society to advocate equalitarian feminism. Crystal became a member of its executive committee and further volunteered to serve on the literature committee, handling publicity and outreach alongside the English actress and journalist Cicely Hamilton, who had authored and starred in the play "How the Vote Was Won," a suffrage staple since it premiered in London in 1909.[6]

By May 24, Doris Stevens, NWP vice president, arrived in Paris, and with twenty-five other party members, they opened an informal headquarters at the Hotel Lutetia, a grand Left Bank hotel. On May 27, Stevens held a private summit at which Eastman was not present; nevertheless, she reconstructed the meeting in her article by quoting speakers verbatim as though she had observed the exchanges firsthand. She purported to quote Stevens expressing the desire of the NWP to promote international cooperation among women by applying for formal affiliation with the IWSA: "'We would like to join with you to hasten the day when men and women throughout the universe shall enjoy, if they choose to exercise them, equal political, social, civil, and industrial rights. We offer our strength, our devotion, whatever practical and spiritual forces we have at our command, to the International Woman Movement.'"[7]

Crystal's allegiance to the equalitarians of the NWP remained pronounced throughout her coverage of the congress. Indeed, her equalitarian perspective and purpose served as the engine of the series. In "The Great Rejection, Part II," she highlighted Lady Rhondda's withdrawal of the membership application submitted by the Open Door Council in solidarity with the NWP, quoting Rhondda's statement in full.[8] Crystal's lead in part III consisted of a pointed warning from the now-outraged peeress: "If you vote for the Woman's Party, it is a vote for the future! If you vote against them it is a vote for the past." Crystal ended that third installment by drawing her own conclusions in the first person. Yes, the "I.W.S.A. were social reformers and they rejected us because we were Feminists, but I think that was not the only reason," she ventured. "The trouble with the Woman's Party is that in addition to the purity of its Feminism it has a capacity and reputation for *action*. They were less afraid of what we would think," Crystal pronounced, "than of what we would do."[9]

Crystal reveled in contemplating the future Lady Rhondda had signaled. And she seemed to know now what she wanted to do in light of it: get back in the action, return to the feminist struggle rather than just write about it. When she covered the congress for *The World*, she headlined her own hopes that the moment had come for her to do so. "The feminists of the world must find each other and unite on a policy of action," she announced. "It is thus that the new international will be born."[10] That was clearly the next step for Crystal herself. In *Equal Rights*, she enthusiastically projected herself into the coming fray. "The expedition of the Woman's Party to Paris has demonstrated that there is at present no Feminist international with a purpose and plan of action," she announced. "The future is ours!"[11]

* * *

It would take six months, but in January 1927, she was set for that future to begin. "Your letter came twenty minutes ago, and since it came I have decided to come to America in August to stay and find work," she wrote to Kellogg. "I came aw-fully near it in September but if I had gone then I should have gone on a fight," she explained. "Now I shall go with all hands willing. . . . England holds nothing for me except to drift along as a half-hearted free-lance journalist. I have tried for two years to get a job,—research, organization, editorial, speaking, *anything*," she told him. "I am simply crazy to work."[12]

The obstacles, however, were not only in the arena of work itself. Crystal felt exhausted, and her health had been poor; she had published only one short ar-ticle since "The Great Rejection" series, an exceptionally light lifestyle piece on the tourist value of the English hearthside. Perhaps *Time and Tide* accepted it for publication as a favor.[13] She had nursed her daughter through a long siege with diphtheria the previous spring, then begun a battle against a resulting infantile paralysis in one leg. The prescribed therapy was expensive and involved time-consuming treatments with light, electricity, and massage, followed by a long list of exercises. She remained burdened with worry. "The doctors say it is getting better fast, but I'm not sure it is," she confided to Kellogg. "It has been a constant little anxiety in my mind."[14] Then Jeffrey contracted the mumps, initiating an-other struggle back to health with medical bills lingering afterward.

However, she had taken the children for a relaxing stint in Antibes between her two summer assignments, socializing with Max and others, among them F. Scott and Zelda Fitzgerald, film paramour Rudolph Valentino and his wife, the poet Archibald MacLeish and his wife, and long-time friends John Dos Passos and Floyd Dell.[15] Those months "seem to have given me back myself," she told Kellogg. She felt "rich in health and strength now . . . but they have not made an enthusiastic 'author' out of me."[16]

Crystal reeled off several parts of the plan she had been formulating to relo-cate the family to the United States. Walter, now working at the BBC as editor of *Radio Times*, would be able to find an editorial job at some American magazine covering the radio industry as long as she went ahead of him and found a job to anchor the family. They did not dare to let go of his steady income until she had landed something. "I'll take the children of course," she told Kellogg. Then, she asked him, her old friend and stalwart mentor, to help her start over, essen-tially from scratch. "Paul, will you help me as you did twenty-three years ago? I'll promise to make good again if I can get a start." She beseeched a little: "If you just say that you *think* I can get work and begin to build my life again you will make that happiness last till August."[17]

Kellogg would always help her, steadfastly, but he was honest about the obstacles she faced. "There are practical difficulties in making a fresh start which it does no good to minimize," he told her in reply. "The United States is not as tolerant as England," and she had been a blunt critic of so many powerful people, in both industry and government, all the way up to the president. "Also, interests have shifted a great deal for example, psychology rather than labor legislation is on the map," Kellogg said. Still, she had both assets and liabilities at play. "You have rare powers and a courageous spirit," he told her, "and I don't doubt a lot of your old come-hither."[18]

Kellogg advised her to be patient, to start a long-term plan—much longer than the timetable she had in mind. He suggested she could equip herself in England for six to eighteen months, or perhaps longer, as a stepping stone to a new career back in New York. In the job market of the 1920s, she needed a defined area of expertise, a niche. "Figure out in your own mind the row you want to hoe and start in on a long plan, one which at the end of four or five years would leave you pretty impregnable as a master of something."[19]

Kellogg proposed Crystal become an expert in the new nursery schools, at which point perhaps Vassar or Columbia's Teachers College would put her on the faculty. But a week later he wrote again to tell her about a better idea that had occurred to him—a remarkably prescient one that he thought would capitalize on her early work on workers' compensation, as well as her current residency in England. It was the emerging field of private health insurance. "The success of the compensation movement has, of course, stimulated a lot of the private companies, such as the Metropolitan, to go into group insurance, and to cover not only accidents but sickness," he explained. "Meanwhile, we have had it in the Cornell Clinic here in New York, an experiment in group medicine that is pretty significant. And a committee has been formed to make a study of the general economics of medicine in this country. What we are in for in the next twenty-five years is a general overhauling of the practice of medicine," Kellogg predicted, "and of course the insurance principle will be a big leverage in this."[20]

He urged her to pursue this direction. "Here is a field that is just opening up in the United States; you have special equipment to tackle it; and you are fortunately placed so that you can equip yourself with exceptional knowledge as to the British experience, on which American developments are likely to be built," Kellogg itemized. "Here, I think, is a real lead."[21]

Crystal replied a month later that she had already started pursuing nursery schools, but that health insurance might be a better bet. However, patience had never been her strongest virtue. She was moving ahead with a plan to return to the United States in August, with little advance preparation in England. Her anchor was a few lectures arranged by Frederic Howe, the former New York immigration commissioner and Henry Street Group colleague who was married to her friend Marie Jenney, the Heterodoxy founder. Howe had recently opened a Progressive-minded summer program, the Sconset School of Opinion, on the island of Nantucket off Massachusetts, and invited her to come to give some talks in August. "I cannot afford to come over for a look around this spring," she told Kellogg. "But I can afford to take time when I get there. I shall be pretty well subsidized for the first six months anyhow."[22]

By the end of April—about three months before her departure—Crystal made up her mind what new specialty she would pursue. So much had changed in her life since the days of *Work Accidents and the Law* that she admitted to Kellogg, "I found I have no real interest in insurance, I can't even pretend to have." Rather, it was early childhood education, probably in its connection to the gender revolution she had long contemplated, that fascinated her. "Nursery schools and the whole field of education and training of small children I have a deep and constant interest in. I know a good bit about it already, but I shall take these remaining weeks to learn what England has to tell."[23]

Her most compelling interests now lay at the intersections of feminism and family. She had read in the *Christian Science Monitor* that a study of the changing economic status of women in the modern world was to be conducted at Smith College and immediately sent a cable—not a letter—to the director. "Probably this was a crazy thing to do and it cost a lot of money," she told Kellogg, "but it seemed to be exactly what I'd like to work on, of all things in the world." Besides, she added, "Here is a secret. I expect to come home with a little book on these very subjects, feminism in its relation to marriage and motherhood, partly done. And my talks at Sconset will be on these lines." If people "think I am a back number now," she predicted, "they won't think so in September."[24]

Crystal called Kellogg her "first and best adviser."[25] Nobody but Max ever helped her so much, she told him.[26] In May, the two men worked devotedly to facilitate her plans. They canvassed the lay of the land, exploring various organizations concerned with preschool children and their families, particularly their mothers. Kellogg summarized what they found: "The impression I got from it is that it is very unlikely that you can tie up with anything in advance of coming; that your feminist, even more than your pacifist and radical espousals in the past, is a hurdle; but that this is a field which is going to expand with mounting interest and activity in the next few years, and that if you enter with a concrete hang of the English experience there is a good chance that you can break in."[27]

However, Kellogg warned, "It is not going to be altogether easy to make connections here." What she wanted to do would have been tough enough on her own; the added dimension of a family compounded that. "You and Walter and the children have a much more difficult problem in readjustment and re-engaging lines of work," he told her. "It is the difference, I imagine, between planting seeds and transplanting bulbs, this shuttling back and forth across the Atlantic."[28] She was clearly facing some daunting uncertainties. "Whether you coming pans out professionally is on the laps of the gods," Kellogg ultimately admitted. "For any help I can be, count on me. But with a good lengthy tether of time to look around, make your contacts and try out things, I think you will land," he told her. "And deep down," he offered supportively, "I know you have things big and creative to give in the years ahead."[29]

The first weekend of August 1927, Crystal visited with Walter's parents, presumably to say goodbye. On August 9, she; Jeffrey, ten; and Annis, four months shy of her sixth birthday, set sail on the *Rotterdam* for New York. Crystal carried her two-week lecture booking and possibly a half-written manuscript, now lost, with which to start over again.

* * *

Twenty-six days after they arrived in New York, Crystal received a telegram informing her that Walter was dead. He had died of a brain hemorrhage while on his way home from his BBC office. He was forty-nine. She could not afford the time or money to return to England for the funeral. All she could do was pour out a stunned and punctuation-free wire to Walter's family: "Deep love to you all longing to be there good bye to my Darling Sweet Walter Crystal."[30]

Six days later, Crystal tried to pursue a job lead cultivated for her by Ruth Pickering, now married to her American Union Against Militarism colleague and friend Amos Pinchot. The *Annals of the American Economic Association* was considering a special issue on the economic status of the postsuffrage woman in America and it needed an editor. "Nothing could appeal to me more at the moment," she wrote in a cover letter. However, she was unable to put together her life well enough at that point to update her résumé. After the dated notation for *Work Accidents and the Law*, her vita trails off, dropping out of format entirely; a rough sentence concludes the document, saying only, "during the five or six years following I was active in suffrage, peace and radical movements, both as an organizer and executive and as a journalist."[31] She did not get the job.

Finally, Thanksgiving week, Crystal landed a temporary position organizing the tenth anniversary celebration of Oswald Garrison Villard as editor of *The Nation*. The celebration began with a banquet in Washington on Lincoln's Birthday and include dinners, luncheons, mass meetings, and various kinds of gatherings from coast to coast. A huge public event would serve as the finale: "a genuine rallying of liberal and radical forces as a tribute to the weekly paper that has in the last ten years become a necessity to us all."[32]

Crystal described the position as "promotion, not editorial, 100 a week for four months," but she planned to hold the job for less time than that.[33] She began December 1 and arranged to wrap things up by March so she could travel to London.[34] "I need to see 6 Upper Park Road again,—dispense of everything, and give it up," she told Hallinan. "It will break my heart to come, but it will hurt me more not to come."[35]

At Christmastime, a small box arrived from her sister-in-law Cynthia. It contained a collection of Walter's things, which the family had been unable to part with until now. When she saw the humble store of his remains, she sobbed. "There were my last two letters to Walter, and there was a handkerchief of his—all crumpled up," she wrote her on New Year's Eve. "It must have been in his dear hands and touching his face. I just put my face in it and cried. You don't know how many, many times I've cried in his handkerchiefs and been comforted by him!" With 1928 about to dawn, she confided, "I don't seem to get any happier. You are sad—all of you—to have him out of your lives. But he was fundamental in the very pattern of *my* life. It is so different. Your lives go on as before. Mine goes on—so differently."[36]

Crystal was becoming increasingly ill as she struggled with breadwinning and parenting, and now grief and mourning, almost entirely alone. Her weekends were "spent in 14 hour days trying to catch up with home problems at Croton," she told Hallinan. She felt Walter's loss everywhere in her life. "Oh—Charlie, how I miss Walter in this job," she breathed. "And, what a rare person he was. If he could come back and I could have work, & he could have work too, I think I would know just how to live with him." She blamed herself, her health, her attitude. "My trouble was, largely, that I was never well all those 11 years, never equal to life."[37]

Crystal felt she could not keep the batch of Walter's things from his mother, but asked Cynthia, "will you see that I get it if she dies?" She continued: "I wouldn't wonder if I die first. I'm holding on hard, holding onto the job and everything—but the blood pressure is back where it was and I have the same swollen glands, the same pain on top of my head, etc." Her anguish poured forth. "I am nearly frantic with my life—work in New York—children in Croton—and this good for nothing body of mine. Yes, I have Annis and Jeffrey, with so much of Walter's charm in each of them," she reminded herself as much as Cynthia. "If I can only get well and live to make a happy childhood for them. I don't care about anything else. When that is done I think I'll be pretty tired of life and quite ready to die."[38]

* * *

The Villard anniversary celebration opened March 1, 1928, in Washington, with the liberal senator George Norris of Nebraska as toastmaster at the opening event. It ended in New York on March 13, Villard's birthday. Afterward, Crystal still planned to go to London. "I want to . . . visit everybody—and talk about Walter. I feel I can't bear it if I don't," she told Hallinan.[39] Three weeks later she wrote to Cynthia, "I weaken a little at going to England—only because I don't want to leave Annis. But I guess I will come. Some deep instinct in me demands it. We may not meet for years—you & I and Rosalind and Riss and Dorothy—time will cover over all our precious grief—I think I must talk to you now while we remember everything."[40]

In the end, she did not go. The second annual meeting of the Open Door Council was held in London on May 10, 1927, and though Crystal's name was still listed as a member of the executive committee, no records indicate her travel or her presence at the convention.[41] She was probably too sick to make the trip. Her colleagues at *The Nation* noticed that "she was obviously fighting a tremendous battle."[42] In fact, she was mortally sick by the time she returned to the United States. Her kidneys, damaged so long ago by the scarlet fever that killed her brother Morgan, were now giving out.

Crystal clung to the hope of returning health, going from treatment to treatment, cure to cure, even though, Max thought, many of the supposed healers were "pretty near to a charlatan."[43] Her hopes would rise with each new regimen or powder or diet. "Yesterday and today have been so wonderful that I am happy," she wrote Ruth Pickering Pinchot, "even with this nasty taste in my mouth and every mouthful is more than doubtful,—my eyes almost useless,—and a roaring in my head at night like a train puffing up hill." She had never been the type of person to give up. "It is great to be here with the children. My heart is warm and life is sweet," she expressed. "Tomorrow I am getting a trained nurse dietician. And Monday I am getting a diet. Perhaps I shall just up and get well!"[44] Eventually, however, her mood would plummet when nothing really seemed to help. Characteristically, she kept trying. "I'm starting on a new gland treatment & perhaps that will help," she would report to Cynthia. "I'm not *quite* as discouraged as I sound."[45]

But she was dying. In Crystal's last weeks, the news changed from day to day, as Max explained in a letter to the Fullers. She was admitted to John Harvey Kellogg's famed sanitarium in Battle Creek, Michigan, in early May 1928. "One doctor believed that she might recover, another thought not. She would be better for a day or two, and then worse again," Max recalled. When "she herself finally decided for the second time that she was dying," she asked Max to get her out of Battle Creek and take her to the home of their elder brother, Anstice, now a surgeon in Erie, Pennsylvania. Her doctors approved the plan.[46] There was nothing more they could do for her. A wheelchair was rented and the bills for incidental expenses—a few telegrams, her telephone, the tray service—were tallied.[47] Crystal traveled with a nurse by train to Erie. Max and Anstice went by car. Crystal "was sad but firmly courageous and very eager to go—to be in a home again," Max said.[48]

By the time she was settled onto her brother's porch in Erie, Crystal's outlook had become sunny. "Whether the result of leaving the sanitarium, or merely the progress of the disease" Max did not know, but Crystal became childlike in her joy, "perfectly happy and tranquil and completely convinced that she was getting well. She was full of love towards everybody and delight in everything," he related.[49]

Her dying thoughts went first to her children. A handwritten will, witnessed at Battle Creek before she departed, had bequeathed all her property to her two children, to be divided equally among them.[50] She died with a modest balance of $833 in the bank, with bills for summer camp, school tuition, and home repairs outstanding. There was also a $554 balance due to Battle Creek.[51] On her deathbed she scrawled a note. "Don't forget your darling father," she told Jeffrey and Annis. "He was a darling." Last she gave her children the only inheritance they would receive from either parent: "I want to leave you all my love and all my joy in life." She signed it doubly: "Crystal Mother."[52]

Max documented Crystal's utterances on her deathbed. "I'm so ashamed—so ashamed of the trouble I'm causing—this dying business I mean," she confessed to him. On her last conscious night, she expressed her love for her brother, who slept in a cot by her bedside until the end. "Oh you've been a wonderful friend, a wonderful lover," she said. She seems to have meant it descriptively, not interpersonally—or, as a mother might, in assessing a son as a man. "It's hard being a little bit of father, brother and sweetheart to so many women," she acknowledged. "You've been cruel at times, but oh you've been a good friend."[53]

Max attended to his sister for four days. It was a relief to have her ensconced in a family home, but still he found it "heart-sickening," as he wrote to Ruth, to see Crystal losing herself, losing her "terrible restless will."[54] "Quiet was not her natural medium," Freda Kirchwey lamented in her obituary in *The Nation*. But Kirchwey's elegy expressed her unending faith in Crystal's spirit, a life force she conjured as a torch, even mightier than a beacon. "She was to thousands of young women and young men a symbol of what the free woman might be."[55]

Crystal Eastman died at 3:34 a.m. on Saturday, July 28, 1928. At the end, Max said, she was "in a state of sweet and affectionate happiness," full of hope for what could happen in the world. She closed her eyes for the last time on Friday morning and passed away without waking again, not long before sunrise on a hot summer day.

EPILOGUE

In 1929, Jeffrey and Annis Fuller were adopted by Crystal's longtime colleague Agnes Brown Leach and her husband. Leach had been a principal benefactor of the Woman's Peace Party and American Union Against Militarism and a member of the National Woman's Party executive committee. Her husband, Henry Goddard Leach, was an editor of *The Forum* and president of the Scandinavian Foundation and the Poetry Society of America. The children were raised in the Leaches' Park Avenue mansion.

Immediately upon hearing of Crystal's death, Cynthia Fuller expressed her eagerness to adopt the children, but as correspondence evolved it appeared that finances might necessitate splitting them between two households within the family.[1] That seemed a cruel separation for the siblings, ages six and eleven, who had been orphaned by the deaths of both parents within nine months. Moreover, Crystal had protested as she was dying that she wanted the children to be *hers*, which would only really happen if they remained in the United States. She did not want them "to be brought up in England, to be Walter Fuller's children," Ruth Pickering reminded Max.[2] "It was Crystal's deepest desire to have them grow up here," Paul Kellogg said shortly after her death. "She put every ounce of courage and strength into her effort to work out a scheme of life for them back here."[3]

In her will, Crystal appointed Max as legal guardian for her son and daughter, and he promised her he would follow her wishes regarding their care.[4] She believed he would adopt them himself.[5] But Max "wasn't a family man," according to his widow, "he wasn't a daddy type."[6] At the time, Max told close friends he planned to "put on my best bib and tucker to find those children a good home."[7] In fact, it was Paul Kellogg who first broached the subject with Agnes Leach. And when he did, she told him the same thought had occurred to her. The Leaches had no children, and they too felt the children would find loving hearts and a rare home with them. Kellogg told Hallinan, the Leaches "would have the means and intention of giving the very

Crystal Eastman. Amy Aronson, Oxford University Press (2020).
© Oxford University Press.
DOI: 10.1093/oso/9780199948734.001.0001

best opportunity in life to both. But they have more than this world's goods to give," he said. "They have things of the spirit. Walter knew and loved them, as did Crystal."[8]

Kellogg felt sure the Leaches would make it possible for the children to visit and revisit England, "to really be members in a true sense of Walter's family. But at the same time they could give both children a home, surroundings, a chance in life that would be kindred to all the hopes Crystal and Walter cherished for them."[9] In the end, Jeff and Annis saw little of their English relatives growing up and visited them and their children only on occasion as adults.[10] It is not clear why.

Ten years after Crystal's death, in 1938, she was interred in Woodlawn Cemetery in Canandaigua, New York. Her grave is in a family plot first occupied by her brother Morgan, then by Annis Eastman by his side. Crystal must have been cremated, just as her mother was. Annis once told her daughter she wanted to die with one of her letters "put into my hands. . . . It will keep me even in the burning—I want to be burned—I have always enjoyed burning things—It's the only way to make a clean sweep and begin all over again."[11]

There is no record of where Crystal's casket traveled from Buffalo on the day she died, or with whom; or when she was cremated; or who kept her ashes all those years. There is no headstone at Woodlawn. But the cemetery records show she was buried on June 26, the day after her birthday, almost as if to suggest her final resting place, once found, might begin her story anew.

NOTES

INTRODUCTION

1. The characterization comes from Christine Stansell, *American Moderns: Bohemian New York and the Creation of a New Century* (New York: Henry Holt, 2000). See also Ross Wetzsteon, *Republic of Dreams: Greenwich Village: The American Bohemia* (New York: Simon & Schuster, 2003).
2. Max Eastman, "The Old Bohemia—Noble, Crazy Glorious," *Village Voice*, June 24, 1959, 1.
3. Margaret Lane to Jeffrey Fuller, November 10, 1931, courtesy of Rebecca Young.
4. See John Fabian Witt, *Patriots & Cosmopolitans: Hidden Histories in American Law* (Cambridge, MA: Harvard University Press, 2007), 181.
5. "'Miss' Eastman Seeks Divorce, Scorns Alimony," *Chicago Tribune*, February 29, 1916.
6. Patricia Sullivan, *Lift Every Voice: The NAACP and the Making of the Civil Rights Movement* (New York: New Press, 2009). See also Flint Kellogg, "Oswald Villard, the NAACP and *The Nation*," *The Nation*, July 2, 2009, https://www.thenation.com/article/oswald-villard-naacp-and-nation/.
7. Dorothy Fuller original drawing, courtesy of Peter Winnington.
8. "Mrs. Benedict Due Today," *Washington Herald*, March 10, 1914, 5; "Beautiful American Suffragettes in Austria," *Mail Tribune*, May 29, 1913, 6.
9. "In the Limelight," *Pearson's*, November 1917, 216.
10. Claude McKay, *A Long Way from Home* (New Brunswick, NJ: Rutgers University Press, 1937), 28.
11. Roger Baldwin, unpublished audio interview, courtesy of Rebecca Young.
12. McKay, *A Long Way from Home*, 83. Eastman helped McKay get to Russia, writing to every radical she knew who might be able to help him and booking him on a steamer to Liverpool the same night she was to set sail for London. He carried her bon voyage note with him as inspiration and memento, weeping as he read it for the last time when he learned she had passed away. See *A Long Way from Home*, 122.

13. Clare Sheridan, *Mayfair to Moscow: Clare Sheridan's Diary* (New York: Boni and Liveright, 1921), 71.

14. Walter Fuller to Riss, October 1916, courtesy of Rebecca Young.

15. Blanche Wiesen Cook, "Female Support Networks and Political Activism: Lillian Wald, Crystal Eastman, Emma Goldman," *Chrysalis* 3 (Autumn 1977): 47. See also Cook in *Peace and Freedom*, Women's International League for Peace and Freedom, US Section, 35 (1975): 14.

16. Roger Baldwin, "Recollections of a Life in Civil Liberties, Part I," *Civil Liberties Review* 2, no. 2 (1975): 54.

17. Freda Kirchwey, "Crystal Eastman," *The Nation*, August 8, 1928, 124.

18. "Editorial," *Liberator*, March 1918, 7.

19. Multiple public sources characterize Eastman as one of the country's most neglected women leaders. See Blanche Wiesen Cook, "Crystal Eastman," in *Portraits of American Women: From Settlement to the Present*, ed. G. J. Barker-Benfield and Catherine Clinton (New York: Oxford University Press, 1998), 403–28.

20. Blanche Wiesen Cook, ed., *Crystal Eastman on Women and Revolution* (New York: Oxford University Press, 1978).

21. Cook, *Crystal Eastman on Women and Revolution*, 2.

22. Leila J. Rupp discusses the social penalties paid by straight women who were seen to indulge "unorthodox heterosexuality," particularly within women's organizations in the early twentieth century. See "Sexuality and Politics in the Early Twentieth Century: The Case of the International Women's Movement," *Feminist Studies* 23, no. 3 (Autumn 1997): 577–605. See also "Feminism and the Sexual Revolution in the Early Twentieth Century: The Case of Doris Stevens," *Feminist Studies* 15, no. 2 (Summer 1989): 289–309.

23. Max Eastman, *Enjoyment of Living* (New York: Harper & Brothers, 1948): "libido," 356; "companionship in idealism," 563.

24. Eastman befriended Arthur MacManus, a leading Communist Party politician in Britain whose ashes were placed within the Kremlin Wall acropolis. However, according to the FBI, she did not take an "active part in the movement in England." W. L. Hurley to William J. Burns, Esquire, Director, Bureau of Investigation, January 11, 1923, Federal Bureau of Investigation Records, General Records of the Department of Justice, US National Archives, Record Group 65.

25. Max Eastman briefly joined the Socialist Party on Valentine's Day, 1912. See Eastman, *Enjoyment of Living*, 387. Crystal Eastman to Max Eastman, June 20, 1912, Crystal Eastman Papers (hereinafter CEP), Schlesinger Library, Harvard University, Cambridge, Massachusetts, box 6, folder 191.

26. Crystal Eastman (hereinafter CE) to Max Eastman (hereinafter ME), January 15, 1913, CEP, box 6, folder 192.

27. *Vassar Bulletin*, Class of 1903, Vassar College Archives, Vassar College, Poughkeepsie, New York, 1907.

28. Coined by the legal scholar Kimberlé Crenshaw, the term highlights the interconnections among different forms of injustice. The term was invented to capture the numerous irreducible aspects of identity that interact with each other in systems of inequality and privilege. Kimberlé Crenshaw, "Mapping the Margins: Intersectionality, Identity Politics, and Violence against Women of Color," *Stanford Law Review* 43, no. 6 (July 1991): 1241–99.

29. Eastman certainly engaged in anti-racist advocacy. She worked with African American groups in the suffrage campaigns, denounced the Chinese Exclusion Act of 1882 after it rendered Chinese immigration permanently illegal in 1902 (a ban that lasted until 1943), and controversially included a panel on "the future of colored women" in her Woman's Freedom Congress in 1919. Moreover, she was an outspoken anti-imperialist, effectively advocating international human rights by repeatedly calling for the self-determination of all peoples. As a leading internationalist, she pushed for a foreign policy dedicated to worldwide cooperation, and in 1916 demanded a Pan-American Union to promote cooperation between the United States and Latin America in testimony before the US Congress. These were bold positions in her time, and they clearly acknowledged racism in their formulations and, at times, in their articulations. Still, like too many of her colleagues across movements, she did not always hold racism itself in the foreground of her protests for social justice.

30. Intersectionality is a crucial and evolving concept, now applied in an expanding range of academic disciplines, as well as organizational and public policies. See, for example, Anna Carastathis, "The Concept of Intersectionality in Feminist Theory," *Philosophy Compass* 9, no. 5 (2014): 304–14; Jennifer Nash, "Re-thinking Intersectionality," *Feminist Review* 89 (2008): 1–15; Jennifer Jihye Chun, George Lipsitz, and Young Shin, "Intersectionality as Social Movement Strategy: Asian Immigrant Women Advocates," *Signs* 38, no. 4 (Summer 2013): 917–40; Elizabeth R. Cole, "Coalitions as a Model for Intersectionality: From Practice to Theory," *Sex Roles* 59 (2008): 443–53; and Mieke Verloo, "Intersectional and Cross-Movement Politics and Policies: Reflections on Current Practices and Debate," *Signs* 38, no. 4 (2013): 893–915.

31. Linda Gordon, "'Intersectionality,' Socialist Feminism and Contemporary Activism: Musings by a Second-Wave Socialist-Feminist," *Gender & History* 28, no. 2 (August 2016): 340–57.

32. The idea of history as kaleidoscopic comes from Neil MacGregor, *A History of the World in 100 Objects* (New York: Viking Press, 2010).

33. Patricia H. Collins, "Intersectionality's Definitional Dilemmas," *Annual Review of Sociology* 41 (2015): 1–20.

34. Neil McLaughlin discusses that historical reputation is promoted through affiliation with recognized alliances, institutions, and mentors. These connections are known to impart definition, signal stature, and help to maintain the ideological

intelligibility more readily embraced by historical narrative and collective memory. See "How to Become a Forgotten Intellectual: Intellectual Movements and the Rise and Fall of Erich Fromm," *Sociological Forum* 13, no. 2 (1998): 215–46.

35. Gary Alan Fine discusses the issue of subcultural figures and their divided reputations, which complicate access to cultural memory. See *Difficult Reputations: Collective Memories of the Evil, Inept and Controversial* (Chicago: University of Chicago Press, 2001), 11.

36. Kathleen Gerson, *The Unfinished Revolution: Coming of Age in a New Era of Gender, Work, and Family* (New York: Oxford University Press, 2011).

37. Kirsten Swinth, *Feminism's Forgotten Fight: The Unfinished Struggle for Work and Family* (Cambridge, MA: Harvard University Press, 2018).

38. Crystal Eastman, "Birth Control in the Feminist Program," *Birth Control Review*, January 1918, 1.

39. Cole, "Coalitions as a Model for Intersectionality," 444.

40. Sandra R. Levitsky, "Niche Activism: Negotiating Organizational Heterogeneity in Contemporary American Social Movements," *Mobilization: An International Quarterly* 12, no. 3 (September 2007): 272.

41. Crystal Eastman, "What Feminism Means to Me, An Address Delivered at the First Feminist Meeting Held in Cooper Union, New York City, February 1914," *Vassar Miscellany*, June 15, 1915, 670.

42. Gary Alan Fine discusses these dynamics in "Reputational Entrepreneurs and the Memory of Incompetence: Melting Supporters, Partisan Warriors, and Images of President Harding," *American Journal of Sociology* 101, no. 5 (March 1996): 1159–93. See also Alexi Gugushvili, Peter Kabachnik, and Ana Kirvalidze, "Collective Memory and Reputational Politics of National Heroes and Villains," *Nationalities Papers* 45, no. 3 (2017): 464–84.

43. Michael Kazin characterizes such militancy as the hallmark of the American Left. See *American Dreamers: How the Left Changed a Nation* (New York: Vintage Books, 2012).

CHAPTER 1

1. All seventeen essays in the series are collected in Elaine Showalter, ed., *These Modern Women: Autobiographical Essays from the Twenties* (New York: Feminist Press at CUNY, 1989).

2. Like Crystal, Kirchwey was herself an avowed modern feminist. A well-educated woman, Kirchwey pursued professional aspirations and achieved considerable success; married in 1916, she too kept her own name. Both women embraced working motherhood, continuing to work far into their pregnancies and returning to professional life as soon as possible after their children were born. By the time the series appeared, both women were striving to balance work and family, to forge a life for themselves that censored neither love nor career, a life they both, as feminists,

could define as whole. See Sara Alpern, *Freda Kirchwey: A Woman of The Nation* (Cambridge, MA: Harvard University Press, 1987).

3. Crystal Eastman, "Mother-Worship," *The Nation*, March 16, 1927, 283.

4. Max Eastman, *Enjoyment of Living* (New York: Harper & Brothers, 1948), 277.

5. Eastman, *Enjoyment of Living*, 41.

6. Eastman, *Enjoyment of Living*, 86.

7. Eastman, *Enjoyment of Living*, 78.

8. Eastman, *Enjoyment of Living*, 89.

9. Eastman, *Enjoyment of Living*, 41; Anstice Eastman to Annis Ford Eastman, July 2, 1899, CEP, box 4, folder 172.

10. See Max Eastman, "The Hero as Parent," in *Heroes I Have Known: Twelve Who Lived Great Lives* (New York: Simon & Schuster, 1942), 1–14.

11. Max Eastman, *Love and Revolution: My Journey through an Epoch* (New York: Random House, 1964), 504.

12. Annis Ford Eastman (hereinafter AFE) to Crystal Eastman (hereinafter CE), April 22, 1902, CEP, box 5, folder 125.

13. Eastman, *Enjoyment of Living*, 91.

14. Eastman, *Enjoyment of Living*, 346.

15. Eastman, *Enjoyment of Living*, 51.

16. CE to "Walter's Mother," July 15, 1927, courtesy of Rebecca Young.

17. Eastman, *Enjoyment of Living*, 37–38.

18. Eastman, *Enjoyment of Living*, 55.

19. Eastman, *Enjoyment of Living*, 38.

20. Eastman, *Enjoyment of Living*, 39.

21. Eastman, *Enjoyment of Living*, 51.

22. Eastman, *Enjoyment of Living*, 39.

23. Eastman, *Enjoyment of Living*, 44–49.

24. Eastman, *Enjoyment of Living*, 47–48.

25. Eastman, *Enjoyment of Living*, 48.

26. Eastman, *Enjoyment of Living*, 52.

27. Eastman, *Enjoyment of Living*, 50.

28. "Max Eastman, Late Author, Got Early Schooling Here," *The Daily Messenger*, May 6, 1969, 6.

29. Advertisement for Granger Place School for Girls, 1898.

30. Eastman, *Enjoyment of Living*, 57.

31. Eastman, *Enjoyment of Living*, 50.

32. Eastman, *Enjoyment of Living*, 57.

33. Crystal Eastman, typescript draft of "Mother-Worship," 6-7, courtesy of Rebecca Young. Eastman, *Enjoyment of Living*, 91.

34. Eastman, "Mother-Worship," 284.

35. AFE to CE, February 19, 1903, CEP, box 5, folder 130.

36. AFE to CE, February 3, 1900, CEP, box 5, folder 115.

37. Eastman, *Enjoyment of Living*, 59.

38. Eastman, *Enjoyment of Living*, 82.

39. Eastman, *Enjoyment of Living*, 66.

40. Eastman, *Enjoyment of Living*, 61, 66–67.

41. Eastman, *Enjoyment of Living*, 91.

42. Eastman, *Enjoyment of Living*, 678.

43. Eastman, "Mother-Worship," 284.

44. Eastman, *Enjoyment of Living*, 97.

45. Eastman, *Enjoyment of Living*, 69.

46. Eastman, *Enjoyment of Living*, 72.

47. Eastman, "Mother-Worship," 283.

48. [No headline], *Wellsville Daily Reporter*, November 16, 1895, 3.

49. Max Eastman, "Mark Twain's Elmira," *Harper's*, May, 1938.

50. Eastman, *Enjoyment of Living*, 78.

51. All quotes from Eastman, "Mother-Worship," 284.

52. Eastman, typescript draft of "Mother-Worship," 3.

53. AFE to CE, July 29, 1893, CEP, box 4, folder 97.

54. Max Eastman, *Heroes I Have Known*, 48. See also Rev. John Henry Barrows, *The World's Parliament of Religions: An Illustrated and Popular Story of the World's First Parliament of Religions* (Chicago: Parliament Publishing Company, 1893).

55. They formed the Congregational church of Elmira. Eva Taylor, "History of the Park Church," unpublished paper prepared by the Historical Records Committee of the Park Church, 1946, courtesy of Rebecca Young.

56. Eastman, *Enjoyment of Living*, 97.

57. Eastman, "Mark Twain's Elmira," 620.

58. Eastman, "Mark Twain's Elmira," 623.

59. Mike Hulme, "On the Origin of 'the Greenhouse Effect': John Tyndall's 1859 Interrogation of Nature," *Weather* 64, no. 5 (April 2009): 121–23.

60. Eastman, *Enjoyment of Living*, 623–25.

61. Eastman, *Enjoyment of Living*, 110–11.

62. Eastman, "Mark Twain's Elmira," 625.

63. Eastman, *Enjoyment of Living*, 626.

64. Eastman, *Enjoyment of Living*, 627.

65. Eastman, *Enjoyment of Living*, 107.

66. For this description, I am particularly indebted to Carl Wedekind, unpublished manuscript, courtesy of Annie Wedekind.

67. Eastman, *Enjoyment of Living*, 629.

68. Eastman, *Enjoyment of Living*, 628.

69. Eastman, *Enjoyment of Living*, 159.

70. Eastman, "Mother-Worship," 284.

71. AFE to CE, March 2, 1904, CEP, box 5, folder 137. Annis's reference comes from the Emerson essay, "Swedenborg; or, The Mystic," published in *Representative Men* (1850).

72. Eastman, *Enjoyment of Living*, 118.

73. Annis Ford Eastman, "Havé and Givé," in *Havé and Givé and Other Parables* (Elmira, NY, 1896), 10.

74. Eastman, "Havé and Givé," 23.

75. "Garden (or a girl)," Annis Ford Eastman, "Flower Morals," in *Havé and Givé*, 22; "born to overcome," Eastman, "Hide the Text," in *Havé and Givé*, 34–35.

76. Annis Ford Eastman, "I See," in *Havé and Givé*, 45, 43.

77. AFE to CE, March 27, 1900, CEP, box 5, folder 116.

78. Eastman, *Enjoyment of Living*, 118.

79. Eastman, "Mother-Worship," 284. Crystal's draft claimed Annis was "always" there to tuck you in at night and added a humorous example of motherly devotion, saying Annis was the type of mother who "rubs your chest till you cry for mercy if you have a bad cough." Eastman, typescript draft of "Mother-Worship," 3.

80. "Cousin Adra" was the daughter of Annis's older sister Francis. She later joined Crystal in New York City, working at Greenwich Settlement House by approximately 1905. Author interviews with Philip Wingard, Clover, South Carolina, July 6, 2015; August 18, 2015.

81. AFE to CE, n.d. [1897], CEP, box 4, folder 102. See also Annis Ford Eastman, "Why Do Women Wish to Vote?" [1897], CEP, box 4, folder 86.

82. AFE to CE, October 24, 1897, CEP, box 4, folder 103.

83. AFE to CE, February 14, 1900, CEP, box 5, folder 115. In February 1895, Annis had delivered the introductory religious services at the National Council of Women, an event where Shaw also preached. When Shaw spent a week in Elmira the following May, Annis wrote to Crystal at Granger Place, saying, "I hugged her for you." AFE to CE, May 6, 1898. See also AFE to CE, May 8, 1898, both CEP, box 4, folder 106.

84. Eastman, *Enjoyment of Living,* 128, 127.

85. Eastman, "Mother-Worship," 283.

86. Charlotte Perkins Gilman to AFE, December 6, 1903, CEP, box 5, folder 134.

87. Wykoff Log, July 11, 1907; July 16, 1907; July 24, 1907, courtesy of the Wykoff family.

88. Wykoff Log, August 16, 1907.

89. For example, "Women's Work in the World," August 19, 1907, Wycoff Log.

90. Eastman, "Mother-Worship," 284.

91. See Cherith Log Book, 1901–4; 1904–8; 1909, Max Eastman Papers (hereinafter MEP), Addition 2, The Lilly Library, Indiana University, Bloomington, Indiana.

92. Anstice Eastman to CE, April 9, 1897, Anstice Eastman Papers, The Lilly Library, Indiana University.

93. Wykoff Log, August 28, 1908.

94. Wykoff Log, August 22, 1908.

95. Wykoff Log, August 6, 1908.
96. Wykoff Log, August 6, 1908.
97. See Freda Kirchwey to Oswald Garrison Villard, July 26, 1927, Oswald Garrison Villard Papers, Houghton Library, Harvard University, folder 2073. See also Blanche Wiesen Cook, ed., *Crystal Eastman on Women and Revolution* (New York: Oxford University Press, 1978), 46.
98. Eastman, "Mother-Worship," 284.
99. Suzanna Danuta Walters, *Lives Together/Worlds Apart: Mothers and Daughters in Popular Culture* (Berkeley: University of California Press, 1994).
100. See Ellen Carol Dubois, *Harriot Stanton Blatch and the Winning of Woman Suffrage* (New Haven, CT: Yale University Press, 1999).
101. See Astrid Henry, *Not My Mother's Sister: Generational Conflict and Third Wave Feminism* (Bloomington: Indiana University Press, 2004). See also Susan Faludi, "American Electra: Feminism's Ritual Matricide," *Harper's*, October 2010, 29–42.
102. See Cook, *Crystal Eastman on Women and Revolution*, 46.
103. Crystal Eastman scrapbook, courtesy of Rebecca Young.
104. Eastman, typescript draft of "Mother-Worship," 8–9.
105. Eastman, typescript draft of "Mother-Worship," 9.
106. Annis Ford Eastman, *Have Salt in Yourselves: To Young Ladies* (American Home Missionary Society, n.d.), 2.
107. Eastman, *Have Salt in Yourselves*, 9.
108. Eastman, "Mother-Worship," 284.
109. Eastman, *Enjoyment of Living*, 50.
110. Annis reported the description of herself in AFE to CE, February 9, 1904, CEP, box 5, folder 136.
111. AFE to CE, November 14, 1900, CEP, box 5, folder 118.
112. AFE to CE, September 30, 1897, CEP, box 4, folder 103.
113. AFE to CE, January 19, 1899, CEP, box 4, folder 110.
114. AFE to CE, October 24, 1897, CEP, box 4, folder 103.
115. AFE to CE, April 13, 1903, CEP, box 5, folder 131.
116. AFE to CE, April 25, 1904, CEP, box 5, folder 138.
117. CE to AFE, September 23, 1899, CEP, box 6, folder 172.
118. CE to AFE, October 27, 1899, CEP, box 6, folder 172.
119. AFE to CE, February 15, 1902, CEP, box 5, folder 125.
120. AFE to CE, n.d. [September 1901], CEP, box 5, folder 122.
121. AFE to CE, September 23, 1902, CEP, box 5, folder 126.
122. AFE to CE, September 7, 1905, CEP, box 5, folder 143.
123. AFE to CE, May 19, 1904, CEP, box 5, folder 139.
124. AFE to CE, May 10, 1903, CEP, box 5, folder 131.
125. CE to AFE, December 30, 1907, CEP, box 6, folder 183.
126. Eastman, typescript draft of "Mother-Worship," 9.

CHAPTER 2

1. William Jennings Bryan, July 8, 1896, http://www.let.rug.nl/usa/documents/ 1876-1900/william-jennings-bryan-cross-of-gold-speech-july-8-1896.php.

2. CE to ME, November 8, 1900, CEP, box 5, folder 118.

3. Mark Twain and Charles Dudley Warner, *The Gilded Age: A Tale of Today* (New York: Harper & Brothers, 1893).

4. Annis Ford Eastman, "The Coming Man," March 5, 1893, CEP, box 1, folder 1.

5. Walter Lippmann to ME, April 2, 1913, MEP, box 1.

6. See Ronald Steel, *Walter Lippmann and the American Century* (New York: Routledge, 1999).

7. See John Reed's mock-epic poem, "A Day in Bohemia," cited in Jeremy McCarter, *Young Radicals: In the War for American Ideals* (New York: Random House, 2017), 14.

8. Walter Lippmann, 1912, cited in Christine Stansell, *American Moderns*, 44.

9. Henry James, *The Bostonians* (1895), cited by Michael Kimmel, *Manhood in America: A Cultural History* (New York: Free Press, 1996), 120.

10. Kimmel, *Manhood in America*, 120–87.

11. Both quotes from Kimmel, *Manhood in America*, 182.

12. See Stansell, *American Moderns*, 28–29.

13. Max Eastman, *Love & Revolution* (New York: Random House, 1964), 26.

14. Mathew B. Fuller, "A History of Student Financial Aid," *Journal of Student Financial Aid* 44, no. 1 (2014): 42–62; Vassar Encyclopedia, "A History of the Curriculum, 1865–1970s," http://vcencyclopedia.vassar.edu/curriculum/a-history-of-the-curriculum-1865-1970s.html.

15. See Vassar Encyclopedia, "Inez Milholland," https://vcencyclopedia.vassar.edu/ alumni/inez-milholland.html.

16. Fuller, "History of Financial Aid," 45.

17. CE to AFE, December 17, 1899, CEP, box 4, folder 113.

18. AFE to CE, November 19, 1898, CEP, box 4, folder 109.

19. AFE to CE, April 13, 1897, CEP, box 4, folder 102.

20. AFE to CE, March 11, 1898, CEP, box 4, folder 106.

21. AFE to CE, October 18, 1898, CEP, box 4, folder 109.

22. AFE to CE, n.d., CEP, box 4, folder 106.

23. AFE to CE, n.d., CEP, box 4, folder 106.

24. AFE to CE, October 18, 1898, CEP, box 4, folder 108.

25. AFE to CE, October 24, 1898, CEP, box 4, folder 108.

26. AFE to CE, May 20, 1900, CEP, box 5, folder 117.

27. CE to AFE, October 27, 1899, CEP, box 4, folder 113.

28. CE to AFE, January 21, 1907, CEP, box 5, folder 155.

29. See Sylvia Law, "Crystal Eastman: Organizer for Women's Rights, Peace and Civil Liberties in the 1910s," *Valparaiso University Law Review* 28, no. 4 (1994): 1305–26.

30. Anstice Eastman to AFE, July 2, 1899, CEP, box 4, folder 97.

31. CE to AFE, July 11, 1899, CEP, box 4, folder 112.

32. CE to AFE, September 27, 1899, CEP, box 4, folder 113.

33. CE to AFE, September 27, 1899, CEP, box 4, folder 113.

34. CE to AFE, October 16, 1899, CEP, box 4, folder 113.

35. CE to AFE, January 21, 1900, CEP, box 5, folder 115.

36. CE to AFE, October 16, 1899, CEP, box 4, folder 113.

37. CE to ME, March 3, 1903, CEP, box 5, folder 130.

38. Both quotes from CE to ME, January 20, 1899, CEP, box 4, folder 110.

39. CE to AFE, January 25, 1900, CEP, box 5, folder 115.

40. Carroll Smith-Rosenberg, "The Female World of Love and Ritual: Relations between Women in Nineteenth Century America," in *The Girls' History and Culture Reader: The Nineteenth Century*, ed. Miriam Forman-Brunell and Leslie Paris (Urbana: University of Illinois Press, 2011), 150.

41. Rikki Novetsky, "College Girls: What Was the Barnard College Crush?," *Columbia Spectator*, October 23, 2014, http://features.columbiaspectator.com/blog/2014/10/23/college-girls/. See also Rona M. Wilk, "'What's a Crush?': A Study of Crushes and Romantic Friendships at Barnard College, 1900–1920," *Magazine of History* 18, no. 4 (July 2004): 20–22.

42. "Dandy," CE to ME, February 24, 1900, CEP, box 5, folder 115; "versatility," CE to ME, March 4, 1900, CEP, box 5, folder 116.

43. CE to ME, April 15, 1900, CEP, box 5, folder 116.

44. CE to ME, January 20, 1900, CEP, box 5, folder 115.

45. CE to AFE, n.d. [1900], CEP, box 5, folder 116.

46. AFE to CE, November 1, 1900, CEP, box 5, folder 118.

47. AFE to CE, March 12, 1902, CEP, box 5, folder 116.

48. CE to ME, n.d. [1903], CEP, box 5, folder 134.

49. *Vassarion*, 1902, Vassar College Archives, Vassar College, Poughkeepsie, New York.

50. *Vassarion*, 1902; *Vassarion*, 1903, Vassar College Archives.

51. CE to ME, September 29, 1903, CEP, box 5, folder 133.

52. "Hands," CE to ME, April 30, 1900, CEP, box 5, folder 116; "taking it up," CE to ME, May 25, 1900, CEP, box 5, folder 117.

53. CE to ME, April 22, 1900, CEP, box 5, folder 116.

54. Crystal was a member of a social club called 66666, with Lucy Burns, Elsie Clapp, and others, as well as the Philatelis Club and the German Club, according to the *Vassarion*, 1901. The other clubs that followed are noted in *Vassarion*, 1902, and *Vassarion*, 1903, Vassar College Archives.

55. *Vassarion*, 1901; 1902; 1903, Vassar College Archives.

56. CE to ME, March 31, 1906, CEP, box 5, folder 149.

57. Crystal Eastman surviving diary entries, Monday, May 15, 1902, courtesy of Rebecca Young.

58. CE to ME, February 26, 1903, CEP, box 5, folder 130.

59. CE to ME, August 13, 1902, CEP, box 5, folder 126.

60. American Sociological Association, "Franklin H. Giddings," http://www.asanet. org/about-asa/asa-story/asa-history/past-asa-officers/past-asa-presidents/ franklin-h-giddings. Giddings's emphasis on like-mindedness, on consciousness of kind, was a driving force in his arguments about the imperialism and the integration of Western nations. See Evander Bradley McGilvary, "Review of *Democracy and Empire* by Franklin Henry Giddings," *Philosophical Review* 9, no. 6 (November 1900): 651–56.

61. F. H. Hankins, "Franklin Henry Giddings, 1855–1931: Some Aspects of His Sociological Theory," *American Journal of Sociology* 37, no. 3 (1931): 360.

62. The term comes from Charles Camic and Yu Xie (1994), as cited by David D. McFarland, "Adding Machines and Logarithms: Franklin H. Giddings and Computation for the Exact Science of Sociology," *Social Science Computer Review* 22, no. 2 (Summer 2004): 249.

63. McFarland, "Adding Machines and Logarithms," 250, 253.

64. McFarland, "Adding Machines and Logarithms," 254.

65. John Fabian Witt, *Patriots & Cosmopolitans: Hidden Histories of American Law* (Cambridge, MA: Harvard University Press, 2007), 165.

66. Crystal Eastman, "Daniel Raymond" (master's thesis, Columbia University, 1904, Columbia University Archives), 12.

67. Eastman, "Daniel Raymond" (both quotes), 18. Crystal nevertheless undertook a critical assessment of Raymond's critique of Smith. Raymond's neglect of his own earlier reasoning in failing to distinguish between wealth and capital in *The Wealth of Nations*, she wrote, "almost suggests a willful, deliberate misunderstanding" of Smith that "makes this criticism of little use." See Eastman, "Daniel Raymond," 45–47.

68. Eastman, "Daniel Raymond," 18, 52.

69. Eastman, "Daniel Raymond," 14. She did use personal pronouns in her preface, outlining, for example, "my inducement in writing" about Raymond on the first preface page.

70. Eastman, "Daniel Raymond," 51.

71. Eastman, "Daniel Raymond," 26.

72. Eastman, "Daniel Raymond," 26–27.

73. Eastman, "Daniel Raymond," 34.

74. Eastman, "Daniel Raymond," 28–29.

75. Eastman, "Daniel Raymond," 28–29.

76. Eastman, "Daniel Raymond," (all quotes), 29.

77. Eastman, "Daniel Raymond," 3.

78. Eastman, "Daniel Raymond," 47.

79. Eastman, "Daniel Raymond," 33.

80. Eastman, "Daniel Raymond," 52.

81. National Center for Education Statistics, *120 Years of American Education: A Statistical Portrait* (US Department of Education, 1993), Table 28, 82.

82. CE to ME, October 12, 1903, CEP, box 5, folder 133.

83. CE to ME, October 12, 1903, CEP, box 5, folder 133.

84. Susan Goodier and Karen Pastorello, *Women Will Vote: Winning Suffrage in New York State* (Ithaca, NY: Cornell University Press, 2017), 122.

85. CE to AFE, October 27, 1899, CEP, box 4, folder 113.

86. For example, CE to ME, February 11, 1902, CEP, box 5, folder 125; August 4, 1902, CEP, box 5, folder 126; March 31, 1903, CEP, box 5, folder 130.

87. Crystal Eastman surviving diary entries, June 9 [1902], courtesy of Rebecca Young.

88. CE to ME, March 9, 1905, CEP, box 5, folder 142.

89. CE to ME, February 10, 1905, CEP, box 5, folder 142.

90. CE to AFE, October 30, 1906, CEP, box 5, folder 153.

91. All quotes from CE to AFE, December 17, 1906, CEP, box 6, folder 180.

92. Crystal Eastman surviving diary entries, May 4, 1904, courtesy of Rebecca Young.

93. Crystal Eastman surviving diary entries, May 15, 1904, courtesy of Rebecca Young.

94. Max Eastman, *Enjoyment of Living*, 138.

95. CE to ME, March 9, 1905, CEP, box 5, folder 142.

96. CE to ME, March 29, 1905, MEP, box 10.

97. CE to ME, March 9, 1905, CEP, box 5, folder 142.

98. *Vassar 1903 First Annual Class Bulletin*, May 1904, Vassar College Archives.

99. Phyllis Eckhaus, "Restless Women: The Pioneering Alumni of NYU Law School," *NYU Law Review* 66 (1991): 1996.

100. Eckhaus, "Restless Women," 1996.

101. *Vassar 1903 Second Annual Class Bulletin*, May 1905, Vassar College Archives.

102. All quotes from CE to ME, November 28, 1904, CEP, box 5, folder 140.

103. CE to ME, February 18, 1905, CEP, box 5, folder 142.

104. See Mary Simkhovitch, *Neighborhood; My Story of Greenwich House* (New York: W. W. Norton, 1938), 90–91. See also Herbert Stroup, *Social Welfare Pioneers* (Chicago: Nelson-Hall Publishers, 1986), 243–44.

105. While almost all historical accounts credit Jane Addams with starting the settlement house movement in the United States, New York's University Settlement, founded by Stanton Coit three years earlier as "The Neighborhood Guild," hails itself as the first in the country. See http://www.unhny.org/about/history.

106. The figure is cited in Stansell, *American Moderns*, 61.

107. Some, notably both Hull House and the Henry Street Settlement, were secular. Miriam Cohen, "Women and the Progressive Movement," The Gilder Lehrman Institute of American History, https://www.gilderlehrman.org/history-by-era/politics-reform/essays/women-and-progressive-movement#_ftn5.

108. This movement "motto" is widely noted. See, for example, Walter I. Trattner, *From Poor Law to Welfare State: A History of Social Welfare in America*, 6th ed. (New York: Free Press, 1998), 171.

109. Wendy B. Sharer, *Vote and Voice: Women's Organizations and Political Literacy 1915–1930* (Carbondale: Southern Illinois University Press, 2004).

110. See Robyn Muncy, *Creating a Female Domain in American Reform 1890–1935* (Oxford: Oxford University Press, 1991). See also Kathryn Kish Sklar, *Florence Kelley and the Nation's Work: The Rise of Women's Political Culture, 1830–1900* (New Haven, CT: Yale University Press, 1995).

111. Noted in Tracey Briggs, "Twenty Years at Greenwich House" (PhD diss., Department of History, University of Toledo, 2008), note 96, 33.

112. CE to ME, April 8, 1905, CEP, box 5, folder 142.

113. CE to ME, February 18, 1905, CEP, box 5, folder 142.

114. Mary White Ovington, *Black and White Sat Down Together: The Reminiscences of an NAACP Founder* (New York: Feminist Press, 1995). Cited in Briggs, "Twenty Years at Greenwich House," 144.

115. "Edward T. Devine," Social Welfare History Project, https: //socialwelfare.library.vcu.edu/people/devine-edward-t-3/.

116. Edward T. Devine, *American Social Work in the Twentieth Century* (Cambridge, MA: Frontier Press, 1921). Quoted in Briggs, "Twenty Years at Greenwich House," 36.

117. Figure cited by Sylvia Law, "Crystal Eastman: NYU Law Graduate," *NYU Law Review* 66 (1991): 1981.

118. CE to AFE, December 17, 1906, CEP, box 6, folder 180.

119. CE to AFE, October 11, 1906, CEP, box 6, folder 168.

120. CE to AFE, September 30, 1906, CEP, box 6, folder 179.

121. CE to AFE, January 15, 1907, CEP, box 6, folder 181.

122. CE to AFE, November 19, 1906, CEP, box 6, folder 180.

123. CE to AFE, n.d., CEP, box 6, folder 168.

124. CE to AFE, February 1, 1907, CEP, box 6, folder 181.

125. CE to AFE, January 23, 1907, CEP, box 6, folder 181.

126. CE to AFE, November 19, 1906, CEP, box 6, folder 180.

127. CE to AFE, October 4, 1906, CEP, box 5, folder 153.

128. CE to AFE, October 19, 1906, CEP, box 6, folder 179.

129. CE to AFE, October 4, 1906, CEP, box 6, folder 180.

130. CE to ME, March 31, 1903, CEP, box 5, folder 130.

131. CE to AFE, October 30, 1906, CEP, box 6, folder 179.

132. Ross Wetzsteon, *Republic of Dreams: Greenwich Village: The American Bohemia, 1910–1960* (New York: Simon & Schuster, 2003), 6–13.

133. Most famously, between 1912 and 1914, the American heiress and arts patron Mabel Dodge Luhan hosted a weekly salon at her home at 23 Fifth Avenue, which catered to both the artistic and radical-political energies of the area and era. It became a fixture of the intellectual, political, artistic, and social scene in the Village. See Wetzsteon, *Republic of Dreams*, 6. See also Allen Churchill, *The Improper Bohemians* (New York: Ace Books, 1959); Robert A. Rosenstone, "The Salon of Mabel Dodge," in *Affairs of the Mind: The Salon in Europe and America from the Eighteenth to the*

Twentieth Century, ed. Peter Quennell (New York: New Republic Books, 1980), 131–49; and Gerald W. McFarland, *Inside Greenwich Village: A New York City Neighborhood 1898–1918* (Amherst: University of Massachusetts Press, 2001).

134. Joanna Levin, *Bohemia in America 1858–1920* (Stanford, CA: Stanford University Press, 2009), 356.

135. CE to AFE, October 4, 1906, CEP, box 5, folder 153.

136. CE to ME, February 18, 1905, CEP, box 5, folder 142.

137. Crystal Eastman, "Charles Haag, An Immigrant Sculptor of His Kind," *Charities and the Commons*, January 5, 1907, 615–16.

138. Only small numbers of black intellectuals lived anywhere in Manhattan at the time, and by the time the "New Negroes" touted by the press appeared in the 1920s, Harlem was their home. When Crystal first moved to the Village, black thinkers, writers, reformers, and radicals might have faced precious little neighborliness from people and businesses in the area. See Stansell, *American Moderns*, 66–69. See also Joy James, *Transcending the Talented Tenth: Black Leaders and American Intellectuals* (New York: Routledge, 1996); and William M. Banks, *Black Intellectuals: Race and Responsibility in American Life* (New York: W. W. Norton, 1996).

139. CE to AFE, June 25, 1907, CEP, box 5, folder 157.

140. CE to ME, February 18, 1905, CEP, box 5, folder 142.

141. Max Eastman, *Enjoyment of Living* (New York: Harper and Brothers, 1948), 291.

142. See ME to CE, December 15, 1906, MEP, box 10.

143. CE to ME, December 1906, CEP, box 5, folder 154.

144. ME to CE, December 20, 1906, MEP, box 10.

145. CE to AFE, January 4, 1907, CEP, box 6, folder 181.

146. CE to AFE, January 6, 1907, CEP, box 6, folder 181.

147. CE to AFE, January 24, 1907, CEP, box 6, folder 181.

148. Madeleine Zabriskie Doty, *Society's Misfits* (New York: Century, 1916).

149. CE to AFE, September 30, 1906, CEP, box 6, folder 179.

150. CE to AFE, November 19, 1906, CEP, box 6, folder 179.

151. Doty and Baldwin married in 1919. The couple divorced in 1925.

152. CE to AFE, September 30, 1906, CEP, box 6, folder 179.

153. Christoph Irmscher devotes considerable attention to Max Eastman's social life and relationships in *Max Eastman: A Life* (New Haven, CT: Yale University Press, 2017).

154. The New York State Men's League was founded in 1909, and Max Eastman was its first executive secretary. See Max Eastman, "Early History of the Men's League," *Woman Voter*, October 1912, 221–22.

155. CE to ME, July 10, 1908, CEP, box 6, folder 187.

156. After speaking at a conference on industrial accidents and workers' compensation in January 1910, Crystal came home "with a fat fifty dollar wad in my bag. I've got to share it with somebody and I guess it must be with you—in these days of joy.

Please take this in token of my other gladness." CE to ME, January 4, 1910, CEP, box 6, folder 189.

157. Ada James to CE, April 13, 1912, Ada James Papers, reel 6.

158. See Irmscher, *Max Eastman*. See also Elise K. Kenney, Earl Davis, and Rebecca Zurier, *Art for the Masses: A Radical Magazine and Its Graphics 1911–1917* (Philadelphia: Temple University Press, 1988).

159. CE to AFE, January 4, 1907, CEP, box 6, folder 181.

160. CE to AFE, January 6, 1907, CEP, box 6, folder 181.

161. CE to AFE, March 16, 1907, CEP, box 6, folder 182.

162. CE to AFE, February 17, 1907, CEP, box 6, folder 181.

163. CE to AFE, January 15, 1907, CEP, box 6, folder 181.

164. Irmscher focuses on the play of these feelings in *Max Eastman,* particularly chap. 2, "Dearest of All Lovers," 27–47.

165. CE to ME, March 8, 1907, CEP, box 6, folder 182.

166. CE to AFE, March 6, 1907, CEP, box 6, folder 182.

167. CE to AFE March 6, 1907, CEP, box 6, folder 182.

168. CE to AFE, March 13, 1907, CEP, box 6, folder 182.

169. CE to ME, April 29, 1907, box 6, folder 182.

170. Both quotes from Eastman, *Love and Revolution*, 504.

171. ME to CE, February 26, 1904, CEP, box 5, folder 141.

172. ME to CE, January 14, 1903, MEP, box 10.

173. ME to CE, February 26, 1904, CEP, box 5, folder 141.

174. ME to CE, March 29, 1904, CEP, box 5, folder 141.

175. ME to CE, n.d. [January?], 1907, MEP, box 10.

176. ME to CE, March 11, 1907, MEP, box 10.

177. "On the scene" and "small flat," CE to AFE, January 24, 1907; "living *with* people," CE to AFE, February 12, 1907, CEP, box 6, folder 181.

178. CE to AFE, June 7, 1907, CEP, box 6, folder 182.

179. ME to AFE, September 23, 1908, MEP, box 10.

180. See CE to ME, March 24, 1909, CEP, box 6, folder 171; CE to ME, August 10, 1909, CEP, box 6, folder 171.

181. CE to ME, "Friday afternoon," n.d. [1909], CEP, box 6, folder 171.

CHAPTER 3

1. Roger Daniels, *Guarding the Golden Door: American Immigration Policy and Immigrants since 1882* (New York: Hill and Wang, 2005). See also David A. Gerber, *American Immigration: A Very Short Introduction* (New York: Oxford University Press, 2011).

2. Kerry Abrams, "Polygamy, Prostitution, and the Federalization of Immigration Law," *Columbia Law Review* 105, no. 3 (2005): 641–716.

3. CE to AFE, June 25, 1907, CEP, box 5, folder 155.

4. *New York Evening World*, December 14, 1908.

5. CE to AFE, June 8, 1907, CEP, box 6, folder 182.

6. "Portia Appointed by the Governor," *New York Herald*, April 24, 1910.

7. Wykoff Log, July 25, 1907, courtesy of the Wykoff Family.

8. CE to AFE, February 9, 1908, CEP, box 6, folder 186.

9. It was a reader, a probation officer of the Alleghany juvenile court in Pittsburgh, Alice B. Montgomery, who was so gripped by the report that she contacted Kellogg to ask if the magazine might appoint a special investigator to study the social conditions in and around Pittsburgh. See Clarke A. Chambers, *Paul U. Kellogg and The Survey: Voices for Social Welfare and Social Justice* (Minneapolis: University of Minnesota Press, 1971), 33.

10. All quotes from Edward T. Devine, "Results of the Pittsburgh Survey," *American Journal of Sociology* 14, no. 5 (March 1909): 661–62.

11. Chambers, *Paul U. Kellogg and The Survey*, 38.

12. Chambers, *Paul U. Kellogg and The Survey*, 34. See also Maurine Weiner Greenwald and Margo J. Anderson, eds., *Pittsburgh Surveyed: Social Science and Social Science Reform in the Early Twentieth Century* (Pittsburgh: University of Pittsburgh Press, 2011), 6–7.

13. The entire Pittsburgh Survey was published as Paul Kellogg, ed., *Wage-Earning Pittsburgh* (New York: Survey Associates, 1914), and has been digitized in full: https://archive.org/stream/pittsburghsurvey05kelluoft/pittsburghsurvey05-kelluoft_djvu.txt.

14. For further context on the two men, see Jeffrey Mirel, *Patriotic Pluralism: Americanization Education and European Immigrants* (Cambridge, MA: Harvard University Press, 2010) and David A. Zonderman, *Uneasy Allies: Working for Labor Reform in Nineteenth-Century Boston* (Amherst: University of Massachusetts Press, 2011).

15. See Russell Freedman, *Kids at Work: Lewis Hine and the Crusade against Child Labor* (New York: Clarion Books, 1994), 9–19.

16. Lynn Gordon, "Women and the Anti-Child Labor Movement in Illinois, 1890–1920," *Social Service Review* 51, no. 2 (June 1977): 228–48.

17. Maurine W. Greenwald, "Elizabeth Beardsley Butler," in *American National Biography* (New York: Oxford University Press, 2004). On the history of women in the labor force, see Alice Kessler-Harris, *Women Have Always Worked: A Concise History*, 2nd rev. ed. (Champaign: University of Illinois Press, 2018).

18. See Julie Des Jardins, *Women and the Historical Enterprise in America: Gender, Race and the Politics of Memory, 1880–1945* (Chapel Hill: University of North Carolina Press, 2003).

19. "In Memoriam, Margaret Byington, 1877–1952," *Social Service Review* 26, no. 4 (1952): 486. The book went on to three printings through 1919 by the Russell Sage

Foundation, which republished it as a free e-book in January 1970: https://www.russellsage.org/what-social-workers-should-know-about-their-own-communities.

20. Edward T. Devine, "Results of the Pittsburgh Survey," *American Journal of Sociology* 14, no. 5 (March 1909): 661. See also Greenwald and Anderson, *Pittsburgh Surveyed*, 17.

21. Devine, "Results of the Pittsburgh Survey," 660.

22. Greenwald and Anderson, *Pittsburgh Surveyed*, 16.

23. John Fabian Witt, "Toward a New History of American Accident Law: Classical Tort Law and the Cooperative First-Party Insurance Movement," *Harvard Law Review* 114 (2001): 690–841. See also Witt, *Patriots and Cosmopolitans*, 167.

24. Jack B. Hood et al., *Workers' Compensation and Employment Protection Law* (New York: West Publishing, 1999), cited by Erin F. Davis, "Love's Labors Lost?: Crystal Eastman's Contribution to Workers' Compensation Reform," Stanford Legal Women's History Project, Fall 2002.

25. Devine, "Results of the Pittsburgh Survey," 662.

26. CE to AFE, September 17, 1907, CEP, box 6, folder 183.

27. CE to AFE, September 18, 1907, CEP, box 6, folder 183.

28. CE to AFE, September 18, 1907, CEP, box 6, folder 183. Note that these quotations are drawn from two letters to Crystal written and postmarked on the same day.

29. Joan Waugh, "Florence Kelley and the Anti-Sweatshop Campaign of 1892–1893," *UCLA Historical Journal* 3 (1982): 21–35.

30. See Kathryn Kish Sklar, *Florence Kelley and the Nation's Work: The Rise of Women's Political Culture, 1830–1900* (New Haven, CT: Yale University Press, 1995).

31. The following year, for example, the NCL spearheaded a campaign for a minimum wage that presaged passage of similar laws in fourteen other states. See "Florence Kelley," Welfare History Project, April 3, 2008, http://socialwelfare.library.vcu.edu/people/kelley-florence/.

32. See "Muller v. State of Oregon," Women Working, 1800–1930, Harvard University Library Open Collections Program, http://ocp.hul.harvard.edu/ww/muller.html.

33. "Muller v. State of Oregon."

34. CE to AFE, September 24, 1907, CEP, box 6, folder 183.

35. CE to AFE, September 18, 1907, CEP, box 6, folder 183.

36. Crystal Eastman, *Work Accidents and the Law* (New York: Russell Sage Foundation, 1910), 55.

37. Eastman, *Work Accidents*, 41–42, 45.

38. Eastman, *Work Accidents*, 50.

39. Eastman, *Work Accidents*, 74.

40. Eastman's tabulations show forty-eight of seventy-one deaths occurred this way, comprising 67 percent of the total. See Eastman, *Work Accidents*, table 7, 51.

41. Eastman, *Work Accidents*, 38.

42. Eastman, *Work Accidents*, 68.

43. Both quotes from CE to AFE, September 18, 1907, CEP, box 6, folder 183.

44. CE to ME, January 7, 1908, CEP, box 6, folder 185.

45. Eastman, *Work Accidents*, 121.

46. Eastman, *Work Accidents*, 223, 226.

47. Eastman, *Work Accidents*, 229.

48. Crystal paraphrased the notion consistently proffered by managers, putting it in quotes: " 'Well, I've been in business for fifteen years and I can tell you one thing right now,' they would say, '95% of our accidents are due to the carelessness of the man who gets hurt. Why, you simply wouldn't believe the things they'll do' " (Eastman, *Work Accidents*, 84).

49. This explanation is particularly indebted to Carl Wedekind, unpublished manuscript, courtesy of Annie Wedekind.

50. This explanation too is particularly indebted to Carl Wedekind, unpublished manuscript, courtesy of Annie Wedekind.

51. Crystal Eastman, "Employer's Liability and Its Relation to Injured Workmen," *Trenton Evening Times*, March 9, 1908.

52. Both quotes from CE to AFE, October 10, 1907, CEP, box 6, folder 183.

53. The full book has been digitized. See Crystal Eastman, *Work Accidents and the Law* (New York: Russell Sage Foundation, 1910), http://www.russellsage.org/sites/all/files/Eastman&Kellog_Work%20Accidents_0.pdf.

54. CE to AFE, April 26, 1908, CEP, box 6, folder 186.

55. CE to ME, July 6, 1908, CEP, box 6, folder 187.

56. CE to AFE, January 18, 1908, CEP, box 6, folder 185.

57. CE to AFE, October 1, 1907, CEP, box 6, folder 183.

58. CE to AFE, October 9, 1907, CEP, box 6, folder 183.

59. James Forbes, "The Reverse Side," in *Wage-Earning Pittsburgh*, ed. Paul Kellogg (New York: Survey Associates, 1914), 366, 384.

60. CE to AFE, December 31, 1907, CEP, box 6, folder 183.

61. CE to AFE, December 31, 1907, CEP, box 6, folder 183.

62. CE to AFE, December 9, 1907, CEP, box 6, folder 183.

63. CE to AFE, January 14, 1908, CEP, box 6, folder 185.

64. CE to AFE, December 31, 1907, CEP, box 6, folder 183.

65. CE to AFE, December 31, 1907, CEP, box 6, folder 183.

66. CE to AFE, January 28, 1908, CEP, box 6, folder 185.

67. CE to AFE, January 28, 1908, CEP, box 6, folder 185.

68. CE to AFE, April 21, 1908, CEP, box 6, folder 186.

69. CE to Paul Kellogg, August 15, 1908, Paul U. Kellogg Papers (hereinafter Kellogg Papers), Social Welfare History Archives, Elmer L. Andersen Library, University of Minnesota, box 42.

70. CE to Paul Kellogg (hereinafter PK), August 15, 1908, Kellogg Papers, box 42.

71. "College Girls Form Club to Promote Exercise for Women," *Evening Telegram*, November 10, 1909.

72. CE to PK, August 15, 1908, Kellogg Papers, box 42.

73. CE to AFE, April 27, 1908, CEP, box 6, folder 186.

74. CE to AFE, December 5, 1906, CEP, box 6, folder 180.

75. Vladimir Simkhovitch (hereinafter VS) to CE, n.d. [Monday afternoon], CEP, box 6, folder 196.

76. CE to AFE, March 6, 1907, CEP, box 6, folder 181.

77. AFE to CE, June 16, 1906, CEP, box 5, folder 152.

78. CE to AFE, September 26, 1906, CEP, box 6, folder 179.

79. CE to AFE, September 30, 1906, CEP, box 6, folder 179.

80. CE to AFE, December 5, 1907, CEP, box 6, folder 183.

81. CE to VS, March 16, 1908, CEP, box 6, folder 196.

82. AFE to CE, March 13, 1906, CEP, box 5, folder 149.

83. Indeed, Mary Simkhovitch spoke glowingly of Crystal in her 1938 memoir, saying, "Crystal Eastman, brilliant suffragist and especially known for her masterly work on the Pittsburgh Survey, and her work on industrial accidents, was one of us." Mary Kingsbury Simkhovitch, *Neighborhood; My Story of Greenwich House* (New York: W. W. Norton, 1938), 149. See also CE to Mary Simkhovitch, May 21, 1912, James Papers, reel 7.

84. CE to AFE, March 30, 1907, CEP, box 6, folder 181.

85. CE to AFE, n.d. [March 1907], CEP, box 6, folder 181.

86. CE to AFE, March 30, 1907, CEP, box 6, folder 181.

87. VS to CE, n.d. [Sunday], CEP, box 6, folder 196.

88. VS to CE, May 20, 1907, CEP, box 6, folder 196.

89. VS to CE, n.d., Tuesday afternoon [presumably May 21, 1907], CEP, box 6, folder 197.

90. CE to ME, June 15, 1909, CEP, box 6, folder 171.

91. VS to CE, n.d., CEP, box 6, folder 197.

92. Paul Kellogg, introduction to *Wage-Earning Pittsburgh*, iii.

93. CE to Irene Osgood, January 20, 1909, Papers of the American Association for Labor Legislation (hereinafter AALL), reel 1.

94. Crystal Eastman, "Employers' Liability, a Criticism Based on Fact," New York Branch of the American Association of Labor Legislation, vol. 1, no. 1, January 1, 1909.

95. CE to John R. Commons, March 17, 1909, AALL, reel 1. The original figures derive from Crystal Eastman, "A Year's Work Accidents and Their Cost," *Charities and the Commons*, March 1909: 1143–74.

96. CE to Commons, May 5, 1909, AALL, reel 2.

97. ME to AFE, October 1, 1909, MEP, box 10.

98. CE to ME, June 15, 1909, CEP, box 6, folder 171.

99. ME to AFE, October 26, 1909, MEP, box 10.

100. Crystal Eastman, "The Philosophy of the Poor" and "Workers under Trial," *Eau Claire Sunday Leader*, January 10, 1909.

101. Crystal Eastman, "The American Way of Distributing Industrial Accident Losses," *American Economic Association Quarterly*, 3rd ser., 10, no. 1. Papers and Discussions of the Twenty-First Annual Meeting, Atlantic City, NJ, December 28–31, 1908 (April 1909), 120.

102. CE to AFE, March 28, 1908, CEP, box 6, folder 186.

103. CE to AFE, March 28, 1909, CEP, box 5, folder 159.

104. Eastman, *Enjoyment of Living*, 297.

105. "Portia Appointed by Governor," *New York Herald*, April 24, 1910.

106. CE to ME, n.d. [1909], CEP, box 6, folder 188.

107. Morris Hillquit and Mary Beard were also among the fifty men and women who attended what Sinclair called a first "lively meeting." See Max Horn, *The Intercollegiate Socialist Society, 1905–1921: Origins of the Modern Student Movement* (Boulder, CO: Westview Press, 1979).

108. "Teacher Pleases Socialists; Dr. Bonn Applauded for Saying 'To Hell with the Government,'" *New York Times*, January 15, 1910, 16.

109. "Would Call on Women to Strike," *Flushing Daily Times*, December 2, 1910.

110. "Votes for Women Week," *New York Times*, March 7, 1910. See also "Women Folk in Limelight," *Syracuse Post Standard*, March 7, 1910; and "Suffragists and Antis Meet. In Annual Hearing before Judiciary Committees in Albany," *Dunkirk Evening Observer*, March 10, 1910.

111. Report of the Employer Liability Commission, New York Historical Society, New York State Legislature, Senate Documents, 1910, vol. 25, no. 38, fiche 5, 5.

112. "Pound Away at Pittsburgh," *New York Tribune*, February 5, 1910, 3.

113. Crystal Eastman, "Work Accidents and Employers' Liability," *Survey*, September 3, 1910.

114. Commission Report, New York Historical Society, New York State Legislature, Senate Documents, 1910, vol. 25, no. 38, fiche 5, 44.

115. "Portia Appointed by the Governor," *New York Herald*, April 24, 1910.

116. Evidentiary Hearing, Employer Liability Commission, New York State Legislature, Senate Documents, 1910, December.

117. See Philip S. Foner, *History of the Labor Movement in the United States*, vol. 2, *From the Founding of the A. F. of L. to the Emergence of American Imperialism* (New York: International Publishers, 1975). See also Ronald L. Filippelli, *Labor Conflict in the United States: An Encyclopedia* (New York: Garland Publishing, 1990); and Erik Loomis, *A History of America in Ten Strikes* (New York: The New Press, 2018).

118. Textile workers across New England received pay raises, and other industries followed. See Christine Stansell, *American Moderns: Bohemian New York and the Creation of a New Century* (New York: Henry Holt, 2000), 180–82 See also Bruce Watson, *Bread and Roses: Mills, Migrants, an. d the Struggle for the American Dream* (New York: Penguin, 2006).

119. Paul Kellogg, "The Field before the Commission on Industrial Relations," *Political Science Quarterly* 28, no. 4 (December 1913): 593.

120. "Woman Gets Federal Place," *Christian Science Monitor*, November 1, 1913. See also "Suffragists Win Another Office," *The Day*, November 15, 1913.

121. Kellogg, "The Field before the Commission on Industrial Relations," 593.

122. Crystal Eastman, "Industrial Relations and the Law," US Commission on Industrial Relations, 1912–1915, unpublished records of the Division of Research and Investigation: Reports, Staff Studies, and Background Research Materials, reel 6.

123. "Proposes to Increase Employers' Liability," *Syracuse Post Standard*, March 22, 1910. This discussion is deeply indebted to Carl Wedekind, unpublished manuscript, courtesy of Annie Wedekind.

124. New York's mandatory workers' compensation scheme set in motion the passage of a predecessor form of the state's current law. See the brief history provided in Mary L. D'Agostino, "New York State's 2007 Workers' Compensation Reform: Success or Failure?," *Albany Law Review* 76, no. 1 (2013): 367–402. See also New York State Workers' Compensation Board, Centennial: Celebrating 100 Years of New York State Workers' Compensation, 2014, http://www.wcb.ny.gov/WCB_Centenial_Booklet.pdf.

125. "Address of Miss Crystal Eastman," Addresses Made at the Fourth Annual Meeting of the Employer Liability Association, October 20, 1910, *Records of the Employer Liability Association 1908–1910*, 6.

126. "Address of Miss Crystal Eastman," 6.

127. *New York Times*, October 21, 1910.

128. See Witt, *Patriots & Cosmopolitans: Hidden Histories of American Law* (Cambridge, MA: Harvard University Press, 2007), 168–69.

129. Eastman, *Enjoyment of Living*, 344, 345–46.

130. Excerpt from Jervis Langdon diary, from private collection of Irene Langdon, Elmira, New York, cited in Carl Wedekind, unpublished manuscript, courtesy of Annie Wedekind.

131. Matthew Mark Silver, *Louis Marshall and the Rise of Jewish Ethnicity in America* (Syracuse, NY: Syracuse University Press, 2013), xi, 207–8.

132. *Ives v. South Buffalo Railroad Company*, 94 N.E. 431 (1911), in *Negligence and Compensation Cases Annotated,* vol. 1, ed. Callaghan and Company 1912 (Chicago: FB & C Limited, 2017), 526.

133. *New York Times*, January 17, 1911.

134. *Ives v. South Buffalo Railroad Company*, 94 N.E. 431 (1911), 528.

135. *Ives v. South Buffalo Railroad*, 529.

136. *Ives v. South Buffalo Railroad*, 536.

137. On May 4, 1911, Wisconsin became the first state to adopt a workers' compensation law that was upheld; it passed constitutional muster because the law

was optional, not mandatory. However, it advanced the framework of workers' compensation because it extended protection to all workers, not just those employed in the most dangerous trades. See John D. Buenker and William Fletcher Thompson, *The History of Wisconsin*, vol. 4, *The Progressive Era, 1893–1914* (Madison: State Historical Society of Wisconsin, 1998), 544–48.

138. CE to ME, April 1, 1911, CEP, box 6, folder 190.
139. Crystal Eastman, "Three Essentials for Accident Prevention," *Annals of the American Academy of Political and Social Science* 38, no. 1 (July 1911): 98–99.

CHAPTER 4

1. CE to ME, November 6, 1911, CEP, box 6, folder 190.
2. See Theodora W. Youmans, "How Wisconsin Women Won the Ballot," *Wisconsin Magazine of History* 5, no. 1 (September 1921): 3–32.
3. Cited in Jo Freeman, "The Rise of Political Women in the Election of 1912," *Women's Political History*, JoFreeman.com, http://www.jofreeman.com/polhistory/1912.htm.
4. Mrs. Smith to Ada James, n.d., Women's Suffrage in Wisconsin, part 2: The Papers of Ada Lois James (hereinafter James Papers), reel 4.
5. Ada James to Belle Case LaFollette, April 19, 1912, James Papers, reel 6.
6. Women in Norway gained equal suffrage in 1913 and in Denmark in 1915.
7. Catherine M. Smith to Ada James, James Papers, reel 4.
8. Anna Howard Shaw to Gwendolin [*sic*] Willis, February 23, 1912, Women's Suffrage in Wisconsin, part 1: Records of the Wisconsin Woman Suffrage Association, 1892–1925, reel 1.
9. Anna Howard Shaw to Ada James, November 9, 1911, James Papers, reel 4.
10. The vote in the senate was sixteen for, four against; the assembly vote was fifty-nine for, twenty-nine against. See "Brief Legislative History of the Woman's Suffrage Movement in Wisconsin thru 1915," Woman Suffrage in Wisconsin, part 1, reel 17.
11. CE to ME, June 29, 1911, CEP, box 6, folder 190.
12. "To Make Labor Safe," *New York Times*, June 5, 1910, 32.
13. "Crystal Eastman, Woman of the Strenuous Life, Is in Madison," *Wisconsin State Journal*, June 17, 1910, 10.
14. Max Eastman, *Enjoyment of Living* (New York: Harper & Brothers, 1948), 341.
15. Eastman, *Enjoyment of Living*, 341.
16. CE to ME, April 3, 1911, CEP, box 6, folder 190.
17. Eastman, *Enjoyment of Living*, 341.
18. CE to ME, n.d. [Summer 1911], CEP, box 6, folder 190.
19. CE to ME, June 29, 1911, CEP, box 6, folder 190.
20. "Mrs. W.J. Benedict Admitted to the Bar," *Milwaukee Journal*, September 28, 1911.

21. CE to ME, October 4, 1911, CEP, box 6, folder 190.

22. CE to ME, October 4, 1911, box 6, folder 190.

23. *Vassar 1903 Class Bulletin*, February 1910, Vassar College Archives.

24. All quotes from CE to ME, June 29, 1911, CEP, box 6, folder 190.

25. CE to ME, July 25, 1911, CEP, box 6, folder 190.

26. CE to ME, July 25, 1911, CEP, box 6, folder 190.

27. CE to ME, June 29, 1911, CEP, box 6, folder 190.

28. CE to ME, July 25, 1911, CEP, box 6, folder 190.

29. CE to ME, November 6, 1911, CEP, box 6, folder 190.

30. CE to ME, June 29, 1911, CEP, box 6, folder 190.

31. CE to ME, June 29, 1911, CEP, box 6, folder 190.

32. CE to ME, October 4, 1911, CEP, box 6, folder 190.

33. CE to ME, June 20, 1912, CEP, box 6, folder 190.

34. All quotes are CE to ME, October 17, 1911, CEP, box 6, folder 190.

35. John Fabian Witt, *Patriots & Cosmopolitans: Hidden Histories in American Law* (Cambridge, MA: Harvard University Press, 2007), 165.

36. CE to Mrs. Julia Lovejoy, April 15, 1912, cited in Sylvia Law, "Crystal Eastman: Organizer for Women's Rights, Peace, and Civil Liberties in the 1910s," *Valparaiso Law Review* 28, no. 4 (1994): 1305–26.

37. CE to Ada James, November 6, 1911, James Papers, reel 4. The Pankhurst visit was especially unusual since many prominent American suffrage leaders had refused to travel to Wisconsin to speak, or had agreed, then reneged. See Law, "Crystal Eastman: Organizer for Women's Rights, Peace, and Civil Liberties in the 1910s."

38. CE to ME, November 6, 1911, CEP, box 6, folder 190.

39. CE to Ada James, November 6, 1911, James Papers, reel 4.

40. CE to ME, November 6, 1911, CEP, box 6, folder 190.

41. Anna Howard Shaw to Ada James, November 17, 1911, James Papers, reel 4.

42. Shaw to James, November 9, 1911, James Papers, reel 4.

43. All quotes from Shaw to James, November 29, 1911, James Papers, reel 4.

44. L. E. S. [Lucy Strong] to Ada James, November 5, 1911, James Papers, reel 4.

45. Theodora Youmans to Ada James, December 11, 1911, James Papers, reel 5. Youmans soon came to like and appreciate Eastman very much, and addressed her concerns about organizational money management directly and professionally with her colleague. "We are spending a good deal of money nowadays," she told her about halfway through the campaign, "and I think we should be pretty careful to have things done regularly and in order." Youmans to CE, April 15, 1912, James Papers, reel 6.

46. Theodora Youmans to Ada James, December 11, 1911, James Papers, reel 5.

47. Anna Howard Shaw to Ada James, March 25, 1912, James Papers, reel 6.

48. Harriet Grimm to Ada James, December 24, 1911, James Papers, reel 5.

49. Ross Wetzsteon, *Republic of Dreams: Greenwich Village: The American Bohemia, 1910–1960* (New York: Simon & Schuster, 2003), 53.

50. Max Eastman, "Confessions of a Suffrage Orator," *The Masses*, November 1915, 9.

51. Ada James to CE, April 13, 1912, Ada James Papers, reel 6.

52. Anna Howard Shaw to Ada James, November 17, 1911, James Papers, reel 4.

53. Theodora Youmans to "Girls," 1912 [?], James Papers, reel 12.

54. Noted in Mari Jo Buhle, *Women and American Socialism: 1870–1920* (Urbana: University of Illinois Press, 1981), 231.

55. "Canvassing for the Cause," *Woman's Journal*, November 16, 1912, 7.

56. Mrs. Smith to Ada James, n.d. [1912], James Papers, reel 4.

57. Theodora Youmans to "Girls" of the PEL, n.d. [1912 ?], James Papers, reel 12.

58. Jane Addams made similar arguments for suffrage in women's magazines, for example. See Jennifer Scanlon, *Inarticulate Longings: The Ladies' Home Journal and the Promises of Consumer Culture* (New York: Routledge, 1995), 109–36.

59. Crystal Eastman Benedict, "The Political Recognition of Women," *Report of the Sixteenth Annual Meeting of the State Bar Association of Indiana*, July 10–11, 1912, 259.

60. Crystal Eastman Benedict, "The Political Recognition of Women," 260.

61. According to a magazine called *Time* (not the currently published magazine of the same name founded by Henry Luce in 1923), "the ignorant and purchasable vote is cast for the side having the most money." *Time*, January 18, 1890, 2.

62. "An Opinion," *Life*, vol. 55, part 2, January 18, 1890, 200.

63. Crystal Eastman Benedict, "The Political Recognition of Women," 262.

64. Crystal Eastman Benedict, "The Political Recognition of Women," 264.

65. Crystal Eastman, "Wisconsin Women Active along Many Lines," *Woman's Journal*, May 4, 1912, 139.

66. PEL form letter "To the Suffragists of _____ County," James Papers, reel 17.

67. CE to Mrs. Thomas, May 13, 1912, James Papers, reel 12.

68. Youmans, "How Wisconsin Women Won the Ballot," 32.

69. See Ama Ansah, "Votes for Women Means Votes for Black Women," National Women's History Museum, August 16, 2018, https://www.womenshistory.org/articles/votes-women-means-votes-black-women. See also Rosalyn Terborg-Penn, *African American Women in the Struggle for the Vote, 1850–1920* (Bloomington: Indiana University Press, 1998)).

70. CE to Ovington, August 1, 1912, James Papers, reel 9. See also Mary White Ovington to CEB, July 25, 1912, James Papers, reel 9; and Mary White Ovington to CEB, July 29, 1912, James Papers, reel 8.

71. CE to Jane Addams, April 22, 1912, Jane Addams Papers, Swarthmore College Peace Collection, Swarthmore College, reel 6.

72. Detailed historical discussions of campaign strategy can be found in Genevieve G. McBride, *On Wisconsin Women: Working for Their Rights from Settlement to Suffrage* (Madison: University of Wisconsin Press, 1993). See also Marilyn Grant, "The 1912 Suffrage Referendum: An Exercise in Political Action," *Wisconsin Magazine of History* 4, no. 2 (1980–81): 116–18.

73. She attracted considerable news coverage wherever she went. See, for example, "Mrs. Benedict to Speak on Lake Front," *Milwaukee Sentinel*, July 13, 1911.

74. *La Crosse Tribune*, August 27, 1912, cited in Kenneth W. Duckett, "Suffragettes on the Stump: Letter from the Political Equality League of Wisconsin, 1912," *Wisconsin Magazine of History* 38, no. 1 (Autumn 1954): 31.

75. Mrs. P. M. Clark to CEB, June 27, 1912, cited in Duckett, "Suffragettes on the Stump," 32.

76. See Youmans, "How Wisconsin Women Won the Ballot," 21.

77. Mrs. Rex McCreery to Ada James, July 23, 1912, James Papers, reel 8.

78. Zona Gale to Ada James, July 5, 1912, James Papers, reel 8.

79. CE to Mrs. C. W. Steele, July 12, 1912, cited in Duckett, "Suffragettes on the Stump," 33.

80. "Things packed in a box and taken to the State Fairs," Woman Suffrage in Wisconsin, reel 1.

81. See, for example, M. Quackenbush to PEL, August 26, 1912, James Papers, reel 9.

82. Ada James to Belle Case LaFollette, April 19, 1912, James Papers, reel 6.

83. "Mrs. LaFollette Is Leader," *New York Times*, September 11, 1912, 6.

84. Ada James to Mrs. B. C. Guden, September 21, 1912, cited in Duckett, "Suffragettes on the Stump," 31.

85. Letter from Crystal Eastman to Jesse Ashley, March 21, 1912, Ada James Papers, cited in Law, "Crystal Eastman," 1312.

86. Crystal Eastman, "Wisconsin Has High Hopes," *Woman's Journal*, September 14, 1912, 290.

87. Theodore Roosevelt, speech at the New York State Agricultural Association, Syracuse, New York, September 7, 1903, http://www.memorablequotations. com/SquareDeal.htm

88. "Wisconsin Women Active," *New York Times*, October 6, 1912, 32.

89. Catherine M. Smith to Ada James, November 26, 1911, James Papers, reel 4.

90. CE to Mrs. Bradley, October 7, 1912, James Papers, reel 11.

91. CE to Mrs. H. C. Bradley, Madison, October 7, 1912, Ada James Papers, reel 11.

92. CE to Attorney General L. H. Bancroft, March 22, 1912; CE to Secretary of State James A. Frear, both in James Papers, reel 6. Additional correspondence March 25, 26, 27, 29, 1912, all in James Papers, reel 6.

93. Both quotes from Frear to CE, March 26, 1912, James Papers, reel 6.

94. Orton & Osborne to CE, August 26, 1912, James Papers, reel 9.

95. James A. Frear to CE, September 6, 1912, pt. 2, reel 10.

96. Mrs. Clara [Bewick] Colby, "Election Tricks in Wisconsin," *Woman's Journal*, November 16, 1912.

97. Crystal Eastman, "Why We Lost in Wisconsin," November 25, 1912, James Papers, reel 12.

98. CE to ME, November 26, 1911, CEP, box 6, folder 190.

99. CE to Fola LaFollette, May 6, 1912, James Papers, reel 6.

100. CE to ME, June 4, 1912, CEP, box 6, folder 191.

101. CE to ME, July 15, 1911, CEP, box 6, folder 190.

102. Ada James to Bela La Follette, December 7, 1912, James Papers, reel 12.

103. "Weds New York Woman: Wallace J. Benedict Surprises Friends by Announcement of Marriage," *Milwaukee Sentinel*, May 6, 1911.

104. Interview with Monica Dehn Wilson, London, England, August 3, 2011.

105. CE to ME, October 17, 1911, CEP, box 6, folder 190.

106. CE to ME, June 20, 1912, CEP, box 6, folder 191.

107. CE to ME, January 15, 1913, CEP, box 6, folder 192.

108. Inez Haynes Irwin, *The Story of the Woman's Party* (New York: Harcourt, Brace & Co., 1921), 13.

109. Crystal Eastman, "Feminism, a Statement Read at the First Feminist Congress in the United States," *Liberator*, May 1919, 37.

110. In the end, at least four states marched in the procession as integrated units: Michigan, Illinois, Delaware, and Eastman's home state of New York.

111. Amelia R. Fry, "Conversations with Alice Paul," Suffragists Oral History Project, University of California, Berkeley, 1976, transcript page 65.

112. *Chicago Tribune,* March 4, 1913, 2, cited by "Marching for the Vote: Remembering the Woman Suffrage Parade of 1913," US Library of Congress, Washington, DC, https://memory.loc.gov/ammem/awhhtml/aw01e/aw01e.html.

113. "Will Ride as Heralds; Four Suffragists to Play Part of Paul Revere," *Washington Post*, January 27, 1913.

114. CE to Lucinda, January 1913, National Woman's Party Papers, US Library of Congress, (hereinafter NWPP), cited in Law, "Crystal Eastman," 1316.

115. CE to ME, n.d. [1913], CEP, box 6, folder 192.

116. CE to ME, n.d. [1913], CEP, box 6, folder 192.

117. Eastman and Addams both spoke at the late session on Friday afternoon, June 20, from 5 to 7:00 p.m. in the convention hall. Addams spoke on "How to Reach the Women Social Workers" and Crystal on "How to Reach the Women of Higher Education." See *Report of the Seventh Congress of the International Woman Suffrage Alliance* (Manchester, UK: Hotspur Press, 1919).

118. *Washington Herald*, June 15, 1913.

119. CE to ME, July 4, 1913, CEP, box 6, folder 192.

120. Crystal Eastman Benedict, "A Comment," *Jus Suffragii*, July 15, 1913, 5.

121. CE to ME, n.d. [1913], CEP, box 6, folder 192.

122. CE to ME, March 29, 1913, CEP, box 6, folder 192.

123. Art Young, *On My Way: Being the Book of Art Young in Text and Picture* (New York: Liveright, 1928), 286.

124. CE to ME, March 29, 1913, CEP, box 6, folder 192.

125. Sandra Adickes discusses Young's description and his later recalibrating of Vorse. See *To Be Young Was Very Heaven: Women in New York before the First World War* (New York: St. Martins, 1997), 47.

126. Mabel Dodge Luhan, *Intimate Memories*, vol. 3, *Movers and Shakers* (New York: Harcourt, Brace & Co., 1936), 143.

127. CE to ME, March 29, 1913, CEP, box 6, folder 192.
128. CE to ME, March 29, 1913, CEP, box 6, folder 192.
129. CE to ME, n.d. [1913]; CE to ME, March 18, 1913; CE to ME, March 29, 1913; CE to ME, May 31, 1913, all in CEP, box 6, folder 192.
130. CE to ME, July 14, 1913, CEP, box 6, folder 192.
131. CE to ME, July 4, 1913, CEP, box 6, folder 192.
132. "New Jersey Women Will Be Honored," *Washington Times*, October 28, 1913; "Plans of Suffrage Hosts Are Complete," *Washington Herald*, January 10, 1914; "Mrs. Benedict Due Today," *Washington Herald*, March 10, 1914.
133. Lucy Burns to Alice Paul, January 15, 1914, NWPP, cited in Mary Walton, *A Woman's Crusade: Alice Paul and the Battle for the Ballot* (New York: St. Martin's, 2010), 94.
134. Mary Beard to Alice Paul, January 8, 1914, NWPP, reel 6.
135. "Talk on Feminism Stirs Crowd," *New York Times*, February 18, 1914; "Feminists Ask for Equal Chance," *New York Times*, February 21, 1914.
136. For more on Heterodoxy, see Judith Schwarz, *Radical Feminists of Heterodoxy: Greenwich Village 1912–1940* (Norwich, VT: New Victoria Publishers, 1986).
137. Crystal Eastman, "What Feminism Means to Me, an Address Delivered at the First Feminist Meeting Held in Cooper Union, New York City, February 1914," *Vassar Miscellany*, June 15, 1915, 670.
138. Testimony of Mrs. Crystal Eastman Benedict of New York City, Hearings before the Committee on the Judiciary, US House of Representatives, Sixty-Third Congress, On Woman Suffrage, March 3, 1914.
139. "Votes or Fight, Women's Threat; Remember the Ides of November, Suffragist Tells House Democrats," *Washington Herald*, March 4, 1914. See also "Mrs. Benedict's Challenge," *Mahoning Dispatch*, March 6, 1914.
140. *Report of the Congressional Union for Woman Suffrage: For the Year 1914 with Outline of Congressional Work during the Preceding Year* (Washington, DC: Model Print Company), 22.
141. CE to Wallace J. Benedict, March 12, 1914, NWPP, reel 8.
142. CE to Lucy Burns, March 19, 1914, NWPP, reel 8.
143. CE to Lucy Burns, March 21, 1914, NWPP, reel 8.
144. CE to Lucy Burns, March 24, 1914, NWPP, reel 8.
145. In April 1914, Eastman was hospitalized in Michigan for several days, and ordered to stay in bed for several weeks. She didn't, so in May, she was ill for a week; in June, she was in the hospital for two weeks back in New York. This was the second bout of ill health to affect Eastman's early career. See Crystal Eastman to Henry R. Seager, February 3, 1911, American Association for Labor Legislation Papers, Kheel Center for Labor-Management Documentation and Archives, Cornell University; scc also Wainwright Commission Staff to J. Mayhew Wainwright, as cited in Witt, *Patriots and Cosmopolitans*, 197.
146. CE to Lucy Burns, April 3, 1914, NWPP, reel 9.
147. CE to Alice Paul, April 9, 1914, NWPP, reel 9.

148. Inez Milholland 1916 speech, Inez Milholland Papers, Schlesinger Library, Harvard University, folder 29, cited by Adickes, *To Be Young Was Very Heaven*, 99.

149. See Aileen S. Kraditor, *The Ideas of the Woman Suffrage Movement: 1890–1920* (New York: W. W. Norton, 1981). See also Eleanor Flexner, *Century of Struggle: The Woman's Rights Movement in the United States*, 3rd rev. ed. (New York: Belknap Press, 1996). For more on Catt, see Jacqueline Van Voris, *Carrie Chapman Catt: A Public Life* (New York: The Feminist Press, 1996).

150. "Newport's Conference Politically Momentous," *New York Herald-Tribune*, September 6, 1914.

151. "Newport's Conference Politically Momentous."

152. "Clayton Act Bars Way to Freedom of Labor," *Evening Star*, May 16, 1915. See also "Man-Politician Taken to Task," *Washington Herald*, June 6, 1915.

153. CE to Alice Paul, September 1914, NWPP, reel 12.

154. Brenda Ueland, *Me* (St. Paul: Schubert Club, 1983), 149.

155. Ueland, *Me*, 148–49.

156. Ueland, *Me,* 161.

157. "'Alimony Relic of Dark Ages,' Says Mrs. Eastman," *Gazette-Telegraph*, March 12, 1916. See also "Mrs. Benedict Gives Feminist Platform," *Washington Herald*, February 19, 1918.

158. "Suffragist Tires of Marital Link," *Milwaukee Sentinel*, October 27, 1915. Her statement was widely discussed in the press, including *Day Book*, February 19, 1916; *New York Tribune*, March 1, 1916; *New York Evening World*, March 1, 1916; and *Ogden Standard*, March 3, 1916. Later the phrase became "a link, not a chain," in *New York Tribune*, December 14, 1919. Crystal herself also restated the case in the later years, for example, in the *Washington Herald*, February 19, 1918.

159. Ueland, *Me*, 162.

160. "Crystal Eastman Married," *New York Times*, November 14, 1916.

161. By summer of 1921, newspapers across the country announced that Crystal was on the executive board of the Lucy Stone League, a group founded to lobby for women to be able to keep their maiden names. Also on the board were friends and colleagues, including Zona Gale, Charlotte Perkins Gilman, Susan Glaspell, Fola La Follette, and Ruth Pickering; Katherine Anthony was also involved. For more on "Lucy Stoners," see Alice Stone Blackwell's 1930 biography *Lucy Stone: Pioneer of Woman's Rights* (Charlottesville: University Press of Virginia, 2001). See also Sally G. McMillen, *Lucy Stone: An Unapologetic Life* (New York: Oxford University Press, 2015).

162. Crystal Eastman Benedict, "Millions of Unpaid Wives," *Washington Herald*, May 26, 1915.

CHAPTER 5

1. "Women Pacifists Demand Action," *New York Times*, November 16, 1915. Judging from the quoted material in press accounts, Eastman drew the bulk of this speech

from her article "A Platform of Real Preparedness," published in the *Survey* three days before.

2. Initially, Italy did not enter the war because of an earlier defensive pact with Germany and Austria. However, as more nations entered, reorganizing alliances, Italy joined on the side of the Allies.

3. See Adam Hochschild, *To End All Wars: A Story of Loyalty and Rebellion, 1914–1918* (Boston and New York: Houghton Mifflin Harcourt, 2011), 142.

4. Just four days after entering the conflict, the British Parliament passed the Defense of the Realm Act—with no debate. The legislation gave the government new powers to seize economic resources, including land and buildings, for the war effort. It overrode civil liberties, allowing the British government to search private property and arrest or imprison people, all without a warrant. And information deemed critical of government policy, or likely to excite resistance to the war effort, could now be censored more or less at will. See Hochschild, *To End All Wars*, 148.

5. Figures about casualties vary. Adam Hochschild writes that the Allies alone saw over two hundred thousand men killed and wounded. See *To End All Wars*, 156. My totals are taken from Richard Stowers, *Bloody Gallipoli* (2005), as reported by the government of New Zealand, https://nzhistory.govt.nz/media/interactive/gallipoli-casualties-country.

6. Numerous sources give the number of American deaths as 124. Michael Kazin cites "more than 120," noting a number of sources that dispute the figure. See *A War against War: The American Fight for Peace, 1914–1918* (New York: Simon & Schuster, 2017), 59.

7. "Women Pacifists Demand Action," *New York Times*, November 16, 1915.

8. "To Promote Preparedness for Peace," *Survey*, January 9, 1915, 394–95. PK to George Nasmyth, September 22, 1914, Addams Papers, cited by Donald Johnson, "American Civil Liberties Union: 1914–1924" (PhD diss., Columbia University, Department of History, 1960), 3.

9. C. Roland Marchand, *The American Peace Movement and Social Reform 1898–1918* (Princeton, NJ: Princeton University Press, 1972), 8–10.

10. Marchand, *The American Peace Movement*, 8–10.

11. Marchand, *The American Peace Movement*, 8–10. See also Kazin, *War against War*, 5–8.

12. Marchand, *The American Peace Movement*, 8–10. See also Kazin, *War against War*, 5–8.

13. The coinage "new peace movement" comes from William I. Hull, "The New Peace Movement: A Series of Addresses Delivered in 1908–09: How Far Has the World Progressed Toward Peace?" (Philadelphia: Sunday School Times Company, 1911), William Isaac Hull Papers, Swarthmore College Peace Collection, Swarthmore College, Swarthmore, Pennsylvania.

14. See Marchand, *The American Peace Movement*, 263.

15. Jane Addams, *Newer Ideals of Peace: The Moral Substitutes for War* (Chester, NY: Anza Publishing, 2005), 11.

16. Kazin, *War against War*, 11.

17. Eastman spoke alongside the legendary civil rights attorney Clarence Darrow at this hearing. "Says Vote Will Bring New Eden," *Washington Herald*, May 18, 1915.

18. "'Votes for Women' First Words of Miss Liberty by the Sea," *New York Tribune*, July 6, 1915, 5.

19. "Suffrage Debaters Picked," *The Sun*, October 28, 1915, 5.

20. "Saleswoman Is Auto Rage," *Los Angeles Times*, February 23, 1915.

21. "Women to Conquer Ways to Salaries," *New York Times*, March 5, 1915.

22. Louise Knight, *Jane Addams: Spirit in Action* (New York: W. W. Norton, 2010), 189.

23. CE, "Memorandum," June 14, 1917, Records of the American Union against Militarism, (hereinafter AUAM Records), reel 1.

24. Max Eastman, *Enjoyment of Living* (New York: Harper & Brothers, 1948), 129. Annis wrote a stinging critique of masculinity and militarism, for example, in a letter to her daughter from Berlin. CE to AFE, November 23, 1901, CEP, box 6, folder 174.

25. William I. Hull, *The New Peace Movement* (Boston: World Peace Foundation, 1912), vi.

26. Bryant was quoting a leading pacifist in the piece. See Louise Bryant, "The Pacifists at 70 Fifth Avenue," *New York Tribune*, March 18, 1917.

27. Anne Wiltsher writes that Crystal, Doty, and Rauh together handled publicity for the Carnegie Hall event, resulting in the rapid formation of Woman's Peace Party branches in Boston and Philadelphia. See *Most Dangerous Women: Feminist Peace Campaigners of the Great War* (London: Pandora, 1985), 51.

28. Emmeline Pethick-Lawrence, "Union of Women for Constructive Peace," *Survey*, December 5, 1914, 230. See also Pethick-Lawrence, "Motherhood and War," *Harper's Weekly*, December 5, 1914, 542.

29. Crystal Eastman, "British Women Fire First Gun in Their Second Suffrage Battle," *Equal Rights*, February 27, 1926.

30. See Wiltsher, *Most Dangerous Women*. See also Harriet Hyman Alonso, *Peace as a Woman's Issue: A History of the U.S. Peace Movement for World Peace and Women's Rights* (Syracuse, NY: Syracuse University Press, 1993).

31. Cited in David S. Patterson, *Search for Negotiated Peace: Women's Activism and Citizen Diplomacy* (New York: Routledge, 2008), 42.

32. Charlotte Perkins Gilman, *The Man-Made World* (New York: Cosimo Classics, 2007), 90. See also "Masculinism at Its Worst," *Forerunner*, October 1914, 257–58.

33. See Michael Kimmel, *Manhood in America: A Cultural History* (New York: Oxford University Press, 2016).

34. Pethick-Lawrence, "Union of Women for Constructive Peace," 230.

35. Anna Garlin Spencer, Preamble to Woman's Peace Party Platform, in Mary Louise Degen, *The History of the Woman's Peace Party* (New York: Burt Franklin Reprints, 1974), 41. See also "Women for Peace: The Organization of the First Woman's Peace Party," *The Independent*, January 25, 1915, 120–24.

36. Pethick-Lawrence, "Motherhood and War," 542.

37. "Protesting Women March in Mourning," *New York Times*, August 30, 1914, 11.

38. Spencer, Preamble to the Woman's Peace Party Platform, 40.

39. Emmeline Pethick-Lawrence notes Crystal's immediate founding and naming of the organization in *My Part in Changing the World* (London: Hyperion Press, 1938), 309. Harriet Hyman Alonso characterizes it as I have in *Peace as a Women's Issue*, 59.

40. Pethick-Lawrence, *My Part in Changing the World*, 308–9; Pethick-Lawrence, "Women and War," *Suffragist*, November 21, 1914, 2.

41. Addams to Catt, December 14, 1914, NAWSA Correspondence, box 1, cited in Barbara Jean Steinson, "Female Activism in World War I: The American Women's Peace, Suffrage, Preparedness, and Relief Movements, 1914–1919" (PhD diss., Department of History, University of Michigan, 1977), 1:25.

42. Alonso, *Peace as a Women's Issue*, 62.

43. Jane Addams to Lucia Ames Mead, December 28, 1914, cited in Alonso, *Peace as a Women's Issue*, 62.

44. CE to Jane Addams, June 28, 1917, Jane Addams Papers, reel 10.

45. CE to Jane Addams, June 28, 1917, Jane Addams Papers, reel 10.

46. See Degen, *The History of the Woman's Peace Party*, 40–42.

47. "Use Belgium's Fate as Warning to U.S.," *New York Times*, June 15, 1915.

48. Alonso, *Peace as a Women's Issue*, 63.

49. "Speeches from the Mass Meeting, January 10, 1915," Woman's Peace Party Papers (hereinafter WPPP), Swarthmore College Peace Collection, Swarthmore College, Swarthmore, Pennsylvania, box 1, folder 6.

50. See Walter I. Trattnor, "Julia Grace Wales and the Wisconsin Plan for Peace," *Wisconsin Magazine of History* 44 (1961): 204–6.

51. Indeed, a number of the Woman's Peace Party's earlier resolutions, including the formula for how the war should end, passed at The Hague in 1915, were remarkably similar to the ideas of Wilson's later Fourteen Points. See Alonso, *Peace as a Women's Issue*, 78.

52. On Ford, see Steven Watts, *The People's Tycoon: Henry Ford and the American Century* (New York: Vintage, 2006).

53. CE to Addams, November 27, 1915; CE to Addams, December 3, 1915, both in WPPP, reel 12.8.

54. A thorough and detailed account of efforts for a mediated peace is Patterson, *Search for Negotiated Peace*.

55. Crystal Eastman, "'Now I Dare to Do It': An Interview with Dr. Aletta Jacobs, Who Called the Woman's Peace Congress at The Hague," *Survey*, October 9, 1915.

56. *New York Times*, April 13, 1915.

57. The "hysterical women" is from the *Globe*; "folly" from *Sunday Pictorial*. Both are cited in Wiltsher, *Most Dangerous Women*, 88. The congress program puts attendance at 1,500 people, but several later tallies come to a total of 1,136. The

complete program can be found in WPPP, reel 12.3. See also Jane Addams, Emily G. Balch, and Alice Hamilton, *Women at The Hague: The International Congress of Women and Its Results*, ed. Harriet Hyman Alonso (Chicago: University of Illinois Press, 2003).

58. CE to Alice Lewisohn, February 21, 1916, Swarthmore College Peace Collection, cited in Blanche Wiesen Cook, ed., *Toward the Great Change: Crystal and Max Eastman on Feminism, Antimilitarism and Revolution* (New York: Garland Publishing, 1976), 23.

59. Eastman, " 'Now I Dare to Do It.' "

60. See Kenneth E. Miller, *From Progressive to New Dealer: Frederic C. Howe and American Liberalism* (University Park, PA: Penn State University Press, 2010).

61. Lillian Wald to William Dean Howells, September 22, 1914, cited in Johnson, "American Civil Liberties Union," 3.

62. See Marjorie N. Feld, *Lillian Wald: A Biography* (Chapel Hill: University of North Carolina Press, 2008).

63. Lee K. Frankel, "An Insurance Company Seeks to Improve Individual and Public Health," *Modern Hospital* 111, no. 5 (November 1914): 283–88. Just before the end of World War II, in 1944, it officially became an independent entity, the Visiting Nurse Service of New York.

64. See Doris Groshen Daniels, *Always a Sister: The Feminism of Lillian D. Wald* (New York: Feminist Press, 1995), 52.

65. The mission statement is quoted in Daniels, *Always a Sister*, 99.

66. Stella Franklin to CE, July 23, 1912, James Papers, reel 8.

67. Wald continued to view the league as valuable, although in her memoir, *Windows on Henry Street*, she wrote that she herself had added no value to the league. See Daniels, *Always a Sister*, 99–100.

68. Cited in Robert F. Wesser, *Charles Evans Hughes: Politics and Reform in New York 1905–1910* (Ithaca, NY: Cornell University Press, 2009), 326.

69. A brief summary is Sidney Milkis, "Theodore Roosevelt: Campaigns and Elections," The Miller Center, University of Virginia, 2017, https://millercenter.org/president/roosevelt/campaigns-and-elections.

70. See Daniels, *Always a Sister*, 100–101.

71. Crystal Eastman, "To Make War Unthinkable," Letter to the Editor, *New Republic*, July 24, 1915.

72. *Woman's Peace Party of New York City: First Annual Report* (New York [?]: Woman's Peace Party, 1916), 4.

73. See *Woman's Peace Party of New York City: First Annual Report*.

74. Crystal Eastman, "Why Study War and Peace," *New York Tribune*, October 17, 1915.

75. Henry Street Group Minutes, November 15, 24, 29, 1915, Paul Kellogg Papers, Social Welfare History Archives, University of Minnesota, box 32.

76. All quotes from Crystal Eastman, "A Platform of Real Preparedness," *Survey*, November 13, 1915. The Pan-American Union, an organization formed in 1890, worked for cooperation among the countries of the Americas to reach agreements

on both juridical and commercial problems. In 1948, it became the Organization of American States.

77. Eastman, "A Platform of Real Preparedness."

78. See Arthur S. Link, *Wilson: The Struggle for Neutrality, 1914–15* (Princeton, NJ: Princeton University Press, 1960).

79. AUAM Minutes, February 26, 1916, AUAM Records, reel 10.1.

80. US House of Representatives, Committee on Military Affairs, Hearings on H.R. 12766, To Increase the Military Establishment of the United States, Sixty-Fourth Congress, First Session, January 6–February 11, 1916.

81. Woodrow Wilson, "Speech before the Manhattan Club," in *The New Democracy: Presidential Messages, Addresses and Other Papers*, ed. Ray Stannard Baker and William E. Dodd (New York: Harper & Brothers, 1926), 384–92, cited in Blanche Wiesen Cook, "Woodrow Wilson and the Antimilitarists 1914–1917" (PhD diss., Johns Hopkins University, Department of History, 1980), 35.

82. "Statement Concerning the Anti-Militarism Committee," December 1915, AUAM Records, reel 10.1.

83. "Typescript of AUAM History," reel 1. A few of these original signatories resigned within a short time, notably Florence Kelley, who left the organization as of March 20, 1916, less than three weeks after Crystal became executive secretary of the group. AUAM Minutes, March 20, 1916, AUAM Records, reel 10.1.

84. Crystal Eastman, "Limitation of Armaments," *Year Book of the Woman's Peace Party, The Section for the United States of the International Committee of Women for Permanent Peace*, 1916, 16–17.

85. Eastman, "A Platform of Real Preparedness." She used the metaphor of the burning roof frequently in press interviews, and lengthy excerpts of this article were also published in the mainstream press, such as, for example, in the *New York Times*, November 16, 1915.

86. Eastman, "A Platform of Real Preparedness."

87. Eastman, "Limitation of Armaments."

88. "Militarism Opposed by S. Fraser Langford," *Sacramental Union*, November 22, 1915.

89. Commission for Enduring Peace, Hearings before the Committee on Foreign Affairs, US House of Representatives, Sixty-Fourth Congress, First Session, January 11, 1916, 9.

90. Commission for Enduring Peace, Hearings before the Committee on Foreign Affairs, US House of Representatives, Sixty-Fourth Congress, First Session, January 11, 1916, 9.

91. Commission for Enduring Peace, Hearings before the Committee on Foreign Affairs, US House of Representatives, Sixty-Fourth Congress, First Session, January 11, 1916, 10.

92. Minutes of the Anti-Preparedness Committee, January 24, 1916, AUAM Records, reel 10.1.

93. Mass Meeting at Cooper Union announcement, January 31, 1916, Mary Ware Dennett Papers, Schlesinger Library, reel 32. Despite their efforts, the measures passed and were approved by Governor Whitman in May 1916. The WPP-NYC planned a state-wide campaign for repeal but gained little momentum on the question.

94. Minutes of Anti-Preparedness Committee, January 31, 1916, AUAM Records, reel 10.1. See also *New York Times*, February 23, 1916.

95. Margaret Lane to Mrs. William I. Thomas, February 25, 1916, WPPP, reel 12.4.

96. Press release, May 15, 1916, WPPP, cited in Alonso, *Peace as a Woman's Issue*, 70.

97. G. Peter Winnington, *Walter Fuller: The Man Who Had Ideas* (London: Letterworth Press, 2014), 82.

98. *New York Sun*, October 31, 1915, cited in Winnington, *Walter Fuller*, 154.

99. Jane Addams, *Twenty Years at Hull House*, 122, cited in Winnington, *Walter Fuller*, 119.

100. Walter Fuller (hereinafter WF) to Riss, mid-September 1915, cited in Winnington, *Walter Fuller*, 143.

101. WF to Riss "Dear Girl," October 1916, cited in Winnington, *Walter Fuller*, 144.

102. WF to Riss, mid-September 1915, cited in Winnington, *Walter Fuller*, 143.

103. WF to Riss, mid-September 1915, cited in Winnington, *Walter Fuller*, 143.

104. WF to Riss, mid-September 1915, cited in Winnington, *Walter Fuller*, 144.

105. WF to Riss, mid-September 1915, and Walter Fuller to sisters, September 22, 1915, cited together in Winnington, *Walter Fuller*, 150.

106. WF to Riss, mid-September 1915, cited in G. Peter Winnington, *Walter Fuller*, 144, 150.

107. Edward Bernays, widely acknowledged as the founder of American public relations, touted film's ability to "establish a reciprocal understanding" between producers and viewers. In discussing the "mechanics of propaganda" in his seminal 1928 book, *Propaganda*, he further hails the motion picture as "the greatest conveyor of public opinion today." Bernays, *Propaganda* (New York: Horace Liveright, 1928), 156, available at https://www.voltairenet.org/IMG/pdf/Bernays_Propaganda_in_english_.pdf.

108. The critic James Agee quoted Griffith about *Birth of a Nation* that "Above all . . . I am trying to make you see," cited in Richard Corliss, "D.W. Griffith's *The Birth of a Nation* 100 Years Later: Still Great, Still Shameful," *Time*, March 3, 2015, http://time.com/3729807/d-w-griffiths-the-birth-of-a-nation-10/.

109. See Leslie Midkiff DeBauche, *Reel Patriotism: The Movies and World War I* (Madison: University of Wisconsin Press, 1997). See also Gordon Thomas, "A Film Divided against Itself: D. W. Griffith's *Birth of a Nation* (1915)," *Bright Lights Film Journal*, June 26, 2016, http://brightlightsfilm.com/film-divided-d-w-griffiths-birth-nation-1915/#.WZRzhFWGMdU.

110. The intertitle quote is cited in Corliss, "D.W. Griffith's *The Birth of a Nation* 100 Years Later."

111. Available in AUAM Records, reel 10.2.

112. See "Use Belgium's Fate as Warning to U.S." See also Manuel Franz, "Preparedness Revisited: Civilian Societies and the Campaign for American Defense, 1914–1920," *Journal of the Gilded Age and Progressive Era* 17, no. 4 (2018): 663–76.

113. "Preparedness Is Favored," *New York Times*, February 23, 1916.

114. Minutes of the Anti-Preparedness Committee, February 14, 1916, AUAM Records, reel 10.1.

115. WF to Riss, mid-September 1915, cited in Winnington, *Walter Fuller*, 150.

116. At the time, half of all American incomes fell between $3,000 and $10,000 per year. "Statistics of Income, Compiled from the Returns of 1916," Treasury Department, United States Internal Revenue, Document number 2817 (Washington, DC: Government Printing Office, 1918), available at https://www.irs.gov/pub/irs-soi/16soirepar.pdf.

117. "Secretary's Report," March 20, 1916, AUAM Records, reel 10.1.

118. WF to Riss, mid-September 1915, cited in Winnington, *Walter Fuller*, 143–44.

119. WF to Riss, ca. December 5, 1915, cited in Winnington, *Walter Fuller*, 157.

120. Fuller's extensive plan is published in Winnington, *Walter Fuller*, 146–48.

121. See AUAM Minutes, February 14, 1916, AUAM Records, reel 1. See also Winnington, *Walter Fuller*, 172.

122. See Winnington, *Walter Fuller*, 171.

123. Statement to the Press, May 7, 1916, AUAM Records, reel 10.1.

124. Memo from CE to Committee Members, March 4, 1916, AUAM Records, reel 10.1. Memo, "Hearing before the President," n.d., AUAM Records, reel 10.2.

125. Max Eastman, *Enjoyment of Living*, 546.

126. "President on Defenses: In Speech to Antimilitarists Says Force Must Back Up Opinion," *New York Times,* May 9, 1916.

127. Press Release, May 9, 1916, AUAM Records, reel 10.2.

128. AUAM Minutes, May 8, 1916, AUAM Records, reel 10.1.

129. Press Release, May 9, 1916, AUAM Records, reel 10.2.

130. "Suggestions for 1916–1917," October 1916, AUAM Records, reel 10.2.

131. AUAM Bulletin #57, August 25, 1916, AUAM Records, reel 10.2.

132. AUAM Minutes, October 24, 1916, AUAM Records, reel 10.1.

133. Charles Hallinan to CE, October 23, 1916, Lillian Wald Papers (hereinafter LWP), Columbia University Library, New York, New York, box 88.

134. *New York Times*, June 30, 1916. Different reports and subsequent scholarly treatments supply different figures for the numbers killed and captured.

135. For an accessible introduction, see Frank McLynn, *Villa and Zapata: A History of the Mexican Revolution* (New York: Basic Books, 2002). See also the photographic account by Anita Brenner, *The Wind That Swept Mexico: The Story of the Mexican Revolution of 1910–1942* (Austin: University of Texas Press, 1984).

136. *New York Tribune*, June 22, 1916, 1. See also "American Cavalry Ambushed by Mexican Troops. Scores, Including a Mexican General, Were Reported Slain," *New York Times*, June 22, 1916, 3.

137. Lillian Wald, *Windows on Henry Street* (Boston: Little Brown, 1934), 293.

138. Bulletin 53, July 15, 1916, AUAM Records, reel 10.2.

139. "Call for Mediation from Peace Union," *New York Times*, June 24, 1916.

140. Minutes of the Special Conference, June 21, 1916, at 4:30 p.m., AUAM Records, reel 10.1.

141. Cable to Mexico from Margaret Lane, June 1916, WPPP, cited in Alonso, *Peace as a Woman's Issue*, 72. The WPP of Boston, which rarely agreed with the New York City group, also sent a telegram of protest to Wilson.

142. "Suggestions for 1916–1917," AUAM Records, reel 10.2.

143. Paul Kellogg, "Hostages of Appeasement," Speech before Social Workers' Committee, Spanish Refugee Campaign, February 1, 1940, 3, courtesy of Rebecca Young.

144. "Some Inside Information on the Mexican Crisis," Bulletin #53, July 15, 1916, AUAM Records, reel 10.2.

145. See "Bryan Asked to Try to Prevent War," *Washington Times*, June 23, 1916.

146. Bulletin #53, July 15, 1916, AUAM Records, reel 10.2.

147. Kellogg, "Hostages of Appeasement," 2.

148. "House Approves Draft of Militia," *New York Times*, June 24, 1916.

149. AUAM Minutes, June 26, 1916, AUAM Records, reel 10.1.

150. "Some Inside Information on the Mexican Crisis," Bulletin 53, July 15, 1916, AUAM Records, reel 10.2.

151. "Some Inside Information on the Mexican Crisis."

152. "Catastrophe in War with Mexico," *New York Times*, July 6, 1916. Pinchot agreed to pay for one ad; Wald and Lewisohn split the cost of the other. AUAM Minutes, June 25, 1916, AUAM Records, reel 1.

153. Crystal Eastman, *The Mexican-American League* (Mexican-American Peace Committee of the AUAM), 1916.

154. Kellogg, "Hostages of Appeasement," 5.

155. Eastman, *Love and Revolution*, 28.

156. "Suggestions to the AUAM for 1916–17," AUAM Records, reel 10.2.

157. Crystal Eastman, "War and Peace," *Survey*, December 30, 1916, 363.

CHAPTER 6

1. Eleanor Karsten, Office Secretary to Jane Addams, June 1, 1916, WPPP, reel 12.1.

2. "Suffrage Plank Sought by Women," *Sacramento Union*, June 6, 1916.

3. CE to Lillian Wald, July 14, 1916, LWP, box 88.

4. Margaret Lane told the papers that speeches against preparedness would be in progress all day at the store. Unidentified press clipping, "Banner to Oppose Views of Paraders," WPPP, reel 12.3.

5. "Women Will Spend a Big Party Fund," *Washington Times*, July 18, 1916, 14.

6. "Republican Women Aid Whole Ticket," *New York Times*, August 5, 1916, 4.

7. "Women Ask Fund to Beat Wilson," *New York Tribune*, August 30, 1916, 7. See also "Suffrage Fund Increasing," *New York Times*, August 30, 1916, 9.

8. CE to ME, November 8, 1900, CEP, box 5, folder 118.

9. CE to ME, June 4, 1912, CEP, box 6, folder 191. No extant evidence suggests Crystal considered the Socialist ticket of Eugene Debs and Emil Seidel.

10. All quotes from Woodrow Wilson, Speech of Acceptance, September 2, 1916, accessed via http://millercenter.org/president/wilson/speeches/speech-3795.

11. AUAM Minutes, n.d. [September 7, 1916], AUAM Records, reel 1.

12. Blanche Wiesen Cook, "Woodrow Wilson and the Antimilitarists" (PhD diss., Johns Hopkins University, Department of History, 1980), 165.

13. CE to Amos Pinchot, February 3, 1916, Amos Pinchot Papers, US Library of Congress, box 24.

14. AUAM Minutes, October 1916, AUAM Records, reel 1.

15. Quoted in Blanche Wiesen Cook, ed., *Crystal Eastman on Women and Revolution* (New York: Oxford University Press, 1978), 17.

16. Michael Kazin, *A War against War: The American Fight for Peace 1914–1918* (New York: Simon & Schuster, 2017), 124–25.

17. WF to Dorothy Fuller, October 5, 1915, cited in Winnington, *Walter Fuller*, 144.

18. Winnington, *Walter Fuller*, 189.

19. Margaret Lane to WPP-NYC, WPPP, reel 12.20.

20. CE to Jane Addams, November 14, 1916, Jane Addams Papers, reel 10.

21. "Peace Cry to Greet 1917," *New York Herald*, December 31, 1916, 4.

22. Cited in Linda J. Lumsden, *Inez: The Life & Times of Inez Milholland* (Bloomington: Indiana University Press, 2004), 172.

23. Quotation from *The Suffragist* is cited in Blanche Wiesen Cook, "Crystal Eastman," in *Portraits of American Women: From Settlement to the Present*, ed. G. J. Barker-Benfied and Catherine Clinton (New York: Oxford University Press, 1998), 415.

24. Walton, *A Woman's Crusade*, 148.

25. See Walton, *A Woman's Crusade*, 171–72.

26. CE and ME to Lucy Burns, June 21, 1917, NWPP, reel 44. The banner protest is described by Walton, *A Woman's Crusade*, 172.

27. "'Neutral Conference' Now Moves for Peace," *New York Times*, January 4, 1917, 3.

28. Telegram to President Wilson from the American Union Against Militarism, February 1, 1917, Records of the AUAM, reel 2.

29. Minutes, February 5, 1916, AUAM Records, reel 1.

30. "Pacifists Demand War Referendum," *New York Times,* February 5, 1917, 7.

31. Telegrams, February 6, 1917, WPPP, reel 12.4.

32. Telegram, February 9, 1917, 3:13 a.m., WPPP, reel 12.4.

33. CE to AUAM Members, March 1, 1917, AUAM Records, reel 1.

34. Telegram, February 9, 1917, 3:13 a.m., WPPP, reel 12.4.

35. Goodier and Pastorello, *Women Will Vote*, 155.

36. "Pilgrims for Peace to Visit Congress," *New York Times*, February 9, 1917, 11. See also "War Offer Causes War for the Suffs," *New York Herald*, February 9, 1917, 14.

37. CE to Mrs. Leigh French, February 28, 1917, cited in June Sochen, *The New Woman: Feminism in Greenwich Village, 1910–1920* (New York: Quadrangle Books, 1972), 105.

38. Reported in letter from Margaret Lane to Mrs. Louis F. Post, March 23, 1917, WPPP, reel 12.4. Post replied to Lane that Crystal's letter to Catt was excellent and that she hopes by now they have received a reply from her. Mrs. Post to Margaret Lane, March 27, 1917, WPPP, reel 12.4.

39. Kellogg to Addams, February 9, 1917, Addams Papers, cited in Donald Johnson, "American Civil Liberties Union: 1914–1924" (PhD diss., Columbia University, Department of History, 1960), 16. AUAM Minutes, February 1917, June 25, 1917, AUAM Records, reel 1. See also Oswald Garrison Villard, *Fighting Years: Memoirs of a Liberal Editor* (New York: Harcourt, Brace and Co., 1939), 323.

40. Paul L. Murphy, *World War I and the Origin of Civil Liberties in the United States* (New York: W. W. Norton, 1975), 55.

41. Carleton J. H. Hayes, "Which? War without a Purpose? Or Armed Neutrality with a Purpose?," *Survey*, February 10, 1917, 537. Cited in Kazin, *A War against War*, 162.

42. Telegram from American Union against Militarism to Mrs. Malcolm Forbes, Boston, February 5, 1917, AUAM Records, reel 1. "Pacifists Approve President's Action," *New York Times*, February 27, 1917.

43. AUAM Minutes, February 14, 1916, AUAM Records, reel 1.

44. "Suggestions Regarding a Policy of Non-Intercourse with Germany," n.d. [February 1917], AUAM Records, reel 1.

45. AUAM Minutes, February 20, 1916, AUAM Records, reel 1.

46. See *Four Lights*, March 10, 1917, cited in Steinson, "Female Activism in World War I," 225.

47. CE, AUAM Minutes, February 27, 1917, AUAM Records, reel 1.

48. See James Peter Warbasse, "Are We for Armed Neutrality?," reprinted from the *New York Evening Post* of February 10, 1917, by the Committee for Democratic Control, March 1, 1917, Mary Ware Dennett Papers, reel 33.

49. The talking points were discussed in detail by the executive committee at the February 27, 1917, meeting. AUAM Minutes, AUAM Records, reel 1.

50. Max Eastman, "Statement Made to the President," February 28, 1917, AUAM Records, reel 1. Kellogg's "Statement to the President" is also preserved in AUAM Records, reel 1.

51. Jane Addams, *Peace and Bread in Time of War* (Urbana: University of Illinois Press, 2002), 38.

CHAPTER 7

1. Woodrow Wilson, "War Message," delivered to Congress April 2, 1917, accessed via https://wwi.lib.byu.edu/index.php/Wilson's_War_Message_to_Congress.

2. Julian F. Jaffe, *Crusade against Radicalism: New York during the Red Scare 1914–1924* (Port Washington, NY: Kennikat Press, 1972), 67–69.

3. All quotations by George Creel cited in John Hollitz, *Contending Voices: Biographical Explorations of the American Past*, vol. 2, *Since 1865* (Belmont, CA: Wadsworth Publishing, 2010), 97.

4. George Creel, *How We Advertised America: The First Telling of the Amazing Story of the Committee on Public Information That Carried the Gospel of Americanism to Every Corner of the Globe* (New York: Harper and Brothers, 1920), 4.

5. Margaret Lane to WPP-NYC board, April 14, 1917. See also WPP-NYC press release, April 18, 1917, WPPP, reel 12.13.

6. Lillian Wald and others to Woodrow Wilson, April 16, 1917, cited in John A. Thompson, *Reformers and War: Progressive Publicists and the First World War* (New York: Cambridge University Press, 2003), 223.

7. Thompson, *Reformers and War*, 223–24.

8. Woodrow Wilson to Max Eastman, September 18, 1917, cited in Samuel Walker, *In Defense of American Liberties: A History of the ACLU* (Carbondale: Southern Illinois University Press, 1990), 12.

9. Paul L. Murphy, *World War I and the Origin of Civil Liberties in the United States* (New York: W. W. Norton, 1979), 71.

10. Albert S. Burleson, quoted in Walker, *In Defense of American Liberties*, 14.

11. See Witt, *Patriots & Cosmopolitans*, 191.

12. For an organizational chart of the standard league office nationwide, see Bill Mills, *The League: The True Story of Average Americans on the Hunt for WWI Spies* (New York: Skyhorse Publishing, 2013), 27–28.

13. Mills, *The League*, 15.

14. Walker, *In Defense of American Liberties*, 15.

15. For more on the APL, see Joan Jensen, *The Price of Vigilance* (Chicago: Rand McNally, 1968).

16. *Four Lights*, January 27, 1917.

17. Addams then asked the New York branch to be exceptionally careful to advertise itself as the source of its actions and utterances, so nothing would be confused with the national organization. CE to Jane Addams, January 27, 1916; Addams to CE, January 30, 1917, WPPP, reel 12.5. See also Alice Thatcher Post to Jane Addams, February 3, 1917, WPPP, reel 12.9.

18. See Floyd Dell, "Indictment on Criminal Libel," *The Masses*, January 1914. See also the AP's editorial in response, *New York Times*, March 7, 1914, and Amos Pinchot, "Mr. Pinchot's Reply," *New York Sun*, March 9, 1914, all available at https://www.marxists.org/history/etol/writers/eastman/works/1910s/libel.htm.

19. Only when Max Eastman demanded to be shown the specific violations did government attorneys cite the eight items. See Christopher Finan, *From the Palmer Raids to the Patriot Act: A History of the Fight for Free Speech in America* (Boston: Beacon Press, 2008), 19.

20. A fine overview is John Sayer, "Art and Politics, Dissent and Repression: *The Masses* Magazine versus the Government, 1917–1918," *American Journal of Legal History* 32, no. 1 (January 1988): 42–78. Numerous documents from the case files of the two *Masses* trials are available at https://catalog.archives.gov/id/7595376.

21. CE to Randolph Bourne, November 20, 1917, WPPP, reel 12.20.

22. All quotes from Crystal Eastman, *Our War Record: A Plea for Tolerance* (Woman's Peace Party of New York City, January 1, 1918), 1-2, Mary Ware Dennett Papers, Schlesinger Library, reel 33.

23. See "To the Editor," *New York Tribune*, August 28, 1917. See also "Proposed Announcement for Press," September 24, 1917, LWP, reel 102.

24. The scrawl is mentioned in "Memoir of Frances Witherspoon and Tracy Mygatt," Oral History Collection, Columbia University, cited in Charles Chatfield, "World War I and the Liberal Pacifist in the United States," *American Historical Review* 75, no. 7 (December 1970): 1920–37.

25. AUAM Memorandum to the Organization, April 1917, AUAM Records, reel 1.

26. Telegram to the President of the United States, April 16, 1917, LWP, reel 102.

27. *The Wartime Program of the American Union Against Militarism*, May 1917, AUAM Records, reel 1.

28. Crystal Eastman, "War and Peace," *Survey*, December 30, 1916, 363–64.

29. Oswald Garrison Villard, "Universal Military Training: Our Latest Cure-All," AUAM Records, reel 2.

30. AUAM Minutes, April 30, 1917, AUAM Records, reel 1.

31. The AUAM sent a letter to Secretary of War Newton Baker describing the claim for exemption from military service for conscientious objectors and asking for his review and comments. AUAM to Baker, April 12, 1917, LWP, reel 102.

32. CE to Amos Pinchot, June 13, 1917; Pinchot to CE, June 15, 1917, Amos Pinchot Papers, box 30, US Library of Congress, cited in Blanche Wiesen Cook, "Woodrow Wilson and the Antimilitarists" (PhD diss., Johns Hopkins University, Department of History, 1980), 213.

33. Roger Baldwin to Sir, May 23, 1917, AUAM Records, reel 1.

34. "Conscription and the Conscientious Objector—Facts Regarding Military Service under the Conscription Act," AUAM Records, reel 2.

35. Statement on Conscientious Objectors, LWP, reel 102.

36. AUAM Minutes, June 1, 1917, AUAM Records, reel 1.

37. AUAM Minutes, June 1, 1917; June 4, 1917; July 2, 1917, AUAM Records, reel 1.

38. Crystal Eastman as quoted in Murphy, *World War I and the Origin of Civil Liberties in the United States*, 156.

39. "Bureau to Defend Lovers of Peace," *New York Times*, July 3, 1917, 5.

40. Blanche Wiesen Cook, "Democracy in Wartime: Antimilitarism in England and the United States, 1914–1918," *American Studies* 13 (Spring 1972): 60–61, cited in Murphy, *World War I and the Origins of Civil Liberties in the United States*, 56.

41. CE to Lillian Wald, May 23, 1917, LWP, reel 102.

42. Crystal Eastman, "Urgent Letter to American Union Members, Local Committees and Affiliated Organizations," July 13, 1917, AUAM Records, reel 1.

43. "Malone Aids Fight of Anti-Draft Press," *New York Times*, July 14, 1917, 7.

44. Lillian Wald to CE, August 26, 1917, AUAM Records, reel 10; *New York Times*, July 4, 1917, cited in Robert Cottrell, *Roger Nash Baldwin and the American Civil Liberties Union* (New York: Columbia University Press, 2001), 55.

45. Lillian Wald, *Windows on Henry Street* (Boston: Little, Brown, 1934), 311.

46. Lillian Wald to Jane Addams, November 13, 1917, Addams Papers, reel 11.

47. Crystal Eastman, "Memorandum," June 14, 1917, AUAM Records, reel 1.

48. Crystal Eastman, "Memorandum," June 14, 1917, AUAM Records, reel 1.

49. All quotes from Crystal Eastman, "Memorandum," June 14, 1917, AUAM Records, reel 1.

50. Crystal Eastman, "Memorandum," June 14, 1917, AUAM Records, reel 1.

51. On this internationalist dilemma, see John Fabian Witt, *Patriots & Cosmopolitans: Hidden Histories in American Law* (Cambridge, MA: Harvard University Press, 2007), 157–208.

52. Crystal Eastman, "Memorandum," June 14, 1917, AUAM Records, reel 1.

53. PK to Jane Addams, June 12, 1917, Jane Addams Papers, reel 10.

54. "Rough Draft of Possible Basis for Immediate Statement to the Press," June 15, 1917, AUAM Records, reel 1.

55. Statement to the Press, July 2, 1917, AUAM Records, reel 1, cited in Blanche Wiesen Cook, ed., *Crystal Eastman on Women and Revolution* (New York: Oxford University Press, 1978), 21.

56. *Announcing the Civil Liberties Bureau*, AUAM Records, reel 2.

57. "The Purposes of the People's Council," *Northwest Worker*, August 9, 1917.

58. Although the *Bulletin* bore no mention of its writers or editors, probably to avoid legal entanglements, Walter's biographer makes the case that he mainly edited it, at least in its first, active year between August 1917 and September/October 1918. See Winnington, *Walter Fuller*, 239.

59. "Tentative Program of Discussion for the First American Conference on Democracy and Terms of Peace," WPPP, reel 12.4.

60. Cited in Records of the People's Council for Democracy and Peace, Swarthmore College Peace Collection, https://www.swarthmore.edu/library/peace/CDGA.M-R/pcadp.htm.

61. See, for example, "Women Are Disloyal," *Ogden Standard*, September 3, 1917.

62. "Enemies Within," *New York Tribune*, August 26, 1917. See also "Undesirables Organizing," *Labor Advocate*, June 30, 1917; and "American Pacifists: How They Are Treated," *Northern Star*, January 2, 1918.

63. AUAM Minutes, August 6, 1917, AUAM Records, reel 1.

64. Lillian Wald to Jane Addams, November 13, 1917, Jane Addams Papers, reel 11.

65. Lillian Wald to CE, August 25, 1917, AUAM Records, reel 1.

66. AUAM Minutes, August 30, 1917, reel 1.

67. Lillian Wald to Joseph Tumulty, September 12, 1917, cited in Charles Chatfield, *Peace Movements in America* (New York: Schocken Books, 1972), 55.

68. Charles Hallinan to Oswald Garrison Villard, September 18, 1917, AUAM Records, reel 1.

69. CE to Lillian Wald, September 6, 1917, LWP, reel 102.

70. AUAM Minutes, September 13, 1917, AUAM Records, reel 1.

71. CE to Lillian Wald, September 13, 1917, LWP, reel 102.

72. AUAM Minutes, September 13, 1917, AUAM Records, reel 1.

73. AUAM Minutes, September 13, 1917, AUAM Records, reel 1.

74. AUAM Minutes, September 13, 1917, AUAM Records, reel 1.

75. AUAM Minutes, June 15, 1917, AUAM Records, reel 1.

76. CE to Executive Committee, September 25, 1917, AUAM Records, reel 1.

77. Lillian Wald to CE, September 27, 1917, AUAM Records, reel 1.

78. Jane Addams to CE, September 28, 1917; James Maurer to CE, September 27, 1917, AUAM Records, reel 1.

79. A. A. Berle to CE, September 27, 1917, AUAM Records, reel 1.

80. Norman Thomas to CE, September 27, 1917, AUAM Records, reel 1.

81. Emergency Meeting of the Executive Committee, February 10, 1916, AUAM Records, reel 1.

82. Quoted in Walker, *In Defense of American Liberties*, 37. See also Baldwin, "Recollections of a Life in Civil Liberties, part I," *Civil Liberties Review* 2, no. 2 (1975): 31–72.

83. AUAM Minutes, March 5, 1917, AUAM Records, reel 1.

84. CE to Lillian Wald, March 13, 1917, LWP, reel 102.

85. Walker, *In Defense of American Liberties*, 37. Donald Johnson provides additional detail, having interviewed Baldwin for "American Civil Liberties Union: 1914–1924" (PhD diss., Columbia University, Department of History, 1960), 24.

86. In September 1918, Baldwin created a test case of himself on the legality of the draft. After refusing counsel, pleading guilty, and refusing bail, he was briefly jailed. He wrote to Wald from his cell, joking, "It was a telegram from you that brought me on from St. Louis to start a job which has meant growth and a high privilege—and which, in a sense, has landed me where I am!" Roger Baldwin to Lillian Wald, January 3, 1919, Wald Papers, New York Public Library, box 88, cited in Johnson, "American Civil Liberties Union: 1914-1924," 26. Baldwin elsewhere recalled that Crystal "had been hospitalized with a serious illness," rather than a

difficult delivery after a pregnancy. See Baldwin, "Recollections of a Life in Civil Liberties, part I," 51.

87. Baldwin, "Recollections of a Life in Civil Liberties, part I," 52.

88. Crystal Eastman uses the phrase in "Socialist Women of Eighteen Countries Meet at Marseilles," *Equal Rights*, September 26, 1925.

89. Walker, *In Defense of American Liberties*, 31.

90. Baldwin, "Recollections of a Life in Civil Liberties," 54.

91. Baldwin, "Recollections of a Life in Civil Liberties," 54. Walker is one of a number of scholars who discuss a "remarkably similar outlook" between Baldwin and Eastman. While the two did share a deep commitment to conscientious objectors and to civil liberties in wartime, that kind of meeting of the minds is rendered uncertain by Baldwin's recollections of their relationship. See Walker, *In Defense of American Liberties*, 17.

92. Oswald Garrison Villard to Charles Hallinan, December 3, 1917, cited in Blanche Wiesen Cook, ed., *Toward the Great Change: Crystal and Max Eastman on Feminism, Antimilitarism and Revolution* (New York: Garland Publishing, 1976), 27. See also Walker, *In Defense of American Liberties*, 11.

93. Johnson interview with Roger Baldwin, cited in "American Civil Liberties Union," 24.

94. Cynthia Fuller to her parents, April 24, 1917, cited in Winnington, *Walter Fuller*, 215.

95. Margaret Lane to Mrs. Louis F. Post, March 23, 1917, WPPP, reel 12.4.

96. At the time, Crystal had been told "Jeffrey is flourishing," but noted, "I haven't seen him yet!" CE to ME, n.d. [1917], CEP, box 6, folder 192.

97. CE to Lillian Wald, n.d. [1917], LWP, reel 102.

98. CE to Paul Kellogg, April 20, 1917, Kellogg Papers, box 42.

99. AUAM Minutes, April 2 and April 4, 1917, AUAM Records, reel 1.

100. CE to Wald, n.d. [April 1917], LWP, reel 102.

101. CE to Lillian Wald, n.d. [1917], LWP, reel 102.

102. CE to Amos Pinchot, cited in Marchand, *American Peace Movement*, 80n, 255. Both cited in Witt, *Patriots & Cosmopolitans*, 197.

103. Crystal Eastman, "Secretary's Recommendations," AUAM Records, reel 1. See also Witt, *Patriots & Cosmopolitans*, 196.

104. See CE to AUAM Members on financing the Civil Liberties Bureau, August 1, 1917; CE and Roger Baldwin to AUAM Locals and Affiliates, August 31, 1917, both in AUAM Records, reel 1. See also Selected AUAM Members to Woodrow Wilson, August 9, 1917, LWP, reel 102.

105. AUAM Minutes, October 9, 1917, AUAM Records, reel 1.

106. John Fabian Witt discusses the genealogy of the term in Anglo-American law and political theory in "Crystal Eastman and the Internationalist Beginnings of American Civil Liberties," *Duke Law Journal* 54, no. 3 (2004): 705–63.

107. Witt, *Patriots & Cosmopolitans*, 202.

108. A comprehensive biographical account of Baldwin's life at the ACLU is Robert C. Cottrell, *Roger Nash Baldwin and the American Civil Liberties Union* (New York: Columbia University Press, 2001).

109. AUAM Minutes, October 9, 1917, AUAM Records, reel 1.

110. AUAM Minutes, October 22, 1917, AUAM Records, reel 1.

111. AUAM Minutes, November 12, 1917, AUAM Records, reel 1. See also "The American Union Against Militarism, headquarters 70 Fifth Avenue, announced yesterday its reorganization as the AMERICAN UNION FOR A DEMOCRATIC PEACE," November 12, 1917, AUAM Records, reel 1.

112. AUAM Minutes, October 29, 1917, AUAM Records, reel 1.

113. CE to Jane Addams, October 30, 1917, Jane Addams Papers, reel 11.

114. CE to Jane Addams, November 14, 1917, Jane Addams Papers, reel 11.

115. Both occurred at the same meeting. AUAM Minutes, November 27, 1917, AUAM Records, reel 1.

116. AUAM Minutes, June 18, 1919, AUAM Records, reel 1.

CHAPTER 8

1. CE to Jane Addams, November 28, 1917, WPPP, reel 12.3. Also available in Jane Addams Papers, reel 11.

2. CE to Jane Addams, June 28, 2917, Jane Addams Papers, reel 10.

3. CE to Jane Addams, June 28, 1917, Jane Addams Papers, reel 10

4. John A. Thompson, *Reformers and War: American Progressive Publicists and the First World War*, 155–56.

5. CE to Oswald Garrison Villard, November 16, 1917, AUAM Records, reel 1.

6. AUAM Minutes, November 26, 1917, AUAM Records, reel 1.

7. CE to Oswald Garrison Villard, November 16, 1917, AUAM Records, reel 1.

8. Kristen R. Ghodsee, "Why Women Had Better Sex under Socialism," Sunday Review, *New York Times*, August 12, 2017. See also *Mary Jo Buhle, Women and American Socialism 1870–1920* (Urbana: University of Illinois Press, 1981).

9. Philip S. Foner, *The Bolshevik Revolution: Its Impact on American Radicals, Liberals, and Labor, A Documentary Study* (New York: International Publishers, 1967), 20–23.

10. The *Four Lights*, March 24, 1917.

11. Max Eastman, *Love and Revolution: My Journey through an Epoch* (New York: Random House, 1964), 70.

12. Christine Stansell relates that Reed had taken the Patterson assignment as a respite from the mainstream political journalism he was doing at the muckraking *American* magazine (1906–56), then rather accidentally lucked into a series of contacts that fostered his career. In a security sweep of the area around the Patterson strike, Reed was arrested and found himself placed in the same cell as the anarchist Carlo Tresca.

Tresca soon introduced him to key sources in left-wing politics, including "Big Bill" Haywood, of the Industrial Workers of the World and Socialist Party of America. See Christine Stansell, *American Moderns: Bohemian New York and the Creation of a New Century* (New York: Henry Holt, 2000), 192–93.

13. The meeting is cited in Stansell, *American Moderns*, 193.

14. Ross Wetzsteon coins this moniker in *Republic of Dreams: Greenwich Village: The American Bohemia 1910–1960* (New York: Simon & Schuster, 2003), 37.

15. Stansell quotes Reed's letters to his editor, Carl Hovey, in which he admits, "I have never done such awful work." See Stansell, *American Moderns*, 194.

16. John Reed, *The War in Eastern Europe, Pictured by Boardman Robinson* (New York: Charles Scribner's Sons, 1916), ix.

17. See Stansell, *American Moderns*, 195.

18. Eastman, *Love and Revolution*, 70.

19. AUAM Minutes, January 31, 1918, AUAM Records, reel 1.

20. E. W. Scripps to Kate Crane Gartz, October 8, 1916, MEP, box 1.

21. Eastman, *Love and Revolution*, 70.

22. Eastman, *Love and Revolution*, 70.

23. Eastman, *Love and Revolution*, 78.

24. Eastman, *Love and Revolution*, 72.

25. In fact, the United States was the last great power to accord recognition to the Soviet Union. It was not until November 16, 1933, that President Franklin Roosevelt established full diplomatic relations between the United States and the Soviet Union, writing to Soviet Foreign Minister Maxim Litvinov that he hoped the two nations "may co-operate for their mutual benefit and for the preservation of the peace of the world." See Foner, *The Bolshevik Revolution*, 51.

26. Unsigned editorial, *Liberator*, February 1919.

27. Unsigned editorial, *Liberator*, June 1919.

28. Foner quotes Robert K. Murray's description of this coverage at some length. "Cartoonists . . . picture[d] the Bolshevik government as a smoking gun, a bomb, a hangman's noose; others show[ed] cultured women cleaning the streets and officers of high rank, businessmen, and professors selling newspapers to keep from starving. The Bolsheviki, meanwhile, were described as riding around in automobiles, dining in fashionable restaurants, and otherwise amusing themselves." Robert K. Murray, *Red Scare: A Study in National Hysteria 1919–20*, cited in Foner, *The Bolshevik Revolution*, 28.

29. Eastman, *Love and Revolution*, 137.

30. Unsigned editorial, *Liberator*, March 1919.

31. The friend who spoke of "colors flying" was Margaret Sanger. Eastman, *Love and Revolution*, 70.

32. Eastman, *Love and Revolution*, 70.

33. Eastman, *Love and Revolution*, 77.

34. Both quotes from Eastman, *Love and Revolution*, 79.

35. Until June 1918, the magazine was called the *New World*. Fuller's job description and contributions to the magazine are described in some detail in G. Peter Winnington, *Walter Fuller*, 248–49, 257–59.

36. Eastman, *Love and Revolution*, 79.

37. "Cooking and eating" is from CE to Paul Kellogg, July 25, 1918 [?], Kellogg Papers, box 42. The Croton crowd is named in Eastman, *Love and Revolution*, 65.

38. "Reed Won't Be Opposed as Bolshevik Consul," *New York Tribune*, February 3, 1918, 4.

39. Vladimir Lenin, "Brest-Litovsk—A Brigands' Peace," *Liberator*, October 1918.

40. Crystal Eastman, "Radicals Here Offer Lives to Russia," *New York Evening Call*, February 28, 1918, cited in Foner, *The Bolshevik Revolution*, 76.

41. Eastman, *Love and Revolution*, 144.

42. Some records show the title as simply "We Are Coming, Father Abraham." Benjamin Tubb, *Music of the American Civil War*, accessible at http://www.civilwarpoetry.org/union/songs/coming.html.

43. "Hopes for Socialist U.S.," *New York Tribune*, March 26, 1919, 7.

44. Crystal Eastman, "Impressions of the AF of L Convention," *Liberator*, August 1918, 6.

45. Crystal Eastman, "The Socialist Vote," *Liberator*, December 1918, 33.

46. Crystal Eastman, "The Mooney Congress," *Liberator*, March 1919, 19, 20.

47. Crystal Eastman, *A Program for Voting Women* (Woman's Peace Party of New York, March 1919).

48. The program and some details are available in Mary Ware Dennett Papers, Schlesinger Library, Harvard University, reel 33.

49. Lucia Ames Mead to Jane Addams, July 13, 1915, WPPP, reel 12.8.

50. *The Advocate of Peace*, March 1918, 83–84.

51. Lucia Ames Mead, "Do Suffragists Care about Our Mad Militarism?," *Woman Voter*, July 1913: 11–12; Anon, "English Suffragettes' Methods Are Scorned," *Brooklyn Daily Eagle*, March 20, 1912, 7. See also Anon, "Not Good Sports," *Remonstrance*, October 1912, 3.

52. John M. Craig, "Red-Baiting, Pacifism and Free Speech: Lucia Ames Mead and Her 1926 Lecture Tour in Atlanta and the Southeast," *Georgia Historical Quarterly* 71, no. 4 (Winter 1987): 601–22.

53. Crystal Eastman, "British Labor Is Moving," *Liberator*, September 1919, 28, 30.

54. Crystal Eastman, "The Workers of the Clyde," *Liberator*, October 1919, 28.

55. Eastman, "The Workers of the Clyde," 28

56. Crystal Eastman, "The Socialist Party Convention," *Liberator*, July 1920, 24.

57. Winnington discusses Fuller's editorial talent in *Walter Fuller*, particularly 281–312.

58. WF to Mother, August 10, 1918, courtesy of Rebecca Young.

59. WF to Mother, August 10, 1918, courtesy of Rebecca Young.

60. WF to Mother, August 10, 1918, courtesy of Rebecca Young.

61. WF to CE, August 12–August 14, 1918, CEP, box 6, folder 192. This correspondence is very helpfully contextualized in Winnington, *Walter Fuller*, 250–57.

62. All quotes from WF to CE, August 12–August 14, 1918, CEP, box 6, folder 192. See also Winnington, *Walter Fuller*, 255.

63. WF to CE, August 12–August 14, 1918, CEP, box 6, folder 192. See also Winnington, *Walter Fuller*, 256.

64. WF to CE, August 12–August 14, 1918, CEP, box 6, folder 192. See also Winnington, *Walter Fuller*, 253.

65. John Read, "Letter," *Liberator*, September 1918, 34.

66. Eastman, *Love and Revolution*, 108–9.

67. CE to John Reed, July 25, 1918, John Reed Papers, Houghton Library, Harvard University, folder 406.

68. CE to John Reed, July 25, 1918, John Reed Papers, Houghton Library, Harvard University, folder 406.

69. Lukacs chaired panels on "What Can Men Do to Help the Movement for Woman Suffrage? Representatives of the Government and the City," and "Woman Suffrage and Men's Economicel [*sic*], Ethical and Political Interest." Program from the IWSA Congress 1913, Schwimmer-Lloyd Collection, Manuscript Division, New York Public Library, series II, box 500, folder 9.

70. Crystal Eastman, "In Communist Hungary," *Liberator*, August 1919, 7, 8, 5.

71. All quotes from Crystal Eastman, "In Communist Hungary," 8.

72. Crystal Eastman, "In Communist Hungary," 8.

73. Crystal Eastman, "In Communist Hungary," 9.

74. "Crystal Eastman in Hungary," *Liberator*, July 1919, 35. See also "Miss Eastman Obtained Passport Legitimately," *New York Tribune*, June 12, 1919, which briefly describes her remarks in Budapest.

75. Crystal Eastman, "In Communist Hungary," 9.

76. Crystal Eastman, "In Communist Hungary," 9.

77. One of several full-page ads appeared in front of the *Liberator*, July 1919.

78. Crystal Eastman, "In Communist Hungary," 9.

79. International Congress of Women after the War delegate list, December 1918, WPPP, reel 14.

80. Ross Wetzsteon argues that the liberal Villagers of Crystal's cohort believed "the quickest way to win the revolution was to live as if the revolution had already been won." See *Republic of Dreams*, 13.

81. See Leila J. Rupp, "Feminism and the Sexual Revolution in the Early Twentieth Century: The Case of Doris Stevens," *Feminist Studies* 15, no. 2 (Summer 1989): 289–309.

82. See Leila J. Rupp, "Sexuality and Politics in the Early Twentieth Century: The Case of the International Women's Movement," *Feminist Studies* 23, no. 3 (Autumn 1997) : 577–605.

83. See Leila J. Rupp, *Worlds of Women: The Making of an International Women's Movement* (Princeton, NJ: Princeton University Press, 1997).

84. Kathryn Kish Sklar and Beverly Palmer erroneously claim that Eastman did not attend the Zurich conference. They go on to say that she was not even missed, remarking, "many WILPF members were not displeased when Eastman was refused a passport in 1919 and could not attend the Zurich conference." While it is impossible to assess how anyone felt about an absence that did not, in fact, occur, their assumption presumably arises from legitimate scholarly inference about Eastman's reputation or position within the organization at that time. See Kathryn Kish Sklar and Beverly Palmer, *Selected Letters of Florence Kelley 1869–1931* (Champaign: University of Illinois Press, 2009), 259.

85. HPT to Jane Addams, March 14, 1917, Jane Addams Papers.

86. Mrs. Philip Snowden, *A Political Pilgrim in Europe* (New York: George H. Doran Company, 1921), 82, cited in Anne Wiltsher, *Most Dangerous Women: Feminist Peace Campaigners of the Great War* (London: Pandora, 1985), 206.

87. This issue climbed high on the "to do" list for both US and international feminists in the 1920s. In the NWP, a number of its high-profile members, including Harriot Stanton Blatch and Inez Milholland, had been affected by it well before Crystal was. The 1922 Cable Act provided some relief but didn't equalize citizenship rights. As a result, bills were proposed through the twenties to try to remove the remaining citizenship inequalities affecting such married women. By the 1930s, the NWP had shifted its strategy to the Equality Nationality Treaty, rather than attempting to further amend the Cable Act.

88. *Report of the International Congress of Women at Zurich*, 16.

89. David Crossland, "Germany Set to Make Final World War I Reparation Payment," ABC News, September 29, 2010, http://abcnews.go.com/International/germany-makes-final-reparation-payments-world-war/story?id=11755920.

90. Margaret MacMillan, *Paris 1919: Six Months That Changed the World* (New York: Random House, 2002). See also Hochschild, *To End All Wars* (New York: Houghton Mifflin Harcourt, 2011).

91. The resolution is printed in "The Zurich International Congress of Women," authored by an anonymous "Special Correspondent" in the *Bulletin of the People's Council of America*, July–August, 1919, reel 3.2. Kristen E. Gwinn emphasizes that the women at Zurich were the first to publicly rebuke the official terms of peace decided at Versailles. See Gwinn, *Emily Greene Balch: The Long Road to Internationalism* (Champaign: University of Illinois Press, 2010), 117.

92. Crystal Eastman, Memorandum, June 14, 1917, AUAM Records, reel 1. The United States rejected the Treaty of Versailles in 1919 and failed to ratify it or join the League of Nations, but for other reasons.

93. *Report of the International Congress of Women at Zurich*, 78.

94. *Report of the International Congress of Women at Zurich*, 174.

95. *Report of the International Congress of Women at Zurich*, 124.

96. *Report of the International Congress of Women at Zurich*, 124.

97. *Report of the International Congress of Women at Zurich*, 126.

98. *Report of the International Congress of Women in Zurich*, 129.

99. *Report of the International Congress of Women in Zurich*, 128.

100. *Report of the International Congress of Women in Zurich*, 129. Additional coverage can be found in a special single issue of the *Four Lights* dedicated to the congress, June 12, 1919, WPPP, reel 23.01.

101. Crystal Eastman, "The Mooney Congress," *Liberator*, March 1919, 124.

102. Crystal Eastman, "In Communist Hungary," 6.

103. Special Correspondent, "The Zurich International Congress of Women," *Bulletin of the People's Council of America*, July–August 1919, Papers of the People's Council of America, reel 3.2.

104. Another article in the *Bulletin* is attributed to the same anonymous correspondent, who is claimed to be female. It is "Glimpses of Soviet Hungary," published in the same issue. It too may be Crystal's work, polished by Walter. See *Bulletin of the People's Council of America*, July–August 1919, Papers of the People's Council of America, reel 3.2.

105. Vladimir Simkhovitch to Jeffrey Fuller c/o Henry Goddard Leach, February 23, 1939, courtesy of Rebecca Young.

106. Vladimir Simkhovitch to Jeffrey Fuller c/o Henry Goddard Leach, February 23, 1939, courtesy of Rebecca Young.

107. Walter Fuller to Albert DeSilver, August 5, 1919, ACLU Archives, cited in John Fabian Witt, "Crystal Eastman and the Internationalist Beginnings of American Civil Liberties," *Duke Law Journal* 58, no. 705 (2004): 758. See also the discussion of the proceedings in Samuel Walker, *In Defense of American Liberties: A History of the ACLU* (Carbondale: Southern Illinois University Press, 1990).

108. ME to Florence Deshon, September 20, 1919, Florence Deshon Papers, The Lilly Library, Indiana University, Bloomington, Indiana, box 1.

109. Records of the New York State Legislature, Joint Legislative Committee to Investigate Seditious Activities, New York State Archives, L0038, reel 4.

110. Records of the Women's International League for Peace and Freedom, series C, box 5, reel 42.

111. "Bela Kun Declared No Sympathizer with 'Reds,'" *New York Tribune*, November 16, 1919, 3. Famine relief, particularly in the war-devastated countries affected by the blockade—Germany, Austria, and Hungary—was one of the earliest campaigns of the newly established WILPF in 1919.

112. Records of the New York State Legislature, Joint Legislative Committee to Investigate Seditious Activities, L0038, reel 4.

113. Department of State to W. H. Moran, January 26, 1920, Secret Service General Correspondence, US Department of Treasury, Record Group 87, box 215.

114. In her speech, Eastman now seemed to recognize the possibility that she was being watched. She refused to reveal how she had done it, saying, according to the citizen spy, that she "might find it necessary to go to Europe again and she did not want her method known." W. L. Hurley to Mr. Moran, February 4, 1920, Secret Service General Correspondence, US Department of Treasury, Record Group 87, box 215.

115. "Stephens Refuses to Read 'Liberator,'" *Sacramento Union*, April 9, 1920.

116. *Liberator Publishing Company vs. David E. White et al.*, Equity Case number 539, US District Court, Northern District of California, San Francisco, filed May 12, 1920 (decided September 22, 1921), 6–7.

117. *Liberator Publishing Company vs. David E. White et al.*, 6, 7. See also "Liberator Company Sues Police Head," *Berkeley Daily Gazette*, May 13, 1920.

118. *Liberator Publishing Company vs. David E. White et al.*, 8.

119. For years, Crystal had been eager to take to the courts, not only over government censorship practices, but also over local, informal repression and smear tactics like those brandished against the magazine now. In September 1917, for example, she and her more radical allies on the AUAM executive committee wanted to pursue a case against "hysterical 'patriots' or unintelligent secret service men" who labeled them "pro-German" and "under investigation" in order to execute a "chilling effect on their rights of free speech and assembly." The union never pursued this case. See AUAM Press Release, September 1, 1917, AUAM Records, reel 1.

120. CE to Cynthia Fuller, September 27, 1920, courtesy of Rebecca Young.

121. CE to "Family in Bournemouth," May 22, 1920, courtesy of Rebecca Young.

122. Upton Sinclair's novel about Sacco and Vanzetti, *Boston*, made the case that the two men had been executed for the two murders because of their radical politics, but many years later, Sinclair's biographer uncovered evidence that the muck-raking author of *The Jungle* possessed convincing evidence from the men's lawyer that the two were, in fact, guilty. See Anthony Arthur, *Radical Innocent: Upton Sinclair* (New York: Random House, 2006).

123. By 1926, with their executions coming the next year, Vanzetti said publicly, "If we have to die for a crime of which we are innocent, we ask for revenge, revenge in our names and in the names of our living and our dead." See Beverly Gage, *The Day Wall Street Exploded* (New York: Oxford University Press, 2009), 328.

124. CE to Cynthia, September 1920, courtesy of Rebecca Young.

125. CE to Cynthia, November 1, 1920, courtesy of Rebecca Young.

126. In the immediate aftermath of her trip to Zurich and Hungary, Crystal returned to the United States "terribly sick—[with] measles, acute bronchitis, a slight pneumonia, influenza—in that order." Eastman, *Love and Revolution*, 180.

127. All quotes from Eastman, *Love and Revolution*, 180.

128. William L. O'Neill discusses these dynamics, as diagnosed to Max by Dr. Ely Jetcliffe, one of America's first Freudian psychoanalysts. Dr. A. A. Brill agreed: "I

think you have a strong mother-fixation," O'Neill quotes. "Your pattern is that you want to get away from mother and yet be with her." See O'Neill, *The Last Romantic: A Life of Max Eastman* (New York: Oxford University Press, 1978), particularly 11–14. See also Irmscher, *Max Eastman*.

129. AFE to CE, March 20, 1904, CEP, box 5, folder 137.

130. ME to Florence Deshon, January 19, 1920, Florence Deshon Papers, box 1. See also Eastman, *Love and Revolution*, 180.

131. Editorial, *Liberator*, January 1921.

132. "Mylius Says He Only 'Borrowed' $4000," *New York Times*, December 2, 1921. Mylius had the gall to write to Max, offering him advice on how the *Liberator* could economize to stay afloat after he stole the magazine's financial reserve. E. F. Mylius to ME, October 19, 1921, MEP.

133. "Max Eastman Replies to 'E.F. Mylius' Letter," *New York Times*, December 3, 1921.

CHAPTER 9

1. Crystal Eastman, "Feminism; a Statement Read at the First Feminist Congress in the United States, New York, March 1, 1919," *Liberator*, May 1919, 37.

2. Erika Kuhlman, "'Women's Ways in War': The Feminist Pacifism of the New York City Woman's Peace Party," *Frontiers* 18, no. 1 (1997): 99.

3. Program for the Woman's Freedom Congress, Mary Ware Dennett Papers, Schlesinger Library, reel 33. Crystal and Byrns had been friends since law school. They wrote a play together in March 1907: "Miss Byrns and I have just written a short play, which the classes are going to give. It will mean some work for us, putting it through, but it will be worthwhile. We saved them from giving a stupid, stale, vulgar thing." CE to AFE, March 13, 1907, CEP, box 5, folder 156. They also studied for exams together that May: "It is just before my hardest exam and I've been on Staten Island all day studying with Elinor Byrns." CE to AFE, May 8, 1907, CEP, box 5, folder 157. A leading voice in the Women's Peace Union, Byrns joined with Caroline Lexow Babcock to draft a federal amendment to outlaw war; it was introduced in every congressional session from 1926 to 1939. See Scott H. Bennett and Charles F. Howlett, eds., *Antiwar Dissent and Peace Activism in World War I America: A Documentary Reader* (Lincoln: University of Nebraska Press, 2014).

4. Eastman, "Feminism; a Statement Read at the First Feminist Congress in the United States," 37.

5. Several of the most prominent leaders submitted a group resignation letter. See Fanny Garrison Villard, Elinor Byrns, Katherine Devereaux Blake, Mary Ware Dennett, Lucy Watson, Rose Hicks, Edna Kearns, Caroline Lexow Babcock, Gartia Gollar to Members of the Women's International League, September 12, 1919, Mary Ware Dennett Papers, Schlesinger Library, reel 33. See also Minutes of the Women's International League, September 4, 1919, Dennett Papers, reel 33.

6. Crystal Eastman, "Practical Feminism," *Liberator*, January 1920, 40.

7. Anon, "Woman's Party Leaders Confer on President and Future Plans," *Suffragist*, October 1920, 232–33.

8. "Minutes of the Monthly Executive Meeting of the National Woman's Party," September 10, 1920, Doris Stevens Papers, Schlesinger Library, Harvard University, folder 7.

9. Crystal Eastman, "London Letter—The Married Teacher," *Equal Rights*, January 30, 1926.

10. Crystal Eastman, "What Next?," *The Suffragist*, November 1920, 278.

11. Eastman, "What Next?," 279.

12. Eastman, "What Next?," 278–79.

13. Crystal Eastman, "Now We Can Begin," *Liberator*, December 1920, 23.

14. Eastman, "Now We Can Begin," 23.

15. See Crystal Eastman, "Suffragists Ten Years After," *New Republic*, June 27, 1923, 118–19.

16. Crystal Eastman, "Alice Paul's Convention," *Liberator*, April 1921, 10

17. Eastman, "Alice Paul's Convention," 10.

18. The twenties saw the rise of new forms of political engagement centered around people's identities as consumers. See Meg Jabobs, *Pocketbook Politics: Economic Citizenship in Twentieth-Century America* (Princeton: Princeton University Press, 2005). See also Lawrence B. Glickman, "The Strike in the Temple of Consumption: Consumer Activism and Twentieth-Century American Culture," *Journal of American History* 88 (2001): 99–128.

19. Nancy Cott, "Feminist Politics in the 1920s: The National Woman's Party," *Journal of American History* 71, no. 1 (June 1984): 47.

20. The lost terrain of feminist solidarity between 1910 and 1930 is the argument of Nancy Cott's authoritative *The Grounding of Modern Feminism* (New Haven: Yale University Press, 1987).

21. All quotes from Eastman, "Alice Paul's Convention," 9–10.

22. Eastman, "Alice Paul's Convention," 9–10.

23. "Woman's Party Will Work for Feminism Only," *New York Tribune*, February 19, 1921.

24. Cott, "Feminist Politics in the 1920s," 48. Ellen Carol DuBois points out the importance of collective process in women's organizing from the dawn of the American movement in *Feminism and Suffrage: The Emergence of an Independent Women's Movement in America* (Ithaca: Cornell University Press, 1978).

25. Eastman, "Alice Paul's Convention," 10.

26. "Woman's Party Will Work for Feminism Only," *New York Tribune*, February 19, 1921.

27. All quotes from Eastman, "Alice Paul's Convention," 10. Paul's dictatorial style was an issue for an array of feminist leaders, particularly in the post-suffrage era. Mary White Ovington opposed Paul's relegation of race and racism as outside the

mandate for feminism at the February 1921 NWP convention. Florence Kelley complained about Paul's dismissal of intersecting social issues including labor rights and antimilitarism. Doris Stevens dedicated her 1920 book on the woman's party to Paul, but also compared her to Vladimir Lenin. See Doris Stevens, *Jailed For Freedom* (New York: Boni & Liveright, 1920), 17. These examples are raised in Cott, *The Grounding of Modern Feminism*, 56–57.

28. Cott, "Feminist Politics in 1920s," 48.

29. CE to PK, n.d. [April 1921?], Survey Associates Records, Social Welfare History Archives, University of Minnesota, box 67.

30. The Provincetown Players, who included Reed and Max, joined together in 1915 to produce artistic, anticommercial, alternative theater over six seasons in New York, taking as their first stage the Provincetown wharf of Mary Heaton Vorse. Under the direction of the playwright Susan Glaspell and her husband, George Cram "Gig" Cook, the group produced important plays by women writers whom Crystal knew from downtown Manhattan and the *Liberator*, including Glaspell, Neith Boyce, Edna St. Vincent Millay, and Djuna Barnes. The Provincetown Players also helped launch the career of Eugene O'Neill. In 1919, their Provincetown Playhouse opened at 133 MacDougal Street, less than three blocks from Crystal's house.

31. CE c/o C. W. Crooker to Walter Fuller at 116 West 13 Street, courtesy of Peter Winnington.

32. WF to parents, March 20, 1922, courtesy of Rebecca Young.

33. CE to Cynthia, March 21, 1922, courtesy of Rebecca Young.

34. PK to CE, January 20, 1927, Survey Associate Records, box 67.

35. CE to Cynthia, March 21, 1922, courtesy of Rebecca Young.

36. The *Survey Graphic* became an independent magazine in 1933 and remained that way until it ceased publication in 1952.

37. CE to WF, April 14, 1922, courtesy of Rebecca Young. See also G. Peter Winnington, *Walter Fuller: The Man Who Had Ideas* (London: Letterworth Press, 2014), 315–16.

38. WF to PK, May 18, 1922, Survey Associates Records, box 67.

39. CE to Arthur Kellogg, June 3, 1922, Paul Kellogg Papers, Social Welfare History Archives, University of Minnesota, box 42.

40. PK to CE, June 15, 1922, Survey Associates Records, box 67.

41. "Memorandum in Re: Crystal Eastman," February 11, 1926, General Records of the Justice Department, US National Archives, Record Group 60.

42. CE to Samuel Eastman, June 7, 1922, courtesy of Rebecca Young.

43. CE to WF "Darling" June 27, 1922, courtesy of Rebecca Young.

44. Walter's activities, including details about the background and evolution of these friendships, is discussed at length in Winnington, *Walter Fuller*, 316–18.

45. CE to WF "Darling" June 27, 1922, courtesy of Rebecca Young.

46. Bertrand Russell to WF, March 15, 1923; Walter Fuller to G. B. Shaw, March 21, 1924; G. B. Shaw to WF, March 26, 1924; H. G. Wells to CE, n.d., all courtesy of Rebecca Young.

47. Winnington, *Walter Fuller*, 320-21.

48. CE to WF, August 20, 1922, courtesy of Rebecca Young.

49. Cited in Winnington, *Walter Fuller*, 321. The full title of the Ibanez novel is *The Four Horsemen of the Apocalypse*. Originally published in 1916, an English translation in 1919 became a bestseller in the United States.

50. PK to CE, September 7, 1922, Survey Associates Records, box 67.

51. CE to WF, August 20, 1922, courtesy of Rebecca Young.

52. See Winnington, *Walter Fuller*, 317.

53. CE to WF, August 29, 1922, courtesy of Rebecca Young.

54. CE to "Walter darling," September 3, 1922, courtesy of Rebecca Young.

55. CE to WF, September 14, 1922, courtesy of Rebecca Young.

56. "Women Abroad Puzzle Over Nationality," *Oakland Tribune*, January 7, 1923, 33. See also "Married Women and Passports," *London Daily Herald*, November 22, 1922.

57. Crystal Eastman, "Rome, May 14, 1923," *London Daily Herald*, May 1923.

58. Eastman, "Suffragists Ten Years After," 119.

59. Crystal Eastman, "1848–1923," *Time and Tide*, July 27, 1923, 753–54. The historical genealogy was more complicated than Crystal admitted. Excellent comprehensive accounts pertaining to this history include: Eleanor Flexner, *Century of Struggle: The Woman's Rights Movement in the United States* (New York: Atheneum, 1971); Anne F. Scott and Andrew M. Scott, *One Half the People: The Fight for Women Suffrage* (Champaign: University of Illinois Press, 1982); Suzanne M. Marilley, *Suffrage and the Origins of Liberal Feminism in the United States, 1820–1920* (Cambridge, MA: Harvard University Press, 1996); Mary Jo Buhle, *The Concise History of Woman Suffrage: Selections from History of Woman Suffrage* (Cambridge, MA: Harvard University Press, 2005); Lisa Tetrault, *The Myth of Seneca Falls: Memory and the Women's Suffrage Movement, 1848–1898* (Chapel Hill: University of North Carolina Press, 2017).

60. Crystal Eastman, "Personalities and Powers: Alice Paul," *Time and Tide*, July 20, 1923, 731.

61. Eastman, "Personalities and Powers," 731.

62. Eastman, "What Next?," 278.

63. Crystal Eastman, "An Acid Test for Suffragists," *London Daily Herald*, June 1925. Note that this is the date Crystal herself recorded in her scrapbook, but I have been unable to locate the day of publication.

64. Numerous prominent sources, from Blanche Cook to Vassar College to the American Civil Liberties Union to the National Women's Hall of Fame, credit Eastman as a coauthor of the Equal Rights Amendment (ERA). Cook has said that Eastman was one of four authors involved; numerous other scholars have called Alice Paul the sole author of the amendment. NWP records show meetings were held to debate the language of the ERA beginning in 1921. Multiple NWP feminists, particularly

selected lawyers, were definitely involved in a months-long drafting process. Crystal was in the United States during 1921 and into 1922, departing for England in September. When she returned to the country in the summer of 1924 to head the Women for Congress Campaign, she was accepted into the hierarchy of the NWP leadership. But documentary details about the specific contributions of anyone involved in the drafting process are scarce. To date, I have not been able to definitively delineate Eastman's hand in the evolution of the amendment, nor have I been able to rule it out. Some mention of meetings connected to the drafting process can be found in National Woman's Party Papers, Group II, box 200, folder 10.

65. Cott, "Feminist Politics in the 1920s," 62.

66. Cott, "Feminist Politics in the 1920s," 62.

67. PK to CE, April 30, 1926, Survey Associates Records, box 67.

68. See Rosalind Rosenberg, *Beyond Separate Spheres: Intellectual Roots of Modern Feminism* (New Haven, CT: Yale University Press, 1983), 110.

69. Mary Anderson (as told to Mary N. Winslow), *Women at Work: The Autobiography of Mary Anderson* (Minneapolis: University of Minnesota Press, 1951), 159–72.

70. Cott, "Feminist Politics in the 1920s," 60. See also Nancy Woloch, *A Class by Herself: Protective Labor Laws for Women Workers, 1890s–1990s* (New York: Oxford University Press, 2015).

71. PK to CE, April 30, 1926, Survey Associates Records, box 67.

72. PK to CE, April 30, 1926, Survey Associates Records, box 67. On subsequent developments, see Martha F. Davis, "Equal Rights Amendment: Then and Now," *Columbia Journal of Gender and Law* 17, no. 3 (2008): 419–60.

73. Crystal Eastman, "Equality or Protection?," *Equal Rights*, March 15, 1923, 53.

74. Crystal Eastman, "English Feminism and Special Labor Laws for Women," *Equal Rights*, April 18, 1925, 77.

75. Crystal Eastman, "Protective Legislation in England," *Equal Rights*, October 3, 1925, 269–70.

76. Crystal Eastman, "English Feminism and Special Labor Laws for Women," *Equal Rights*, April 18, 1925, 77.

77. Both quotes from *Equal Rights*, August 30, 1924, cited in "Women for Congress: The NWP's Campaign to Elect Women to Represent Women's Concerns," National Woman's Party, http://nationalwomansparty.org/women-for-congress-the-nwps-campaign-to-elect-women-to-represent-womens-concerns/.

78. Crystal Eastman, "Feminists Must Fight," *The Nation*, November 12, 1924, 523.

79. Eastman, "Feminists Must Fight," 523.

80. *New York Telegram and Evening Mail*, October 31, 1924.

81. Crystal Eastman, "Equal Rights Amendment," *New Republic*, November 19, 1924, 6.

82. See National Woman's Party, "Women for Congress."

83. The NWP revived the WCC for a second go-round in 1926, under the leadership of Doris Stevens. This time, no WCC-supported candidates were elected. See National Woman's Party, "Women for Congress."

84. CE to WF, November 4, 1924, CEP, box 6, folder 192.

85. CE to WF, November 4, 1924, CEP, box 6, folder 192.

86. Crystal Eastman, "Justice for the Prostitute—Lady Astor's Bill," *Equal Rights*, September 19, 1925.

87. Crystal Eastman, "London Letter—The Married Teacher," *Equal Rights*, January 30, 1926.

88. See Crystal Eastman, "British Women Fire the First Gun in Their Second Suffrage Battle," *Equal Rights*, February 27, 1926; "Recent Developments in England," *Equal Rights*, January 22, 1927; "Women, Rights and Privileges," *London Outlook*, February 5, 1927; "What Is Real Protection," *Equal Rights*, February 19, 1927; "Equalitarian vs. Reformer," *Equal Rights*, June 4, 1927. Overall, between 1923 and 1927, Eastman also produced some thirty articles on crisscrossing political subjects and women's issues for magazines and newspapers on both sides of the Atlantic.

89. Crystal Eastman, "What Is Real Protection?," *Equal Rights*, February 19, 1927.

90. Ellen Carol DuBois, among other eminent feminist scholars, has discussed that the internal division over equality versus difference remains a defining feature of the American women's movement. See DuBois, *Woman Suffrage and Women's Rights* (New York: New York University Press, 1998), 132. See also DuBois, *Harriot Stanton Blatch and the Winning of Woman Suffrage* (New Haven, CT: Yale University Press, 1999), 216–22.

91. The party now moved to "work for Equal Rights and recognition for men and women not only in the United States but in any international association or gathering to which our country should become a party." Crystal Eastman, "International Cooperation," *Equal Rights*, May 9, 1925, 101.

92. Eastman, "International Cooperation," 101 (all quotes).

CHAPTER 10

1. Crystal Eastman, "Modern Adventures in Maternity," typescript of early or initial draft, unpublished manuscript, n.d. [1920s], courtesy of Rebecca Young, 1.

2. Crystal Eastman, "Modern Adventures in Maternity," typescript of revised draft, unpublished manuscript, n.d. [1920s], courtesy of Rebecca Young, 1.

3. Crystal Eastman, "Is Woman's Place the Home?," *Equal Rights*, June 13, 1925.

4. See Sandra L. Adickes, *To Be Young Was Very Heaven: Women in New York Before the First World War* (New York: St. Martin's, 1997), 45.

5. Gilman and Rodman are mutually discussed in Patricia Carter, "Guiding the Working Class Girl: Henrietta Rodman's Curriculum for the New Woman, 1913," *Frontiers* 38 (November 1, 2017): 124–55. A brief summary of Rodman's plan can be found in June Sochen, *The New Woman in Greenwich Village, 1910–1920* (New York: Quadrangle, 1972), 51–52.

6. AFE to CE, December 11, 1903, CEP, box 5, folder 134.

7. See Susan D. Becker, *The Origins of the Equal Rights Amendment: American Feminism Between the Wars* (Westport, CT: Greenwood, 1981), 132.

8. Becker, *Origins of the Equal Rights Amendment*, 8.

9. Becker, *Origins of the Equal Rights Amendment*, 132. Christine Stansell suggests the rejection of motherhood became almost an article of faith among feminist moderns. See Christine Stansell, *American Moderns: Bohemian New York and the Creation of a New Century* (New York: Henry Holt, 2000), 246–47.

10. Crystal Eastman, "Birth Control in the Feminist Program," *Birth Control Review*, January 1918, 1.

11. Crystal Eastman, "Now We Can Begin," *Liberator*, January 1920.

12. Eastman, "Birth Control in the Feminist Program," 1.

13. Crystal Eastman, "What Shall We Do with the Woman's Page?," *Time and Tide*, May 20, 1927, 470.

14. Both quotes from Eastman, "Now We Can Begin," 23.

15. Margaret Sanger, *My Fight for Birth Control* (New York: Farrar & Rinehart, 1931), 83.

16. *New York World-Telegram*, March 23, 1931, cited in Roger Streitmatter, *Voice of Revolution: The Dissident Press in America* (New York: Columbia University Press, 2001), 163.

17. A 1918 law allowed women to use contraception for therapeutic purposes, and then a 1936 decision by the appeals court of New York ruled that birth control information was not obscene and allowed doctors to legally distribute contraceptives across state lines.

18. See Constance M. Chen, *"The Sex Side of Life": Mary Ware Dennett's Pioneering Battle for Birth Control and Sex Education* (New York: New Press, 1997).

19. "To Lecture to Women on Boon of 'Twilight Sleep,'" *Washington Herald*, January 23, 1915, 6. Within a month of its first meeting in January 1915, the association announced a "blacklist" of doctors who didn't administer the treatment correctly.

20. See John M. Craig, "'The Sex Side of Life': The Obscenity Case of Mary Ware Dennett," *Frontiers: A Journal of Women's Studies* 15, no. 3 (1995): 145–56. See also Linda Gordon, *The Moral Property of Women: The History of Birth Control in America* (Champaign: University of Illinois Press, 2002.

21. Sanger, *My Fight for Birth Control*, 80.

22. Margaret Sanger, "Prevention of Conception," *Woman Rebel*, March 1914.

23. Cited in Joan M. Jensen, "The Evolution of Margaret Sanger's 'Family Limitation' Pamphlet, 1914–1921," *Signs* 6, no. 3 (Spring 1981): 548–67.

24. The article was "Suppression," *Woman Rebel*, June 1914, cited in Joan M. Goulard, "Woman Rebel: The Rhetorical Strategies of Margaret Sanger and the American Birth Control Movement, 1912–1938" (PhD diss., Indiana University, 1978), 33.

25. See Margaret Sanger, "The New Feminists," *Woman Rebel*, March 1914. See also Ellen Chesler, *Woman of Valor: Margaret Sanger and the Birth Control Movement*

in America (New York: Simon & Schuster, 1992); and David M. Kennedy, *Birth Control in America: The Career of Margaret Sanger* (New Haven, CT: Yale University Press, 1970).

26. Eastman, "Birth Control in the Feminist Program," 15.

27. Eastman, "Birth Control in the Feminist Program," 15 (both quotes).

28. Eastman, "Birth Control in the Feminist Program," 1.

29. Eastman, "Birth Control in the Feminist Program," 1 (both quotes).

30. Eastman, "What Next?," *The Suffragist*, November 1920, 279.

31. Eastman, "Now We Can Begin," 23.

32. Crystal Eastman, "Boys and Girls," *Time and Tide*, January 4, 1924, 5.

33. Eastman, "Now We Can Begin," 23.

34. Crystal Eastman, "Bed-Makers and Bosses," *Time and Tide*, October 12, 1923, 1028.

35. The book is *The Dominant Sex*, published in translation by Allen & Unwin, 1923.

36. This is the organizing idea of Michael Kimmel in *The Gendered Society* (New York: Oxford University Press, 2000). The era's discussion of the politics of gender socialization all but began with Charlotte Perkins Gilman. See *Women & Economics*, ed. Michael Kimmel and Amy Aronson (Berkeley: University of California Press, 1998).

37. Eastman, "Bed-Makers and Bosses," 1028.

38. All quotes from Eastman, "Bed-Makers and Bosses," 1028.

39. Crystal Eastman, "Caroline Haslett and the Women Engineers," *Equal Rights*, April 10, 1926.

40. Eastman, "Boys and Girls," 5.

41. Writing on the issue surfaced in the feminist press beginning around 1925. See Rebecca Hourwich, "Why Can't Daddy Help?," *Equal Rights*, October 31, 1925; "Editorial: Their Mutual Contributions," *Equal Rights*, August 22, 1925; "Editorial: Wages for Wives," *Equal Rights*, December 4, 1926; Frances Perkins, "Wage Earning Wives," *Equal Rights*, January 3, 1931; Editorial: "Wives and Family Incomes," *Equal Rights*, July 21, 1934. See also Doris Stevens, "Wages for Wives," *Nation*, January 27, 1926, 405–6. On later developments, see Louise Toupin, *Wages for Housework: A History of an International Feminist Movement, 1972–77* (Vancouver: University of British Columbia Press, 2018).

42. Mary Ware Dennett in *The Freewoman*, May 9, 1912, cited in Delap, *The Feminist Avant-Garde*, 205.

43. Eastman, "Boys and Girls," 5.

44. All three ideas are discussed by Delap, *The Feminist Avant-Garde*, 185. Harriot Stanton Blatch's book on this subject is *Mobilizing Woman Power* (New York: The Womans Press, 1918).

45. Cited in Delap, *The Feminist Avant-Garde*, 189–90. See also Johanna Alberti, *Beyond Suffrage: Feminists in War and Peace, 1914–28* (London: Palgrave Macmillan, 1989).

46. Delap, *The Feminist Avant-Garde*, 189–90.

47. Some research suggests the support of these women's organizations was decisive in securing the widespread enactment of maternity pensions that occurred in the United States through the 1910s. See Theda Skocpol, Marjorie Abend-Wein, Christopher Howard, and Susan Goodrich Lehmann, "Women's Association and the Enactment of Mothers' Pensions in the United States," *American Political Science Review* 87, no. 3 (September 1993): 686–701.

48. Delap, *The Feminist Avant-Garde*, 189–90.

49. Letter to the Editor of *Time and Tide*, March 18, 1927, in Blanche Wiesen Cook, ed., *Crystal Eastman on Women and Revolution* (New York: Oxford University Press, 1978), 225.

50. Eastman, "Now We Can Begin," 23.

51. Eastman, "Now We Can Begin," 23.

52. Eastman, "Modern Adventures in Maternity," typescript of original or early draft, 3.

53. Peter Winnington describes a creative, sometimes brilliant soul who flashed and whisked into his life and resisted settling down. See G. Peter Winnington, *Walter Fuller: The Man Who Had Ideas* (London: Letterworth Press, 2014).

54. WF to Rosalind Fuller, July 6, 1917, cited in Winnington, *Walter Fuller*, 189.

55. CE to WF, August 23, n.d., courtesy of Rebecca Young.

56. CE to Cynthia Fuller, September 9, 1923, courtesy of Rebecca Young.

57. CE to Cynthia Fuller, n.d., cited in Winnington, *Walter Fuller*, 333.

58. CE to WF, December 14, 1924, courtesy of Rebecca Young.

59. CE to WF, November 4, 1924, courtesy of Rebecca Young.

60. WF to Riss "Dear Girl," October 1916, cited in Winnington, *Walter Fuller*, 144.

61. WF to Riss "Dear Girl," October 1916, cited in Winnington, *Walter Fuller*, 144.

62. Crystal Eastman, "Marriage under Two Roofs," *Cosmopolitan*, December 1923, 100.

63. Eastman, "Marriage under Two Roofs," 100.

64. Eastman, "Marriage under Two Roofs," 100.

65. Hazel Hunkins Hallinan Diary, Hazel Hunkins Hallinan Papers, Schlesinger Library, Harvard University, subseries D, folder 13.8.

66. Author interviews with Rebecca Young, New York City, September 20, 2010; March 22, 2011. Author interview with Cordelia Fuller, by email, August 22, 2008.

67. CE to Cynthia Fuller, January 22, 1925, courtesy of Rebecca Young.

68. See Arlie Hochschild with Anne Machung, *The Second Shift: Working Parents and the Revolution at Home* (New York: Avon Books, 1989).

69. All quotes from Eastman, "Now We Can Begin," 23.

70. Crystal Eastman, "Is Woman's Place the Home?," *Equal Rights*, June 13, 1925.

71. "Modern Fiction" first appeared in the *Times Literary Supplement* in April 1919, then was slightly revised and republished under the title "Modern Fiction" in *The Common Reader*, published by the Hogarth Press in 1925.

72. Crystal may have made the acquaintance of Virginia Woolf through *Time and Tide*, which published both women in the 1920s, or through her numerous connections to the Bloomsbury Group formed through Walter and her own political work. She met Leonard Woolf, a Socialist and leading antimilitarist, as well as a noted author, editor, and publisher, most likely in 1924. In April, he penned a notation in his calendar in April that appears to record an appointment with "C. Eastman." Diary for 1924, Leonard Woolf Archive, Manuscript Division, University of Sussex, Brighton, UK.

73. All quotes from Crystal Eastman, "Anna Wickham; a Poet without a Wife," *Equal Rights*, June 5, 1925, 183.

74. Crystal Eastman, "Now We Can Begin," 23.

75. "Lady Rhondda Contends That Women of Leisure Are 'Menace,'" *Christian Science Monitor*, March 8, 1927.

76. Crystal Eastman, "Who Is Dora Black?," *Equal Rights*, June 5, 1926, 135. See also Stephen Brooke, "The Body and Socialism: Dora Russell in the 1920s," *Past & Present* 189, no. 1 (November 2005): 147–77.

77. All quotes from Eastman, "Who Is Dora Black?," 135.

78. Crystal Eastman, "Bertrand Russell on Bringing Up Children," *Children: The Magazine for Parents*, March 1927, 19.

79. Crystal Eastman, "Are Wives Partners or Dependents?," typescript unpublished article, n.d. [1920s], courtesy of Rebecca Young, 1.

80. Eastman, "Are Wives Partners or Dependents?," 2. See also Michelle Chen, "The Absurdly Rational Logic of Wages for Wives," *Nation*, April 7, 2015, 1–9.

81. Both quotes from Eastman, "Modern Adventures in Maternity," typescript of early or initial draft, courtesy of Rebecca Young, 2.

82. Eastman, "Modern Adventures in Maternity," typescript of revised draft, 2.

83. Regina G. Kunzel, *Fallen Women, Problem Girls: Unmarried Mothers and the Professionalization of Social Work, 1890–1945* (New Haven, CT: Yale University Press, 1993).

84. Eastman, "Modern Adventures in Maternity," typescript of revised draft, 5.

85. Karen Chow, "Popular Sexual Knowledges and Women's Agency in 1920s England: Marie Stopes's 'Married Love' and E. M. Hull's 'The Sheik,'" *Feminist Review* 63, no. 64 (1999): 64–87.

86. Eastman, "Modern Adventures in Maternity," typescript of early or initial draft, 2.

87. Eastman, "Modern Adventures in Maternity," typescript of revised draft, 3.

88. Eastman, "Modern Adventures in Maternity," typescript of revised draft, 17.

89. Eastman, "Modern Adventures in Maternity," typescript of revised draft, 3.

90. The redefinition of the family unit as a mother with her child or children is the subject of Martha Fineman, *The Neutered Mother, the Sexual Family and Other Twentieth Century Tragedies* (New York: Routledge, 1995).

91. Eastman, "Modern Adventures in Maternity," typescript of revised draft, 8.

92. Eastman, "Modern Adventures in Maternity," typescript of revised draft, 8.

93. Eastman, "Modern Adventures in Maternity," typescript of revised draft, 16.

94. Eastman, "Modern Adventures in Maternity," typescript of revised draft, 15. See also Graham Richards, "Britain on the Couch: The Popularization of Psychoanalysis in Britain 1918–1940, *Science in Context* 13, no. 2 (2000): 183–230.

95. All quotes from Eastman, "Modern Adventures in Maternity," typescript of revised draft, 17. See also Mari Jo Buhle, *Feminism and Its Discontents: A Century of Struggle with Psychoanalysis* (Cambridge, MA: Harvard University Press, 2000).

96. All quotes from Eastman, "Modern Adventures in Maternity," typescript of revised draft, 18.

97. Crystal Eastman, typescript proposal for new column, n.d. [1927], CEP, box 6, folder 192.

98. Crystal Eastman, "Women at the Cross-Roads," typescript proposal for a new column, n.d. [1927], courtesy of Rebecca Young; Andy Heath to CE, March 2, 1927, CEP, box 6, folder 192.

99. Crystal Eastman, "What Shall We Do With the Women's Page?," *Time and Tide*, May 20, 1927, 470.

CHAPTER 11

1. CE to PK, February 18, 1926, Survey Associates Records, box 67.

2. PK to CE, April 30, 1926, Survey Associates Records, box 67.

3. See "Socialist Women of Eighteen Countries Meet at Marseilles," *Equal Rights*, September 26, 1925, 262–63.

4. "League Labor Body Flayed. Woman Protection Clause Draws Wrath of Feminist," *Spokesman Review*, June 3, 1926.

5. Crystal Eastman, "The Great Rejection: Part I," *Equal Rights*, June 19, 1926, 149.

6. Open Door Council First Annual Report 1926–27, April 4, 1927, National Woman's Party Papers, Group II, box 262, folder 2. Rhondda had previously founded another feminist society, the Six Point Group, in 1921. See The Viscountess Rhondda, *This Was My World* (London: Macmillan and Company, 1933); Angela V. John, *Turning the Tide: The Life of Lady Rhondda* (London: Parthian Books, 2014). See also Catherine Clay, "'The Modern Weekly for the Modern Woman': *Time and Tide*, Feminism and Interwar Print Culture," *Women: A Cultural Review* 27, no. 4 (2016): 397–411.

7. Crystal Eastman, "The Great Rejection, Part I," 149.

8. Crystal Eastman, "The Great Rejection, Part II," *Equal Rights*, June 26, 1926, 157.

9. Crystal Eastman, "The Great Rejection, Part III," *Equal Rights*, July 3, 1926, 167.

10. Crystal Eastman, "Woman's Party Accepts Paris Repulse as Spur to a World-Wide Feminist Movement," *The World*, June 27, 1926, 3.

11. Eastman, "The Great Rejection, Part III," 167.

12. CE to PK, January 6, 1927, Survey Associates Papers (hereinafter Survey Papers), box 67.

13. Crystal Eastman, "Boosting England: An American View," *Time and Tide*, October 29, 1926, 925.

14. All quotes from CE to PK, February 18, 1926, Survey Papers, box 67.

15. F. Scott Fitzgerald letter from Antibes in summer 1926, cited in Sadie Stein, "On the Occasion of Zelda Fitzgerald's Birthday," *Paris Review* blog, July 24, 2013, https://www.theparisreview.org/blog/2013/07/24/on-the-occasion-of-zelda-fitzgeralds-birthday/. Also cited by Garrison Keillor, *The Writer's Almanac*, www.publicradio.org.

16. CE to PK, January 6, 1927, Survey Papers, box 67.

17. CE to PK, January 6, 1927, Survey Papers, box 67.

18. PK to CE, January 20, 1927, Survey Papers, box 67.

19. PK to CE, January 20, 1927, Survey Papers, box 67.

20. PK to CE, January 27, 1927, Survey Papers, box 67.

21. PK to CE, January 27, 1927, Survey Papers, box 67.

22. All quotes from CE to PK, March 2, 1927, Survey Papers, box 67.

23. CE to PK, April 25, 1927, Survey Papers, box 67.

24. CE to PK, April 25, 1927, Survey Papers, box 67.

25. CE to PK, April 24, 1926, Survey Papers, box 67.

26. CE to PK, March 2, 1927, Survey Papers, box 67.

27. PK to CE, May 12, 1927, Survey Papers, box 67.

28. PK to CE, May 12, 1927, Survey Papers, box 67.

29. PK to CE, May 12, 1927, Survey Papers, box 67.

30. CE to the Fuller family, September 17, 1927, courtesy of Rebecca Young.

31. CE to Dr. King, September 23, 1927, courtesy of Rebecca Young.

32. Crystal Eastman, fundraising letter, January 5, 1928, Survey Papers, box 67.

33. CE to Charles Hallinan, December 5, 1927, CEP, box 6, folder 192.

34. CE to Cynthia Fuller, December 31, 1927, courtesy of Rebecca Young.

35. CE to Charles Hallinan (with note to Hazel inside), December 5, 1927, CEP, box 6, folder 192.

36. CE to Cynthia Fuller, New Year's Eve, 1927, courtesy of Rebecca Young.

37. CE to Charles Hallinan (with note to Hazel inside), December 5, 1927, CEP, box 6, folder 192.

38. CE to Cynthia Fuller, New Year's Eve, 1927, courtesy of Rebecca Young.

39. CE to Charles Hallinan (with note to Hazel inside), December 5, 1927, CEP, box 6, folder 192.

40. CE to Cynthia Fuller, New Year's Eve, 1927, courtesy of Rebecca Young.

41. National Woman's Party Papers, Group II, box 262, US Library of Congress, Washington, DC.

42. Lewis Gannett to Max Eastman, quoted in Max Eastman, *Love and Revolution: My Journey through an Epoch* (New York: Random House, 1964), 504.

43. Eastman, *Love and Revolution*, 505.

44. CE to Ruth Pickering Pinchot, Friday, n.d., courtesy of Rebecca Young.

45. CE to Cynthia Fuller, December 31, 1927, courtesy of Rebecca Young.

46. ME to the Fuller sisters, July 31, 1928, courtesy of Rebecca Young.

47. CE Estate Papers, CEP, box 7, folder 200, folder 201.

48. ME to the Fuller sisters, July 31, 1928, courtesy of Rebecca Young.

49. ME to the Fuller sisters, July 31, 1928, courtesy of Rebecca Young.

50. Westchester County Archives, Elmsford, New York.

51. CE Estate Papers, CEP, box 7, folder 200, folder 201.

52. Crystal Eastman note to her children, n.d., courtesy of Rebecca Young.

53. Max Eastman, "Crystal's Last Words on Her Death-Bed," unpublished notes, courtesy of Rebecca Young. Upon Crystal's death, Ruth Pickering Pinchot replied to a letter from Max, saying, "You have been so good, and Crystal was so happy with you. I'm so glad she thought you loved her all alone—," Ruth Pickering Pinchot at Maidstone Inn, East Hampton, to ME, Sunday, n.d. [July 29, 1928], courtesy of Rebecca Young.

54. ME to Ruth Pickering Pinchot, July 3, 1928, courtesy of Rebecca Young.

55. Freda Kirchwey, "Crystal Eastman," *The Nation*, August 8, 1928, 128. See also Katharine Ward Fisher, "Crystal Eastman," *Equal Rights*, August 18, 1928, 219–20.

EPILOGUE

1. ME to Cynthia Fuller, August 11, 1928, courtesy of Rebecca Young.

2. Ruth Pickering Pinchot to ME, September 20, 1928, courtesy of Rebecca Young.

3. PK to Charles Hallinan, May 20, 1929, courtesy of Rebecca Young.

4. Ruth Pickering Pinchot to ME, September 20, 1928, courtesy of Rebecca Young.

5. Author interview with Yvette Eastman, New York City, September 20, 2007.

6. Author interview with Yvette Eastman, New York City, September 20, 2007.

7. Author interview with Nancy Hallinan, New York City, July 30, 2008.

8. All quotes from PK to Charles Hallinan, May 20, 1929, courtesy of Rebecca Young.

9. PK to Charles Hallinan, May 20, 1929, courtesy of Rebecca Young.

10. Author interview with Rebecca Young, New York City, September 20, 2010. Author interview with Charles Young, Martha's Vineyard, Massachusetts, April 3, 2010.

11. AFE to CE, May 10, 1903, CEP, box 5, folder 131.

BIBLIOGRAPHY

MANUSCRIPT COLLECTIONS

Columbia University Archival Collections, Columbia University, New York, New York
- Papers of Lillian D. Wald, 1895–1936

Houghton Library, Harvard University, Cambridge, Massachusetts
- John Reed Papers
- Oswald Garrison Villard Papers

Kathryn and Shelby Cullom Davis Library, St. John's University, New York, New York
- Records of the Liability Insurance Association, 1908–10

Kheel Center for Labor-Management Documentation and Archives, Cornell University, Ithaca, New York
- American Association for Labor Legislation Papers

Lilly Library Manuscript Collections, Indiana University, Bloomington, Indiana
- Florence Deshon Papers
- Max Eastman Papers
- Anstice Eastman Papers

New York Public Library, Manuscript Division, New York, New York
- Lillian D. Wald Papers, 1889–1957
- Schwimmer-Lloyd Collection

New York State Archives, Albany, New York
- Records of the New York State Legislature, Joint Legislative Committee to Investigate Seditious Activities

Schlesinger Library, Harvard University, Cambridge, Massachusetts
- Crystal Eastman Papers
- Hazel Hunkins Hallinan Papers
- Inez Milholland Papers
- Mary Ware Dennett Papers

Social Welfare History Archives, Elmer L. Andersen Library, University of Minnesota
- Paul U. Kellogg Papers
- Survey Associates Records

Swarthmore College Peace Collection, Swarthmore College, Swarthmore, Pennsylvania
- American Union against Militarism Records
- Jane Addams Papers
- Papers of the People's Council of America for Democracy and Peace Collected Records
- Records of the Women's International League for Peace and Freedom
- William Isaac Hull Papers
- Woman's Peace Party Papers

University of Sussex Library Special Collections, University of Sussex, Brighton, UK
- Leonard Woolf Archive

US Library of Congress, Washington, DC
- Amos Pinchot Papers
- National Woman's Party Records

US National Archives, Washington, DC
- General Records of the US Department of Treasury
- Records of the US Department of State, Secret Service Division
- Records of the US Department of Justice, Bureau of Investigation

Vassar College Archives, Vassar College, Poughkeepsie, New York

Westchester County Archives, Elmsford, New York

Wisconsin Historical Society Archives
- Papers of Ada Lois James, Part Two: Women's Suffrage in Wisconsin (microfilm collection)

BOOKS, ARTICLES, PROCEEDINGS

Abrams, Kerry. "Polygamy, Prostitution, and the Federalization of Immigration Law." *Columbia Law Review* 105, no. 3 (2005): 641–716.

Adams, Katherine H., and Michael L. Keene. *Alice Paul and the American Suffrage Campaign*. Champaign: University of Illinois Press, 2008.

Addams, Jane. *Newer Ideals of Peace: The Moral Substitutes for War*. Chester, NY: Anza Publishing, 2005.

Addams, Jane. *Peace and Bread in Time of War*. Urbana: University of Illinois Press, 2002.

Addams, Jane. *Twenty Years at Hull House*. Edited by James Hurt. Champaign: University of Illinois Press, 1990.

Addams, Jane, Emily G. Balch, and Alice Hamilton. *Women at The Hague: The International Congress of Women and Its Results*. Edited by Harriet Hyman Alonso. Chicago: University of Illinois Press, 2003.

Adickes, Sandra. *To Be Young Was Very Heaven: Women in New York before the First World War*. New York: St. Martins, 1997.

Alberti, Johanna. *Beyond Suffrage: Feminists in War and Peace, 1914–28*. London: Palgrave Macmillan, 1989.

Alonso, Harriet Hyman. *Peace as a Women's Issue: A History of the U.S. Peace Movement for World Peace and Women's Rights*. Syracuse, NY: Syracuse University Press, 1993.

Alpern, Sara. *Freda Kirchwey: A Woman of The Nation*. Cambridge, MA: Harvard University Press, 1987.

American Sociological Association. "Franklin H. Giddings." ASANet. 2004. http://www.asanet.org/about-asa/asa-story/asa-history/past-asa-officers/past-asa-presidents/franklin-h-giddings.

Anderson, Mary, as told to Mary N. Winslow. *Women at Work: The Autobiography of Mary Anderson*. Minneapolis: University of Minnesota Press, 1951.

Ansah, Ama. "Votes for Women Means Votes for Black Women, National Women's History Museum." https://www.womenshistory.org/articles/votes-women- means-votes-black-women.

Arthur, Anthony. *Radical Innocent: Upton Sinclair*. New York: Random House, 2006.

Associated Press. "Editorial." *New York Times*, March 7, 1914.

Baldwin, Roger. "Recollections of a Life in Civil Liberties, Part I." *Civil Liberties Review* 2, no. 2 (1975): 31–72.

Banks, William M. *Black Intellectuals: Race and Responsibility in American Life*. New York: W. W. Norton, 1996.

Barrows, John Henry. *The World's Parliament of Religions: An Illustrated and Popular Story of the World's First Parliament of Religions*. Chicago: Parliament Publishing Company, 1893.

Becker, Susan D. *The Origins of the Equal Rights Amendment: American Feminism between the Wars*. Westport, CT: Greenwood Press, 1981.

Bekken, Jon. "These Great and Dangerous Powers: Postal Censorship of the Press." *Journal of Communication Inquiry* 15, no. 1 (Winter 1991): 55–71.

Belknap, Michal, "The Mechanics of Repression: J. Edgar Hoover, the Bureau of Investigation and the Radicals 1917–1925." *Crime and Social Justice* 7 (Spring–Summer 1977): 49–58.

Bennett, Scott H., and Charles F. Howlett, eds. *Antiwar Dissent and Peace Activism in World War I America: A Documentary Reader*. Lincoln: University of Nebraska Press, 2014.

Berkeley Daily Gazette. "Liberator Company Sues Police Head." May 13, 1920.

Bernays, Edward. *Propaganda*. New York: Horace Liveright, 1928.

Blackwell, Alice Stone. *Lucy Stone: Pioneer of Woman's Rights*. Edited by Randolph Hollingworth. Charlottesville: University Press of Virginia, 2001.

Blatch, Harriot Stanton. *Mobilizing Woman Power*. New York: The Woman's Press, 1918.

Brenner, Anita. *The Wind That Swept Mexico: The Story of the Mexican Revolution of 1910–1942*. Austin: University of Texas Press, 1984.

Brooke, Stephen. "The Body and Socialism: Dora Russell in the 1920s." *Past & Present* 189, no. 1 (2005): 147–77.

Brooklyn Daily Eagle. "English Suffragettes' Methods Are Scorned." March 20, 1912.

Bryan, William Jennings. "Cross of Gold Speech, July 8, 1896." *American History from Revolution to Reconstruction and Beyond*. http://www.let.rug.nl/usa/documents/1876-1900/william-jennings-bryan-cross-of-gold-speech-july-8-1896.php.

Bryant, Louise. "The Pacifists at 70 Fifth Avenue." *New York Tribune*, March 18, 1917.

Buenker, John D., and William Fletch Thompson. *The History of Wisconsin*. Vol. 4, *The Progressive Era, 1893–1914*. Madison: State Historical Society of Wisconsin, 1998.

Buhle, Mari Jo. *Concise History of Woman Suffrage: Selections from the History of Woman Suffrage*. Cambridge, MA: Harvard University Press, 1981.

Buhle, Mari Jo. *Feminism and Its Discontents: A Century of Struggle with Psychoanalysis*. Cambridge, MA: Harvard University Press, 2000.

Buhle, Mari Jo. *Women and American Socialism: 1870–1920*. Urbana: University of Illinois Press, 1981.

Carastathis, Anna. "The Concept of Intersectionality in Feminist Theory." *Philosophy Compass* 9, no. 5 (2014): 304–14.

Carter, Patricia. "Guiding the Working Class Girl: Henrietta Rodman's Curriculum for the New Woman, 1913." *Frontiers* 38 (November 1, 2017): 124–55.

Chambers, Clarke A. *Paul U. Kellogg and The Survey: Voices for Social Welfare and Social Justice*. Minneapolis: University of Minnesota Press, 1971.

Chatfield, Charles. *Peace Movements in America*. New York: Schocken Books, 1972.

Chatfield, Charles. "World War I and the Liberal Pacifist in the United States." *American Historical Review* 75, no. 7 (December 1970): 1920–37.

Chen, Constance M. *"The Sex Side of Life": Mary Ware Dennett's Pioneering Battle for Birth Control and Sex Education*. New York: New Press, 1997.

Chen, Michelle. "The Absurdly Rational Logic of Wages for Wives." *Nation*, April 7, 2015.

Chesler, Ellen. *Woman of Valor: Margaret Sanger and the Birth Control Movement in America*. New York: Simon & Schuster, 1992.

Chicago Tribune. "'Miss' Eastman Seeks Divorce, Scorns Alimony." February 29, 1916.

Chow, Karen. "Popular Sexual Knowledges and Women's Agency in 1920s England: Marie Stopes's 'Married Love' and E. M. Hull's 'The Sheik.'" *Feminist Review* 63 (Autumn 1999): 64–87.

Christian Science Monitor. "Woman Gets Federal Place." November 1, 1913.

Chun, Jennifer Jihye, George Lipsitz, and Young Shin. "Intersectionality as Social Movement Strategy: Asian Immigrant Women Advocates." *Signs* 38, no. 4 (Summer 2013): 917–40.

Churchill, Allen. *The Improper Bohemians*. New York: Ace Books, 1959.

Clay, Catherine. "'The Modern Weekly for the Modern Woman': *Time and Tide*, Feminism and Interwar Print Culture." *Women: A Cultural Review* 27, no. 4 (2016): 397–411.

Cohen, Miriam. "Women and the Progressive Movement." Gilder Lehrman Institute of American History. https://www.gilderlehrman.org/history-by-era/politics-reform/essays/women-and-progressive-movement#_ftn5.

Cole, Elizabeth R. "Coalitions as a Model for Intersectionality: From Practice to Theory." *Sex Roles* 59, no. 5/6 (2008): 443–53.

Collins, Patricia H. "Intersectionality's Definitional Dilemmas." *Annual Review of Sociology* 41 (2015): 1–20.

Commission for Enduring Peace. Hearings before the Committee on Foreign Affairs, U.S. House of Representatives, Sixty-Fourth Congress, First Session, January 11, 1916.

Committee on Military Affairs, Hearings on H.R. 12766, To Increase the Military Establishment of the United States, Sixty-Fourth Congress, First Session, US House of Representatives, January 6–February 11, 1916.

Cook, Blanch Wiesen. "Crystal Eastman." In *Portraits of American Women: From Settlement to the Present*, edited by G. J. Barker-Benfield and Catherine Clinton, 403–28. New York: Oxford University Press, 1998.

Cook, Blanche Wiesen, ed. *Crystal Eastman on Women and Revolution*. New York: Oxford University Press, 1978.

Cook, Blanche Wiesen. "Democracy in Wartime: Antimilitarism in England and the United States, 1914–1918." *American Studies* 13 (Spring 1972): 60–61.

Cook, Blanche Wiesen. "Female Support Networks and Political Activism: Lillian Wald, Crystal Eastman, Emma Goldman." *Chrysalis* 3 (Autumn 1977): 43–61.

Cook, Blanche Wiesen, ed. *Toward the Great Change: Crystal and Max Eastman on Feminism, Antimilitarism and Revolution*. New York: Garland Publishing, 1976.

Corliss, Richard. "D.W. Griffith's *The Birth of a Nation* 100 Years Later: Still Great, Still Shameful." *Time*, March 3, 2015.

Cott, Nancy. "Feminist Politics in the 1920s: The National Woman's Party." *Journal of American History* 71, no. 1 (June 1984): 33–68.

Cott, Nancy. *The Grounding of Modern Feminism*. New Haven, CT: Yale University Press, 1987.

Cottrell, Robert C. "Roger Nash Baldwin, the National Civil Liberties Bureau, and Military Intelligence during World War I." *The Historian* 60, no. 1 (Fall 1997): 87–106.

Cottrell, Robert. *Roger Nash Baldwin and the American Civil Liberties Union*. New York: Columbia University Press, 2001.

Craig, John M. "'The Sex Side of Life': The Obscenity Case of Mary Ware Dennett." *Frontiers: A Journal of Women's Studies* 15, no. 3 (1995): 145–56.

Craig, John M. "Red-Baiting, Pacifism and Free Speech: Lucia Ames Mead and Her 1926 Lecture Tour in Atlanta and the Southeast." *Georgia Historical Quarterly* 71, no. 4 (Winter 1987): 601–22.

Creel, George. *How We Advertised America: The First Telling of the Amazing Story of the Committee on Public Information That Carried the Gospel of Americanism to Every Corner of the Globe*. New York: Harper and Brothers, 1920.

Crenshaw, Kimberle. "Mapping the Margins: Intersectionality, Identity Politics, and Violence against Women of Color." *Stanford Law Review* 43, no. 6 (July 1991): 1241–99.

Crossland, David. "Germany Set to Make Final World War I Reparation Payment." ABC News, September 29, 2010. http://abcnews.go.com/International/germany-makes-final-reparation-payments-world-war/story?id=11755920.

D'Agostino, Mary L. "New York State's 2007 Workers' Compensation Reform: Success or Failure?" *Albany Law Review* 76, no. 1 (2013): 367–402.

The Daily Messenger. "Max Eastman, Late Author, Got Early Schooling Here." May 6, 1969.

Daniels, Doris Groshen. *Always a Sister: The Feminism of Lillian D. Wald*. New York: Feminist Press, 1995.

Daniels, Roger. *Guarding the Golden Door: American Immigration Policy and Immigrants since 1882*. New York: Hill and Wang, 2005.

Davis, Erin F. "Love's Labors Lost?: Crystal Eastman's Contribution to Workers' Compensation Reform." Unpublished article, Stanford Legal Women's History Project, Fall 2002.

Davis, Martha F. "The Equal Rights Amendment: Then and Now." *Columbia Journal of Gender and Law* 17, no. 3 (2008): 419–60.

The Day. "Suffragists Win Another Office." November 15, 1913.

DeBauche, Leslie Midkiff. *Reel Patriotism: The Movies and World War I*. Madison: University of Wisconsin Press, 1997.

DeLap, Lucy. *The Feminist Avant-Garde: Transatlantic Encounters of the Early Twentieth Century*. Cambridge: Cambridge University Press, 2007.

Dell, Floyd. "Indictment on Criminal Libel." *The Masses*, January 1914.

Dell, Floyd. *Love in Greenwich Village*. New York: George H. Doran Company, 1926.

Dell, Floyd. "Memories of the Old Masses." *American Mercury*, April 1949.

Dell, Floyd. *Women as World Builders, Studies in Modern Feminism*. Chicago: Forbes and Company, 1913.

Des Jardins, Julie. *Women and the Historical Enterprise in America: Gender, Race and the Politics of Memory, 1880–1945*. Chapel Hill: University of North Carolina Press, 2003.

Devine, Edward T. *American Social Work in the Twentieth Century*. Cambridge: Frontier Press, 1921.

Devine, Edward T. "Results of the Pittsburgh Survey." *American Journal of Sociology* 14, no. 5 (March 1909): 660–67.

Doty, Madeleine Zabriskie. *Society's Misfits*. New York: Century, 1916.

DuBois, Ellen Carol. *Feminism and Suffrage: The Emergence of an Independent Women's Movement in America*. Ithaca: Cornell University Press, 1978.

Dubois, Ellen Carol. *Harriot Stanton Blatch and the Winning of Woman Suffrage*. New Haven, CT: Yale University Press, 1999.

DuBois, Ellen Carol. *Woman Suffrage and Women's Rights*. New York: New York University Press, 1998.

Duckett, Kenneth W. "Suffragettes on the Stump: Letter from the Political Equality League of Wisconsin, 1912." *Wisconsin Magazine of History* 38, no. 1 (Autumn 1954): 31–36.

Dumenil, Lynn. *The Modern Temper: American Culture and Society in the 1920s*. 2nd ed. New York: Hill and Wang, 1996.

Dunkirk Evening Observer. "Suffragists and Antis Meet in Annual Hearing before Judiciary Committees in Albany." March 10, 1910.

Eastman, Annis Ford. *Have and Give and Other Parables*. Elmira, NY, 1896.

Eastman, Annis Ford. *Have Salt in Yourselves: To Young Ladies*. New York: American Home Missionary Society, n.d.

Eastman, Crystal. "An Acid Test for Suffragists." *London Daily Herald*, June 1925.

Eastman, Crystal. "Address of Miss Crystal Eastman." *Addresses Made at the Fourth Annual Meeting of the Employer Liability Association, October 20, 1910*. Records of the Liability Insurance Association, 1908–1910. Kathryn and Shelby Cullom Davis Library, St. John's University.

Eastman, Crystal. "Aeroplanes and Jails." *Liberator*, November 1918.

Eastman, Crystal. "Alice Paul's Convention." *Liberator*, April 1921.

Eastman, Crystal. "The American Way of Distributing Industrial Accident Losses." *American Economic Association Quarterly*, 3rd ser., 10, no. 1. In *Papers and Discussions of the Twenty-First Annual Meeting. Atlantic City, N.J., December 28–31, 1908* (April 1909): 119–34.

Eastman, Crystal. "Are Wives Partners or Dependents?" Unpublished article, n.d. [1920s], courtesy of Rebecca Young.

Eastman, Crystal. "Bed-Makers and Bosses." *Time and Tide*, October 12, 1923.

Eastman, Crystal. "Bertrand Russell on Bringing Up Children." *Children: The Magazine for Parents*, March 1927.

Eastman, Crystal. "Birth Control in the Feminist Program." *Birth Control Review*, January 1918, 1.

Eastman, Crystal. "Boosting England: An American View." *Time and Tide*, October 29, 1926.

Eastman, Crystal. "Boys and Girls." *Time and Tide*, January 4, 1924.

Eastman, Crystal. "British Labor Is Moving." *Liberator*, September 1919.

Eastman, Crystal. "British Women Fire First Gun in Their Second Suffrage Battle." *Equal Rights*, February 27, 1926.

Eastman, Crystal. "Caroline Haslett and the Women Engineers." *Equal Rights*, April 10, 1926.

Eastman, Crystal. "Crystal Eastman in Hungary." *Liberator*, July 1919.

Eastman, Crystal. "Daniel Raymond." Master's thesis, Columbia University, 1904, Columbia University Archives.

Eastman, Crystal. "Debs and His Contemporaries." *Liberator*, May 1921.

Eastman, Crystal. "1848–1923." *Time and Tide*, July 27, 1923.

Eastman, Crystal. *Employers' Liability, a Criticism Based on Fact*. New York: American Association of Labor Legislation, January 1, 1909.

Eastman, Crystal. "Employer's Liability and Its Relation to Injured Workmen." *Trenton Evening Times*, March 9, 1908.

Eastman, Crystal. "English Feminism and Special Labor Laws for Women." *Equal Rights*, April 18, 1925.

Eastman, Crystal. "Equalitarian vs. Reformer." *Equal Rights*, June 4, 1927.

Eastman, Crystal. "Equality or Protection?" *Equal Rights*, March 15, 1923.

Eastman, Crystal. "Equal Rights Amendment." *New Republic*, November 19, 1924.

Eastman, Crystal. "Feminism, a Statement Read at the First Feminist Congress in the United States." *Liberator*, May 1919.

Eastman, Crystal. "Feminists Must Fight." *The Nation*, November 12, 1924.

Eastman, Crystal. "The Great Rejection: Part I." *Equal Rights*, June 19, 1926.

Eastman, Crystal. "The Great Rejection, Part II." *Equal Rights*, June 26, 1926.

Eastman, Crystal. "The Great Rejection, Part III." *Equal Rights*, July 3, 1926.

Eastman, Crystal. "Impressions of the AF of L Convention." *Liberator*, August 1918.

Eastman, Crystal. "In Communist Hungary." *Liberator*, August 1919.

Eastman, Crystal. "Industrial Relations and the Law." US Commission on Industrial Relations, 1912–1915. Unpublished Records of the Division of Research and Investigation: Reports, Staff Studies, and Background Research Materials, reel 6.

Eastman, Crystal. "International Cooperation." *Equal Rights*, May 9, 1925.

Eastman, Crystal. "Is Woman's Place the Home?" *Equal Rights*, June 13, 1925.

Eastman, Crystal. "Justice for the Prostitute—Lady Astor's Bill." *Equal Rights*, September 19, 1925.

Eastman, Crystal. "Lady Rhondda Contends That Women of Leisure Are 'Menace.'" *Christian Science Monitor*, March 8, 1927.

Eastman, Crystal. "Letter to the Editor of *Time and Tide*." *Time and Tide*, March 18, 1927.

Eastman, Crystal. "Limitation of Armaments." *Year Book of the Woman's Peace Party, the Section for the United States of the International Committee of Women for Permanent Peace*, 1916: 16–17.

Eastman, Crystal. "Lindbergh's Mother." *Time and Tide*, May 27, 1927.

Eastman, Crystal. "London Letter—The Married Teacher." *Equal Rights*, January 30, 1926.

Eastman, Crystal. "Marriage under Two Roofs." *Cosmopolitan*, December 1923.

Eastman, Crystal. *The Mexican-American League*. New York: Mexican-American Peace Committee of the AUAM, 1916.

Eastman, Crystal. "Modern Adventures in Maternity." Unpublished manuscripts, n.d. [1920s], courtesy of Rebecca Young.

Eastman, Crystal. "The Mooney Congress." *Liberator*, March 1919.

Eastman, Crystal. "Mother-Worship." *The Nation*, March 16, 1927.

Eastman, Crystal. "'Now I Dare to Do It': An Interview with Dr. Aletta Jacobs, Who Called the Woman's Peace Congress at The Hague." *Survey*, October 9, 1915.

Eastman, Crystal. "Now We Can Begin." *Liberator*, December 1920.

Eastman, Crystal. *Our War Record: A Plea for Tolerance*. Woman's Peace Party of New York City, January 1, 1918.

Eastman, Crystal. "Personalities and Powers: Alice Paul." *Time and Tide*, July 20, 1923.

Eastman, Crystal. "Philosophy of the Poor." *Eau Claire Sunday Leader*, January 10, 1909.

Eastman, Crystal. "A Platform of Real Preparedness." *Survey*, November 13, 1915.

Eastman, Crystal. "Practical Feminism." *Liberator*, January 1920.

Eastman, Crystal. *A Program for Voting Women*. New York: Woman's Peace Party of New York, March 1919.

Eastman, Crystal. "Protective Legislation in England." *Equal Rights*, October 3, 1925.

Eastman, Crystal. "Radicals Here Offer Lives to Russia." *New York Evening Call*, February 28, 1918.

Eastman, Crystal. "Recent Developments in England." *Equal Rights*, January 22, 1927.

Eastman, Crystal. "Rome, May 14, 1923." *London Daily Herald*, May 1923.

Eastman, Crystal. "Signs of the Times." *Liberator*, December 1918.

Eastman, Crystal. "The Socialist Party Convention." *Liberator*, July 1920.

Eastman, Crystal. "The Socialist Vote." *Liberator*, December 1918.

Eastman, Crystal. "Socialist Women of Eighteen Countries Meet at Marseilles." *Equal Rights*, September 26, 1925.

Eastman, Crystal. "Suffragists Ten Years After." *New Republic*, June 27, 1923.

Eastman, Crystal. "Three Essentials for Accident Prevention." In *Annals of the American Academy of Political and Social Science* 38, no. 1 (July 1911): 98–107.

Eastman, Crystal. "To Make War Unthinkable." *New Republic*, July 24, 1915.

Eastman, Crystal. "War and Peace." *Survey*, December 30, 1916.

Eastman, Crystal. "What Feminism Means to Me, an Address Delivered at the First Feminist Meeting Held in Cooper Union, New York City, February 1914." *Vassar Miscellany*, June 15, 1915.

Eastman, Crystal. "What Is Real Protection?" *Equal Rights*, February 19, 1927.

Eastman, Crystal. "What Next?" *The Suffragist*, November 1920.

Eastman, Crystal. "What Shall We Do with the Woman's Page?" *Time and Tide*, May 20, 1927.

Eastman, Crystal. "Who Is Dora Black?" *Equal Rights*, June 5, 1926.

Eastman, Crystal. "Why Study War and Peace." *New York Tribune*, October 17, 1915.

Eastman, Crystal. "Woman's Party Accepts Paris Repulse as Spur to a World-Wide Feminist Movement," *The World*, June 27, 1926.

Eastman, Crystal. "Women at the Cross-Roads." Unpublished manuscript, n.d. [1920s], courtesy of Rebecca Young.

Eastman, Crystal. "Women, Rights and Privileges." *London Outlook*, February 5, 1927.

Eastman, Crystal. "Work Accidents and Employers' Liability." *Survey*, September 3, 1910.

Eastman, Crystal. *Work Accidents and the Law*. New York: Russell Sage Foundation, 1910.

Eastman, Crystal. "The Workers of the Clyde." *Liberator*, October 1919.

Eastman, Crystal. "Workers under Trial." *Eau Claire Sunday Leader*, January 10, 1909.

Eastman, Crystal. "A Year's Work Accidents and Their Cost." *Charities and the Commons*, March 1909.

Eastman (Benedict), Crystal. "A Comment." *Jus Suffragii*, July 15, 1913.

Eastman (Benedict), Crystal. "Millions of Unpaid Wives." *Washington Herald*, May 26, 1915.

Eastman (Benedict), Crystal. "The Political Recognition of Women." In *Report of the Sixteenth Annual Meeting of the State Bar Association of Indiana; South Bend, July 10 and 11, 1912*, 257–67. Indianapolis: State Bar Association of Indiana, 1912.

Eastman (Benedict), Crystal. "Why We Lost Wisconsin." James Papers, November 25, 1912, reel 12.

Eastman (Benedict), Crystal. "Wisconsin Has High Hopes." *Woman's Journal*, September 14, 1912.

Eastman (Benedict), Crystal. "Wisconsin Women Active along Many Lines." *Woman's Journal*, May 4, 1912.

Eastman, Max. "Confessions of a Suffrage Orator." *The Masses*, November 1915.

Eastman, Max. "Crystal's Last Words on Her Death-Bed." Unpublished notes, courtesy of Rebecca Young.

Eastman, Max. "Early History of the Men's League." *Woman Voter*, October 1912.

Eastman, Max. *Enjoyment of Living*. New York: Harper & Brothers, 1948.

Eastman, Max. "The Hero as Parent." In *Heroes I Have Known: Twelve Who Lived Great Lives*, edited by Max Eastman, 1–14. New York: Simon & Schuster, 1942.

Eastman, Max. *Love and Revolution: My Journey through an Epoch*. New York: Random House, 1964.

Eastman, Max. "Mark Twain's Elmira." *Harper's*, May 1938.

Eastman, Max. "The Old Bohemia—Noble, Crazy Glorious." *Village Voice*, June 24, 1959.

Eckhaus, Phyllis. "Restless Women: The Pioneering Alumni of NYU Law School." *NYU Law Review* 66 (1991): 1996–2013.

"Editorial: Their Mutual Contributions." *Equal Rights*, August 22, 1925.

"Editorial: 'Wages for Wives.'" *Equal Rights*, December 4, 1926.

"Editorial: Wives and Family Incomes." *Equal Rights*, July 21, 1934.

Editorial (unsigned). *Liberator*, March 1918.

Editorial (unsigned). *Liberator*, February 1919.

Editorial (unsigned). *Liberator*, March 1919.

Editorial (unsigned). *Liberator*, June 1919.

Editorial (unsigned). *Liberator*, January 1921.

Employer Liability Commission. Report of the Employer Liability Commission, New York Historical Society, New York State Legislature, Senate Documents, 1910, vol. 25, no. 38, fiche 5.

Evening Star. "Clayton Act Bars Way to Freedom of Labor." May 16, 1915.

Evening Telegram. "College Girls Form Club to Promote Exercise for Women." November 10, 1909.

Evidentiary Hearing, Employer Liability Commission, New York State Legislature, Senate Documents, 1910.

Faludi, Susan. "American Electra: Feminism's Ritual Matricide." *Harper's*, October 2010, 29–42.

Feld, Marjorie N. *Lillian Wald: A Biography.* Chapel Hill: University of North Carolina Press, 2008.

Filippelli, Ronald L. *Labor Conflict in the United States: An Encyclopedia.* New York: Garland Publishing, 1990.

Finan, Christopher. *From the Palmer Raids to the Patriot Act: A History of the Fight for Free Speech in America.* Boston: Beacon Press, 2008.

Fine, Gary Alan. *Difficult Reputations: Collective Memories of the Evil, Inept and Controversial.* Chicago: University of Chicago Press, 2001.

Fine, Gary Alan. "Reputational Entrepreneurs and the Memory of Incompetence: Melting Supporters, Partisan Warriors, and Images of President Harding." *American Journal of Sociology* 101, no. 5 (March 1996): 1159–93.

Fineman, Martha. *The Neutered Mother, The Sexual Family and Other Twentieth Century Tragedies.* New York: Routledge, 1995.

Fisher, Katharine Ward. "Crystal Eastman." *Equal Rights*, August 18, 1928.

Flexner, Eleanor. *Century of Struggle: The Woman's Rights Movement in the United States*, 3rd rev. ed. New York: Belknap Press, 1996.

Flushing Daily Times. "Would Call on Women to Strike." December 2, 1910.

Foner, Philip S. *The Bolshevik Revolution: Its Impact on American Radicals, Liberals, and Labor, a Documentary* Study. New York: International Publishers, 1967.

Foner, Philip S. *History of the Labor Movement in the United States.* Vol. 2, *From the Founding of the A. F. of L. to the Emergence of American Imperialism.* New York: International Publishers, 1975.

Forbes, James. "The Reverse Side." In *Wage-Earning Pittsburgh*, edited by Paul Kellogg, 366–85. New York: Survey Associates, 1914.

Frankel, Lee K. "An Insurance Company Seeks to Improve Individual and Public Health." *Modern Hospital* 111, no. 5 (November 1914): 283–88.

Franz, Manuel. "Preparedness Revisited: Civilian Societies and the Campaign for American Defense, 1914–1920." *Journal of the Gilded Age and Progressive Era* 17, no. 4 (2018): 663–76.

Freedman, Russell. *Kids at Work: Lewis Hine and the Crusade against Child Labor.* New York: Clarion Books, 1994.

Freeman, Jo. "The Rise of Political Women in the Election of 1912." *Women's Political History*. http://www.jofreeman.com/polhistory/1912.htm.

Fry, Amelia R. "Conversations with Alice Paul: Woman Suffrage and the Equal Rights Amendment." In *Suffragists Oral History Project*. Berkeley: University of California, 1976.

Fuller, Mathew B. "A History of Student Financial Aid." *Journal of Student Financial Aid* 44, no. 1 (2014): 42–62.

Gage, Beverly. *The Day Wall Street Exploded*. New York: Oxford University Press, 2009.

Gazette-Telegraph. "'Alimony Relic of Dark Ages,' Says Mrs. Eastman." March 12, 1916.

Gerber, David A. *American Immigration: A Very Short Introduction*. New York: Oxford University Press, 2011.

Gerson, Gerson. *The Unfinished Revolution: Coming of Age in a New Era of Gender, Work, and Family*. New York: Oxford University Press, 2011.

Ghodsee, Kristen R. "Why Women Had Better Sex under Socialism." Sunday Review, *New York Times*, August 12, 2017.

Gilman, Charlotte Perkins. *The Home, Its Work and Influence*. New York: McClure Phillips, 1903.

Gilman, Charlotte Perkins. *The Man-Made World*. New York: Cosimo Classics, 2007.

Gilman, Charlotte Perkins. "Masculinism at Its Worst." *Forerunner*, October 1914.

Gilman, Charlotte Perkins. "Maternity Benefits and Reformers." *Forerunner*, March 1916.

Gilman, Charlotte Perkins. *Women and Economics: A Study of the Economic Relation between Men and Women as a Factor in Evolution*. Edited by Michael Kimmel and Amy Aronson. Berkeley: University of California Press, 1998.

Goodier, Susan, and Karen Pastorello. *Women Will Vote: Winning Suffrage in New York State*. Ithaca, NY: Cornell University Press, 2017.

Gordon, Linda. "'Intersectionality,' Socialist Feminism and Contemporary Activism: Musings by a Second-Wave Socialist-Feminist." *Gender & History* 28, no. 2 (August 2016): 340–57.

Gordon, Linda. *The Moral Property of Women: The History of Birth Control in America*. Champaign: University of Illinois Press, 2002.

Gordon, Lynn. "Women and the Anti-Child Labor Movement in Illinois, 1890–1920." *Social Service Review* 51, no. 2 (June 1977): 228–48.

Grant, Marilyn. "The 1912 Suffrage Referendum: An Exercise in Political Action." *Wisconsin Magazine of History* 4, no. 2 (1980–1981): 116–18.

Greenwald, Maurine W. "Elizabeth Beardsley Butler." In *American National Biography*, edited by John A. Garraty and Mark C. Carnes, 803. New York: Oxford University Press, 2004.

Greenwald, Maurine Weiner, and Margo J. Anderson, eds. *Pittsburgh Surveyed: Social Science and Social Science Reform in the Early Twentieth Century*. Pittsburgh: University of Pittsburgh Press, 2011.

Gugushvili, Alexi, Peter Kabachnik, and Ana Kirvalidze. "Collective Memory and Reputational Politics of National Heroes and Villains." *Nationalities Papers* 45, no. 3 (2017): 464–84.

Gwinn, Kristen E. *Emily Greene Balch: The Long Road to Internationalism.* Champaign: University of Illinois Press, 2010.

Hankins, F. H. "Franklin Henry Giddings, 1855–1931: Some Aspects of His Sociological Theory." *American Journal of Sociology* 37, no. 3 (1931): 349–66.

Hayes, Carleton J. H. "Which? War Without a Purpose? Or Armed Neutrality with a Purpose?" *Survey*, February 10, 1917.

Henry, Astrid. *Not My Mother's Sister: Generational Conflict and Third Wave Feminism.* Bloomington: Indiana University Press, 2004.

Hochschild, Adam. *To End All Wars: A Story of Loyalty and Rebellion, 1914–1918.* Boston and New York: Houghton Mifflin Harcourt, 2011.

Hochschild, Arlie, with Anne Machung. *The Second Shift: Working Parents and the Revolution at Home.* New York: Avon Books, 1989.

Hollitz, John. *Contending Voices: Biographical Explorations of the American Past.* Vol. 2, *Since 1865.* Belmont, CA: Wadsworth Publishing, 2010.

Hood, Jack B., Benjamin A. Hardy Jr., and Harold S. Lewis Jr. *Workers' Compensation and Employment Protection Law.* 3rd ed. New York: West Publishing, 1999.

Horn, Max. *The Intercollegiate Socialist Society, 1905–1921: Origins of the Modern Student Movement.* Boulder, CO: Westview Press, 1979.

Hourwich, Rebecca. "Why Can't Daddy Help?" *Equal Rights*, October 31, 1925.

Hull, William I. "The New Peace Movement: A Series of Addresses Delivered in 1908–09: How Far Has the World Progressed Toward Peace?" Philadelphia: Sunday School Times Company, 1911.

Hull, William I. *The New Peace Movement.* Boston: World Peace Foundation, 1912.

"In Memoriam, Margaret Byington, 1877–1952." *Social Service Review* 26, no. 4 (1952): 486.

The Independent. "Women for Peace: The Organization of the First Woman's Peace Party." January 25, 1915.

International Woman Suffrage Alliance. *Report of the Seventh Congress of the International Woman Suffrage Alliance.* Manchester: Hotspur Press, 1919.

Irmscher, Christoph. *Max Eastman: A Life.* New Haven, CT: Yale University Press, 2017.

Irwin, Inez Haynes. *The Story of the Woman's Party.* New York: Harcourt, Brace & Co., 1921.

Ives v. South Buffalo Railroad Company, 94 N.E. 431 (1911). In *Negligence and Compensation Cases Annotated*, vol. 1, edited by Callaghan and Company 1912, 526–36. Chicago: FB & C Limited, 2017.

Jaffe, Julian F. *Crusade against Radicalism: New York during the Red Scare 1914–1924.* Port Washington, NY: Kennikat Press, 1972.

James, Joy. *Transcending the Talented Tenth: Black Leaders and American Intellectuals*. New York: Routledge, 1996.

Jensen, Joan M. "The Evolution of Margaret Sanger's 'Family Limitation' Pamphlet, 1914–1921." *Signs* 6, no. 3 (Spring 1981): 548–67.

Jensen, Joan. *The Price of Vigilance*. Chicago: Rand McNally, 1968.

JLD. "A History of the Curriculum, 1865–1970s." *Vassar Encyclopedia*. 2005. http://vcencyclopedia.vassar.edu/curriculum/a-history-of-the-curriculum-1865-1970s.html.

John, Angela V. *Turning the Tide: The Life of Lady Rhondda*. London: Parthian Books, 2014.

Kazin, Michael. *American Dreamers: How the Left Changed a Nation*. New York: Vintage Books, 2012.

Kazin, Michael. *A War Against War: The American Fight for Peace, 1914–1918*. New York: Simon & Schuster, 2017.

Kellogg, Flint. "Oswald Villard, the NAACP and *The Nation*." *The Nation*, July 2, 2009. https://www.thenation.com/article/oswald-villard-naacp-and-nation/.

Kellogg, Paul. "The Field before the Commission on Industrial Relations." *Political Science Quarterly* 28, no. 4 (December 1913): 593–609.

Kellogg, Paul. "Hostages of Appeasement." Speech before Social Workers' Committee, Spanish Refugee Campaign, February 1, 1940, courtesy of Rebecca Young.

Kellogg, Paul. "To Promote Preparedness for Peace." *Survey*, January 9, 1915.

Kennedy, David M. *Birth Control in America: The Career of Margaret Sanger*. New Haven, CT: Yale University Press, 1970.

Kenney, Elise K., Earl Davis, and Rebecca Zurier. *Art for the Masses: A Radical Magazine and Its Graphics 1911–1917*. Philadelphia: Temple University Press, 1988.

Kessler-Harris, Alice. *Women Have Always Worked: A Concise History*. 2nd ed. Champaign: University of Illinois Press, 2018.

Kimmel, Michael. *The Gendered Society*. New York: Oxford University Press, 2000.

Kimmel, Michael. *Manhood in America: A Cultural History*. New York: Free Press, 1996.

Kirchwey, Freda. "Crystal Eastman." *The Nation*, August 8, 1928, 124.

Knight, Louise. *Jane Addams: Spirit in Action*. New York: W. W. Norton, 2010.

Koven, Seth, and Sonya Michel, eds. *Mothers of a New World: Maternalist Politics and the Origins of Welfare States*. New York: Routledge, 1993.

Kraditor, Aileen S. *The Ideas of the Woman Suffrage Movement: 1890–1920*. New York: W. W. Norton, 1981.

Kuhlman, Erika. "'Women's Ways in War': The Feminist Pacifism of the New York City Woman's Peace Party." *Frontiers* 18, no. 1 (1997): 80–100.

Kunzel, Regina G. *Fallen Women, Problem Girls: Unmarried Mothers and the Professionalization of Social Work, 1890–1945*. New Haven, CT: Yale University Press, 1993.

The Labor Advocate. "Undesirables Organizing." June 30, 1917.

Law, Sylvia. "Crystal Eastman: NYU Law Graduate." *NYU Law Review* 66 (1991): 1963–95.

Law, Sylvia. "Crystal Eastman: Organizer for Women's Rights, Peace and Civil Liberties in the 1910s." *Valparaiso University Law Review* 28, no. 4 (1994): 1305–26.

Lenin, Vladimir. "Brest-Litovsk—A Brigands' Peace." *Liberator*, October 1918.

Levin, Joanna. *Bohemia in America 1858–1920*. Stanford: Stanford University Press, 2009.

Levitsky, Sandra R. "Niche Activism: Negotiating Organizational Heterogeneity in Contemporary American Social Movements." *Mobilization: An International Quarterly* 12, no. 3 (September 2007): 272.

Life. "An Opinion." January 18, 1890.

Loomis, Erik. A History of America in Ten Strikes. New York: The New Press, 2018.

Link, Arthur S. *Wilson: The Struggle for Neutrality, 1914–15*. Princeton, NJ: Princeton, 1960.

London Daily Herald. "Married Women and Passports." November 22, 1922.

Los Angeles Times. "Saleswoman Is Auto Rage." February 23, 1915.

Lower Cost Gazette. "New Ideas About Alimony." February 28, 1916.

Luhan, Mabel Dodge. *Intimate Memories*. Vol. 3, *Movers and Shakers*. New York: Harcourt, Brace & Co., 1936.

Lumsden, Linda J. *Inez: The Life & Times of Inez Milholland*. Bloomington: Indiana University Press, 2004.

MacGregor, Neil. *A History of the World in 100 Objects*. New York: Viking Press, 2010.

MacMillan, Margaret. *Paris 1919: Six Months That Changed the World*. New York: Random House, 2002.

Mahoning Dispatch. "Mrs. Benedict's Challenge." March 6, 1914.

Mail Tribune. "Beautiful American Suffragettes in Austria." May 29, 1913.

Marchand, C. Roland. *The American Peace Movement and Social Reform 1898–1918*. Princeton, NJ: Princeton University Press, 1972.

Marilley, Suzanne M. *Suffrage and the Origins of Liberal Feminism in the United States, 1820–1920*. Cambridge, MA: Harvard University Press, 1996.

McBride, Genevieve G. *On Wisconsin Women: Working for Their Rights from Settlement to Suffrage*. Madison: University of Wisconsin Press, 1993.

McCarter, Jeremy. *Young Radicals: In the War for American Ideals*. New York: Random House, 2017.

McFarland, David D. "Adding Machines and Logarithms: Franklin H. Giddings and Computation for the Exact Science of Sociology." *Social Science Computer Review* 22, no. 2 (Summer 2004): 249–55.

McFarland, Gerald W. *Inside Greenwich Village: A New York City Neighborhood 1898–1918*. Amherst: University of Massachusetts Press, 2001.

McGilvary, Evander Bradley. "Review of *Democracy and Empire* by Franklin Henry Giddings." *Philosophical Review* 9, no. 6 (November 1900): 651–56.

McGovern, James R. "The American Woman's Pre–World War I Freedom in Manners and Morals." *Journal of American History* 55 (September 1968): 315–33.

McKay, Claude. *A Long Way from Home*. New Brunswick, NJ: Rutgers University Press, 1937.

McLaughlin, Neil. "How to Become a Forgotten Intellectual: Intellectual Movements and the Rise and Fall of Erich Fromm." *Sociological Forum* 13, no. 2 (1998): 215–46.

McLynn, Frank. *Villa and Zapata: A History of the Mexican Revolution*. New York: Basic Books, 2002.

McMillen, Sally G. *Lucy Stone: An Unapologetic Life*. New York: Oxford University Press, 2015.

Mead, Lucia Ames. "Do Suffragists Care about Our Mad Militarism?" *Woman Voter*, July 1913: 11–12.

Milkis, Sidney. "Theodore Roosevelt: Campaigns and Elections." Miller Center, University of Virginia. https://millercenter.org/president/roosevelt/campaigns-and-elections.

Miller, Kenneth E. *From Progressive to New Dealer: Frederic C. Howe and American Liberalism*. University Park: Penn State University Press, 2010.

Mills, Bill. *The League: The True Story of Average Americans on the Hunt for WWI Spies*. New York: Skyhorse Publishing, 2013.

Milwaukee Journal. "Mrs. W.J. Benedict Admitted to the Bar." September 28, 1911.

Milwaukee Sentinel. "Mrs. Benedict to Speak on Lake Front." July 13, 1911.

Milwaukee Sentinel. "Suffragist Tires of Marital Link." October 27, 1915.

Milwaukee Sentinel. "Weds New York Woman: Wallace J. Benedict Surprises Friends by Announcement of Marriage." May 6, 1911.

Mirel, Jeffrey. *Patriotic Pluralism: Americanization Education and European Immigrants*. Cambridge, MA: Harvard University Press, 2010.

MPB. "Inez Milholland." *Vassar Encyclopedia*. 2006. http://vcencyclopedia.vassar.edu/alumni/inez-milholland.html.

Muncy, Robyn. *Creating a Female Domain in American Reform 1890–1935*. Oxford: Oxford University Press, 1991.

Murphy, Paul L. *World War I and the Origin of Civil Liberties in the United States*. New York: W. W. Norton, 1975.

Murray, Robert K. *Red Scare: A Study in National Hysteria, 1919–20*. Minneapolis: University of Minnesota Press, 1955.

Nash, Jennifer. "Re-thinking Intersectionality." *Feminist Review* 89 (2008): 1–15.

National Center for Education Statistics. *120 Years of American Education: A Statistical Portrait*. US Department of Education, 1993, Table 28.

National Woman's Party. "Women for Congress: The NWP's Campaign to Elect Women to Represent Women's Concerns." National Woman's Party. http://nationalwomansparty.org/women-for-congress-the-nwps-campaign-to-elect-women-to-represent-womens-concerns/.

New York Herald. "Peace Cry to Greet 1917." December 31, 1916.

New York Herald. "Portia Appointed by the Governor." April 24, 1910.

New York Herald. "War Offer Causes War for the Suffs." February 9, 1917.

New York Herald-Tribune. "Newport's Conference Politically Momentous." September 6, 1914.

New York State Workers' Compensation Board. *Centennial: Celebrating 100 Years of New York State Workers' Compensation*. 2014. http://www.wcb.ny.gov/WCB_Centenial_Booklet.pdf.

New York Telegram and Evening Mail. "Feminist for Equality, Not 'Women as Women': Crystal Eastman Explains She Favors Election of Congressional Candidates on Account of Their Principles, Not Their Sex." October 31, 1924.

New York Times. "Bureau to Defend Lovers of Peace." July 3, 1917.

New York Times. "Call for Mediation from Peace Union." June 24, 1916.

New York Times. "Catastrophe in War with Mexico." July 6, 1916.

New York Times. "Crystal Eastman Married." November 14, 1916.

New York Times. "Feminists Ask for Equal Chance." February 21, 1914.

New York Times. "House Approves Draft of Militia." June 24, 1916.

New York Times. "Malone Aids Fight of Anti-Draft Press." July 14, 1917.

New York Times. "Max Eastman Replies to 'E.F. Mylius' Letter." December 3, 1921.

New York Times. "Mrs. LaFollette Is Leader." September 11, 1912.

New York Times. "Mylius Says He Only 'Borrowed' $4000." December 2, 1921.

New York Times. "'Neutral Conference' Now Moves for Peace." January 4, 1917.

New York Times. "Pacifists Approve President's Action." February 27, 1917.

New York Times. "Pacifists Demand War Referendum." February 5, 1917.

New York Times. "Pilgrims for Peace to Visit Congress." February 9, 1917.

New York Times. "Preparedness Is Favored." February 23, 1916.

New York Times. "President on Defenses: In Speech to Antimilitarists Says Force Must Back Up Opinion." May 9, 1916.

New York Times. "Protesting Women March in Mourning." August 30, 1914.

New York Times. "Republican Women Aid Whole Ticket." August 5, 1916.

New York Times. "Talk on Feminism Stirs Crowd." February 18, 1914.

New York Times. "Teacher Pleases Socialists; Dr. Bonn Applauded for Saying 'To Hell with the Government.'" January 15, 1910.

New York Times. "To Make Labor Safe." June 5, 1910.

New York Times. "Use Belgium's Fate as Warning to U.S." June 15, 1915.

New York Times. "Votes for Women Week." March 7, 1910.

New York Times. "Wisconsin Women Active." October 6, 1912.

New York Times. "Women Pacifists Demand Action." November 16, 1915.

New York Times. "Women to Conquer Ways to Salaries." March 5, 1915.

New York Tribune. "Bela Kun Declared No Sympathizer with 'Reds.'" November 16, 1919.

New York Tribune. "Enemies Within." August 26, 1917.

New York Tribune. "Hopes for Socialist U.S." March 26, 1919.

New York Tribune. "Miss Eastman Obtained Passport Legitimately." June 12, 1919.

New York Tribune. "Pound Away at Pittsburgh." February 5, 1910.

New York Tribune. "Reed Won't Be Opposed as Bolshevik Consul." February 3, 1918.

New York Tribune. "'Votes for Women' First Words of Miss Liberty by the Sea." July 6, 1915.

New York Tribune. "Woman's Party Will Work for Feminism Only." February 19, 1921.

New York Tribune. "Women Ask Fund to Beat Wilson." August 30, 1916.

Nielsen, Kim E. *Un-American Womanhood: Antiradicalism, Antifeminism and the First Red Scare.* Columbus: Ohio State University Press, 2001.

Northern Star. "American Pacifists: How They Are Treated." January 2, 1918.

Northwest Worker. "The Purposes of the People's Council." August 9, 1917.

Novetsky, Rikki. "College Girls: What Was the Barnard College Crush?" *Columbia Spectator,* October 23, 2014. http://features.columbiaspectator.com/blog/2014/10/23/college-girls/.

O'Neill, William. *The Last Romantic: A Life of Max Eastman.* New York: Oxford University Press, 1978.

Oakland Tribune. "Women Abroad Puzzle Over Nationality." January 7, 1923.

Ogden Standard. "Miss Eastman Spurns Alimony." March 3, 1916.

Ogden Standard. "Women Are Disloyal." September 3, 1917.

Ovington, Mary White. *Black and White Sat Down Together: The Reminiscences of an NAACP Founder.* New York: Feminist Press, 1995.

Patterson, David S. *Search for Negotiated Peace: Women's Activism and Citizen Diplomacy.* New York: Routledge, 2008.

Perkins, Frances. "Wage Earning Wives." *Equal Rights,* January 3, 1931.

Pethick-Lawrence, Emmeline. "Motherhood and War." *Harper's Weekly,* December 5, 1914.

Pethick-Lawrence, Emmeline. *My Part in Changing the World.* London: Hyperion Press, 1938.

Pethick-Lawrence, Emmeline. "Union of Women for Constructive Peace." *Survey,* December 5, 1914.

Pethick-Lawrence, Emmeline. "Women and War." *Suffragist,* November 21, 1914.

Pinchot, Amos. "Mr. Pinchot's Reply." *New York Sun,* March 9, 1914.

Reed, John. "Letter." *Liberator,* September 1918.

Reed, John. *Ten Days That Shook the World. New York.* Boni & Liveright, 1919. https://www.marxists.org/archive/reed/1919/10days/10days/.

Reed, John. *The War in Eastern Europe.* New York: Charles Scribner's Sons, 1916.

The Remonstrance. "Not Good Sports." October 1912.

Report of the Congressional Union for Woman Suffrage: For the Year 1914 with Outline of Congressional Work during the Preceding Year. Washington, DC: Model Print Company, 1914.

Rhondda, The Viscountess. *This Was My World*. London: Macmillan and Company, 1933.

Richards, Graham. "Britain on the Couch: The Popularization of Psychoanalysis in Britain 1918–1940." *Science in Context* 13, no. 2 (2000): 183–230.

Roosevelt, Theodore. "Speech at the New York State Agricultural Association, Syracuse, New York, September 7, 1903." http://www.memorablequotations.com/SquareDeal.htm.

Rosenberg, Rosalind. *Beyond Separate Spheres: Intellectual Roots of Modern Feminism*. New Haven, CT: Yale University Press, 1983.

Rosenstone, Robert A. "The Salon of Mabel Dodge." In *Affairs of the Mind: The Salon in Europe and America from the Eighteenth to the Twentieth Century*, edited by Peter Quennell, 131–49. New York: New Republic Books, 1980.

Rupp, Leila J. "Feminism and the Sexual Revolution in the Early Twentieth Century: The Case of Doris Stevens." *Feminist Studies* 15, no. 2 (Summer 1989): 289–309.

Rupp, Leila J. "Sexuality and Politics in the Early Twentieth Century: The Case of the International Women's Movement." *Feminist Studies* 23, no. 3 (Autumn 1997): 577–605.

Rupp, Leila J. *Worlds of Women: The Making of an International Women's Movement*. Princeton, NJ: Princeton University Press, 1998.

Rupp, Leila J., and Verta Taylor. *Survival in the Doldrums: The American Women's Rights Movement 1945–1960s*. New York: Oxford University Press, 1987.

Sacramento Union. "Militarism Opposed by S. Fraser Langford." November 22, 1915.

Sacramento Union. "Stephens Refuses to Read 'Liberator.'" April 9, 1920.

Sacramento Union. "Suffrage Plank Sought by Women." June 6, 1916.

Sanger, Margaret. *My Fight for Birth Control*. New York: Farrar & Rinehart, 1931.

Sanger, Margaret. "The New Feminists." *Woman Rebel*, March 1914.

Sanger, Margaret. "Prevention of Conception." *Woman Rebel*, March 1914.

Sayer, John. "Art and Politics, Dissent and Repression: *The Masses* Magazine versus the Government, 1917–1918." *American Journal of Legal History* 32, no. 1 (January 1988): 42–78.

Scanlon, Jennifer. *Inarticulate Longings: The Ladies' Home Journal and the Promises of Consumer Culture*. New York: Routledge, 1995.

Schwarz, Judith. *Radical Feminists of Heterodoxy: Greenwich Village 1912–1940*. Norwich: New Victoria Publishers, 1986.

Scott, Anne F., and Andrew M. Scott. *One Half the People: The Fight for Women Suffrage*. Champaign: University of Illinois Press, 1982.

Sharer, Wendy B. *Vote and Voice: Women's Organizations and Political Literacy 1915–1930*. Carbondale: Southern Illinois University Press, 2004.

Sheridan, Clare. *Mayfair to Moscow: Clare Sheridan's Diary*. New York: Boni and Liveright, 1921.

Showalter, Elaine. *These Modern Women: Autobiographical Essays from the Twenties*. New York: Feminist Press at CUNY, 1989.

Silver, Matthew Mark. *Louis Marshall and the Rise of Jewish Ethnicity in America*. Syracuse: Syracuse University Press, 2013.

Simkhovitch, Mary. *Neighborhood; My Story of Greenwich House*. New York: W. W. Norton, 1938.

Sklar, Kathryn Kish. *Florence Kelley and the Nation's Work: The Rise of Women's Political Culture, 1830–1900*. New Haven, CT: Yale University Press, 1995.

Sklar, Kathryn Kish, and Beverly Palmer. *Selected Letters of Florence Kelley 1869–1931*. Champaign: University of Illinois Press, 2009.

Skocpol, Theda, Marjorie Abend-Wein, Christopher Howard, and Susan Goodrich Lehmann. "Women's Association and the Enactment of Mothers' Pensions in the United States." *American Political Science Review* 87, no. 3 (September 1993): 686–701.

Smith-Rosenberg, Carroll. "The Female World of Love and Ritual: Relations between Women in Nineteenth Century America." In *The Girls' History and Culture Reader: The Nineteenth Century*, edited by Miriam Forman-Brunell and Leslie Paris, 149–78. Urbana: University of Illinois Press, 2011.

Snowden, Mrs. Philip. *A Political Pilgrim in Europe*. New York: George H. Doran Company, 1921.

Sochen, June. *The New Woman: Feminism in Greenwich Village, 1910–1920*. New York: Quadrangle Books, 1972.

Social Welfare History Project. "Edward T. Devine (1867–1948)." *Social Welfare History Project*. 2011. http://socialwelfare.library.vcu.edu/people/devine-edward-t-3/.

Social Welfare History Project. "Florence Kelley." *Social Welfare History Project*. 2008. http://socialwelfare.library.vcu.edu/people/kelley-florence/.

Special Correspondent. "Glimpses of Soviet Hungary." *Bulletin of the People's Council of America*, July–August 1919.

Special Correspondent. "The Zurich International Congress of Women." *Bulletin of the People's Council of America*, July–August 1919.

"Speeches from the Mass Meeting, January 10, 1915." Unknown source newspaper, WPPP, box 1, folder 6.

Spencer, Anna Garlin. "Preamble to Woman's Peace Party Platform." In *The History of the Woman's Peace Party* by Mary Louise Degen, 40–41. New York: Burt Franklin Reprints, 1974.

Spokesman Review. "League Labor Body Flayed. Woman Protection Clause Draws Wrath of Feminist." June 3, 1926.

Stansell, Christine. *American Moderns: Bohemian New York and the Creation of a New Century*. New York: Henry Holt, 2000.

Steel, Ronald. *Walter Lippmann and the American Century*. New York: Routledge, 1999.

Stein, Sadie. "On the Occasion of Zelda Fitzgerald's Birthday." *Paris Review* blog, July 24, 2013. https://www.theparisreview.org/blog/2013/07/24/on-the-occasion-of-zelda-fitzgeralds-birthday.

Steinson, Barbara J. *American Women's Activism in World War I*. New York: Garland Press, 1982.

Stevens, Doris. *Jailed for Freedom*. New York: Boni & Liveright, 1920.

Stevens, Doris. "Wages for Wives." *The Nation*, January 27, 1926.

Stowers, Richard. "From *Bloody Gallipoli* (2005)." As reported by the government of New Zealand. https://nzhistory.govt.nz/media/interactive/gallipoli-casualties-country.

Streitmatter, Roger. *Voice of Revolution: The Dissident Press in America*. New York: Columbia University Press, 2001.

Stroup, Herbert. *Social Welfare Pioneers*. Chicago: Nelson-Hall Publishers, 1986.

Suffragist. "Woman's Party Leaders Confer on President and Future Plans." October 1920.

Sullivan, Patricia. *Lift Every Voice: The NAACP and the Making of the Civil Rights Movement*. New York: New Press, 2009.

The Sun. "Suffrage Debaters Picked." October 28, 1915.

Swinth, Kirsten. *Feminism's Forgotten Fight: The Unfinished Struggle for Work and Family*. Cambridge, MA: Harvard University Press, 2018.

Syracuse Post Standard. "Proposes to Increase Employers' Liability." March 22, 1910.

Syracuse Post Standard. "Women Folk in Limelight." March 7, 1910.

Taylor, Eva. "History of the Park Church." Unpublished paper prepared by the Historical Records Committee of the Park Church, 1946.

Terborg-Penn, Rosalyn. *African American Women in the Struggle for the Vote, 1850-1920*. Bloomington: Indiana University Press, 1998.

Testimony of Mrs. Crystal Eastman Benedict of New York City, Hearings before the Committee on the Judiciary, US House of Representatives, Sixty-Third Congress, On Woman Suffrage, March 3, 1914.

Tetrault, Lisa. *The Myth of Seneca Falls: Memory and the Women's Suffrage Movement, 1848–1898*. Chapel Hill: University of North Carolina Press, 2017.

Thomas, Evan. *The War Lovers: Roosevelt, Lodge, Hearst, and the Rush to Empire*. New York: Basic Books, 2011.

Thomas, Gordon. "A Film Divided against Itself: D. W. Griffith's *Birth of a Nation* (1915)." *Bright Lights Film Journal*, June 26, 2016. http://brightlightsfilm.com/film-divided-d-w-griffiths-birth-nation-1915/#.WZRzhFWGMdU.

Thompson, John A. *Reformers and War: Progressive Publicists and the First World War*. New York: Cambridge University Press, 2003.

Time. "New York: January 18, 1890." January 18, 1890.

Trattner, Walter I. *From Poor Law to Welfare State: A History of Social Welfare in America*. 6th ed. New York: Free Press, 1998.

Trattner, Walter I. "Julia Grace Wales and the Wisconsin Plan for Peace." *Wisconsin Magazine of History* 44 (1961): 204–6.

Twain, Mark, and Charles Dudley Warner. *The Gilded Age: A Tale of Today*. New York: Harper & Brothers, 1893.

Ueland, Brenda. *Me*. St. Paul: Schubert Club, 1983.

United States Internal Revenue. "Statistics of Income, Compiled from the Returns of 1916." United States Treasury Department, Document number 2817. Washington, DC: Government Printing Office, 1918.

Unites States Library of Congress. "Marching for the Vote: Remembering the Woman Suffrage Parade of 1913." *American Memory*. https://memory.loc.gov/ammem/awhhtml/aw01e/aw01e.html.

Van Voris, Jacqueline. *Carrie Chapman Catt: A Public Life*. New York: The Feminist Press, 1996.

Verloo, Mieke. "Intersectional and Cross-Movement Politics and Policies: Reflections on Current Practices and Debate." *Signs* 38, no. 4 (2013): 893–915.

Villard, Oswald Garrison. *Fighting Years: Memoirs of a Liberal Editor*. New York: Harcourt, Brace and Co., 1939.

Wald, Lillian. *Windows on Henry Street*. Boston: Little Brown, 1934.

Walker, Samuel. *In Defense of American Liberties: A History of the ACLU*. Carbondale: Southern Illinois University Press, 1990.

Walters, Suzanna Danuta. *Lives Together/Worlds Apart: Mothers and Daughters in Popular Culture*. Berkeley: University of California Press, 1994.

Walton, Mary. *A Woman's Crusade: Alice Paul and the Battle for the Ballot*. New York: St. Martin's, 2010.

Warbasse, James Peter. "Are We for Armed Neutrality?" *New York Evening Post*, February 10, 1917.

Washington Herald. "Man-Politician Taken to Task." June 6, 1915.

Washington Herald. "Mrs. Benedict Due Today." March 10, 1914.

Washington Herald. "Mrs. Benedict Gives Feminist Platform." February 19, 1918.

Washington Herald. "Plans of Suffrage Hosts Are Complete." January 10, 1914.

Washington Herald. "Says Vote Will Bring New Eden." May 18, 1915.

Washington Herald. "To Lecture to Women on Boon of 'Twilight Sleep.'" January 23, 1915.

Washington Herald. "Votes or Fight, Women's Threat; Remember the Ides of November, Suffragist Tells House Democrats." March 4, 1914.

Washington Post. "Will Ride as Heralds; Four Suffragists to Play Part of Paul Revere." January 27, 1913.

Washington Times. "Bryan Asked to Try to Prevent War." June 23, 1916.

Washington Times. "New Jersey Women Will Be Honored." October 28, 1913.

Washington Times. "Women Will Spend a Big Party Fund." July 18, 1916.

Watson, Bruce. *Bread and Roses: Mills, Migrants, and the Struggle for the American Dream*. New York: Penguin, 2006.

Watts, Steven. *The People's Tycoon: Henry Ford and the American Century*. New York: Vintage, 2006.

Waugh, Joan. "Florence Kelley and the Anti-Sweatshop Campaign of 1892–1893." *UCLA Historical Journal* 3 (1982): 21–35.

Wellsville Daily Reporter. [No Headline, Thomas Beecher on Annis Ford Eastman ordination]. November 16, 1895.

Wesser, Robert F. *Charles Evans Hughes: Politics and Reform and New York 1905–1910*. Ithaca, NY: Cornell University Press, 1967.

Wetzsteon, Ross. *Republic of Dreams: Greenwich Village: The American Bohemia, 1910–1960*. New York: Simon & Schuster, 2003.

Wilk, Rona M. "'What's a Crush?': A Study of Crushes and Romantic Friendships at Barnard College, 1900–1920." *Magazine of History* 18, no. 4 (July 2004): 20–22.

Wilson, Woodrow. "Speech before the Manhattan Club." In *The New Democracy: Presidential Messages, Addresses and Other Papers*, edited by Ray Stannard Baker and William E. Dodd, 384–92. New York: Harper & Brothers, 1926.

Wilson, Woodrow. "Speech of Acceptance, September 2, 1916." http://millercenter.org/president/wilson/speeches/speech-3795.

Wilson, Woodrow. "War Message, Delivered to Congress April 2, 1917." 1917. https://wwi.lib.byu.edu/index.php/Wilson's_War_Message_to_Congress.

Wiltsher, Anne. *Most Dangerous Women: Feminist Peace Campaigners of the Great War*. London: Pandora, 1985.

Winnington, G. Peter. *Walter Fuller: The Man Who Had Ideas*. London: Letterworth Press, 2014.

Wisconsin State Journal. "Crystal Eastman, Woman of the Strenuous Life, Is in Madison." June 17, 1910, 10.

Witt, John Fabian. "Crystal Eastman and the Internationalist Beginnings of American Civil Liberties." *Duke Law Journal* 54, no. 3 (December 2004): 705–63.

Witt, John Fabian. *Patriots & Cosmopolitans: Hidden Histories in American Law*. Cambridge, MA: Harvard University Press, 2007.

Witt, John Fabian. "Toward a New History of American Accident Law: Classical Tort Law and the Cooperative First-Party Insurance Movement." *Harvard Law Review* 114 (2001): 690–841.

Woloch, Nancy. *A Class by Herself: Protective Labor Laws for Women Workers, 1890s–1990s*. New York: Oxford University Press, 2015.

Woman's Journal. "Canvassing for the Cause." November 16, 1912.

Woman's Peace Party of New York City. *First Annual Report*. New York [?]: Woman's Peace Party, 1916.

Women's International League for Peace and Freedom. *Report of the International Congress of Women at Zurich, May 12 to 17, 1919*. Geneva [?]: Women's International League for Peace and Freedom, 1920.

Working Women. "Muller v. State of Oregon." *Harvard University Library Open Collections Program*. 1800–1930. http://ocp.hul.harvard.edu/ww/muller.html.

Youmans, Theodora W. "How Wisconsin Women Won the Ballot." *Wisconsin Magazine of History* 5, no. 1 (September 1921): 3–32.

Young, Art. *On My Way: Being the Book of Art Young in Text and Picture*. New York: Liveright, 1928.

Zonderman, David A. *Uneasy Allies: Working for Labor Reform in Nineteenth-Century Boston*. Amherst: University of Massachusetts Press, 2011.

DISSERTATIONS

Briggs, Tracey. "Twenty Years at Greenwich House." PhD diss., Department of History, University of Toledo, 2008.

Cook, Blanche Wiesen. "Woodrow Wilson and the Antimilitarists 1914–1917." PhD diss., Department of History, John Hopkins University, 1980.

Galatola, Antoinette. "From Bohemianism to Radicalism: The Art and Political Context of the Liberator, 1918–1924." PhD diss., Department of Art History, City University of New York, 2000.

Goulard, Joan Marie. "Woman Rebel: The Rhetorical Strategies of Margaret Sanger and the American Birth Control Movement, 1912–1938." PhD diss., Department of Speech Communication and the Program in American Studies, Indiana University, 1978.

Johnson, Donald. "American Civil Liberties Union: 1914–1924." PhD diss., Columbia University, Department of History, 1960.

Steinson, Barbara Jean. "Female Activism in World War I: The American Women's Peace, Suffrage, Preparedness, and Relief Movements, 1914–1919." Vol. 1. PhD diss., Department of History, University of Michigan, 1977.

Stricker, Frank A. "Socialism, Feminism and the New Morality: The Separate Freedoms of Max Eastman, William English Walling, and Floyd Dell, 1910–1930." PhD diss., Department of History, Princeton University, 1974.

Thomas, William Henry Jr. "The United States Department of Justice and Dissent during the First World War." PhD diss., Department of History, University of Iowa, 2002.

Zimmerman, Loretta Ellen. "Alice Paul and the National Woman's Party, 1912–1920." PhD diss., Department of History, Tulane University, 1964.

AUTHOR INTERVIEWS

Conrad Dehn, London, England, June 21, 2009.

Monica Dehn, London, England, June 30, 2009.

Yvette Eastman, New York City, September 20, 2007.

Anne Fuller, New York City, April 17, 2012.

Joyce Fuller, New York City, November 3, 2008.

Nancy Hallinan, New York City, July 30, 2008.

Philip Wingard, Clover, South Carolina, April 16, 2014; May 3, 2016.

Charles Young, Martha's Vineyard, Massachusetts, April 3, 2010.

Rebecca Young, New York City, September 16, 2008; September 20, 2010; October 3, 2011; March 9, 2012; February 6, 2013; June 7, 2014; March 22, 2015.

INDEX

For the benefit of digital users, indexed terms that span two pages (e.g., 52–53) may, on occasion, appear on only one of those pages.